Reparations and the Theological Disciplines

Reparations and the Theological Disciplines

Prophetic Voices for Remembrance, Reckoning, and Repair

Edited by Michael Barram, Drew G. I. Hart,
Gimbiya Kettering, and Michael J. Rhodes

LEXINGTON BOOKS
Lanham • Boulder • New York • London

Rowman & Littlefield
Bloomsbury Publishing Inc, 1359 Broadway, New York, NY 10018, USA
Bloomsbury Publishing Plc, 50 Bedford Square, London, WC1B 3DP, UK
Bloomsbury Publishing Ireland, 29 Earlsfort Terrace, Dublin 2, D02 AY28, Ireland
www.bloomsbury.com

First published in the United States of America 2023
Paperback edition published 2025

Copyright © 2023 by The Rowman & Littlefield Publishing Group, Inc.

All rights reserved. No part of this publication may be: i) reproduced or transmitted in any form, electronic or mechanical, including photocopying, recording or by means of any information storage or retrieval system without prior permission in writing from the publishers; or ii) used or reproduced in any way for the training, development or operation of artificial intelligence (AI) technologies, including generative AI technologies. The rights holders expressly reserve this publication from the text and data mining exception as per Article 4(3) of the Digital Single Market Directive (EU) 2019/790.

British Library Cataloguing in Publication Information available

Library of Congress Cataloging-in-Publication Data

Names: Barram, Michael D., 1966- editor. | Hart, Drew G. I., editor. | Kettering, Gimbiya, editor. | Rhodes, Michael J., 1985- editor.
Title: Reparations and the theological disciplines : prophetic voices for remembrance, reckoning, and repair / edited by Michael Barram, Drew G.I. Hart, Gimbiya Kettering, Michael J. Rhodes.
Description: Lanham : Lexington Books, [2023] | Includes bibliographical references and index. | Summary: "Biblical scholars, theologians, and religious historians have largely ignored the issue of reparations. The time is now to engage with and make the case. Written for students, scholars, and pastors, the essays in Reparations and the Theological Disciplines emphatically advocate for a reparational ethic of remembrance, reckoning, and repair"– Provided by publisher.
Identifiers: LCCN 2023031533 (print) | LCCN 2023031534 (ebook) | ISBN 9781666922462 (cloth) | ISBN 9781666922479 (ebook)
Subjects: LCSH: African Americans–Reparations. | Reparations for historical injustices–Biblical teaching.
Classification: LCC E185.89.R45 R45 2023 (print) | LCC E185.89.R45 (ebook) | DDC 362.8496/073–dc23/eng/20230905
LC record available at https://lccn.loc.gov/2023031533
LC ebook record available at https://lccn.loc.gov/2023031534

For product safety related questions contact productsafety@bloomsbury.com.

Contents

Abbreviations	ix
Introduction: Toolbox for a Journey of Remembrance, Reckoning, and Repair *Michael Barram, Drew G. I. Hart, Gimbiya Kettering, and Michael J. Rhodes*	xi
PART ONE: REPARATIONS AND THE BIBLE	**1**
Chapter One: Reparations in Exodus *Matthew Schlimm*	3
Chapter Two: Bypassing the Bible: Why Exodus 21 and Deuteronomy 15 Did Not Influence and Have Not Influenced Reparations Proposals *Stacy Davis*	17
Chapter Three: Witness: The Job: How to Talk to White People About Reparations *Gimbiya Kettering*	35
Chapter Four: From Here to Jubilee: Reading Torah in Dialogue with Darity and Mullen's Case for Reparations *Michael J. Rhodes*	43
Chapter Five: Reparational Reasoning: The Biblical Jubilee as Moral Formation for a More Just Future *Michael Barram*	63
Chapter Six: Witness: Zacchaeus and the Call to Repair: A Sermon on Luke 19:1–10 *Duke L. Kwon*	79

Chapter Seven: You Cannot Pay Back What You Have Never Owned: A Conversation on Reparations and Paul's Letter to Philemon 91
Angela N. Parker

Chapter Eight: Philemon as a Plea for Reparations Then and Now 107
Michael J. Gorman

PART TWO: REPARATIONS AND CHRISTIAN THEOLOGY 123

Chapter Nine: The Reparational God 125
Mark Labberton

Chapter Ten: Myth, Belonging, and Reparative Ethics: A Theological and Pedagogical Account 137
Drew G. I. Hart

Chapter Eleven: "Don't Make Me Feel Guilty": Why Penal Substitution Interferes with Reparations and Reconciliation 155
Mako A. Nagasawa

Chapter Twelve: Witness: Reparations or Atonement: Searching for an Appropriate Vessel 179
Rodney S. Sadler Jr.

Chapter Thirteen: Reparations NOW: For the Glory of God 193
Ekemini Uwan

Chapter Fourteen: Catholic Social Thought and Reparations 209
Christina McRorie

PART THREE: REPARATIONS IN HISTORY AND CONTEMPORARY PRAXIS 237

Chapter Fifteen: The DC Compensated Emancipation Act as Precedent for Reparations 239
Renee K. Harrison

Chapter Sixteen: Reparation as Reckoning 259
Malcolm Foley

Chapter Seventeen: Witness: The Call for Truth and Reparations in Minnesota 271
Jim Bear Jacobs, Pamela R. Ngunjiri, and Curtiss Paul DeYoung

Chapter Eighteen: "Bear Fruits Worthy of Repentance": A Black
    Administrator's Perspective on the Challenge and Promise of
    the Virginia Theological Seminary Reparations Program   281
    Joseph Downing Thompson Jr.

Conclusion   299
    Drew G. I. Hart

Author/Subject Index   303

Scripture Index   311

About the Contributors   319

Abbreviations

AEL	*Ancient Egyptian Literature.* Edited by Miriam Lichtheim. 3 vols. Berkeley: University of California Press, 1971–1980.
ANET	*Ancient Near Eastern Texts Relating to the Old Testament.* Edited by J. B. Pritchard. 3rd ed. Princeton: Princeton University Press, 1969.
ANF	*Ante-Nicene Fathers: The Writings of the Fathers Down to A.D. 325.* Edited by Alexander Roberts, James Donaldson, A. Cleveland Coxe, and Allan Menzies. Peabody, MA: Hendrickson, 1994.
Ant.	*Jewish Antiquities*
b. Sanh.	*Babylonian Sanhedrin*
BDB	Brown, F., S. R. Driver, and C. A. Briggs. *The Brown-Driver-Briggs Hebrew and English Lexicon: With an Appendix Containing the Biblical Aramaic.* Peabody, MA: Hendrickson, 1999.
CEB	Common English Bible
DDD	*Dictionary of Deities and Demons in the Bible.* Edited by Karel Van Der Toorn, Bob Becking, and Pieter W. Van der Horst. 2nd ed. Leiden: Brill, 1999.
GKC	*Gesenius' Hebrew Grammar.* Edited by E. Kautzsch. Translated by A. E. Cowley. 2nd ed. Oxford: Clarendon, 1910.
IBC	Interpretation: A Bible Commentary for Teaching and Preaching
IBHS	Waltke, Bruce K., and M. O'Connor. *An Introduction to Biblical Hebrew Syntax.* Winona Lake, IN: Eisenbrauns, 1990.
ITC	International Theological Commentary
JBL	*Journal of Biblical Literature*

JEOL	*Jaarbericht van het Vooraziatisch-Egyptisch Gezelschap (Genootschap) Ex oriente lux*
Joüon	Joüon, Paul. *A Grammar of Biblical Hebrew*. Translated and revised by T. Muraoka. 2 vols. Subsidia biblica 14/1–2. Rome: Editrice Pontificio Istituto Biblico, 1991.
LCL	Loeb Classical Library
Marc.	*Against Marcion*
MGWJ	*Monatschrift für Geschichte und Wissenschaft des Judentums*
Moses	*On the Life of Moses*
MT	Masoretic Text
NASB	New American Standard Bible
NET	New English Translation
NIDOTTE	*New International Dictionary of Old Testament Theology and Exegesis.* Edited by Willem A. VanGemeren. 5 vols. Grand Rapids: Zondervan, 1997.
NIV	New International Version (1984)
NIV11	New International Version (2011)
NRSV	New Revised Standard Version
NRSVue	New Revised Standard Version, Updated Edition
OBO	Orbis biblicus et orientalis
OEANE	*The Oxford Encyclopedia of Archaeology in the Near East.* Edited by E. M. Meyers. 5 vols. American Schools of Oriental Research. New York: Oxford University Press, 1997.
OIP	Oriental Institute Publications
OTL	Old Testament Library
RB	*Revue biblique*
RSV	Revised Standard Version
TDOT	*Theological Dictionary of the Old Testament.* Edited by G. Johannes Botterweck, Helmer Ringgren, and Heinz-Josef Fabry. Translated by John T. Willis et al. 15 vols. Grand Rapids, Eerdmans, 1974–2006.
VT	*Vetus Testamentum*
WBC	Word Biblical Commentary
ZAW	*Zeitschrift für die alttestamentliche Wissenschaft*

Introduction

Toolbox for a Journey of Remembrance, Reckoning, and Repair

Michael Barram, Drew G. I. Hart, Gimbiya Kettering, and Michael J. Rhodes

What do the theological disciplines have to do with reparations? When Ta-Nehisi Coates made his landmark "case for reparations," he began his essay with a quote from Deuteronomy 15:12–14 and brought his argument to a crescendo by speaking of a "national reckoning that would lead to spiritual renewal." Coates's appeal to the biblical text and his summons to spiritual renewal may be surprising to some readers. After all, Coates himself is an atheist, and the Christian theological disciplines have tended to ignore or avoid discussing reparations. The essays in the present volume, however, argue that the Bible and Christian theology provide the theological academy important reasons to embrace reparations for Black Americans. Indeed, we believe that the time for the theological disciplines to make the case for reparations is *now*.

The idea for this book began as members of our editorial team realized that it was long *past* time to consider reparations biblically and theologically. Three of us (Michael Barram, Drew Hart, and Michael Rhodes) had gotten to know one another through our participation in the Forum on Missional Hermeneutics, an Affiliate Program of the Society of Biblical Literature (SBL). All of us had written about scripture, theology, race, and economics. But while Barram and Rhodes had each written books on the Bible and economic ethics, neither had specifically engaged the issue of reparations. Hart pointed this out to Barram in a public review of Barram's *Missional Economics*, while another contributor to this volume, Duke Kwon, pushed

Rhodes on the similar gap in *Practicing the King's Economy*. (For the record, Barram and Rhodes are both enormously grateful for the gracious, prophetic push they received from their brothers!)

These conversations inspired Barram, Hart, and Rhodes to help put together a conference session on reparations and the Bible, jointly sponsored by the Forum on Missional Hermeneutics and the Ethics and Biblical Interpretation Section, during the 2020 Annual Meetings of the Society of Biblical Literature. Following an open call for papers, Barram, Rhodes, and Matthew Schlimm (another contributor to the present volume) each explored reparations by engaging with the biblical text. Reflecting on biblical literature in that context convinced us that scripture could dramatically transform the way we think about reparations. Indeed, our research and conference discussions demonstrated to us that engaging the issue of reparations can open our eyes to new aspects of scripture's witness as well.

That experience made us wonder: what would happen if our colleagues within the theological disciplines—biblical scholars, theologians, and religious historians—were to take up the case for reparations? What arguments might surface? Could reparations become a major topic of academic research and discussion? If so, how might our various disciplines be affected? And how might raising the issue of reparations in connection with scripture and theology contribute to wider efforts, well beyond the theological disciplines, to foster a more equitable and just society?

Soon, Gimbiya Kettering, a creative essayist and activist who has led many workshops about racism and gospel-based social justice in the church and beyond, joined the conversation. Kettering, too, recognized the need for the theological disciplines to commit to this conversation, and—once becoming part of the editorial team—played a pivotal role in imagining and shaping a volume that could capture the heads, hearts, and imaginations of its readers.

The four of us approached the eventual contributors to this volume with a specific invitation: would you be willing to explore how your discipline might make the case for reparations for Black Americans? Their willingness to say *yes* is what unites this collection. We are a diverse group. We come to the issue of reparations with different academic backgrounds and disciplines, with various racial and ethnic identities, and from differing ecclesial contexts, socio-economic locations, and theological commitments. Perhaps not surprisingly, we do not agree on everything. But while we have disagreements, what unites us is the belief that the Christian scriptures, theology, and history and praxis offer powerful reasons for pursuing reparations for Black Americans.

Our dream is that *Reparations and the Theological Disciplines* will help people of faith—particularly those in churches and in theological classrooms—to pursue a deep and enduring process of remembrance, reckoning, and repair that emerges logically, organically, and authentically from our encounter with the God revealed to us in Jesus and to whom scripture bears witness. At the same time, we hope that this volume may inspire a shift in focus in academic theological circles, such that reparations would become a more central and urgent topic of research, discussion, and engagement. Indeed, we believe that the character and subject matter of the theological disciplines themselves demand that we do so.

After all, many of us are not accustomed or well equipped to speak about reparations. So, together we set out to gather a collection of essays that would help churches and theological institutions across the country wrestle with reparations theologically. As we began to compile this anthology, we increasingly recognized that the diversity of our contributors' perspectives was a strength, not a weakness. Precisely because these essays draw on various theological disciplines and reflect a diversity of perspectives in addressing reparations, the collection as a whole can serve as something of a "toolbox" for readers. Just as a toolbox holds many different implements for basic repairs and projects, we have tried to bring together various philosophical and rhetorical approaches for thinking, talking, teaching, and preaching about reparations. *Reparations and the Theological Disciplines* offers diverse ideas from diverse perspectives for a diverse readership, yet all of them are oriented toward a shared cause and mission: engaging theology in the work of *remembering, reckoning with, and repairing* the injustice perpetrated against Black people in America, especially through race-based slavery and its enduring legacies.

As with toolboxes that we store in our homes, space is limited and the system of organization can be flexible. Again, while the editors and various contributors do not agree with one another on everything, we agree, despite our diverse perspectives, that making reparation for past and continuing injustice is essential. We anticipate that readers will find some arguments more persuasive than others. But we hope that you will find wrestling with each of these essays enriching, and that you will find particular contributions that resonate deeply with your own context. As you search for the tools that will best fit your needs, we encourage you to explore the bibliographies at the end of each essay, which are full of additional resources that can be helpful.

The present volume is divided into three sections: "Reparations and the Bible," "Reparations and Christian Theology," and "Reparations in History and Contemporary Praxis." In the first, biblical scholars bring the question of reparations into deep dialogue with scriptural texts. Matthew Schlimm explores the so-called "plundering" of the Egyptians as an example of reparations, while Stacy Davis explores why laws in Exodus 21 and Deuteronomy 15 *failed* to influence the debate about reparations, particularly among white Christians. Michael J. Rhodes explores the Torah's teaching on theft and the

Year of Jubilee in dialogue with one recent proposal for reparations, while Michael Barram explores the moral reasoning at work in that same Jubilee text. Finally, both Angela N. Parker and Michael J. Gorman turn to Paul's letter to Philemon, each arguing in different ways that the letter ought to influence theological engagement with reparations today.

In the second section, "Reparations and Christian Theology," our contributing theologians come at the task from a variety of angles. Mark Labberton argues that the character of the God of the Bible ought to drive Christians toward reparations. Drew G. I. Hart reflects on a theology of memory and pedagogy that might help theological students move toward an ethic of liberation and repair. Mako Nagasawa argues that a penal substitutionary view of atonement wrongly impedes efforts at reparations and argues for an alternative approach. Ekemini Uwan makes a biblically shaped, theological argument for reparations, placing the debate within the broad sweep of the biblical story. Finally, Christina McRorie makes a distinctly Catholic case for reparations, drawing deeply on the resources of Catholic Social Thought.

Each of the essays in the third section of the book, "Reparations in History and Contemporary Praxis," examines reparations by exploring the past. Renee K. Harrison's essay probes the painful history of the decision, enacted through the DC Compensated Emancipation Act, to pay reparations to *enslavers,* rather than the enslaved. Malcolm Foley summons us to examine the connection between economic injustice and the lynching of Black people in America, arguing that contemporary debates about reparations must reckon with the deeply economic roots of white supremacy. Finally, Joseph Thompson Jr. considers the "challenge and promise" of Virginia Theological Seminary's attempt to "bear fruits worthy of repentance" in relation to the descendants of people enslaved by the Seminary.

Interspersed throughout the three sections of the book are a series of chapters that we refer to as *Witness* essays. These *Witness* chapters imagine what it would look like for a theological case for reparations to come alive in our world today. Gimbiya Kettering offers a searing meditation on the complexity of talking about reparations in American churches, and the high price activists often pay for doing so. Duke L. Kwon contributes a sermon on reparations drawn from the story of Zacchaeus (Lk. 19:1–10), illustrating the way a reparational ethic might be proclaimed from the pulpits of American churches. Biblical scholar Rodney S. Sadler Jr. shares his experience working with activists and civic leaders on the ground in North Carolina, as well as their journey toward the terminology of "atonement" in relation to their work. Finally, Jim Bear Jacobs, Pamela Ngunjiri, and Curtiss Paul DeYoung tell the story of the Minnesota Council of Churches' pursuit of "truth and reparations" in their community.

At the outset, we want to acknowledge a significant lacuna in this book: for the purposes of this project, we felt the need to limit the scope to arguments for reparations for Black Americans. As a consequence, we do not substantively or consistently engage the case for reparations for indigenous peoples in the United States—even as we recognize that this, too, is a pressing moral issue facing Christian theology. We hope that the essays in this volume will inspire readers to consider and participate in a Christian ethic of repair in relation to indigenous peoples in the US and around the world.

Further, in the midst of a conversation about reparations, we feel called to acknowledge that these essays represent the unpaid labor of our contributors. For some, this work falls within the roles and responsibilities of paid work and careers. For other contributors, their essays represent a passion project carried out when they are not doing the work that pays the bills and provides the health insurance. The benefits of being published in an academic text are as unevenly distributed as access to the rewards of higher education and the ivory tower. As a result, some potential contributors could not join the project as it would pull them away from necessary paid responsibilities or unpaid familial obligations. Our hope is that soon there will be many more voices speaking out and books written about the necessity of reparations—with adequate support for all of the contributing writers.

Let us return for a moment to the toolbox metaphor. If this book were an actual toolbox, it would come with a safety warning. Beyond a possible papercut or a bruised toe—should you drop the hardback edition on your own foot—this volume poses no physical danger. That said, we hope this anthology leads to robust dialogue in churches and theological classrooms—and, by necessity, talking about reparations involves entering into the taboo realms of race, religion, economics, and politics. There is always the risk that we may say the wrong thing, find out that a friend or colleague has views that seem irreconcilable with our own, and—even more horrifyingly—recognize that we have to face our own insecurities, fears, and biases. The pain is real when we realize that the faith that has informed us has also profited from the exploitation of Black people—and yet such pain is crucial for spiritual renewal, growth, and real change.

While reparations will require that we come to terms with who, what, and where we are—and how and why we got here—endless theoretical dialogue is insufficient. Ultimately, we hope that this volume forms and equips people of faith to *act*. For Christians, this work for reparations is, in fact, central to our mission—gospel work that is deeply consonant with the reign of God as described in Christian scripture and proclaimed and embodied by Jesus of Nazareth. Together, as Jesus's followers, we are called into a communal journey of remembrance, reckoning, and repair—a way that must be *lived*. Being found and seen by Jesus, Zacchaeus discovers his own liberation—"Today salvation has come to this house" (Luke 19:9)—even as he participates in fostering justice and liberation for others: "Look, half of my possessions, Lord, I will give to the poor; and if I have defrauded anyone of anything, I will pay back four times as much" (Luke 19:8). As it was for Zacchaeus, so for us: the time is *now*—today!

—Michael Barram, Drew G. I., Hart, Gimbiya Kettering, and Michael J. Rhodes

BIBLIOGRAPHY

Barram, Michael. *Missional Economics: Biblical Justice and Christian Formation.* Grand Rapids, MI: Eerdmans, 2018.

Coates, Ta-Nehisi. "The Case for Reparations." *The Atlantic*, June 15, 2014. Accessed May 23, 2023. https://www.theatlantic.com/magazine/archive/2014/06/the-case-for-reparations/361631/.

Hart, Drew. *Trouble I've Seen.* Harrisonburg, VA: Herald Press, 2016.

Rhodes, Michael, and Robby Holt, with Brian Fikkert. *Practicing the King's Economy: Honoring Jesus in How We Work, Earn, Spend, Save, and Give.* Grand Rapids, MI: Baker, 2018.

PART ONE

Reparations and the Bible

Chapter One

Reparations in Exodus[1]

Matthew Schlimm

Christian interpreters of the Bible usually see themselves as God's chosen people. We relate to people like Abraham and Sarah, Isaac and Rebekah, and Jacob and Rachel. When reading a book like Exodus, we naturally think of ourselves as the Israelites rather than the Egyptians. Since childhood, most of us have been taught to read the Bible this way. It allows us to feel like we're on the right side of history. We prefer not to identify with the bad guys.[2]

In an essay called "Why I Stopped Talking about Racial Reconciliation and Started Talking about White Supremacy," Korean American writer Erna Kim Hackett characterizes such interpretive practices as "Disney princess theology." In a quote from the essay that went viral in 2020, she points out why it's so problematic that White Christians see themselves as the princess in every story:

> For the citizens of the most powerful country in the world, who enslaved both Native and Black people, to see itself as Israel and not Egypt when studying Scripture is a perfect example of Disney princess theology. And it means that as people in power, they have no lens for locating themselves rightly in Scripture or society—and it has made them blind and utterly ill-equipped to engage issues of power and injustice.[3]

In actuality, White Americans more closely resemble the Egyptians than the Israelites. Unlike the Egyptians, however, White people have failed to pay reparations for the legacy of slavery.

If you've never heard that the Egyptians paid reparations to the Hebrews for the time that they spent in slavery, it's not entirely your fault. "The Israelites," says Exodus, " . . . had asked the Egyptians for jewelry of silver and gold and for clothing, and the Lord had given the people favor in the sight of the Egyptians, so that they let them have what they asked. And so, they plundered the Egyptians" (12:35–36; NRSVue). The first sentence sounds like the Egyptians are engaging in a practice remarkably similar to reparations. Coins had not yet been invented, so in lieu of currency, the Egyptians gave the greatest valuables they owned.[4] But what about the plundering? One definition of plunder is "to take something wrongfully." Why would God encourage seizing someone else's property wrongfully? Are the Israelites doing something good, receiving what is owed to them for centuries of working without pay? Or are they stealing?[5]

Some interpreters like George Coats have suspected that when the Israelites asked for such precious items, they only asked to borrow them. By leaving Egypt for good with these treasures, the Israelites thus plundered the Egyptians.[6] There are at least four problems with this way of treating the text, however. First, this approach presupposes that the Egyptians were foolish enough to lend out jewelry in mass quantities without worry about their return.[7] Second, this line of interpretation comes out of a sad habit among biblical interpreters of seeing the Israelites—and Semites in general—as morally suspect. Several interpreters have spotted and rejected such anti-Semitism.[8] Third, Exodus 3:21 and 11:3's talk of YHWH giving favor to the Israelites in the eyes of the Egyptians suggests that the Egyptians gave gifts freely, not that they were deceived.[9] Finally, the biblical text never says unambiguously that the Israelites only asked to borrow the valuables.[10]

The Hebrew word translated "plundered" in Exodus 12:35–36 (and 3:22) appears more than 200 times in the Bible.[11] In a handful of cases, it appears in violent contexts (see 2 Chron 20:25). Exodus 12:35–36, by contrast, talks about the Israelites asking Egyptians for valuables and the Egyptians giving tremendous gifts. That doesn't sound like theft or warfare. It sounds more like a wedding reception or a baby shower. The Egyptians give great gifts to make sure that the Israelites have a good start in their new lives.[12] It sounds even more like the Egyptians realized their treatment of the Israelites was fundamentally wrong, and they tried to make reparations.

From early to modern times, interpreters have seen the giving of gold, silver, and garments as something akin to reparations. Already in the second century BCE, Jubilees 48:18 talks of the transfer of valuables "in return for the fact that [the Israelites] were made to work when [the Egyptians] enslaved them by force."[13] Around the same time, Ezekiel the Tragedian's *Exagoge* makes similar remarks.[14] In (probably) the first century CE, the Wisdom of Solomon appears to allude to the Israelites' gaining Egyptian goods when it says that Wisdom "gave to holy people the reward of their labors (10:17, NRSVue). Near the same time, Philo talks of the Israelites taking from the Egyptians "a bare wage for all their time of service" and "payment long kept back through reluctance to pay what was due."[15] In the early third century

CE, Tertullian speaks of this transfer of goods as "compensation for [the Israelites'] hire, which they were unable in any other way to exact from their masters."[16] The Babylonian Talmud similarly brings the discussion of the Egyptians' gold and silver into conversation with the wages due to the Israelites (*b. Sanh. 91a*).[17]

This interpretive strand continued in more recent times. In the mid-nineteenth century, African American Martin R. Delany interprets Exodus 12:35–36 as a basis for taking something akin to reparations:

> Keep this studiously in mind and impress it as an important part of the scheme of organization, that [enslaved persons] must have money, if they want to get free. Money will obtain them every thing necessary by which to obtain their liberty. The money is within all their reach if they only knew it was right to take it. God told the Egyptian slaves to 'borrow from their neighbors'—meaning their oppressors—'all their jewels'; meaning to take their money and wealth wherever they could lay hands upon it, and depart from Egypt. So you must teach them to take all the money they can get from their masters, to enable them to make the strike without a failure.[18]

More recently, Victor Hamilton writes, "Think of all those free man-hours Pharaoh has obtained from the Hebrews. Surely they are entitled to some financial/material compensation."[19] Philip Ryken makes a similar point: "This was God's way of making sure that his people got paid for all the work they did for Pharaoh, which was only fair!"[20] Other modern commentators explicitly use the language of "reparation."[21]

This text from Exodus is hardly the only one in the Bible relevant to the discussions of reparations. Duke L. Kwon and Gregory Thompson's *Reparations: A Christian Call for Repentance and Repair* points to reparations as the church's calling and responsibility. They explain that such reparations need to entail two key elements. The first is restitution, giving back what was wrongfully taken. They reference Zacchaeus, who pays back four times what he wrongfully took (Luke 19:1–10). They show how Zacchaeus's actions entail obedience to texts like Exodus 22:1, which says that thieves need to compensate their victims four or five times over.[22]

The second element of reparations is restoration, making the wronged person whole again. Here, Kwon and Thompson pay careful attention to the parable of the Good Samaritan, who ensures that the robbed person fully recovers and can move forward with health—even though the Samaritan did not personally cause the robbery and injury (Luke 10:25–37).[23]

Kwon and Thompson also look at the passage from Exodus 12.[24] It turns out that the word so oddly translated as "plunder" here almost always means "deliver," "rescue," or "save," as in Ezekiel 14:14.[25] There, Ezekiel talks of saintly people like Noah saving themselves from coming famine. If Exodus is using the word the same way as Ezekiel is, then the Israelites are not robbing the Egyptians—they're saving them. Indeed, just a few verses earlier, the Egyptians urged the Israelites to leave because they feared they would all die (12:33).[26] The Egyptians have already faced an onslaught of plagues, and they dread more coming. The best way to understand Exodus 12:36 (and the closely related 3:22) is that the Israelites rescue the Egyptians from God's ongoing judgment by asking for and receiving their valuables.

This gift giving does not make things perfectly even, but it does symbolize an end to hostilities. It signifies a new beginning. It demonstrates the Egyptians' readiness to relate to the Israelites in new ways. In an act of significant sacrifice, they surrender their greatest valuables with no strings attached. They demonstrate concretely that they are no longer going to exploit the Israelites. They give the Israelites the means to move forward not in destitution, but in prosperity.

And these reparations benefit not just the oppressed but also the oppressors. In Egyptian thinking, all facets of society were supposed to operate smoothly and in concert with one another. The infanticide, slavery, and plagues of Exodus left no doubt that Egyptian society had failed to reach its own goals. The only way to become a functioning society again was to address past wrongs in hopes of avoiding divine judgment.[27]

At their heart, reparations have always been about transforming broken societies into flourishing communities. Ta-Nehisi Coates rooted his groundbreaking essay "The Case for Reparations" in Deuteronomy 15:12–15, in which God commands that the Israelites set their Hebrew slaves free after six years of service.[28] The text also specifies that the Israelites must outfit the freed slaves with an abundance of gifts, including food and wine for the short term and farm animals that would enable former slaves to generate long-term income. Sheep and goats served as a sort of ancient savings account, giving people assets that could be eaten or traded during a drought or other crisis.[29]

These biblical stipulations don't exactly call for forty acres and a mule, but they aren't far removed from such an idea. Indeed, George Fox, the founder of the Quaker movement, appealed directly to this Deuteronomy text in the 1600s when advocating something very similar to reparations. He urged slaveholders to set their slaves free after a period of service, and he added, "When they go, and are made free, *let them not go away empty-handed*, this I say will be very acceptable to the Lord, whose Servants we are."[30]

The promise of restitution for slavery recurs elsewhere in the Hebrew Bible as well. In Genesis 15:14, God promises Abraham that after centuries of slavery, his descendants will leave an oppressive land with great wealth. Then, amid Moses's call, God tells him that the Israelites will go out of Egypt with gold, silver, and clothing, which will be gifts for the next generation (Exod.

3:20–22). Later, just before the original Passover, God tells Moses it's time to fulfill this earlier promise (11:2–3). Finally, as the Israelites get ready to leave Egypt, they ask the Egyptians for silver, gold, and clothing—and the Egyptians freely give it. Much later in the Bible, Psalm 105:37–38 celebrates that these gifts were given.

These repeated references to the Egyptians giving their greatest valuables amid the Israelites' emancipation make clear that the writers of scripture don't want us to miss this essential point: enslavers owe a debt. And, despite many protestations to the contrary, it can be paid by giving valuables that ensure the success of freed slaves and their descendants. In Exodus 3:22, it's clear that these reparations are for the descendants of slaves too. The Egyptians' silver, gold, and clothing will be placed on Israelite children. It's a time of hope in new beginnings for future generations.[31]

Further, understanding texts in the Torah as calling for reparations for slavery, or something very close to it, is consonant with other biblical teachings. In Genesis, gift giving serves to resolve conflicts, facilitate forgiveness, and move past wrongdoings. When Abram's and Lot's shepherds can't get along, Abram lets Lot have his choice of land (Gen 13:5–12). When the Philistines and Isaac come close to violence over who possesses which wells, Isaac cedes land he could claim as his own (Gen 26:12–33). Amid painful strife, Rachel and Leah exchange gifts and privileges to find a way forward (Gen 30:14–18). When Esau looks ready for revenge, Jacob gives an abundance of gifts to make up for terrible wrongdoings (Gen 32:3–21, 33:1–17).[32]

It's not that wrongdoers can pay bribes to make artificial peace. Rather, sacrifices of significance introduce alternate logics and ways of being in the world. They function as catalysts of reconciliation.[33] They work sacramentally as outward and visible signs of inward and invisible changes of attitude. They demonstrate when repentance is real. It's hard to overestimate the costs of reparations, but it's also hard to overestimate their potential for healing.

In one of the most famous sermons in American history, preached on January 1, 1808, Absalom Jones begins by describing Israelite slavery in ways that easily connect with American slavery: "They were compelled to work in the open air, in one of the hottest climates in the world: and, probably, without a covering from the burning rays of the sun."[34] After talking about God's intervention in Egypt, he reminds his listeners that God is the same yesterday, today, and forever. With those words, he pivots from the past to the present, proclaiming that God is now at work in abolishing the transatlantic slave trade:

> Dear land of our ancestors! thou shalt no more be stained with the blood of thy children, shed by British and American hands: the ocean shall no more afford a refuge to their bodies, from impending slavery: nor shall the shores of

the British West India islands, and of the United States, any more witness the anguish of families, parted for ever by a publick sale. For this signal interposition of the God of mercies, in behalf of our brethren, it becomes us this day to offer up our united thanks.[35]

The first time I read that sermon to a group of undergraduate students, a Black student expressed discomfort with the idea that it was already time to offer thanks. He knew that while the slave trade and even slavery itself may have ended, he still wasn't in the promised land. Allen Dwight Callahan makes the same point in *The Talking Book*: for African Americans, the period since the Emancipation Proclamation relates best not to times of thriving in a land of milk and honey but rather to times of wandering in the grueling heat of the desert, not yet free to enjoy the blessings of a good land.[36]

A report from the Economic Policy Institute makes clear just how much the United States still resembles a barren wasteland for many African Americans: "With respect to homeownership, unemployment, and incarceration, America has failed to deliver any progress for African Americans over the last five decades." The median household wealth of Black families is about one-tenth that of White families. Only 41 percent of Black Americans are homeowners, compared with 71 percent of White Americans. For every 100,000 Black Americans, 1,730 are incarcerated, compared with 270 of every 100,000 White Americans. It goes on. The persistent inequalities of both economics and opportunity are staggering.[37]

In the Bible, the Israelites do not wake up in the promised land the day after leaving Egypt. For forty long years, they eked out an existence under oppressive desert heat. What happens to them there is often overlooked—but it is relevant to our American context.

Some of the most disturbing stories in the book of Numbers involve people who try to prevent the Israelites from making it to the promised land. At least four different groups of people do all they can to block the Israelites on their journey (20:14–21, 21:1–3, 21–35, 22:1–24:25). Repeatedly, the Israelites ask in the politest terms possible just to pass through others' land. They promise not to take so much as a drop of water, a grain of barley, or a single grape—in fact, they say that they'll avoid wells, fields, and vineyards altogether. They just need to make it to Canaan.

But the powers and principalities of that age do all they can to block the Israelites. They refuse passage. They deny water. They attack the Israelites instead. They take them captive. They even try to use religion—a famous holy man named Balaam—to try to curse this group of former slaves.

These people never succeed. They instead bring down God's judgment upon themselves. Instead of creating relationships of respect and kindness with the Israelites, those who obstruct their progress end up losing their safety, homes, and lives because they're working against the God who always wants to set the captives free. In their fear of the Israelites, they desperately cling to their land and power, and they lose everything.

The White church in America is becoming increasingly aware of how much it resembles these people in Numbers who deny passageway to the promised land. As it does, it faces questions. Will it continue to forbid entry, or will it recognize that recompense is due? Will it—like the Egyptians—be saved?

NOTES

1. Copyright © 2022 by the *Christian Century*. Reprinted by permission from the Jan 12, 2022, issue of the *Christian Century*, accessed May 19, 2023, https://www.christiancentury.org/article/critical-essay/book-exodus-includes-story-about-reparations-slavery. Endnotes have been added, and some changes have been made. The article's original title in print was "Saving the Egyptians: Exodus 12 Tells a Story of Reparations for Slavery." The original title online was "The Book of Exodus Includes a Story about Reparations for Slavery."

2. Equating the Egyptians with "bad guys" is a problem that this article seeks to address. For more on the topic, see Safwat Marzouk, "The Exodus: A Christian Egyptian Perspective," *HuffPost*, Dec 16, 2014, accessed May 19, 2023, https://www.huffpost.com/entry/the-exodus-a-christian-eg_b_6330118.

3. Erna Kim Hackett, "Why I Stopped Talking about Racial Reconciliation and Started Talking about White Supremacy," *Inheritance*, Mar 25, 2020, accessed May 19, 2023, https://www.inheritancemag.com/stories/why-i-stopped-talking-about-racial-reconciliation-and-started-talking-about-white-supremacy.

4. Benjamin Sass writes, "jewelry is an investment, and in precoinage times (and later) could be used as money" ("Jewelry," *OEANE* 3:238–46, here 238).

5. Some interpreters have claimed that the text envisions an epic battle between Pharaoh (or the gods of Egypt) and the God of Israel (e.g., Godfrey Ashby, *Go Out and Meet God: A Commentary on the Book of Exodus* [ITC; Grand Rapids: Eerdmans, 1998], 24, 50, 58; Brevard S. Childs, *The Book of Exodus: A Critical, Theological Commentary* [OTL; Louisville: Westminster, 1974], 175–77; Thomas B. Dozeman, *Commentary on Exodus* [Grand Rapids: Eerdmans, 2009], 138–39; Donald E. Gowan, *Theology in Exodus: Biblical Theology in the Form of a Commentary* [Louisville: Westminster John Knox, 1994], 136; Waldemar Janzen, *Exodus* [Believers Church Bible Commentary; Waterloo, ON: Herald, 2000], 69–70, 134; Philip Graham Ryken (*Exodus: Saved for God's Glory* [Preaching the Word; Wheaton, IL: Crossway, 2005], 351; cf. John I. Durham, *Exodus* [WBC; Waco, TX: Word, 1987], 168). Because Israel's God gives victory, the Israelites get the spoils of battle. Some parts of Exodus allude to such a battle (e.g., 15:3, 11–12). What the text says explicitly, however, is that the Israelites asked the Egyptians for the most valuable objects of their time—and the Egyptians gave such treasures. Such developments hardly sound like warfare. Josephus even partially credits friendship between Egyptians and Hebrews

(*Ant.* 2.314), and more recently, Carol Meyers speaks of "a close relationship, perhaps a neighborhood network" ("Egyptian Women [Exod 3:22; 11:2]," *Women in Scripture: A Dictionary of Named and Unnamed Women in the Hebrew Bible, the Apocryphal/Deuterocanonical Books, and the New Testament* [ed. Carol Meyers; Grand Rapids: Eerdmans, 2000], 188–89, here 189; see also Göran Larsson, *Bound for Freedom: The Book of Exodus in Jewish and Christian Traditions* [Peabody, MA: Hendrickson, 1999], 94). Cf. the Egyptians' "genuine sympathy" and "gesture of solidarity" described by George V. Pixley, *On Exodus: A Liberation Perspective* (trans. Robert R. Barr; Maryknoll, NY: Orbis, 1987), 59.

6. George Coats, "Despoiling the Egyptians," *VT* 18 (1968): 450–57; cf. Vulgate of 12:36; *Mekilta* 12:35; Julian Morgenstern, "The Despoiling of the Egyptians," *JBL* 68 (1949): 1–28, esp. 3–5; Martin Noth, *Exodus: A Commentary* (OTL; Philadelphia: Westminster, 1962), 93–94, 98.

7. Cf. Terence E. Fretheim, *Exodus* (IBC; Louisville: John Knox, 1991), 67.

8. E.g., Solomon Goldman, *The Book of Human Destiny: From Slavery to Freedom* (London: Abelard-Schuman, 1958), 194–95, 199; Roland Gradwohl, "*Niṣṣal* und *hiṣṣîl* als Rechtsbegriffe im Sklavenrecht," *ZAW* 111 (1999): 187–95, here 188.

9. Cf. Fretheim, *Exodus*, 131.

10. The word שאל appears in Exod 3:22; 11:2; 12:35–36. Although Exod 22:13; 2 Kgs 4:3; 6:5 use this term to talk about borrowing, the word can also refer to a request for a gift, as seen in Judg 5:25; 8:24; 1 Kgs 3:5, 10–11, 13 (//2 Chr 1:7, 11); 1 Kgs 10:13 (//2 Chr 9:12); 2 Chr 11:23; Ps 21:5[4]. According to BDB (specifically its discussion of this word in Exod 3:22, 11:2, and 12:35), "it is . . . not clear that there was any pretext of mere temporary use." See also Durham, *Exodus*, 148; P. Galpaz-Feller, "Silver and Gold, Exodus 3:22," *RB* 109 (2002): 197–209, esp. 199; Benno Jacob, *The Second Book of the Bible: Exodus* (trans. Walter Jacob in association with Yaakov Elman; Hoboken, NJ: KTAV, 1992), 338–46; Morgenstern, "Despoiling," 3–5; Th. C. Vriezen, "A Reinterpretation of Exodus 3:21–22 and Related Texts," *JEOL* 23 (1973–74): 389–401, here 392–94.

11. The word is נצל.

12. Galpaz-Feller ("Silver," esp. 197, see also 207) proposes that "the motif of accepting gifts of silver, gold and garments from Egypt could be a form of literary expression of a common Egyptian custom symbolizing a new status adapted by the Bible and used for theological purposes" (cf. Fretheim, *Exodus*, 142).

13. James C. VanderKam, *Jubilees: A Commentary on the Book of Jubilees* (2 vols.; Hermeneia: A Critical and Historical Commentary on the Bible; Minneapolis: Fortress Press, 2018), 2.1147, 1163–64.

14. Pierluigi Lanfranchi, *L'Exagoge d'Ezéchiel le Tragique: Introduction, texte, traduction et commentaire* (Studia in Veteris Testamenti Pseudepigrapha 21; Leiden: Brill, 2006), 106, 219–20, lines 162–66.

15. *Moses* 1.141–42 (Colson, LCL).

16. *Marc.* 4.24 (*ANF* 3.387); see also 2.20 (*ANF* 3.313).

17. Analogous comments can be found in the Middle Ages in Bachya ben Asher, *Torah Commentary* (trans. Eliyahu Munk; Jerusalem: KTAV, 1998), accessed May 19, 2023, https://www.sefaria.org/Rabbeinu_Bahya%2C_Shemot.11.2.1?lang=bi&with

=About&lang2=en (see comment on *Shemot* 11:2); *Barhebraeus' Scholia on the Old Testament Part I: Genesis—II Samuel* (edited by Martin Sprengling and William Creighton Graham; OIP 13; Chicago: University of Chicago University Press, 1931), 105.

18. Martin R. Delany, *Blake, or the Huts of America* (ed. Jermone McGann; corrected ed.; Cambridge: Harvard University Press, 2017), 44, cf. 318n42.

19. Victor P. Hamilton, *Exodus: An Exegetical Commentary* (Grand Rapids: Baker Academic, 2011), 67–68.

20. Ryken, *Exodus*, 107.

21. William Johnstone, *Exodus 1–19* (Smyth & Helwys Bible Commentary; Macon, GA: Smyth & Helwys, 2014), 236; George A. F. Knight, *Theology as Narration: A Commentary on the Book of Exodus* (Grand Rapids: Eerdmans, 1976), 27, cf. 82–83.

22. Duke L. Kwon and Gregory Thompson, *Reparations: A Christian Call for Repentance and Repair* (Grand Rapids: Brazos, 2021), 133–56, esp. 137–43.

23. Kwon and Thompson, *Reparations*, 157–80, esp. 162–80.

24. Kwon and Thompson, *Reparations*, 156, esp. 239n78.

25. The word נצל appears in the *pi'el* stem in Exod 3:22, 12:36; 2 Chr 20:25, and Ezek 14:14 (though some argue against the MT that יְנַצְּלוּ in Ezek 14:14 should be read as a *nip'al* [e.g., F. L. Hossfeld and B. Kalthoff, "נצל," *TDOT* 9.533–540, here 539] or *hip'il* [e.g., Robert L. Hubbard, "5911 נצל," *NIDOTTE* 3.141–147, here 142]). While there are not many appearances of the word in the *pi'el*, נצל has over 200 appearances in other stems, where the meaning connects with "deliver/rescue/save" much more frequently than "plunder." It can be translated "plunder" only in Gen 31:9, 16; Exod 33:6; 1 Sam 30:22; 2 Chr 20:25; Hos 2:11[9]; cf. 2 Sam 20:6. Elsewhere, the word relates to rescuing, delivering, or a similar concept.

Over 89 percent of the appearances of נצל are in the *hip'il*, where the meaning typically is "to rescue." Although the *pi'el* and *hip'il* should not be conflated, they can have similarities, particularly relating to causation (GKC §52g; *IBHS* §21.2.2c, 24.1i; Christo H. J. van der Merwe, Jacobus A. Naudé, and Jan H. Kroeze, *A Biblical Hebrew Reference Grammar* [2nd ed.; London: Bloomsbury T & T Clark, 2017], 81, §16.4.2.1). As Paul Joüon and T. Muraoka put it, "Some verbs . . . do occur in both Piel and Hifil with scarcely discernible difference in meaning or nuance. . . . It is only rarely possible to distinguish between Piel and Hifil thus used" (Joüon 1.156, §52*d*[3]). Here, it appears that both the *pi'el* and the *hip'il* of נצל basically mean "to cause to be moved" (the movement often being from an undesirable place to a desirable one; so Matthew Richard Schlimm, *70 Hebrew Words Every Christian Should Know* [Nashville: Abingdon, 2018], 85–88). Generally speaking, when the object being moved is a person (or life, or location that includes living inhabitants), the verb means to "rescue." When the object being moved is impersonal, however, then the meaning tends toward "plunder" (Benno Jacob, "Gott und Pharao," *MGWJ* 68 [1924]: 268–89, here 288; Jacob, *Second Book*, 345). Exodus 3:22 and 12:36 are more like the verses where the word should be translated "rescue" because the entity being moved is the Egyptians, not an impersonal object. See also the helpful discussion in Vriezen, "Reinterpretation," 394–400.

26. Josephus asserts that Egyptians gave gifts in hopes that the Israelites would leave quickly so that "Egypt's sufferings would cease" (*Ant.* 2.314 [Thackeray, LCL]; see also David Daube, *The Exodus Pattern in the Bible* [London: Faber and Faber, 1963], 59; Jacob, *Second Book*, 345; Morgenstern, "Despoiling," 22; Pixley, *Exodus*, 23, 59).

27. A core Egyptian concept is *ma'at*, which entails justice and order. When things are rightly ordered and operating in accordance with *ma'at*, then prosperity and goodness ensue. When deviations from *ma'at* occur, then events go badly and divine judgment follows. See, for example, Miriam Lichtheim, *Moral Values in Ancient Egypt* (OBO 155; Göttingen: Vandenhoeck & Ruprecht, 1997), 42–43; Roland E. Murphy, *The Tree of Life: An Exploration of Biblical Wisdom Literature* (2nd ed.; Grand Rapids: Eerdmans, 1996), 115, 161; K. A. D. Smelik, "Ma'at," *DDD* 534–35. For primary texts, see the useful indexes in *AEL* 1.245, 2.239.

Pharaoh in particular was expected to embody the principle of *ma'at*, and the book of Exodus relentlessly portrays pharaoh as unable to live by, rule by, or listen to *ma'at*.

28. Ta-Nehisi Coates, "The Case for Reparations," *The Atlantic*, June 2014, accessed May 19, 2023, https://www.theatlantic.com/magazine/archive/2014/06/the-case-for-reparations/361631/. Links between Exod 3:21–22, 12:35–36, and Deut 15:12–15 are also explored in U. Cassuto, *A Commentary on the Book of Exodus* (trans. Israel Abrahams; Jerusalem: Magnes, 1967), 44; Daube, *Pattern*, 55–61; Gradwohl, "Rechtsbegriffe," 190–93; Moshe Greenberg, *Understanding Exodus* (New York: Behrman, 1969), 86–87; Johnstone, *Exodus 1–19*, 87, 94, 200, 236.

29. Nathan MacDonald, *What Did the Ancient Israelites Eat? Diet in Biblical Times* (Grand Rapids: Eerdmans, 2008), 59. Cf. Gen 47:15–17.

30. George Fox, *Gospel Family-Order, Being a Short Discourse Concerning the Ordering of Families, Both of Whites, Blacks, and Indians* (Ann Arbor: Text Creation Partnership, 2011), 17, accessed May 19, 2023, https://quod.lib.umich.edu/e/evans/N00809.0001.001?rgn=main;view=fulltext.

31. Cf. Jacob, "Gott und Pharao," 288–89.

32. The generosity in some of these episodes is further explored in Matthew R. Schlimm, *From Fratricide to Forgiveness: The Language and Ethics of Anger in Genesis* (Siphrut; Winona Lake, IN: Eisenbrauns, 2011), 145–49, 166–69, 182–83. Gradwohl ("Rechtsbegriffe," 193–94) claims that the treasures received by the enslaved parties should not be seen as gifts but as wages due to them. Given Deut 15:12–15, there may be some truth in this claim. More evidence from Gradwohl would be helpful, however. Furthermore, it is noteworthy that other biblical and ancient Near Eastern texts present giving as a way of alleviating anger and hostilities: Prov 21:14, 25:21–22; "The Story of Idrimi, King of Alalakh," (*ANET*, 557–58); "Emesh and Enten: Enlil Chooses the Farmer-God," pp. 49–51 in S. N. Kramer, *Sumerian Mythology: A Study of Spiritual and Literary Achievement in the Third Millennium B. C.* (Memoirs of the American Philosophical Society; Philadelphia: The American Philosophical Society, 1944); "Horus and Seth" (*AEL* 2:214–23, esp. 215, 222); "Counsels of Wisdom," pp. 96–107 in W. G. Lambert, *Babylonian Wisdom Literature* (London: Oxford University Press, 1975) 101, lines 41–45.

33. Cf. Larsson, *Freedom*, 94.

34. Absalom Jones, "A Thanksgiving Sermon: Preached January 1, 1808, In St. Thomas's, or the African Episcopal, Church, Philadelphia: On Account of the Abolition of the African Slave Trade, On That Day, by the Congress of the United States," in *American Sermons: The Pilgrims to Martin Luther King Jr.* (ed. Michael Warner; New York: The Library of America, 1999), 538–545, here 538.

35. Jones, "Thanksgiving," 541.

36. Allen Dwight Callahan, *The Talking Book: African Americans and the Bible* (New Haven: Yale University Press, 2006), 132–37.

37. Janelle Jones, John Schmitt, and Valerie Wilson, "50 Years after the Kerner Commission," Economic Policy Institute, Feb 26, 2018, accessed May 19, 2023, https://www.epi.org/publication/50-years-after-the-kerner-commission/.

BIBLIOGRAPHY

Ancient Egyptian Literature. Edited by Miriam Lichtheim. 3 vols. Berkeley: University of California Press, 1971–1980.

Ancient Near Eastern Texts Relating to the Old Testament. Edited by J. B. Pritchard. 3rd ed. Princeton: Princeton University Press, 1969.

Ante-Nicene Fathers: The Writings of the Fathers Down to A.D. 325. Edited by Alexander Roberts, James Donaldson, A. Cleveland Coxe, and Allan Menzies. Peabody, MA: Hendrickson, 1994.

Ashby, Godfrey. *Go Out and Meet God: A Commentary on the Book of Exodus.* ITC. Grand Rapids: Eerdmans, 1998.

Bachya ben Asher. *Torah Commentary.* Trans. Eliyahu Munk. Jerusalem: KTAV, 1998. Accessed May 19, 2023. https://www.sefaria.org/Rabbeinu_Bahya?tab=contents.

Barhebraeus' Scholia on the Old Testament Part I: Genesis—II Samuel. Edited by Martin Sprengling and William Creighton Graham. OIP 13. Chicago: University of Chicago University Press, 1931.

Brown, F., S. R. Driver, and C. A. Briggs. *The Brown-Driver-Briggs Hebrew and English Lexicon: With an Appendix Containing the Biblical Aramaic.* Peabody, MA: Hendrickson, 1999.

Callahan, Allen Dwight. *The Talking Book: African Americans and the Bible.* New Haven: Yale University Press, 2006.

Cassuto, U. *A Commentary on the Book of Exodus.* Trans. Israel Abrahams. Jerusalem: Magnes, 1967.

Childs, Brevard S. *The Book of Exodus: A Critical, Theological Commentary.* OTL. Louisville: Westminster, 1974.

Coates, Ta-Nehisi. "The Case for Reparations." *The Atlantic.* June 2014. Accessed May 19, 2023. https://www.theatlantic.com/magazine/archive/2014/06/the-case-for-reparations/361631/.

Coats, George. "Despoiling the Egyptians." *VT* 18 (1968): 450–57.

Daube, David. *The Exodus Pattern in the Bible.* London: Faber and Faber, 1963.

Delany, Martin R. *Blake, or the Huts of America*. Edited by Jerome McGann. Corrected ed. Cambridge: Harvard University Press, 2017.
Dictionary of Deities and Demons in the Bible. Edited by Karel Van Der Toorn, Bob Becking, and Pieter W. Van der Horst. 2nd ed. Leiden: Brill, 1999.
Dozeman, Thomas B. *Commentary on Exodus*. Grand Rapids: Eerdmans, 2009.
Durham, John I. *Exodus*. WBC. Waco, TX: Word, 1987.
Fox, George. *Gospel Family-Order, Being a Short Discourse Concerning the Ordering of Families, Both of Whites, Blacks, and Indians*. Ann Arbor: Text Creation Partnership, 2011. Accessed May 19, 2023. https://quod.lib.umich.edu/e/evans/N00809.0001.001?rgn=main;view=fulltext.
Fretheim, Terence E. *Exodus*. IBC. Louisville: John Knox, 1991.
Galpaz-Feller, P. "Silver and Gold, Exodus 3:22." *RB* 109 (2002): 197–209.
Gesenius' Hebrew Grammar. Edited by E. Kautzsch. Translated by A. E. Cowley. 2nd ed. Oxford: Clarendon, 1910.
Goldman, Solomon. *The Book of Human Destiny: From Slavery to Freedom*. London: Abelard-Schuman, 1958.
Gowan, Donald E. *Theology in Exodus: Biblical Theology in the Form of a Commentary*. Louisville: Westminster John Knox, 1994.
Gradwohl, Roland. "*Niṣṣal* und *hiṣṣîl* als Rechtsbegriffe im Sklavenrecht." *ZAW* 111 (1999): 187–95.
Greenberg, Moshe. *Understanding Exodus*. New York: Behrman, 1969.
Hackett, Erna Kim. "Why I Stopped Talking about Racial Reconciliation and Started Talking about White Supremacy." *Inheritance*. Mar 25, 2020. Accessed May 19, 2023. https://www.inheritancemag.com/stories/why-i-stopped-talking-about-racial-reconciliation-and-started-talking-about-white-supremacy.
Hamilton, Victor. *Exodus: An Exegetical Commentary*. Grand Rapids: Baker Academic, 2011.
Jacob, Benno. "Gott und Pharao." *MGWJ* 68 (1924): 268–89.
———. *The Second Book of the Bible: Exodus*. Trans. Walter Jacob in association with Yaakov Elman. Hoboken, NJ: KTAV, 1992.
Janzen, Waldemar. *Exodus*. Believers Church Bible Commentary. Waterloo, ON: Herald, 2000.
Johnstone, William. *Exodus 1–19*. Smyth & Helwys Bible Commentary. Macon, GA: Smyth & Helwys, 2014.
Jones, Absalom. "A Thanksgiving Sermon: Preached January 1, 1808, In St. Thomas's, or the African Episcopal, Church, Philadelphia: On Account of the Abolition of the African Slave Trade, on That Day, by the Congress of the United States." Pages 538–45 in *American Sermons: The Pilgrims to Martin Luther King Jr*. Edited by Michael Warner. New York: The Library of America, 1999.
Jones, Janelle, John Schmitt, and Valerie Wilson. "50 Years after the Kerner Commission." Economic Policy Institute. Feb 26, 2018. Accessed May 19, 2023. https://www.epi.org/publication/50-years-after-the-kerner-commission/.
Josephus. Translated by H. St. J. Thackeray et al. 10 vols. Loeb Classical Library. Cambridge: Harvard University Press, 1926–1965.

Joüon, Paul. *A Grammar of Biblical Hebrew*. Translated and revised by T. Muraoka. 2 vols. Subsidia biblica 14/1–2. Rome: Editrice Pontificio Istituto Biblico, 1991.

Knight, George A. F. *Theology as Narration: A Commentary on the Book of Exodus*. Grand Rapids: Eerdmans, 1976.

Kramer, S. N. *Sumerian Mythology: A Study of Spiritual and Literary Achievement in the Third Millennium B. C.* Memoirs of the American Philosophical Society. Philadelphia: The American Philosophical Society, 1944.

Kwon, Duke L., and Gregory Thompson. *Reparations: A Christian Call for Repentance and Repair*. Grand Rapids: Brazos, 2021.

Lambert, W. G. *Babylonian Wisdom Literature*. London: Oxford University Press, 1975.

Lanfranchi, Pierluigi. *L'Exagoge d'Ezéchiel le Tragique: Introduction, texte, traduction et commentaire*. Studia in Veteris Testamenti Pseudepigrapha 21. Leiden: Brill, 2006.

Larsson, Göran. *Bound for Freedom: The Book of Exodus in Jewish and Christian Traditions*. Peabody, MA: Hendrickson, 1999.

Lichtheim, Miriam. *Moral Values in Ancient Egypt*. OBO 155. Göttingen: Vandenhoeck & Ruprecht, 1997.

MacDonald, Nathan. *What Did the Ancient Israelites Eat? Diet in Biblical Times*. Grand Rapids: Eerdmans, 2008.

Marzouk, Safwat. "The Exodus: A Christian Egyptian Perspective." *HuffPost*. Dec 16, 2014. Accessed May 19, 2023. https://www.huffpost.com/entry/the-exodus-a-christian-eg_b_6330118.

Meyers, Carol. "Egyptian Women (Exod 3:22; 11:2)." Pages 188–89 in *Women in Scripture: A Dictionary of Named and Unnamed Women in the Hebrew Bible, the Apocryphal/Deuterocanonical Books, and the New Testament*. Edited by Carol Meyers. Grand Rapids: Eerdmans, 2000.

Morgenstern, Julian. "The Despoiling of the Egyptians." *JBL* 68 (1949): 1–28.

Murphy, Roland E. *The Tree of Life: An Exploration of Biblical Wisdom Literature*. 2nd ed. Grand Rapids: Eerdmans, 1996.

New International Dictionary of Old Testament Theology and Exegesis. Edited by Willem A. VanGemeren. 5 vols. Grand Rapids: Zondervan, 1997.

Noth, Martin. *Exodus: A Commentary*. OTL. Philadelphia: Westminster, 1962.

Philo. Translated by F. H. Colson et al. 12 vols. Loeb Classical Library. Cambridge: Harvard University Press, 1954–62.

Pixley, George V. *On Exodus: A Liberation Perspective*. Translated by Robert R. Barr. Maryknoll, NY: Orbis, 1987.

Ryken, Philip Graham. *Exodus: Saved for God's Glory*. Preaching the Word. Wheaton, IL: Crossway, 2005.

Sass, Benjamin. "Jewelry." *OEANE* 3:238–46.

Schlimm, Matthew Richard. *70 Hebrew Words Every Christian Should Know*. Nashville: Abingdon, 2018.

———. *From Fratricide to Forgiveness: The Language and Ethics of Anger in Genesis*. Siphrut. Winona Lake, IN: Eisenbrauns, 2011.

———. "Saving the Egyptians: Exodus 12 Tells a Story of Reparations for Slavery." *Christian Century*. Jan 12, 2022. Accessed May 19, 2023. https://www.christiancentury.org/article/critical-essay/book-exodus-includes-story-about-reparations-slavery.

Smelik, K. A. D. "Ma'at." Pages 534–35 in *Dictionary of Deities and Demons in the Bible*. Edited by Karel Van Der Toorn, Bob Becking, and Pieter W. Van der Horst. 2nd ed. Leiden: Brill, 1999.

Theological Dictionary of the Old Testament. Edited by G. Johannes Botterweck, Helmer Ringgren, and Heinz-Josef Fabry. Translated by John T. Willis et al. 15 vols. Grand Rapids, Eerdmans, 1974–2006.

Van der Merwe, Christo H. J., Jacobus A. Naudé, and Jan H. Kroeze. *A Biblical Hebrew Reference Grammar*. 2nd ed. London: Bloomsbury T & T Clark, 2017.

VanderKam, James C. *Jubilees: A Commentary on the Book of Jubilees*. 2 vols. Hermeneia: A Critical and Historical Commentary on the Bible. Minneapolis: Fortress Press, 2018.

Vriezen, Th. C. "A Reinterpretation of Exodus 3:21–22 and Related Texts," *JEOL* 23 (1973–74): 389–401.

Waltke, Bruce K., and M. O'Connor. *An Introduction to Biblical Hebrew Syntax*. Winona Lake, IN: Eisenbrauns, 1990.

Chapter Two

Bypassing the Bible

Why Exodus 21 and Deuteronomy 15 Did Not Influence and Have Not Influenced Reparations Proposals

Stacy Davis

From 1619 to 1865, the British colonies that eventually became the United States of America utilized Black chattel slavery as one of their economic systems. After independence, the country eventually divided into slave and free states, with both sides using biblical texts and Christian arguments to justify their positions. When the Civil War ended in 1865, the United States had to decide what to do with millions of newly freed enslaved people. Exodus 21:2–11 and Deuteronomy 15:12–18 offered a path; the texts regulate and prescribe compensation for recently freed enslaved people so that they can begin new lives with some financial resources. Yet Republicans who supported the uplift of the newly freed and Democrats who opposed such uplift bypassed both texts, and the United States gave no compensation to former enslaved people during Reconstruction (1863–1877), when it had clear opportunities to do so. Why?

Reparations never materialized due to an emphasis on labor and the rise of the White working class. White emphasis on freed people earning their living through hard work and acquiring capital caused compensation to be viewed as harmful handouts. A new post-slavery White working class did not want to share any financial gains with a Black labor force that they saw as economic competition. Also, the texts in Exodus and Deuteronomy applied to enslaved Hebrew people and Hebrew owners. Because Whites did not see Blacks as kin but as foreign enslaved people (Lev 25:44–46), the laws about reparations need not apply. The missed opportunities of the Reconstruction period, combined with racism, led to the economic disparities between Blacks and Whites that still exist. In order to begin addressing ongoing and expanded race-based economic inequality, the descendants of the enslaved should receive what their ancestors did not—reparations.

Exodus 21:2–11 and Deuteronomy 15:12–18 give laws regarding Israelite male and female enslaved persons. Exodus describes more of a system of indentured servitude, where the men served six years and left debt-free in the seventh year. As John Van Seters notes, "Hebrew slaves purchased from foreigners are to be treated in the same way as those who become enslaved through debt to their creditors with the same right of release after six years of service."[1] If a male enslaved person had established a family during those six years, he either left them behind or stayed with them and became an enslaved person "for life" (Ex 21:6).[2] Female enslaved persons became the wives of their owners or their owners' sons. If the women proved unsatisfactory for some reason, they were redeemed or resold/remarried within another Israelite family. If the owner/husband failed to provide for her material and sexual needs, "she shall go out without debt, without payment of money," free but broke (Ex 21:11). Deuteronomy describes a similar system, except the enslaved people freed in the seventh year are not released

> empty-handed. Provide liberally out of your flock, your threshing floor, and your wine press, thus giving to him some of the bounty with which the Lord your God has blessed you. Remember that you were a slave in the land of Egypt, and the Lord your God redeemed you; for this reason I lay this command upon you today . . . You shall do the same with regard to your female slave. Do not consider it a hardship when you send them out from you free persons, because for six years they have given you services worth the wages of hired laborers; and the Lord your God will bless you in all that you do (Deut 15:12–15, 17b–18).

Those who wanted to remain enslaved, "because he loves you and your household, since he is well off with you," could do so (Deut 15:17).

These texts have not produced large quantities of biblical commentary, in part because they are legal texts[3] and in part because they address what seems to be a self-explanatory response to a particular situation, specifically under what contexts a Hebrew owner frees a Hebrew enslaved person. The Torah presumes three things. First, there is a limited time frame for Israelite slavery. The limit is in part because most slavery in the ancient world was debt slavery, in which a person sold themself in order to pay an outstanding bill. Such a decision had a time limit, unless the male enslaved person decided to remain a slave for life. Notably, the biblical text does not allude to the possibility that owners could have encouraged enslaved men to marry in an attempt to extend their control, similar to the practice of breeding slaves in the US South. Second, how an enslaved person is treated depends upon gender. While Deuteronomy argues that women who become free should receive the same financial compensation as men, Exodus does not. That text leaves an emancipated woman with no financial resources. Because female enslaved persons were often in a sexual relationship with their owners or used for sexual purposes (for example, Hagar in Genesis 16 and Bilhah and Zilpah in Genesis 30), their rights seemed to have been more circumscribed. For example, Bilhah and Zilpah neither name nor have any claim upon the four sons that they bear. Hagar does get to claim Ishmael, but only because Sarah rejects him as an heir in Genesis 21, and Abraham does the same. A similar situation existed in US slavery, where enslaved women bore children as property for their masters and therefore had little control over whether or for how long they would be able to nurture them. Long after slavery ended, Black women spoke candidly about the costs of trying to parent under those conditions.[4] Third, in the biblical text, there is a common enslaved historical memory for owners and their property.

None of these presumptions existed for African slavery in the United States, primarily because slaveowners used biblical texts such as Genesis 9:18–27 and Leviticus 25:44–46 to justify their actions. Applying the curse of Canaan to Africans meant they were destined to be the slaves of Shem and Japheth's descendants. White Americans saw themselves as Japheth's people, so all was well. Furthermore, Leviticus 25 justified lifelong Israelite enslavement of non-Israelites and the passing down of them as property to Israelite heirs. Because White pro-slavery advocates such as Josiah Priest, in *Slavery as It Relates to the Negro or African Race*, and Thornton Stringfellow, in *Slavery: Its Origin, Nature, and History, Considered in the Light of Bible Teachings, Moral Justice, and Political Wisdom*, saw themselves as Japheth's European heirs, and Africans were not Europeans, the law advocating perpetual slavery supported White enslavement of Blacks.[5] So, while the text in Leviticus functioned as a corollary to the US context, Exodus and Deuteronomy could not function as corollaries. The Three-Fifths Clause of the US Constitution made explicit what had been implicit before: people of African descent were not Americans; instead, they were "all other persons." For White Americans to have enslaved other White Americans in perpetuity would have been biblically wrong. What was right was an economic system that created the most amount of profit with the least amount of harm to those in power.

It is difficult to overstate how important slavery was to the US economy. Sven Beckert and Seth Rockman argue that slave labor was at the core of American economic development and prosperity, beginning in the nineteenth century.[6] Such a core could not have been maintained with a rotating labor force. Research has demonstrated the "historical ties to slavery" found in institutions including "banks, insurance firms, and universities."[7]

Enslaved people not only created wealth—they were wealth. Matthew Desmond notes that "the combined value of enslaved people exceeded that of all the railroads and factories in the nation."[8] Daina Ramey Berry writes, "Today we think of compensation for the enslaved as reparations, but rarely do we think about payments being made to those who profited from owning slaves."[9] Owners took out and benefited from life insurance policies on the enslaved.[10] This means an arbitrator determined how much money an enslaved person was worth. Berry asks, "How are we to make sense of the value of black life in a historical context? How are we to make sense of the value of black life in a contemporary moment?"[11] If reparations deals with dollars and cents, then perhaps one place to begin, however potentially distasteful, is with the prices listed in some of those insurance policies, converted into contemporary dollars. For example, "Charlotte, valued at $400" in 1853, would be worth $15,220.92 in October 2021.[12] Human property had financial value during the antebellum period, which is one way to determine what would have been owed in 1865.

Additionally, because the US operated slavery and indentured servitude systems simultaneously until the early nineteenth century, precedent existed before the Civil War for compensating laborers for their work. Law professor Mary Sarah Bilder notes that White indentured servants "constituted property; they were assignable under statutory provisions; they could be sold to satisfy a debt; and they passed by descent pursuant to testamentary laws."[13] The only difference between African enslaved people and White indentured servants was the servants were not permanent property. Like enslaved Hebrews, their labor had a term limit, after which they were free. Furthermore, Bilder writes that "upon the completion of service, indentured servants in most colonies received 'freedom dues.' At first the colonies often made land grants . . . Eventually, however, the colonies turned to either monetary payments or payments in kind by the master. Although early seventeenth-century indentured servants had a degree of economic mobility, by the eighteenth century such mobility had diminished," because very few freed indentured servants received compensation by then.[14] Land distribution allowed the newly freed to support themselves, but as owners began to see the distribution as a reduction of their own wealth, the practice plummeted. Notably, as indentured servitude gave way to White immigration in the nineteenth century, courts began to confirm "that persons, at least when they were white, were not articles of commerce."[15] This became a way to separate and distinguish poor Whites from Black slaves, who were bought and sold. Nevertheless, for a time in the United States, a form of biblical reparations existed.

When the Civil War ended, ideas circulated about compensating the newly freed. As Eric Foner notes in his comprehensive history of Reconstruction, "the creation of the Freedman's Bureau in March 1865 symbolized the widespread belief among Republicans that the federal government must shoulder broad responsibility for the emancipated slaves, including offering them some kind of access to land."[16] The Bureau had the power "to divide abandoned and confiscated land [from Confederates] *into forty-acre plots* for rental to freedmen and loyal refugees and eventual sale."[17] The idea of forty acres, however, predated the Freedmen's Bureau. On January 16, 1865, General William Sherman's Special Field Order Number 15 gave part of South Carolina to Blacks. Foner writes, "Each family would receive forty acres of land, and Sherman later provided that the army could assist them with the loan of mules."[18] The Black hope for land in the South increased, with former slaves arguing that they should now share in the wealth they had helped to create for their former owners in particular and the United States in general.[19]

This hope, however, did not materialize. The Freedmen's Bureau had the land of former Confederates but could not distribute most of it. On May 29, 1865, President Andrew Johnson announced an amnesty program; any Confederate who took a pledge of allegiance to the Union and rejected slavery would be pardoned and have their lands restored. President Johnson also pardoned many wealthy Southerners ineligible for the amnesty program in the summer and fall of 1865 and gave them their land back, even land now being worked by the newly freed under Field Order 15.[20] Johnson actively worked against Freedmen's Bureau efforts at redistributing land to Blacks, vetoing one bill in 1866. Notably, Johnson argued in his veto that Congress had never done anything like this for Whites and doing so would hint that free Blacks "did not have to work for a living."[21] As we will see below, this was not a true statement. When the second bill passed after Johnson's veto, those with land under Sherman's order could only rent or purchase twenty-acre parcels already owned by the US government.[22] This order had only applied to a part of South Carolina, so most Blacks had no access to or opportunity for land. Many in South Carolina lost their land, either when "federal troops evicted them by force" or through becoming sharecroppers and no longer owners.[23]

Even Republicans who favored redistributing land to Blacks were not wholeheartedly in favor of their own proposals. Some emphasized voting rights over property rights. When the Southern Homestead Act passed in 1866, Blacks had the option only of buying land, and many did not have the capital to do so. After the 1867 election, Northern Republicans focused more on reuniting with the South and ending Reconstruction as soon as possible. Southern Republicans, with the exception of those in South Carolina, still focused on land purchase and not land distribution, in the name of equity.[24] This focus did not help formerly enslaved people. In Mississippi, for example, even Blacks with resources to buy small plots of land found it sold to Whites in larger quantities for less money, a hint at the anti-Black racism that finally ended Reconstruction.²⁵ As sharecropping became the dominant economic system, free Blacks were unable to gain the capital needed to buy land. The emphasis on working for a living made the concept of giving anything to Blacks with practically no resources a distasteful option for Whites. Once Democrats began to redeem the South from Republican Reconstruction governments, the focus on Blacks working for their living intensified as an additional means of social control, and Congress showed no interest in land reform.²⁶

The language of redeeming Southern states from Reconstruction was intentionally religious, because the almost immediate White Southern resistance to Black uplift had religious roots. Even before the Civil War ended, White Southerners framed their impending loss as tragic and themselves as noble victims. One Sunday school story encouraged children to reject the Yankees who wanted to enslave them and to resist Reconstruction.²⁷ Confederate soldiers were the true patriots and should not be called "'traitors and criminals.'"²⁸ The end of slavery was not God's will but a source of religious crisis.²⁹ The crisis stemmed in part from a belief in the righteousness of Black slavery,³⁰ since as mentioned earlier, Leviticus 25:44–46 allows Israelites to enslave non-Israelites for life: "they may be your property. You may keep them as a possession for your children after you, for them to inherit as property. These you may treat as slaves." The distinction allowed colonists to treat White indentured servants differently from Black slaves and was a prooftext for slavery in the antebellum South.³¹ It later became a prooftext for the Lost Cause theology that helped to soothe Southerners after military defeat. In that theology, the defeated Southerners were the true patriots, upholding the life and liberty ideals of the Declaration of Independence.³² While one can debate whether this characterization is accurate, what is non-debatable is this: former Southern slaveowners not only had the way paved for their political and economic reintegration into society; in the District of Columbia, they even received financial compensation for their losses in the 1862 District of Columbia Compensated Emancipation Act.

Furthermore, when slavery ended, White wage laborers who had been unable to compete in a system dominated by free labor gained a chance for economic advancement that they did not usually have to share with newly freed Blacks. Historian Keri Leigh Merritt argues as follows:

> They [poor Whites] began by forming "associations," or labor unions, and demanded freedom from competition with slaves and even free blacks, whose wages always undercut their own . . . [after Emancipation], poor white workers were finally able to compete in a free labor economy. But their increasing inclusion in the spoils of whiteness often came at the expense of blacks. While

freedmen waited in vain for forty acres and a mule, some poor whites were *granted* land from the Homestead Acts.[33]

The first one, passed in 1862 and initially proposed by Andrew Johnson in 1846 (the same man opposed to giving land to the newly freed slaves twenty years later) gave over 200 million acres of land in the western United States to men "for nothing more than a small filing fee."[34] Merritt calls the Act "the most comprehensive form of wealth redistribution that has ever taken place in America"; more than 1.5 million households, almost all White, became landowning,[35] a privilege Johnson denied freed Blacks just four years later. Merritt notes, "The number of original (1862) Homestead-recipient descendants living in 2000 was estimated to be around 46 million, about one-quarter of the US adult population."[36] The Act survived until 1934, bringing millions of Whites into the middle class. The 1866 Southern Homestead Act, mentioned earlier, excluded most newly freed enslaved people.[37] Although repealed in 1876, it too helped many Whites raise their economic status in ways that freed Blacks could not: "Largely denied these wealth entitlements, blacks were left landless after years (and generations) of unpaid, coerced, and brutalized labor."[38] Freed poor people were told to earn their way in a system not made for their advancement, the nineteenth-century equivalent of building bricks without straw (Ex 5.6–19).

Merritt's conclusion is the starting point for contemporary conversations about reparations:

> After emancipation, of course, African Americans became the only race in America ever to start out—as an entire people—with close to zero wealth. With no saved, inheritable wealth and assets, loans were nearly impossible to secure ... Without ever owning land, and thus, having nothing else upon which to build or generate wealth, the majority of freedmen had little real chance of breaking the cycles of poverty created by slavery.[39]

The Civil War gave Blacks political freedom on paper while giving many poor Whites land deeds that gave them economic freedom, which was never categorized as a gift or a handout. The disparate treatment of the two groups led to significant real-world consequences, past and present.

As Ibram X. Kendi argues, the White belief in racial progress resulted in a de-emphasis on Black economic progress. He writes, "Each successive generation of white Americans is let off the hook for the legacy of slavery. Politicians and the public alike can claim that this sin remains a part of the past, that the country has rid itself of the stain, and that there is no need for anti-racist remedies like reparations."[40] After the ratification of the Thirteenth, Fourteenth, and Fifteenth Amendments, it was up to Blacks to fend for themselves. The Supreme Court in 1883 struck down the Civil Rights Act of 1875, arguing that Blacks should not receive any special legal treatment. It took nearly a century to correct that misperception, but it returned with the belief that racial preferences are not needed and that economic disparities have no connection to systemic discrimination.[41] The intersection of class and race, which uplifted poor Whites in the post-Civil War United States while limiting the progress of freed Black people, gets bypassed in favor of the beliefs that all can make it if they just work hard enough and that class disparities have nothing to do with the US history of race.

Kendi's call for reparations, however, is not new; instead, it is more than fifty years old. In April 1969, the Black Economic Development Corporation [BEDC] approved the Black Manifesto, a call for "$500 million dollars from white American churches and synagogues as reparation for their complicity in the historical and ongoing economic exploitation of African Americans."[42] On May 4, 1969, James Forman interrupted services at New York City's Riverside Church to read the Manifesto.[43] The Manifesto presumes precisely what US religious arguments about slavery did not—specifically, Black Americans were Americans. Based on the Civil War, three Constitutional amendments, and the civil rights movements, Black people could make a claim on US economic institutions (in this case, churches and synagogues) for debts owed. As the Manifesto states, "We are no longer afraid to demand our full rights as a people in this decadent society." While the document never quoted scripture, it did challenge Christians and Jews to live up to it:

> We call upon all White Christians and Jews to practice patience, tolerance, understanding and nonviolence as they have encouraged, advised and demanded that we as black people should do throughout our entire enforced slavery in the United States. The true test of their faith and belief in the Cross and the words of the prophets will certainly be put to a test as we seek legitimate and extremely modest reparations for our role in developing the industrial base of the Western world through our slave labor.[44]

The reaction was mixed at best. A majority of the church's parishioners walked out in protest but eventually gave "an unspecified percentage of its budget to poverty alleviation, designated for its own programs rather than the United Black appeal,"[45] which was connected to the BEDC. Theologian Edward A. Dowey described the Manifesto as a catalog of "absurd demands" that could lead to socialism.[46] While young Blacks might support it, the proposal would exacerbate racial tensions. Dowey concluded, however, that white Christians should take the Manifesto's call for Black autonomy seriously.[47] Gayraud S. Wilmore Jr. argued against focusing on the word reparations and instead to pay attention to the fact that they [White Americans] and not the blacks evoked the Two Americas, one slave and one free, and that the overdue bill for that evocation must now be paid in full. *The real issue is not the validity or invalidity of reparations, but the fact of black alienation and what white Christians are going to do about it.*[48]

Wilmore argued that churches should "make the money and power available to those who need it to survive our perfidy."[49]

Church historian Hanna Ondrey, writing fifty years later, notes that the Evangelical Covenant Church of America, an historically Swedish Protestant congregation, did respond to the Manifesto, creating a fund that existed until the late 1990s. In 1969, the leadership asked congregations to give an extra dollar per person to organizations working to alleviate Black poverty. While congregations never gave the full amount, they gave over $16,000 in 1969 and in 1970.[50] After 1970, the fund was reclassified "to expand recipients to all ethnic groups."[51] The denomination insisted, however, "that the fund was not a form of reparations."[52] As Ondrey notes, "The Covenant fund was not an act of justice but charity. It addressed the problem of generic poverty rather than the unjust distribution of wealth as the consequence of the particular history of black oppression, with its corollary of white responsibility."[53] Any idea of White people owing Blacks anything not only was rejected, but after just two years, even the charity was distributed as help to all PGMs [people of the global majority] as opposed to Blacks alone.

This resistance to reparations as a debt owed (or even a joyful repayment according to Deuteronomy) does not surprise Jennifer Harvey. Using critical whiteness studies as a foundation for her work, Harvey's thesis is as follows: "There exists in this history the profound absence among white Protestants of a sense of white agency—white *moral* agency, in particular—in the face of the charges of the Black Manifesto."[54] The social construct of Whiteness in combination with slavery and segregation stunted the development of Whites' ethical understanding. Racism became a Black problem to solve, making the Black Manifesto particularly problematic,[55] because "reparations bring white responsibility into view."[56] So, helping poor Black people was acceptable; reparations were not. Evangelicals and Catholics said no to the Manifesto. Protestant groups that responded made sure to distinguish their social service work for Black people from reparations by not giving money to the BEDC, as the Manifesto demanded. Instead, they gave money to the National Committee of Black Churchmen against that committee's own recommendation. These decisions were couched in language that described the problem of Black poverty without mentioning how the problem came to be.[57] The Christian lack of response to the Black Manifesto may have set back any significant discussion of reparations in the late 1960s and early 1970s.

Ta-Nehisi Coates's 2014 article in *The Atlantic*, "The Case for Reparations," brought the issue back to the national stage. Coates's article begins with a quotation of Deuteronomy 15:12–15, the call to send enslaved persons to freedom with gifts. Coates examines the history of theft of Black-owned land beginning in the antebellum period to redlining,[58] which drastically limited Black access to FHA loans and the ability to buy a home, the primary wealth generator in the United States. Consequently, the wealth gap developed and persisted. Coates notes, "Redlining was not officially outlawed until 1968 by the Fair Housing Act. By then the damage was done—and reports of redlining by banks have continued."[59] Redlining exacerbated housing segregation and the persistence of poverty in Black neighborhoods.[60] Even laws like the Social Security Act and the GI Bill did not help, because the Social Security Act excluded domestic and farm workers (mostly Black), and the GI Bill's implementation depended upon individuals at the Veterans Administration and local banks.

Arguing against an 1891 *Chicago Tribune* editorial's claim that learning how to be good, Christian, English-speaking laborers meant former enslaved people were now owed nothing, Coates writes, "Not exactly. Having been enslaved for two hundred and fifty years, black people were not left to their own devices. They were terrorized."[61] Coates calls for a national conversation about reparations, even if the conclusion is that the government cannot afford to pay its debt. The conversation is what matters.

While not on a federal level, the conversation is happening, particularly in Christian communities, which are more receptive now than they were in 1969. Jennifer Harvey notes that in some White Protestant denominations, the conversation began several years before Coates's article.[62] She argues, however, that "without acknowledging and addressing whiteness and white moral agency, that is, the active participation in and perpetuation of racial injustice by white people, attempts to challenge racism remain inadequate."[63] Reparations may help, since they "acknowledge white agency historically and demand ongoing white agency for the repair of racial brokenness."[64] The PCUSA, for example, notes that in the 1960s, it did not recognize the links between racism and social structures and argues now that biblical texts like Zacchaeus's story in Luke 19 justify reparations.[65]

Christian theologians Duke L. Kwon and Gregory Thompson take up the moral call for reparations. They define reparations "*as the deliberate repair of White supremacy, cultural theft through restitution (returning what one wrongfully took) and restoration (returning the wronged to wholeness).*"[66] Acknowledging the multiple government programs that almost exclusively benefited White Americans, they note that native Americans, native Alaskans, and Japanese Americans have received financial reparations from the US government.[67] Kwon and Thompson argue that Christians should support such efforts on behalf of Blacks because of "mission, history, and moral tradition."[68] Mission includes healing historical and contextual wounds; history includes seventeenth- and eighteenth-century Quaker calls for reparations; moral tradition includes biblical texts such as Exodus 21:33–22:5; Leviticus 6:1–7; Numbers 5:5–8; and Luke 19, which show how to restore someone who has been robbed.[69] Notably, the texts in Exodus and Deuteronomy, which clearly mention reparations for the formerly enslaved, are not used here. Instead, the emphasis in these biblical texts is on giving owners of property what they have lost, which is not an exact parallel with giving reparations to newly freed slaves. The problem here is that while the authors want to emphasize the humanity of Black people, they overlook the reality that a rejection of that humanity is exactly what justified enslavement in the first place. Using the reparations passages in Exodus and Deuteronomy would have reinforced the humanity of enslaved peoples while also acknowledging the reality of that enslavement and the White supremacist scaffolding that upheld it for so long. The moral call, while important, overlooks the othering of Black slaves that was necessary in order to justify the institution. No one quotes Leviticus 25, but the text's quiet argument that enslaving those who are not from your community is fine lies just underneath the surface of any discussion about reparations that involves White people. Black people, even with changes to the Constitution and civil rights and voting rights laws, remain other in some way.

As of 2019, only 15 percent of Whites support reparations.[70] The continuing uproar over critical race theory, which reexamines the foundations of US social structures, comes in part out of fear that perhaps US history is more violent, unequal, and even racist than white Americans want to believe. If slavery was an aberration in the United States and not one of its foundations, then reparations are not needed. *The 1619 Project*, another source of White outrage, challenges the presumed history of the United States as a good, Christian, egalitarian nation. If reparations by definition means repair, then they cannot happen without an admission that something was and continues to be broken. The Congressional apologies for slavery in 2008 and 2009 are the only government acknowledgments that this country broke a people.[71] Yet, the 2009 Senate apology ends with the following disclaimer: "Nothing in this resolution—(A) authorizes or supports any claim against the United States; or (B) serves as a settlement of any claim against the United States."[72]

As a scholar of the racist history of interpretation of biblical texts in the United States, I am not optimistic that Black people will even get a more substantive apology, much less reparations. White Christian ignorance and denial run deep. William A. Darity and A. Kirsten Mullen say it best: "At each point that the nation stood at a critical crossroads with respect to its racial future, it chose the wrong fork."[73] With the Supreme Court probably going to end college affirmative action programs in the summer of 2023,[74] the opportunity I had to get an education and a hard-fought ticket to the middle class may disappear for others. The wrong fork looms again. As Darity and Mullen argue, affirmative action "does not compensate for past or ongoing discrimination or the continuing effect of either. In general, stopping an unjust practice is not compensation for the unjust practice."[75] The call for national reparations is an impossible one, but to quote James Baldwin, "the impossible is the least that one can demand."[76] While some White Christians wrestle with the meaning of justice and most pretend that the problem of the color line no longer exists, Black people persist.

NOTES

1. John Van Seters, "Law of the Hebrew Slave: A Continuing Debate," *ZAW* 119 (2007): 169–183 (182).
2. Unless otherwise indicated, all biblical quotations are from the NRSV.
3. Additionally, the Christian lack of interest in Torah commentary outside of the book of Genesis is not new. For example, in the Anchor Bible Commentary, Jewish scholars authored the volumes on Leviticus and Numbers, and a Jewish scholar authored the volume on Leviticus for the Wisdom Commentary Series.
4. For an excellent extended discussion of the lives of US enslaved women, see Alexis Wells-Oghoghomeh's *The Souls of Womenfolk: The Religious Cultures of Enslaved Women in the Lower South* (Chapel Hill: University of North Carolina, 2021).
5. Stacy Davis, *This Strange Story: Jewish and Christian Interpretation of the Curse of Canaan from Antiquity to 1865* (Lanham, MD: University Press of America, 2008), 134–135, 139–140.
6. Sven Beckert and Seth Rockman, "Introduction," in *Slavery's Capitalism: A New History of Economic Development*, ed. Sven Beckert and Seth Rockman (Philadelphia: University of Pennsylvania, 2016), 5, 13.
7. Beckert and Rockman, "Introduction," 6.
8. Matthew Desmond, "Capitalism," in *The 1619 Project: A New Origin Story*, ed. Nikole Hannah-Jones, Caitlin Roper, Ilena Silverman, and Jake Silverstein (New York: One World, 2021), 167.
9. Daina Ramer Berry, "'Broad is de Road dat Leads ter Death': Human Capital and Enslaved Mortality," in *Slavery's Capitalism: A New History of Economic Development*, ed. Sven Beckert and Seth Rockman (Philadelphia: University of Pennsylvania, 2016), 146.
10. Berry, "'Broad,'" 162.
11. Berry, "'Broad,'" 147.
12. Berry, "'Broad,'" 156; "Inflation Calculator" (https://www.officialdata.org/).

13. Mary Sarah Bilder, "The Struggle Over Immigration: Indentured Servants, Slaves, and Articles of Commerce," *Missouri Law Review* 61, 4 (1996): 758. Those who imported indentured servants were compensated; the servants themselves were not. Some importees, however, were more valuable than others, since importing the Irish led to extra taxation. See Bilder, "Struggle," 772, 774.

14. Bilder, "Struggle," 759.

15. Bilder, "Struggle," 807.

16. Eric Foner, *Reconstruction: America's Unfinished Revolution, 1863–1877*, updated edition (New York: Harper Perennial, 2016), 68.

17. Foner, *Reconstruction*, 69; emphasis mine.

18. Foner, *Reconstruction*, 70. The phrase "forty acres and a mule" has been associated with reparations ever since, and it is the name of Spike Lee's production company for that reason.

19. Foner, *Reconstruction*, 104–105.

20. Foner, *Reconstruction*, 158–159, 183.

21. Foner, *Reconstruction*, 247. As Eric Foner concludes on p. 248,
"In appealing to fiscal conservatism, raising the specter of an immense federal bureaucracy trampling upon citizen's rights, and insisting self-help, not dependence on outside assistance, offered the surest road to economic advancement, Johnson voiced themes that to this day have sustained opposition to federal intervention on behalf of blacks."

22. Foner, *Reconstruction*, 161, 163.

23. Trymaine Lee, "Inheritance," in *The 1619 Project: A New Origin Story*, ed. Nikole Hannah-Jones, Caitlin Roper, Ilena Silverman, and Jake Silverstein (New York: One World), 298.

24. Foner, *Reconstruction*, 245–246, 315–316, 374–375, 377.

25. Foner, *Reconstruction*, 403–404.

26. Foner, *Reconstruction*, 419–420, 451.

27. Daniel W. Stowell, *Rebuilding Zion: The Religious Reconstruction of the South, 1863–1877* (New York: Oxford University Press, 1998), 116–117.

28. Stowell, *Rebuilding Zion*, 199.

29. Stowell, *Rebuilding Zion*, 120–121.

30. James W. Watts, "The Historical Role of Leviticus 25 in Naturalizing Anti-Black Racism," *Religions* 12 (2021): 570, accessed May 19, 2023, https://doi.org/10.3390/rel12080570, 2, 3.

31. Watts, "Historical Role," 6, 7; Stacy Davis, *This Strange Story: Jewish and Christian Interpretation of the Curse of Canaan from Antiquity to 1865* (Lanham, MD: University Press of America, 2008), 132, 135.

32. Stowell, *Rebuilding Zion*, 118.

33. Keri Leigh Merritt, *Masterless Men: Poor Whites and Slavery in the Antebellum South* (New York: Cambridge University Press, 2017), 6; emphasis mine.

34. Merritt, *Masterless Men*, 38; 39.

35. Merritt, *Masterless Men*, 38.

36. Merritt, *Masterless Men*, 331.

37. Merritt, *Masterless Men*, 328, 329.

38. Merritt, *Masterless Men,* 331; 330.

39. Merritt, *Masterless Men,* 337.

40. Ibram X. Kendi, "Progress," in *The 1619 Project: A New Origin Story,* ed. Nikole Hannah-Jones, Caitlin Roper, Ilena Silverman, and Jake Silverstein (New York: One World), 432.

41. Kendi, "Progress," 433, 436, 438–439.

42. Hanna Ondrey, "The Covenant Responds to the Black Manifesto (1969)," *The Covenant Quarterly* 77, 2–3 (2019): 3.

43. Ondrey, "Covenant Responds," 6.

44. "Black Manifesto" (1969), accessed May 20, 2023, https://www.episcopalarchives.org/church-awakens/files/original/c20bd83547dd3cf92e788041d7fddfa2.pdf.

45. Ondrey, "Covenant Responds," 8.

46. Edward A. Dowey, "'The Black Manifesto': Revolution, Reparation, Separation," *Theology Today* 26, 3 (1969): 288.

47. Dowey, "The Black Manifesto," 290–291, 293.

48. Gayraud S. Wilmore Jr., "Reparations: Don't Hang Up On a Word," *Theology Today* 26, 3 (1969): 285.

49. Wilmore, "Reparations," 287.

50. Ondrey, "Covenant Responds," 3–4, 9, 14–15, 18–19.

51. Ondrey, "Covenant Responds," 19.

52. Ondrey, "Covenant Responds," 23.

53. Ondrey, "Covenant Responds," 24.

54. Jennifer Harvey, "White Protestants and Black Christians: The Absence and Presence of Whiteness in the Face of the Black Manifesto," *Journal of Religious Ethics* 39, 1 (2011): 126–127.

55. Harvey, "White Protestants and Black Christians," 127–128, 130.

56. Harvey, "White Protestants and Black Christians," 130.

57. Harvey, "White Protestants and Black Christians," 131, 133–134, 137–138, 141–142.

58. As Candace Jackson writes ("What is Redlining?" *The New York Times,* August 17, 2021, accessed May 20, 2023, https://www.nytimes.com/2021/08/17/realestate/what-is-redlining.html.),

"The origins of the term come from government homeownership programs that were created as part of the 1930s-era New Deal." Government maps ranked neighborhoods from A to D, with D neighborhoods excluded from the programs because of the risk of decreasing and already low property values. Jackson notes, "Not coincidentally, most of the 'D' areas were neighborhoods where Black residents lived."

59. Ta-Nehisi Coates, "The Case for Reparations," *The Atlantic,* June 2014, accessed May 20, 2023, https://www.theatlantic.com/magazine/archive/2014/06/the-case-for-reparations/361631/.

60. Writing about the consequences of redlining, Nikole Hannah-Jones ("Justice," 466) observes, "98 percent of the loans the Federal Housing Administration insured from 1934 to 1962 went to white Americans, locking nearly all Black Americans out of the government program credited with building the modern (white) middle class."

61. Coates, "Case for Reparations."
62. Jennifer Harvey, "Which Way to Justice? Reconciliation, Reparations, and the Problem of Whiteness in US Protestantism," *Journal of the Society of Christian Ethics* 31, 1 (2011): 57.
63. Harvey, "Which Way to Justice?," 58.
64. Harvey, "Which Way to Justice?," 64.
65. Harvey, "Which Way to Justice?," 67.
66. Duke L. Kwon and Gregory L. Thompson, *Reparations: A Christian Call for Repentance and Repair* (Ada, MI: Brazos, 2021), 17.
67. Kwon and Thompson, *Reparations*, 25–26, 100–101.
68. Kwon and Thompson, *Reparations,* 101.
69. Kwon and Thompson, *Reparations,* 103, 111, 134–137, 139–142.
70. Scottie Andrew, "Nearly 75% of African Americans support reparations for slavery. Only 15% of white Americans do, a poll says," *CNN*, 28 October 2019, accessed May 20, 2023, https://www.cnn.com/2019/10/28/us/reparations-poll-trnd/index.html.
71. "Congress Apologizes for Slavery, Jim Crow," *NPR*, 30 July 2008, accessed May 20, 2023, www.npr.org/2008/07/30/93059465/congress-apologizes-for-slavery-jim-crow.
72. Senate Concurrent Resolution 26, 2009, accessed May 21, 2023, https://www.congress.gov/111/crec/2009/06/11/CREC-2009-06-11-pt1-PgS6568-3.pdf.
73. William A. Darity Jr., and A. Kirsten Mullen, *From Here to Equality: Reparations for Black Americans in the Twenty-First Century*, (Chapel Hill: University of North Carolina Press, 2020), 4.
74. Adam Liptak, "Supreme Court Seems Ready to Throw Out Race-Based College Admissions," *The New York Times*, 31 October 2022, accessed May 20, 2023, https://www.nytimes.com/2022/10/31/us/supreme-court-harvard-unc-affirmative-action.html.
75. Darity and Mullen, *From Here to Equality*, 249.
76. James Baldwin, *The Fire Next Time* (New York: Laurel Press, 1985), 140.

BIBLIOGRAPHY

Andrew, Scottie. "Nearly 75% of African Americans support reparations for slavery. Only 15% of white Americans do, a poll says." CNN, October 28, 2019. Accessed May 20, 2023. https://www.cnn.com/2019/10/28/us/reparations-poll-trnd/index.html.

Baldwin, James. *The Fire Next Time*. New York: Laurel Press, 1985.

Beckert, Sven, and Seth Rockman. "Introduction: Slavery's Capitalism." In *Slavery's Capitalism: A New History of Economic Development,* edited by Sven Beckert and Seth Rockman, 1–27. Philadelphia: University of Pennsylvania Press, 2016.

Berry, Daina Ramer. "'Broad is de Road dat Leads ter Death': Human Capital and Enslaved Mortality." In *Slavery's Capitalism: A New History of Economic*

Development, edited by Sven Beckert and Seth Rockman, 146–62. Philadelphia: University of Pennsylvania Press, 2016.

Bilder, Mary Sarah. "The Struggle Over Immigration: Indentured Servants, Slaves, and Articles of Commerce." *Missouri Law Review* 61, 4 (1996): 743–824.

"Black Manifesto." 1969. Accessed May 20, 2023. https://www.episcopalarchives.org/church-awakens/files/original/c20bd83547dd3cf92e788041d7fddfa2.pdf.

Coates, Ta-Nehisi. "The Case for Reparations." *The Atlantic,* 2014. Accessed May 20, 2023. https://www.theatlantic.com/magazine/archive/2014/06/the-case-for-reparations/361631/.

"Congress Apologizes for Slavery, Jim Crow," NPR, 30 July 2008. Accessed May 20, 2023. www.npr.org/2008/07/30/93059465/congress-apologizes-for-slavery-jim-crow.

Darity, William A., Jr., and A. Kirsten Mullen. *From Here to Equality: Reparations for Black Americans in the Twenty-First Century.* Chapel Hill: University of North Carolina Press, 2020.

Davis, Stacy. *This Strange Story: Jewish and Christian Interpretation of the Curse of Canaan from Antiquity to 1865.* Lanham, MD: University Press of America, 2008.

Desmond, Matthew. "Capitalism." In *The 1619 Project: A New Origin Story,* edited by Nikole Hannah-Jones, Caitlin Roper, Ilena Silverman, and Jake Silverstein, 165–85. New York: One World, 2021.

District of Columbia Compensated Emancipation Act. 1862. Accessed May 20, 2023. https://www.senate.gov/artandhistory/history/common/civil_war/DCEmancipationAct_FeaturedDoc.htm.

Dowey, Edward A. "'The Black Manifesto': Revolution, Reparation, Separation." *Theology Today* 26, 3 (1969): 288–293.

Foner, Eric. *Reconstruction: America's Unfinished Revolution, 1863–1877.* Updated edition. New York: Harper Perennial, 2014.

Hannah-Jones, Nikole. "Justice." In *The 1619 Project: A New Origin Story,* edited by Nikole Hannah-Jones, Caitlin Roper, Ilena Silverman, and Jake Silverstein, 451–76. New York: One World, 2021.

Harvey, Jennifer. "Which Way to Justice?: Reconciliation, Reparations, and the Problem of Whiteness in US Protestantism." *Journal of the Society of Christian Ethics* 31, 1 (2011): 57–77.

———. "White Protestants and Black Christians: The Absence and Presence of Whiteness in the Face of the Black Manifesto." *Journal of Religious Ethics* 39, 1 (2011): 125–150.

"Inflation Calculator." Accessed May 20, 2023. https://www.officialdata.org/.

Jackson, Candace. "What is Redlining?" *The New York Times,* August 17, 2021. Accessed May 20, 2023. https://www.nytimes.com/2021/08/17/realestate/what-is-redlining.html.

Kendi, Ibram X. "Progress." In *The 1619 Project: A New Origin Story,* edited by Nikole Hannah-Jones, Caitlin Roper, Ilena Silverman, and Jake Silverstein, 421–42. New York: One World, 2021.

Kwon, Duke L., and Gregory Thompson. *Reparations: A Christian Call for Repentance and Repair.* Ada, MI: Brazos Press, 2021.

Lee, Trymaine. "Inheritance." In *The 1619 Project: A New Origin Story*, edited by Nikole Hannah-Jones, Caitlin Roper, Ilena Silverman, and Jake Silverstein, 293–306. New York: One World, 2021.

Liptak, Adam. "Supreme Court Seems Ready to Throw Out Race-Based College Admissions." *The New York Times*, 31 October, 2022. Accessed May 20, 2023. https://www.nytimes.com/2022/10/31/us/supreme-court-harvard-unc-affirmative-action.html.

Merritt, Keri Leigh. *Masterless Men: Poor Whites and Slavery in the Antebellum South*. New York: Cambridge University Press, 2017.

Ondrey, Hanna. "The Covenant Responds to the Black Manifesto (1969)." *The Covenant Quarterly* 77, 2–3 (2019): 3–30.

Senate Concurrent Resolution 26. 2009. Accessed May 21, 2023. https://www.congress.gov/111/crec/2009/06/11/CREC-2009-06-11-pt1-PgS6568-3.pdf.

Stowell, Daniel W. *Rebuilding Zion: The Religious Reconstruction of the South, 1863–1877*. New York: Oxford University Press, 1998.

Van Seters, John. "Law of the Hebrew Slave: A Continuing Debate." *ZAW* 119 (2007): 169–183.

Watts, James W. "The Historical Role of Leviticus 25 in Naturalizing Anti-Black Racism." *Religions* 12 (2021): 570. Accessed May 20, 2023. https://doi.org/10.3390/rel12080570.

Wilmore, Gayraud S., Jr. "Reparations: Don't Hang Up On a Word." *Theology Today* 26, 3 (1969): 284–287.

Chapter Three

Witness: The Job

How to Talk to White People About Reparations

Gimbiya Kettering

Don't. Just don't do it.

You are going to do it anyway. And later, I will say, *I told you so.*

You are going to do it because you feel a calling. I know. I used to feel it too.

At first, it is not a calling to talk about reparations. It is more general. As if it were the voice of God, like an airport loudspeaker, broadcast across your life, calling, *If you see something, say something.* You see the consequences of slavery everywhere. Standing on train platforms, you see it in access to public transport traced on the maps. In your city, those historically preserved school buildings that had been designated for White-only students have limestone steps—the others do not. It is in the pattern of police shootings and also in certain neighbors who expect you to move off the sidewalk when they pass. For all of it, you feel called to say something. Maybe it is not a calling. Maybe, like pulling away when White people reach out to touch your hair, it is only a survival instinct.

Maybe it is a hobby. In fact, you talk about race the way other people talk about sports. You know all the stats. You know the rules, the obscure history going back to the beginning, and you follow each play. You know all the team colors. And you cheer for the blue team. In fact, you see the history of slavery in sports—owners, players sold, profits, and coaches like overseers on the fields. You read books about race. You watch movies about race. You listen to radio programs and podcasts about race. Despite this, all you know about reparations is *forty acres and a mule.* Like an armchair quarterback, from the safety of your living room you yell to turn right instead of left, to duck and to turn down the music as if maybe that could save the next young Black person from being shot. And—because American Christianity and the United States of America are built with enslaved labor—you also talk about religion and politics. You feel called to share your insights over coffee, during family dinners, at office holiday parties, and with strangers you meet on the bus. You might as well get paid for it.

Which is why you apply when your denomination posts a position announcement for The Job.[1]

The Job sounds good on paper. You will be a *director*. It has health insurance, retirement contributions, and a professional development stipend. You can't believe that someone would pay you to talk about race. If you stay in the Job long enough, there is a sabbatical that you imagine using to write a book. The position description includes words like *intercultural-cross-cultural-multicultural-urban-outreach-diversity-celebration-ministry-disciples-of-all-nations*. You think this means talking about social justice, mass incarceration, educational achievement gaps, unconscious bias, neocolonialism, immigration reforms, redlining and its contemporary manifestations in the subprime mortgage crisis. You will be wrong.

The ideal candidate has a seminary degree. You do not. But you attended a faith-based school that equipped you with a scriptural foundation for talking about the connections between race and religion.[2] Integral to your faith journey is the belief that God loves diversity, unity, and peace. At least this is how you explain it in the interview. As part of the interview process, you have to lead your coworkers through a training as if they are the congregational clients. You have never done this before, but you make a few PowerPoint slides, request newsprint and Sharpies, and design an interactive thought experiment. You do not remember what your workshop was about. This is how you meet your future coworkers: they are all White, all have or are getting seminary degrees. The men sit with their arms folded across their chests, and the women scribble in floral-themed notebooks. During your entire presentation, none of them say anything.

You talk and talk to fill up the vacuum of silence, and on the flight home, you will cry. A few weeks later, they will call and tell you that you got The Job. But in order for it to be full time, you have to move. The Job does not include moving expenses, and you do not want to move to a state known for its KKK history. Though maybe that is every state. You ask if you can work remotely. It is pre-pandemic, but there are other full-time, remote employees. When you point that out, you are told, *They are grandfathered in.*

My grandfather was Brethren, too, you tell them. Half joking.[3] Your courage falls short of using that as a teaching moment to explicitly explain that the phrase is now widely acknowledged as rooted in Jim Crow policies that enabled loopholes after Black men were given the vote at the Constitutional level but denied it at local levels via literacy tests. Illiterate White Americans got to vote because their grandfathers voted prior to the 15th Amendment.

When you start The Job, your feeling of being called is particularly urgent, as it is in the midst of a high-publicity case about an unarmed Black teenager shot by a White police officer. But that is not what you will be asked to talk about. Instead, you are invited to give workshops about *hospitality* and *welcome*. To do this, you try to explain to a group of camp directors what it is like to be the only Black kid at camp when you have been called the N-word, are expected to sit in prayer circles with people wearing the Confederate flag, and people touch your hair. During the Q&A, a participant will raise her hand and ask, *So would you say that Black kids would feel more welcome if we served watermelon?*

You realize *hospitality* is code for *recruitment*.

The Job can sound glamorous: You give diversity workshops to faith leaders and volunteers around the country. Your workshops are in church buildings that are too large for their dwindling congregations. You eat lots of cheesy casseroles in fellowship halls. You travel with your own projector. The White American Christians remind you of your own relatives. Even though you list it as your home congregation on all your nametags and all of your aunts and uncles still attend, the congregation where your father was raised never actually invites you. You fly coach. The woman next to you asks what you do; you do not tell her about the watermelon. She says, *Oh! You're an Anti-Racism Practitioner!*

As if it takes only practice to understand how to lead people from racism to anti-racism. As if racism and anti-racism can be practiced, like a tennis serve or a golf swing. As if you are still practicing. When you are an expert, you will have a retort for the watermelon. The experts are the M.Div.'s and D.Min.'s who hold full-time positions. You are part-time and will come to believe that no one asks experts on the intellectual battlegrounds of exegesis and eisegesis and hermeneutics and homiletics about watermelon. No one touches their hair. After presentations, they do not have to listen to confessions from people whose fathers ran stores with *Whites Only* fountains, bathrooms, counters, and who now wait for absolution. Do not ever offer absolution.

Another unarmed Black American Christian teenager is shot by a White man. Another dies in police custody. Then a White police officer asphyxiates a Black American Christian father on the sidewalk. It is captured on camera and uploaded online. Then it happens again. Sometimes it happens to Black women.

Even as this happens, White American Christians, at least the ones you know, have a habit of saying things like: *I don't see color.*

Or, *I don't see your color. I just see you.*

Or, *I don't see myself as White.*

Contradictorily, they also tell you. *I have a Black friend.*

You're not like other Black people. You're so . . . nice.
Can I touch your hair? Does it grow like that?

You feel called to heal their selective blindness. Colorblindness. This would be easier if you had the gift of healing. If you could, like Jesus, spit in the dirt and rub that on their faces. Do not attempt this at home. It won't change how they see, only how they see you. It feels like they will never be ready to talk about reparations.

You ask, *When the police shoot me, will you come to my protest?*
That would never happen, they say. *You're so . . . nice.*

You wish you could believe them because often driving to their congregations means passing one Confederate flag. Then another. The gas station you stop at sells them. You imagine all the worst-case scenarios possible if a flat-tire forces you to wait on the side of the road—or worse, you have to ask for help from one of the darkened homes. It is good for your prayer life. Instead, you imagine that when you are shot for not being White, your White American Christian Brethren and Sisteren will stand with Black Lives Matter leaders as the National Guard advances. You imagine them not as they are but dressed for the occasion in Old Order dress—the men dour and bearded, the women with prayer coverings pinned to their blonde buns. This is a fantasy. You promise God that if you are not shot by someone standing their ground, you will go to a protest for the next person who is.

The position description for The Job could have been a single bullet point:

- Seeking Token BIPOC @ Historically and Predominately White Denomination.

Suddenly, 100,000 White American Christians have a right to claim you as their Black Friend. Your email is public, so is your cell phone number. They can reach out about all their questions about Black people. You used to think that you had heard it *all.* You were wrong. One person writes you to complain about their home healthcare aid who does not want to talk to them about Martin Luther King Jr. Another holds up the phone so you can listen to an upsetting NPR interview with them. They call you to be part of their book clubs when it becomes trendy to read books by Black authors. They find your social media profiles and start following you. For the first time, you begin to wonder if your Twitter feed is "Black enough" to be representative or if you will be fired because it is too Black. Because you are their friend, they think they can touch your hair—which was not included in the position description. The Job, as you will later be reminded, does not have a clause that refers to talking about Black Lives Matter.

Instead of moving toward reparations, White Christian Americans tip the polls and the next president is also racist. Eleven American presidents actually enslaved Black Christians and an additional six were content to be president without signing an executive order to end slavery—so you are not as surprised as the White American Christian progressives who call you in shock and grief the next morning. After they tell you about themselves, they ask you how you feel.

You tell them to read *A Letter from a Birmingham Jail.*

You cannot tell them that you feel like racism is a demon. Nice, self-identified progressive White American Christians no longer believe in the powers and principalities of Evil. It would be easier to end racism if it was something that could be exorcised. One of the denominational districts holds an annual tent revival. If they invite you, you are going to try a laying on of hands. The more evangelical members of your denomination will understand this; they believe in this type of healing even if they do not believe that they are afflicted enough to need it. Of course, you are terrified. When the apostles tried to cast out demons, they were told, *We know Peter and we know Paul. But who are you?* In the end, your faith is never tested because they do not invite you. You are too Black. You might talk about Jesus coming to save the world instead of focusing on individual repentance and salvation.

Your workshops have devolved. You start Bible studies by asking, *What are you all doing here? What are we all doing here?* It is existential. White American Christians will laugh nervously, waiting for the punchline. Afterwards, you preach about liberation in the story of Exodus. Your sermons are about Moses. The Chosen people, the Hebrews, were the slaves. You remind White American Christians that it is the slave owners who are punished with a series of plagues, each more terrible than the last. It is harder to talk about how the Hebrews take the gold and silver of the Egyptians and walk through the parted Red Sea, carrying their plundered reparations. It is not a perfect metaphor; the booty is later melted into the idol of the golden calf. Still, there is scriptural support here for reparations.

You will forget the most important lesson: to talk to White American Christians about reparations, you can never mention the *Dave Chappelle Show* skit. Nor the *Chris Rock Show*'s questions about reparations. Nor anything done by Spike Lee. Talking about race cannot be funny, so do not include Wanda Sykes, Richard Prior, or Key and Peele. If they have heard of these comedians, they won't watch them because those people are *foul-mouthed.*

When you show a video clip about reparations, forgetting that it includes an actor saying the word $#!%, a White American Christian will ask why Black people use so many curse words. The others at the table nod in agreement. Not all Black people, of course. But there does seem to be a lot of that these days. Colored folk used to be so respectable, like Thurgood Marshall and Martin Luther King Jr. To yourself, you think, *Like $#!% Uncle Tom.* Aloud, you say, *Those respectable, good old days when Black people could not cuss in public but White people had picnics at lynchings. Is that the kind of respectable you want to be part of?* Beating a dead horse, you add, *Emmitt Till was not lynched for saying $#!%.*

For the first time in your life, you do not want social reform and an economic package that will even the playing field. You do not want justice for all. You want your *forty acres and a mule* . . . with 150 years of compounding interest. You half hope someone will fire you. Like the Hebrews carrying their treasure to the Promised Land, you are counting in your heart the number of weeks until your sabbatical because you are going to write about all of this $#!%. You are months past being eligible, but your White coworkers claim they have to be first. You thought Jesus said, *The last shall be first and the first shall be last.* Again, you lose your courage and do not tell them you need a break from people trying to touch your hair.

You attend a three-day workshop led by Native Americans.[4] In fact, you are the only person there who is not Native American, and you are not sure you should be there. When they talk about land theft, broken treaties, genocide, and boarding schools, your half Whiteness feels like an ugly beacon. They cry and you do not join them—because you hate it when White American Christians cry before your tears are done. You will cry when you get home. In three days, no one tries touching your hair.

I already told you: Don't. Just don't do it.
But you will take The Job because you feel called.
I used to feel that way too. That is why I can tell you, *I told you so.*
We all have God-given talents, and yours used to be making people uncomfortable at Superbowl parties by mentioning how the team names are actual racial slurs. You should have stopped there. *I told you,* don't talk to White American Christians about reparations. You thought I was worried about how the White American Christians would treat you, what they would say. It was never that.

I knew it would change you. Every step you take, beneath the layers of the enslaved blood of your ancestors, is the stolen land and the layers of blood shed by the people who were here before you. It has always been this way, but now you see it. When Moses saw his people's hard labor he was filled with murderous rage. Witnessing the vengeful killing of the Egyptian overseer, the people asked Moses, *Who made you ruler and judge?* If you cannot judge, you long to flee. You can never again demand *your forty acres* without also acknowledging it has to be carved from land already plundered. It changes the copper mines, the oil pipelines, and Mount Rushmore. Any justice feels stolen, spoiled. You will believe there is no way to make it right. You will feel guilt and shame and hopelessness. You will feel like a White American Christian, one who wants only, only the salvation of Christ without the responsibility to make amends.

You should reread Exodus. Exodus 12 does not say *steal*. It says the Hebrews *asked* the Egyptians for their gold and silver. And that God made the Egyptians *favorably disposed* toward their former slaves. This change of heart—yours, the Egyptians, and even Moses's—is as stunning as walking on dry sand with the sea parted around you, as miraculous as manna falling from the sky, and as life-saving as the water rising from a beaten stone.

For the first time, you understand reparations.

NOTES

1. While I certainly consider *my denomination* as belonging to me as much as it did to my father and his father before him. And his father before him. The denomination is less certain that I belong to it. Not because my mother was not raised in the denomination—many White members marry in and are received in full fellowship. The problem of acceptance is that I am Black. Like my mother and her mother and her mother before her.

2. I did not so much *attend* missionary school as integrate a Historically and Predominately White American Christian missionary school. In Africa. In the 1990s. While my classmates were taking physical education, New Testament history, and biology, I was leading my own Civil Rights Movement. The first time I saw the Norman Rockwell painting of Ruby Bridges bracketed by striding National Guardsmen, what I felt was envy. I could have used that kind of backup at recess.

3. *Grandfathered in:* See Endnote 1.

4. For years people told me to attend the Kairos Blanket Exercise (www.kairosblanketexercise.org). When I asked them why, they would tell me it was so life-changing and could not explain why. I am now telling you to attend it; it was so life-changing in ways that are hard to explain.

Chapter Four

From Here to Jubilee

Reading Torah in Dialogue with Darity and Mullen's Case for Reparations

Michael J. Rhodes

"The origins of the racial wealth gap," the economist William A. Darity Jr., argues, "start with the failure to provide the formerly enslaved with the land grants of 40 acres."[1] For Darity, the solution for this unjust racial wealth gap is a program of reparations for Black Americans. Darity has argued this claim over several decades in book chapters and academic journals, culminating in his landmark 2020 volume, *From Here to Equality: Reparations for Black Americans in the Twenty-First Century*, co-authored with A. Kirsten Mullen.

Darity outlines three components central to any reparations program:

- "acknowledgment of a grievous injustice,
- redress for the injustice,
- closure of the grievances held by the group subjected to the injustice."[2]

Despite their devastating exploration of the injustice suffered by generations of Black Americans, Darity and Mullen ultimately offer a hopeful vision that includes nuanced discussions of the appropriate cost and most effective means of funding and administering an effective reparations program. *If* the injustice is acknowledged, genuine repair and closure are possible.

The primary challenge they see is neither plausibility nor price tag, but political will. The reparations program they pursue is one enacted legislatively, and such a program demands that a "majority of the populace" acknowledge the injustice and accept responsibility for repairing it. Only "when the nation is ready to be transformed," can Congress "legislate a reparations program."[3]

And of course, many Americans are not ready. According to one study, 62 percent of all Americans are "opposed" to reparations, and only 29 percent of white Americans and 7 percent of white evangelicals support reparations.[4]

Do Christians have good reasons to support Darity and Mullen's case? In this chapter, I try to answer that question by bringing their arguments into dialogue with several passages from the Torah, especially the eighth commandment and the Year of Jubilee. As we shall see, these texts offer essential moral resources for Christians considering Darity and Mullen's case for reparations.

A GRIEVOUS INJUSTICE AWAITING ACKNOWLEDGMENT

Darity and Mullen begin their argument by exploring the extent of the injustice suffered by Black Americans. For them, the most important "snapshot" of that injustice lies in the dramatic differences between the net worth of Black and white households: as of 2016, median white household wealth is ten times the median wealth of Black households.[5] This snapshot of injustice is essential because it is extreme, but also because, as the authors state, "wealth is the best single indicator of the cumulative impact of white racism over time" and the "economic measure that best captures individual, family, and household well-being."[6] This is so not least because wealth is one important way, in our present economy at least, families exercise "agency" over their lives.[7]

The origins of this wealth gap lie in the theft of Black labor through slavery coupled with the failure to provide released slaves with the land ownership necessary to provide for themselves at the close of the Civil War.[8] Because of these two failures, upon emancipation

> four million newly liberated slaves found themselves with no bread to eat, no land to cultivate, no shelter to cover their heads . . . [they] were given abstract freedom expressed in luminous rhetoric. But in an agrarian economy [they were] given no land to make liberation concrete.[9]

While many Americans acknowledge the horror of these nineteenth-century injustices, they may also see them as features of America's long distant past. By contrast, Darity and Mullen make a detailed case that the injustice behind the wealth gap *began* during slavery but *continued* long after the close of the Civil War.

For instance, despite the government's failure to provide the promised forty acres and a mule, "black American farmers managed to amass 15 million acres of land" by 1910.[10] Yet in the following decades, "murders of African American landowners, for the purpose of appropriating their property, and coerced public sale of family land resulted in a rapid decline in black American landownership."[11] Many of the more than 4,000 lynchings of Black men and women between 1877 and 1950 "were associated directly with the expropriation of black-owned land."[12] By 1997, Black families had collectively lost more than 12 million acres.[13]

In cities like my hometown of Memphis, Black wealth in the form of home ownership was also stolen through the political process. In 1953, an emerging Black middle-income community was "declared a 'slum'" and demolished with federal slum clearance dollars; the Memphis Housing Authority replaced those Black-owned homes with a 900-unit public housing complex.[14] The homeowners were

> "sick and distressed beyond measure." They wrote that they had toiled for years to pay off their mortgages and fix up their properties, and they'd succeeded in making [theirs] the best neighborhood for blacks in Memphis. Their community was more valuable than any relocation funds the city might provide . . . Their grievances were ignored.[15]

Black households not only had wealth stolen from them, however. They were also barred from the major wealth-building programs that contributed to their white American counterparts' legacy of wealth building. Black families were largely excluded from:

- the Homestead Act, which enriched some 1.6 million white families;[16]
- FHA-backed mortgages through redlining, a practice that both deprived Black families of wealth-building opportunities given to their white counterparts, *and exposed them* to predatory lending practices that further eroded Black wealth;[17]
- the GI Bill, which largely excluded Black veterans from the "guaranteed home, business, and farm loans" made to their white counterparts.[18]

The US government regularly offered white households opportunities to build wealth that were denied to Black households. Drawing on economic and social-science data, Darity and Mullen demonstrate that such past injustices are primary drivers for the wealth gap today. This is so not least because the "major sources of wealth for most" people in the United States come through inheritances and gifts living parents give to their adult children.[19] The roots of the wealth gap in past injustice also at least partially explains why that gap persists even when Black households

> make the choices in family life and education that we often associate with economic success. On average, single white parents have twice the wealth of

married Black parents and Black household heads with a college degree have "about $10,000 less in median net worth than white household heads" who dropped out of high school."[20] *Indeed, Black people "who are working full-time have a lower median net worth than whites who are unemployed."*[21]

These last statistics point to the importance of acknowledging *both* the damage done to Black households, *and* the way that white households have benefitted from that history of harm, even if the present beneficiaries played no active role in the original perpetration of injustice.[22]

Having outlined the extent of the injustice that must be acknowledged, and the way that contemporary white households continue to benefit from that injustice, Darity and Mullen go on to argue for the establishment of a multifaceted "portfolio of reparations." Such a portfolio would include some "direct payments,"[23] but would not rely solely on them, not least because cash transfers that do not increase Black wealth might actually reinforce the wealth gap.[24] Because of this, their reparations portfolio would also include investments in Black institutions and the creation of a "trust fund" to which Black families could apply for education, purchasing a home, establishing a new business, or investing.[25] They believe that such a reparations program is "not only morally justified but practicable," one capable of bringing genuine closure and creating the possibility for the nation as a whole to move forward from "here to equality."[26]

Having briefly explored their argument, we can now ask the question: how might the Bible, and specifically the Torah, shape contemporary faith communities' response?

REPARATIONS AND THE TORAH OUTSIDE LEVITICUS 25

Darity and Mullen's case for reparations begins with a focus on repairing the injustice of *theft*: theft of Black lives, Black labor, Black land, and Black wealth. Their protest against such theft clearly finds support in the eighth commandment's prohibition against stealing (Ex 20:15; Deut 5:19).[27] This may seem obvious to the point of being unhelpful. But scholars increasingly recognize that the biblical teaching that follows the Ten Commandments can be seen as an opening up and unpacking of their meaning.[28] Tracing that unpacking across the Torah reveals a moral and theological logic directly relevant to the contemporary case for reparations.

"OPENING UP" THE SCOPE OF THE EIGHTH COMMANDMENT'S PROHIBITION AND PROVIDING A PATHWAY FOR RESTITUTION

On the one hand, the negative prohibition against theft "opens up" across the rest of the Torah to condemn a much wider variety of economic action. For instance, Leviticus 6:1–3[5:20–22][29] lumps together outright theft with

- "deceiving a neighbor in a matter of a deposit or a pledge"[30]
- "defraud[ing] a neighbor"
- lying about lost property that a person has found.

Exodus 22:5–6 explores outright theft alongside a discussion of what to do when a person inadvertently destroys another person's property,[31] while Deuteronomy 24:14–15 identifies the delay of wages owed a worker as sin.

The logic of the Torah has inspired theological interpreters to see the eighth commandment as condemning a whole host of negative property-related behaviors. Writing on this commandment, for instance, Calvin declares:

> Since God is to be feared and loved by us, we are not to filch by fraud or seize by main force what belongs to another. We are not to catch anyone unawares in bargaining or contracts, either by selling too dear or by buying too cheaply from those who are ignorant of the prices of things; nor are we to lay hands on another's property by any sort of guile whatsoever.[32]

Indeed, for Calvin, the eighth commandment condemns all sorts of "harsh and cruel laws by which the more powerful oppresses and crushes the feeble." While such laws may make a person's actions legal in the eyes of the law, a "different decision is given by God."[33]

The Torah's unpacking of the eighth commandment also includes reflection on what just wisdom requires when a person does in fact commit theft. In the case of stealing *people*, for instance, capital punishment is required to "purge the evil from your midst" (Deut 24:7; Exod 21:16).[34] By contrast, a person who inadvertently destroys another's crop simply repays what was lost. Leviticus 6:1–7[5:23–36] provides particularly important guidance on what is required when a person sins and commits a "trespass against the LORD by deceiving a neighbor" (Lev 6:3b[5:22b]):

> when you have sinned and realize your guilt . . . you shall repay the principal amount and shall add one-fifth to it. You shall pay it to its owner when you realize your guilt. And you shall bring to the priest, as your guilt offering to the LORD, a ram without blemish from the flock, or its equivalent, for a guilt

offering. The priest shall make atonement on your behalf before the LORD, and you shall be forgiven for any of the things that one may do and incur guilt thereby (Leviticus 6:4–7[5:23–25]).

Here Leviticus identifies theft, either by force or by fraud, as both an assault on the neighbor and a crime against God and his creational purposes for his good world. Because of this dual violation, YHWH requires that the perpetrator acknowledge their transgression and repair the damage done both to the neighbor and to YHWH. This occurs through restitution with interest to the injured neighbor and through a sacrifice of atonement offered to God. The result of this process is forgiveness.

Leviticus 6:1–7[5:23–26] thus requires the acknowledgment, redress, and closure that Darity and Mullen argue is central to any program of reparations. At the same time, Leviticus goes beyond Darity and Mullen by including YHWH among the parties to whom acknowledgment and repair must be offered and identifying atonement and forgiveness as the goals of the process. Such theological concepts arguably go far beyond the minimum standard of a "closure" of grievances.

The Torah thus expands the scope of the eighth commandment's prohibition against theft and offers a program of reparations to address violations of that prohibition. As we shall see, this dynamic offers us vital resources for evaluating Darity and Mullen's case for reparations. But first, we need to recognize another way the Torah "unpacks" the eighth commandment.

"OPENING UP" THE POSITIVE SCOPE OF THE EIGHTH COMMANDMENT'S MORAL VISION

The Torah's unpacking of the eighth commandment not only expands the scope and consequence of its prohibitions; it also includes the command that God's people proactively *preserve* the property of their neighbors, and even their enemies.

> When you come upon your enemy's ox or donkey going astray, you shall bring it back.
> When you see the donkey of one who hates you lying under its burden and you would hold back from setting it free, you must help to set it free (Exodus 23:4–5).

The parallel text in Deuteronomy makes clear that this teaching applies to anything lost by one's neighbor (22:3a). Indeed, in the face of a neighbor's lost property, Deuteronomy provocatively declares: "you may not *hide yourself*" (22:3b).[35]

Such Torah reflection on the full force of the eighth commandment lends support to the claim that the Ten Commandments' negative prohibitions "implicitly commend their positive side."[36] The commandments not only warn against "sin which leads to death and judgment"; they also offer us a "gracious gift, pointing to the way of life and joy."[37] Reading the eighth commandment in this way suggests that all in the community of faith must proactively look after the "preservation and well-being of the property of the neighbor, *even if that neighbor is an enemy.*"[38] Once again, Calvin offers an example of this kind of Torah-shaped reasoning:

> But if there is in us any fear or love of God, we are rather to press with every effort to aid either friend or foe, as much as we can with advice and help, to hold onto his possessions, and we are rather to give up our own than take away anything from another. And not this alone, but if they are pressed by any material difficulty, we are to share their needs and relieve their penury with our substance.[39]

From this perspective, the Torah's many commands concerning the need to offer costly, economic support to the neighbor in need are implied by the eighth commandment's "thou shalt not steal." God's people must not "harden their hearts" from lending to their neighbor in need (Deut 15:7) any more than they may "hide themselves" in the face of their enemy's lost donkey.

Fretheim argues that the Ten Commandments are grounded in God's design for his creation.[40] The roots of the eighth commandment's positive and negative exhortations, then, are nothing less than God's creational intention to co-rule his good world through humans who bear the divine image (Gen 1:27–28). Humans do this, in part, by using and enjoying the fruit of good work done in God's good world and in line with God's good purposes. The Torah prohibits stealing and related behaviors because they keep both the victim and the perpetrator from experiencing this creational design.[41] But the Torah also seeks to establish a context and community in which enjoying the fruit of good work done in God's good world is possible for everyone.

One central way the Torah establishes such a community is by ensuring that every household has access to a plot in the promised land. In an agricultural economy, such family farms provided an essential economic and social asset that would enable households to thrive if stewarded well. While the Bible expresses deep suspicion about immoderate wealth accumulation and sees flourishing and security as rooted in one's relationship with YHWH, the Torah's vision of an equitable distribution of land does resonate with aspects of Darity and Mullen's discussion of the role of wealth in family well-being.

Secure access to land would have contributed to an ancient Israelite household's economic agency, improved their chances of achieving a "generous sufficiency,"[42] and offered some level of socio-economic security in ways partially analogous to the role played by home ownership, business ownership, and education in our own economy.

To accomplish the Torah's vision of a relatively equitable distribution of agricultural land, Numbers 33:54 requires the people to divide the land equitably among households. Significant legislation throughout the Torah then seeks to ensure that this land is never permanently lost by any Israelite household. The high point of the Bible's concern that every family have inalienable access to the family farm comes in the Levitical Year of Jubilee.

THE YEAR OF JUBILEE

Leviticus 25:8–55 introduces and unpacks the Year of Jubilee. Every fifty years, Israel is to proclaim a release throughout the entire community. In this year, anybody who had fallen into debt slavery was released, and any family that had lost their family farm over the course of the previous fifty years returned to it. Alongside these acts of liberation, the community spent the entire year on sabbatical; in the Year of Jubilee, YHWH provided for the people's material needs apart from their own organized economic efforts.

The Jubilee makes clear just how far YHWH is willing to go to preserve each family's socio-economic place within the community. On the one hand, the entire community is fully protected from permanently losing their land. On the other hand, doing this requires families that acquire lands and fields beyond their initial holding during the fifty-year period to *return them* to those who lose them in the Year of Jubilee. While the eighth commandment's prohibition against theft assumes some account of private property, such private property is clearly not owned absolutely.[43] While the Year of Jubilee would not end temporary poverty due to natural disaster, poor decision-making, or injustice, it did seek to end *multi-generational* poverty.[44] Strikingly, the Jubilee launches its attack on multi-generational poverty in part by limiting multi-generational affluence.

Ellen Davis argues that the central concern of Leviticus is to help the people become a community "capable of hosting in its midst the radical holiness of God."[45] The Year of Jubilee makes clear that hosting God's holiness requires Israel to acknowledge God as the sole owner of both the *land* and *the Israelites themselves*. Because the land belongs to *YHWH*, no Israelite can claim permanent right to any of it. Because the Israelites are *YHWH's* slaves, no individual Israelite may become a permanent slave of any earthly master

(Lev 25:42).[46] These theological claims are enshrined in the deep structures of Israel's economy through the Jubilee.

THE TORAH AND CONTEMPORARY REPARATIONS DISCOURSE IN DIALOGUE

We have seen that the eighth commandment's prohibition against theft "opens up" to condemn a whole host of negative behaviors. It also provides a process of reparation whereby the perpetrator seeks forgiveness from both their human victim and the LORD himself when violations occur. At the same time, we have tracked the way that the eighth commandment "opens up" to demand a whole host of positive, life-affirming practices whereby one proactively seeks to preserve the well-being of the neighbor. This positive vision is ultimately rooted in creation and comes to full flower in the Year of Jubilee. What might this exploration contribute to our evaluation of Darity and Mullen's case for reparations? I believe we can make at least three important points.

First, the Torah helps us join Darity and Mullen in acknowledging the tremendous injustice that has occurred. The Torah's prescription of capital punishment for kidnapping underscores the heinous evil of the slave trade and agrees with Darity and Mullen that the theft of Black labor and land creates a grievous wrong that must be righted. While these points are fairly obvious, Darity and Mullen go on to tell the long history of wealth-denying injustice against Black Americans in the twentieth and twenty-first century. That history included all sorts of *legal* theft and predatory behavior; Black people were sometimes tricked into losing their land or manipulated into accepting predatory economic contracts designed to force them into selling it. Black people were exposed to both redlining and predatory housing contracts well into the twenty-first century.[47] Based on our discussion, I think it's obvious that the Torah joins Darity and Mullen in calling such predatory behavior what it is: *theft.*

But we can go further. The Torah does not stop at condemning God's people for actively defrauding their neighbor. It also calls them out for passively allowing their neighbor to lose their property, *even if that neighbor is an enemy!* If an Israelite could break God's law by failing to help his enemy's ox out of the ditch, what are we to think of the great masses of white Christians who stood idly by as Black families were terrorized, defrauded, and forced out of their lands and homes? Indeed, who often profited, directly and indirectly, from these injustices? If ignoring the neighbor's ox in the ditch brings guilt, what of our—what of *my*—participation in banking and educational systems often explicitly or implicitly organized against Black economic well-being?

The Torah's unpacking of the eighth commandment *increases the range of culpability*. If our moral imaginations are shaped by the Torah's logic, white Christians like me will be much quicker to *acknowledge* that our white ancestors, and indeed we ourselves, bear responsibility for the injustices against Black people. An Israelite may not have put his enemy's ox in the ditch, but that didn't make them any less guilty if they "hid themselves" from helping it back out again. White Christians like me may not always have proactively taken Black wealth, but we often have "hidden ourselves" while Black wealth was taken or while Black families were denied access to acquiring such wealth. Indeed, given Darity and Mullen's careful demonstration that much present white wealth is the direct result of injustice against Black people in the past, we've ignored the ways that wealth has found its way into our own households.

Second, the Torah agrees with Darity and Mullen that the kind of injustices perpetrated by white Christians against Black Americans must be repaired. When theft occurs, the Torah requires an acknowledgment of that sin. But it also requires a process of *repairing* the damage through repayment to the victim and an offering to YHWH. The Torah celebrates reconciliation between the perpetrator on the one hand, and both God and their human victim on the other. But the Torah also identifies confession and reparation as central to the process of achieving that reconciliation.

If the massive theft of Black labor, land, wages, and wealth constitutes an enormous violation of the eighth commandment, then the Torah demands the perpetrators of these crimes *confess* their sin and seek to *repair* the damage done by repaying what was taken with interest. Moreover, the Torah places this process of repair within a broader theological movement:

> confession of sin > reparation to the victim > sacrifice to and reconciliation with YHWH

Of course, the NT declares the good news that Jesus is a High Priest who wins an eternal redemption for his people through the offering of his own blood as an atoning sacrifice (Heb 9:12). All humanity can receive reconciliation with God through the gracious work of God on our behalf in Jesus. Yet this theological reality does not mean Christians are free from ongoing repentance and confession of sin. Why then would Christians be free from the requirement to *repair* the sins they commit against their neighbor? Indeed, for the author of Hebrews, Christ's sacrifice works by the Spirit to "purify our conscience from dead works to worship the living God!" (Heb 9:14). If Israel was to seek reconciliation with their neighbor through reparation and atonement with God through sacrifice, shouldn't those of us who have experienced atonement with God through Jesus find ourselves empowered for the work of confessing our sin and *seeking to repair its damage* today?

In its own context and within the broader biblical story, then, the Torah exhorts contemporary people of faith to acknowledge and confess violations of the eighth commandment and seek to repair the damage done in concrete ways.

THE QUESTION OF INTERGENERATIONAL REPAIR

These first two points seem sufficient to prove that the Torah agrees with Darity and Mullen that a thief ought to embrace reparations through acknowledgment, restitution, and closure. But Darity and Mullen argue that the present generation of Americans ought to embrace reparations at least partially in response to theft perpetrated by previous generations.[48] For some, it is this intergenerational dynamic that makes Darity and Mullen's case a hard pill to swallow. As Senate Majority Leader Mitch McConnell said during a hearing on reparations, "I don't think reparations for something 150 years ago for whom none of us currently living are responsible is a good idea."[49] What resources does the Torah offer for thinking about intergenerational reparations?

Duke Kwon and Greg Thompson argue that Numbers 5:7 offers evidence that the Torah's reparational ethic includes intergenerational repair.[50] In that text, YHWH outlines a similar process to that of Leviticus 6:1–7[5:20–26]. But then Numbers 5:8 continues:

> But if the individual [who has been wronged] has no close relative to whom reparation can be made for the wrong, the reparation for the wrong must be paid to the LORD for the priest, in addition to the ram of atonement by which atonement is made for him (NET).

At the very least, this passage makes clear that a living perpetrator ought to pay reparations to the family of their victim if that victim is deceased, while also requiring that the perpetrator pay reparations to YHWH in circumstances where this is impossible. But it might also be read as implying that paying reparations becomes increasingly difficult over time. Some might argue that, after a certain point, asking later generations of perpetrators to pay reparations to later generations of victims might be seen as misguided, if not outright unjust.

Yet as bizarre as it seems to many contemporary Christians, the idea that later generations must confess and repair the sins of their ancestors is affirmed in the OT,[51] not least in Leviticus. The jubilary legislation of Leviticus 25 is followed by Leviticus 26's offer of covenantal blessings for obedience and warning of covenantal curses for infidelity. If the community does reject God's way, the ultimate disaster is exile. But even as Leviticus 26 outlines the devastating consequences of rebellion, it offers a glimmer of hope. Even in exile, Yahweh will remember his covenant and their land *if* God's people

> *confess* (ידה) their iniquity and the iniquity of their fathers in their treachery which they committed against me, and . . . if their uncircumcised heart is *humbled* and they *make restitution for* (רצה)[52] their iniquity.[53]

Leviticus 26:40–42 suggests that later generations may be responsible for confessing and making restitution for their own sins *and the sins of their fathers*.

As strange as this may seem to us, acknowledging and repairing the sins of one's ancestors is precisely what Leviticus 25's Year of Jubilee would require *in at least some circumstances*.[54] Consider: the average life expectancy of an Israelite male was probably somewhat less than forty years,[55] and Israelite household heads would typically be well into adulthood when they took over the management of the household. Because of this, if an Israelite obtained their neighbor's land through injustice and refused Leviticus 6:1–7[5:20–26]'s program of reparations to repair that injustice, they might well die and leave what they had taken to their children before the next Jubilee arrived. At the Jubilee Year, then, the descendants of the perpetrator would be required to restore what was taken to the descendants of the victim.

While one household's acquisition of another's land might not be due to injustice,[56] readers of Leviticus would be well aware that injustice frequently caused land loss (cf. Ezek 45:8–9). In the midst of the Jubilee legislation, Leviticus 25 repeatedly exhorts the Israelites not to "oppress" one another (25:14, 17), including through unfair calculations of land-lease prices or exploitative lending. Both practices could easily lead to land loss. Indeed, the Year of Jubilee is announced *on the Day of Atonement*. The Jubilee is thus fixed to the community's annual ritual of atonement and purgation of sin. The text itself thus seems to acknowledge that, on at least some occasions, Jubilee land restoration would repair economic injustices. In such cases, the task for such repair may well have fallen to the descendants of those who originally committed that injustice.

The OT as a whole does not seem to suggest that a person is guilty of their ancestors' sins in the same way that they are guilty of sins they themselves commit. Nevertheless, scripture does suggest a connection.[57]

> Thinking specifically of the Jubilee, people who stole land in the prior generation might be thought of as the original *perpetrators* of economic injustice.

However, if later generations ignore the Year of Jubilee, they become morally culpable as *perpetuators* of that earlier sin. Indeed, the Jubilee identifies the moment where any *perpetuation* of land loss *becomes* an unjust act of *perpetration* in its own right. From the perspective of Leviticus, then, to continually refuse to repair our ancestors' sins is to make them our own. Such continual refusal is nothing less than an assault on Yahweh's presence among his people, and his people's ongoing presence in the land.[58]

Darity and Mullen make a powerful case that, to use Isaiah's language, white Americans have the "plunder from the poor in [our] houses" (Isa 3:14b, NIV). This is true even if we are not the generation that bears primary responsibility for putting it there. The Year of Jubilee suggests that this means we have a responsibility for confessing that injustice and embracing costly action to repair it.

Third, the Torah calls us to costly sacrifice on behalf of our neighbor's economic well-being even in cases where we bear no responsibility for their suffering. According to the Torah's vision, the people of God are called to pursue an economy and society where everyone has a socio-economic place to stand and portion to steward. They are called to do this even when they bear *no* responsibility for their neighbor's economic struggles. Whether our neighbor is struggling due to injustice, disaster, or bad decision-making, the people of God are called to concrete acts of sacrificial love on their behalf.

While we have seen that Leviticus acknowledges the possibility that the Jubilee might require God's people to repair their own or their ancestors' injustice, the Year of Jubilee also demands that God's people return land to those who had lost it, even if their neighbor lost their land through mismanagement and they acquired it through wisdom and hard work.[59] God's commitment to a jubilary economy means his people must seek economic repair they had no part in creating.

Indeed, the Jubilee is simply one particularly powerful example of a broader pattern. God's people restore oxen to their enemies even if they didn't leave the gate open. They give food and provide jobs to refugees even when they did not cause their displacement. They make zero-interest loans to farmers whose struggles they had no part in causing. The Torah does not merely demand that we avoid theft; it requires that we love our neighbors as ourselves *in our economic lives and at our own expense.*

Darity and Mullen offer an ethic of reparation to perpetrators of theft; the Torah both agrees with and expands this ethic. God's breathtaking economic vision requires that his people *repair* economic breakdown wherever and however it occurred. What this means is that even in situations where we might argue that the white Christian church was not directly or even indirectly involved with the injustice perpetrated against Black people, the failure to love our Black neighbors as ourselves through costly economic action constitutes a *massive failure of discipleship*. Beyond questions of guilt, the Torah demands an ethic of repair from God's people in the face of the Black community's experience of serious and sustained injustice and suffering.

CONCLUSION

Many American Christians find the history Darity and Mullen tell deeply lamentable, and indeed, regret the role churches and Christians played within that history. But thus far, the vast majority resist what Darity and Mullen see as a hopeful way forward in light of that history: a concrete program of reparations for Black Americans. In this chapter, I have argued that the Torah's unpacking of the eighth commandment and the Year of Jubilee offer contemporary Christians particularly good reasons for confessing the sins of our ancestors and seeking to repair them through costly economic acts of restitution.

I am not claiming that the Torah provides an exact blueprint for addressing an identical situation to that facing contemporary American Christians, nor that the text offers easy or clear solutions to the practical questions around how reparations ought to be structured. But the interpretation offered here does suggest that the Torah provides a powerful paradigm of jubilary repair that ought to shape and catalyze our moral imaginations and energies for pursuing reparations today.

Many will be quick to claim that the Year of Jubilee "never happened." That claim itself needs to be seriously nuanced, but perhaps the bigger problem is that the Torah recognizes that God's people may not embrace God's economy . . . and threatens them with exile as a result. The difficulty of discipleship does not get God's people off the hook for attempting it.

The flip side to this dismal dynamic is the witness of scripture that God's people *did* occasionally allow the Jubilee to catalyze their moral imaginations. The Year of Jubilee echoes across Ezekiel and Isaiah's prophetic visions, inspires aspects of Nehemiah's advocacy for the poor, gets picked up by the Lord Jesus himself, and arguably inspires aspects of the early church's economic practice.[60] In different ways, each of these examples reminds us of a jubilary dynamic that may surprise us in relation to reparations; the result of a Jubilee economy is *renewal* in the community at large. Responding to Darity and Mullen's case for reparations will be costly. But if scripture is any indication, when God's people embrace this costly work, the result is not only justice, but jubilant *joy*.

NOTES

1. Trymaine Lee, "A Vast Wealth Gap," *New York Times* (August 18, 2019), accessed May 19, 2023, https://pulitzercenter.org/sites/default/files/inline-images/tOJqxJcH01uQisBbPdVFIH4SNopreEKoVbanwgOn5Y2dfneSwF.pdf.
2. William Darity Jr. "Forty Acres and a Mule in the 21st Century," *Social Science Quarterly* 89.3 (2008), 656.
3. William A. Darity Jr., and A. Kirsten Mullen, *From Here to Equality: Reparations for Black Americans in the Twenty-First Century* (Chapel Hill, NC: University of North Carolina Press, 2020), 244.
4. Statistics taken from James Davison Hunter and Carl Desportes Bowman, with Kyle Puetz, "Democracy in Dark Times," (Charlottesville, VA: Finstock & Tew, 2020), 56, 61, accessed May 19, 2023, https://iasculture.org/research/publications/democracy-in-dark-times. In 2004, only 4% of white Americans supported reparations (Darity, "40 Acres," 660).
5. Darity and Mullen, *From Here*, 31.
6. Darity and Mullen, *From Here*, 31.
7. Darity and Mullen, *From Here*, 31.
8. Darity and Mullen, *From Here*, 1–2.
9. Martin Luther King Jr., *Where Do We Go From Here?* (Boston, MA: Beacon Press, 2010), 84.
10. Darity and Mullen, *From Here*, 208.
11. Darity and Mullen, *From Here*, 209.
12. Darity and Mullen, *From Here*, 217.
13. Darity and Mullen, *From Here*, 217.
14. Darity and Mullen, *From Here*, 221–22. See also Preston Lauterbach, "Memphis Burning," *Places Journal* (March 2016) in its entirety; accessed May 19, 2023, https://placesjournal.org/article/memphis-burning.
15. Darity and Mullen, *From Here*, 222.
16. Darity and Mullen, *From Here*, 37.
17. Ta-Nehisi Coates, "The Case for Reparations," *The Atlantic*, June 2014, accessed May 19, 2023, http://www.theatlantic.com/magazine/archive/2014/06/the-case-for-reparations/361631/.
18. Ira Katznelson, "When Affirmative Action Was White," *History & Policy* (November 10, 2005), accessed May 19, 2023, http://historyandpolicy.org/policy-papers/papers/when-affirmative-action-was-white.
19. Darity, "Forty Acres," 661.
20. Darity and Mullen, *From Here*, 33.
21. Darity and Mullen, *From Here*, 33. This paragraph is taken from Michael J. Rhodes, *Just Discipleship: Biblical Justice in an Unjust World* (Downers Grove, IL: IVP Academic, 2023).
22. Darity and Mullen, *From Here*, 4.
23. Darity and Mullen, *From Here*, 264–65. They also devote significant energy to exploring the potential price tag for such a reparations fund, the proper management of such a fund, and who would qualify as a beneficiary.

24. See the discussion in William A. Darity Jr., Bidisha Lahiri, and Dania Frank, "Reparations for African-Americans as a Transfer Problem: A Cautionary Tale," *Review of Development Economics* 14.2 (2010), 249–59.

25. Darity and Mullen, *From Here,* 264–65.

26. Darity and Mullen, *From Here,* 270.

27. A commandment repeatedly reiterated in the New Testament: see Mark 10:19; Luke 18:20; Rom 13:9; Eph 4:28.

28. For scholars arguing that the structure of Deuteronomy's law code is based on the Ten Commandments, see Georg Braulik, "The Sequence of the Laws in Deuteronomy 12–26 and in the Decalogue," in *A Song of Power and the Power of Song*, ed. Duane L. Christensen (Winona Lake, IN: Eisenbrauns, 1993); John H. Walton, "The Decalogue Structure of the Deuteronomic Law," in *Interpreting Deuteronomy: Issues and Approaches*, ed. David G. Firth and Philip S. Johnston (Downers Grove, IL: IVP Academic, 2012).

29. Where there are differences between English and Hebrew verse numbers, I have placed Hebrew verse numbers in brackets.

30. Unless otherwise noted, all biblical quotations are from the NRSV.

31. Such situations require restitution, but without penalty or confession of guilt (cf. Exod 22:5–6).

32. John Calvin, *Institutes of the Christian Religion, 1536 Edition*, Ford Lewis Battles, trans. (Grand Rapids, MI: Eerdmans, 1995), 26.

33. John Calvin, *The Institutes of the Christian Religion*, Henry Beveridge, trans. (Grand Rapids, MI: Christian Classics Ethereal Library), 345, accessed May 19, 2023, https://www.ccel.org/ccel/c/calvin/institutes/cache/institutes.pdf.

34. For a discussion about whether the eighth commandment itself is focused on kidnapping, see the discussion in Brevard S. Childs, *The Book of Exodus*, OTL (Louisville, KY: Westminster John Knox, 1975), 423–24.

35. This appears to be the most literal meaning of the hitpael of עלם (*HALOT*, 835).

36. Terence E. Fretheim, *Exodus,* Interpretation (Louisville, KY: Westminster John Knox, 2010), 221.

37. Childs, *Exodus*, 438.

38. Fretheim, *Exodus,* 236.

39. Calvin, *Institutes*, 1536 ed., 26.

40. Fretheim, *Exodus,* 221–23.

41. Fretheim speaks of the humanity of both thief and victim being "diminished" (*Exodus,* 236).

42. I owe this phrase to Ronald J. Sider, *Just Generosity: A New Vision for Overcoming Poverty in America, 2nd ed.* (Grand Rapids, MI: Baker, 2007), 62.

43. These dynamics are frequent features of Catholic theological reflection on economic matters. See, for instance, the teaching on private property and the universal destination of human goods in the Catechism of the Catholic Church's reflection on the commandment "you shall not steal"; accessed May 19, 2023, http://www.scborromeo.org/ccc/p3s2c2a7.htm.

44. Much of the Torah's economic teaching, however, does seek to alleviate more temporary forms of poverty.

45. Ellen F. Davis, *Opening Israel's Scriptures* (New York, NY: Oxford University Press, 2019), 72.

46. Lev 25 does not, however, prohibit permanent slavery for foreigners (Lev 25:44–46). Fully exploring this difficult aspect of the text lies beyond the scope of this chapter. However, as I have written elsewhere: "it ought to be remembered that often law, as a genre, serves to limit pervasive evil rather than eliminate it" (Gordon Wenham, *Story as Torah: Reading the Old Testament Ethically* [Edinburgh: T&T Clark, 2000], 80). In the case of Lev 25:44–46, Downs notes that "this law is not designed to encourage" such slavery, but "rather to limit it to those who are outside the covenant community of Israel" (David Baker, *Tight Fists or Open Hands? Wealth and Poverty in Old Testament Law* [Grand Rapids, MI: Eerdmans, 2009], 118). Membership in that covenant community, we ought to add, was always porous, as is clear in Israel's laws and stories, and whatever Lev 25:44–46 allows stands under Lev 19:33's command: "When an alien resides with you in your land, you shall not oppress the alien. The alien who resides with you shall be to you as the citizen among you; you shall love the alien as yourself, for you were aliens in the land of Egypt: I am the LORD your God" (Lev 19:33–34). As Matthew Lynch suggests, this admonition not to act like Egyptians is all the more potent given that Pharaoh's harsh oppression in Egypt appears to be alluded to in Lev 25:44–46 through the use of the word פרך here and in the description of Pharaoh's oppression of the Israelites in Exodus (personal communication). "Any Israelite who thought Lev 25:44–46 gave them license to oppress or offer harsh treatment to non-Israelite slaves would thus be corrected by Lev 19:33" (Rhodes, *Just Discipleship*, 163, fn. 43). For an argument that the Jubilee trajectory leads to ever-greater inclusion and justice for outsiders in Ezekiel, see Rhodes, *Just Discipleship*, 189–92.

47. See Rhodes, *Just Discipleship*, 200.

48. Darity and Mullen, *From Here*, 250.

49. Tedd Barrett, "McConnell Opposes Paying Reparations," CNN, June 19, 2019), accessed May 19, 2023, https://www.cnn.com/2019/06/18/politics/mitch-mcconnell-opposes-reparations-slavery/index.html.

50. Duke L. Kwon and Gregory Thompson, *Reparations: A Christian Call for Repentance and Repair* (Grand Rapids, MI: Brazos, 2022), 140–41.

51. For examples of corporate guilt and repentance, see the prayers of repentance in Neh 1:6 and Dan 9:1–20. For scholarly discussions of collective guilt, see Joel S. Kaminsky, *Corporate Responsibility in the Hebrew Bible* (New York, NY: T&T Clark, 1995), 89–94; Mark J. Boda, *"Return to Me": A Biblical Theology of Repentance*, NSBT (Downers Grove, IL: IVP Academic, 2015), 154–9. Milgrom goes so far as to call the doctrine of collective responsibility a "cardinal plank in the structure of priestly theology" (Jacob Milgrom, *Leviticus: A Book of Ritual and Ethics* [Minneapolis, MN: Fortress Press, 2004], 323).

52. Cf. Milgrom, *Leviticus*, 323

53. Author's translation.

54. For a discussion of alternative scenarios also covered by the Jubilee, see below.

55. See Philip J. King and Lawrence E. Stager, *Life in Biblical Israel*, Library of Ancient Israel (Louisville, KY: 2002), 37.

56. See below.

57. Boda speaks of the later generation's "solidarity" with their predecessors (Boda, *Return to Me*, 155). For further discussion, see Rhodes, *Just Discipleship*, 169–71.

58. Rhodes, *Just Discipleship*, 170.

59. Indeed, within Leviticus's vision, a household may have acquired their neighbor's land not through theft, but rather through generosity. The willingness of one's neighbor to "redeem" land on the verge of being lost was part of Israel's social safety net (cf. Lev 25:24–28). But even if a family acquired their neighbor's land as an act of charity in the face of their neighbor's disaster or mismanagement, in the Year of Jubilee they must still return that acquired land to the family that had lost it.

60. For a detailed argument to this effect, see Rhodes, *Just Discipleship*, 177–98.

BIBLIOGRAPHY

Baker, David. *Tight Fists or Open Hands? Wealth and Poverty in Old Testament Law.* Grand Rapids, MI: Eerdmans, 2009.

Barrett, Tedd. "McConnell Opposes Paying Reparations." CNN (June 19, 2019).

Boda, Mark J. *"Return to Me": A Biblical Theology of Repentance.* NSBT. Downers Grove, IL: IVP Academic, 2015.

Braulik, Georg. "The Sequence of the Laws in Deuteronomy 12–26 and in the Decalogue." In *A Song of Power and the Power of Song: Essays on the Book of Deuteronomy*, edited by Duane L. Christensen, 313–35. Winona Like, IN: 1993.

Calvin, John. *Institutes of the Christian Religion, 1536 Edition.* Translated by Ford Lewis Battles. Grand Rapids, MI: Eerdmans, 1995.

———. *The Institutes of the Christian Religion.* Translated by Henry Beveridge. Grand Rapids, MI: Christian Classics Ethereal Library.

Childs, Brevard S. *The Book of Exodus.* Old Testament Library. Louisville, KY: Westminster John Knox, 1975.

Coates, Ta-Nehisi. "The Case for Reparations." *The Atlantic* (June 2014).

Darity, William A., Jr., and A. Kirsten Mullen. *From Here to Equality: Reparations for Black Americans in the Twenty-First Century.* Chapel Hill, NC: UNC Press, 2020.

Darity, William A., Jr., William, Bidisha Lahiri, and Dania Frank. "Reparations for African-Americans as a Transfer Problem: A Cautionary Tale." *Review of Development Economics* 14.2 (2010).

Darity, William, Jr. "Forty Acres and a Mule in the 21st Century." *Social Science Quarterly* 89.3 (2008).

Davis, Ellen F. *Opening Israel's Scriptures.* New York, NY: Oxford University Press, 2019.

Fretheim, Terence E. *Exodus.* Interpretation. Louisville, KY: Westminster John Knox, 2010.

Hunter, James Davison, and Carl Desportes Bowman, with Kyle Puetz. "Democracy in Dark Times." Charlottesville, VA: Finstock & Tew, 2020.

Kaminsky, Joel S. *Corporate Responsibility in the Hebrew Bible.* New York, NY: T&T Clark, 1995.

Katznelson, Ira. "When Affirmative Action Was White." *History & Policy* (November 10, 2005).

King, Martin Luther., Jr. *Where Do We Go From Here?* Boston, MA: Beacon Press, 2010.

King, Philip J., and Lawrence E. Stager. *Life in Biblical Israel.* Library of Ancient Israel. Louisville, KY: 2002.

Lauterbach, Preston. "Memphis Burning." *Places Journal* (March 2016).

Lee, Trymaine. "A Vast Wealth Gap." *New York Times* (August 18, 2019).

Milgrom, Jacob. *Leviticus: A Book of Ritual and Ethics.* Minneapolis, MN: Fortress Press, 2004.

Rhodes, Michael J. *Just Discipleship: Biblical Justice in an Unjust World.* Downers Grove, IL: IVP Academic, 2023.

Sider, Ronald J. *Just Generosity: A New Vision for Overcoming Poverty in America, 2nd ed.* Grand Rapids, MI: Baker, 2007.

Walton, John H. "The Decalogue Structure of the Deuteronomic Law." In *Interpreting Deuteronomy: Issues and Approaches,* edited by David G. Firth and Philip S. Johnston, 93–117. Downers Grove, IL: IVP Academic, 2012.

Wenham, Gordon. *Story as Torah: Reading the Old Testament Ethically.* Edinburgh: T&T Clark, 2000.

Chapter Five

Reparational Reasoning

The Biblical Jubilee as Moral Formation for a More Just Future

Michael Barram

During the last decade, there has been a noticeable resurgence of discussion about reparations for Black and indigenous Americans, inspired, in large part, by Ta-Nehisi Coates's bracing 2014 *Atlantic* essay, "The Case for Reparations."[1] I write not as an expert on reparations, but as an uncommonly privileged, White, male, biblical scholar[2] who has become convinced that (especially White members of) the Christian community in North America must be at the forefront of reflection about and enacting of economic and other social forms of reparations.[3] What follows is a brief attempt to highlight some biblical imagery that may help form and shape churches to begin to address past and present injustices—in part, at least, by means of reparations.[4]

Opposition to reparations—whether to contemporary indigenous, Black, or other communities—often turns on utilitarian and libertarian reasoning, moral logics that are almost as "American" as apple pie, we might say. Of course, racism—in both its interpersonal and enduring structural forms—is no less "American," and it is the fundamental reason that we must now address the topic of reparations today.

Utilitarian and libertarian forms of reasoning regularly serve to underscore both theoretical and practical difficulties involved in making restitution for historical injustices, whether through financial reparations or other types of structural adjustments aimed at restitution (e.g., affirmative action).[5] These logics often fail to foster change and redress that go beyond the superficial and episodic and, in so doing, they can sometimes function as forms of intellectual misdirection and obfuscation, serving to provide a misguided sense of moral "cover" in the face of past and present structures rooted in racist injustice.

The typical outcome—if not necessarily the objective—of utilitarian and libertarian reasoning regarding reparations is to leave the past in the past—to attempt to move toward an eventually less fraught social reality without adequately taking stock of contemporary evidence that past and present injustice continues to have negative impacts.

Ultimately, utilitarian and libertarian forms of moral reasoning are inadequate for Christian discussions of restorative justice and, specifically, reparations. Not only is biblical reasoning unswervingly attentive to historical and contemporary realities "on the ground," but it imagines and encourages radical and creative possibilities in the face of the pragmatic challenges that confound contemporary moral logics. After we consider how utilitarian and libertarian logics fall short, we will turn to Jubilee imagery in Leviticus 25 to explore an alternative and exegetically robust biblical logic that could support arguments in favor of contemporary reparations, despite the theoretical and practical difficulties highlighted by utilitarian and libertarian objections.

UTILITARIAN MORAL REASONING

Utilitarian logics are deeply endemic in the United States, particularly in our economic structures and thought. Indeed, the emergence of contemporary capitalism is almost inconceivable apart from the utilitarian logics that explicate and justify it. From a utilitarian perspective, in which ends ultimately legitimate means, outcomes and consequences are all important.[6] Within this framework, we emphasize efficiencies and outcomes, regularly presuming the moral legitimacy of self-interested and consequentialist reasoning.

Given the intimate historical connection between slavery and the development of capitalism, however, we should not presume the moral neutrality of utilitarian logics—especially when utilitarian reasoning so often provides the rationale and justification for our economic thought and practice. Questioning the legitimacy of reparations from the perspective of utilitarianism arguably reflects an attempt to maintain and justify the master's residence with the same tools that were used to build the master's plantation house in the first place (to extend a seminal turn of phrase by Audre Lorde). Modes of reasoning always emerge within specific contexts, and utilitarianism emerged and operated wtihin socio-cultural and historical systems of inequitable power and privilege. In the United States, then, utilitarian logics necessarily and unavoidably function within—and reinforce—a long-standing complex of racist dynamics.

Inasmuch as utilitarian moral logic focuses almost exclusively on the results of decision-making, and since it is usually impossible to foresee or guarantee such results ahead of time, the range of options for potentially sound decisions may appear to be limited. For example, policies that could eventually threaten the hegemony and status quo of the majority are regularly rejected as legitimate possibilities. Indeed, inequities characteristic of the status quo are often maintained in utilitarian logic through appeal to the impracticalities and unknowns of potentially challenging choices. If the route toward a potentially ideal outcome appears to be challenging, or the end result is largely unpredictable, practical matters—more than explicitly moral considerations—tend to dominate discussion and debate.[7] In short, initiatives aimed at making restitution for past injustice often founder on the rocky shores of *pragmatic* challenges. Obvious and important questions (e.g., Who? Why? In what context? For what reason? In what form? and How?) often function less as invitations for exploration and creativity than as the means by which serious reflection and sustained action in support of reparations can be derailed relatively early in the discussion.

To be sure, utilitarian decision-making is at least theoretically committed to a maximum welfare model—often understood in terms of "the greatest good for the greatest number." *In theory,* utilitarian reasoning enables the widest possible consideration of what should be done in any complex scenario. If the circle of welfare to be maximized is extended far enough—across human and other diversities, species, and generations—choices that would have appeared impractical or even wrongheaded in more circumscribed analyses may begin to seem more reasonable, practical, and even necessary.

In practice, however, maximization of welfare is usually conceptualized in limited terms, both socially and temporally—as is usually the case with reparations. Indeed, utilitarian logic tends to privilege and justify the limited scope of well-being envisioned by societal majorities—or, in real-life contexts characterized by significant power imbalances, by powerful and influential minority perspectives.[8] Social location is, of course, a crucial and often definitive consideration here; those who benefit from the status quo tend to resist change.

The wisdom of a privileged minority is not necessarily wise, however. The inscrutability of the future can effectively shield the potential foolishness of a powerful minority from the scrutiny (through consideration of wider circles of well-being) that status quo "wisdom" deserves. The result is often an insufficiently broad consideration of potential benefits and an inadequately critical engagement with social and historical realities. Potentially misguided calculations regarding risk today versus reward tomorrow are difficult to falsify.[9] Failure to discuss reparations seriously is a case in point.

LIBERTARIAN MORAL REASONING

Libertarian logics take seriously the threat to individual and minority well-being that results from the tendency of utilitarian reasoning to valorize and enshrine majoritarian impulses. Libertarian commitments to autonomy and self-ownership necessitate protection—and thus defense—of individual rights, which naturally leads to an emphasis on present-day contracts and procedures—and the moral responsibility to uphold and abide by them.[10] The potential implications for the future of such present-focused reasoning usually receive less consideration. (Think, for example, about the trope of the anti-tax libertarian who expects to benefit from communal firefighting resources when her house is ablaze.)

Special challenges arise when the limited scope of responsibility envisioned in libertarian moral logic meets past injustice. Arguments that "It wasn't me—I wasn't there" and "I'm not the problem—personally, I don't treat people unfairly" are ubiquitous in the United States, and often carry significant weight in debates about historical injustice and the possibility of making restitution for past wrongs.[11] Many are loath to admit that contemporary social structures and privilege, coupled with widespread inaction (i.e., complicity in the racial injustice), enable them and others to benefit from inequities, past and present. It is difficult for a society to own up to the past when atomized notions of responsibility are considered legitimate.

From a libertarian perspective, consent functions as a moral imperative. As the *sine qua non* for moral reasoning, consent (rooted in the principle of self-ownership) tends to focus deliberation on *present* rights and choices, which can inhibit social change. Libertarian reasoning can certainly take past injustice into account. Robert Nozick, for example, contends that present holdings are just if past exchanges were made justly.[12] At a certain point, however, the depth and ubiquity of past injustices (such as, e.g., stolen land and labor) tends to render the impulse for present change practically unworkable, which, in turn, often limits the scope of debate to recent (and often relatively superficial) situations. Emphasis on consent in the present can relegate the past to the past, since focusing on protecting the right to consent in the present may effectively keep past coercion from receiving the attention that it deserves.[13]

By privileging rational principles over the concrete, often messy, lived situations in which societies find themselves, utilitarian and libertarian forms of reasoning tend to underestimate—and misrepresent—the continuing effects of historically unjust decision-making upon present circumstances, functionally de-historicizing and de-contextualizing past and present social realities.[14] Testimonies of pain and suffering caused or exacerbated by social injustice and structural inequities may provide anecdotal, illustrative evidence of a need for change, but concrete historical realities of this nature too often remain ancillary in moral debate. By contrast, the supra-historical rational principles that give utilitarian and libertarian moral logics their power and appeal can, in effect, function as both judge and jury when deliberations (about, e.g., reparations) are fraught with challenging implications for those with economic, socio-cultural, or political hegemony.

THE BIBLICAL JUBILEE AS FORMATION FOR REPARATIONAL REASONING

While forms of utilitarianism can be found in biblical reasoning, libertarian logics seem largely foreign to the Bible.[15] For its part, Jubilee legislation in Leviticus 25 starts with different assumptions and draws different conclusions than these approaches.

The first thing to note is that every fiftieth year, a Sabbath of Sabbaths, "all rural ancestral land was to be returned to its original owner during the Jubilee year (Lev 25:13, 31)."[16] Land exchanged hands in a variety of ways, including (as presupposed in this legislation) through exploitation and poverty-induced selloffs (often catalyzed by drought, crop failure, and insurmountable indebtedness). As the basic unit of capital in an economy characterized largely by subsistence agriculture, the return of ancestral lands each Jubilee Year would have represented an iterative and concrete redistribution of wealth, at once widespread and tangibly localized in character. Many American Christians, formed more by libertarian than biblical reasoning, "believe that even legal forms of redistribution are fundamentally unjust, especially to those who have wealth." By contrast, "the Jubilee law . . . unequivocally advocates wealth redistribution as *a matter of justice*" for the impoverished.[17]

Second, both utilitarian and libertarian moral reasoning begin with human beings—whether in terms of anticipated results and greater "happiness" or in terms of autonomy and individual rights. Jubilee redistribution, by contrast, begins with God—initiated by divine command: "The land shall not be sold in perpetuity, for the land is mine; with me you are but aliens and tenants" (Lev 25:23).[18] The logical basis for economic and justice-oriented reform here is entirely different from what we find in utilitarian and libertarian approaches. Land belongs to God, the landlord who establishes terms for its occupation and use. Israelite moral reasoning is shaped by the assertion that all land exchange was to be temporary and, effectively, functional. Purchase of land, in fact, represents nothing more than the securing of a number of (potential) harvests (Lev 25:16). Divine land is held in trust by members of the covenantal community and is not to be sold permanently—presumably to prevent the kind of grinding, multi-generational poverty that recurring Jubilee redistribution was intended to mitigate. The moral logic here assumes that the poor must not remain poor in perpetuity, which is why land must not be sold in perpetuity. Land as wealth is a divinely sanctioned and protected means for life and essentially functions as an end in and of itself.

Third, the transitory nature of land ownership in Leviticus 25 is striking. Land holders are metaphorically described in terms normally reserved for some of the most socially and financially vulnerable—they are to be understood as "aliens and tenants" on the land (Lev 25:23). For their part, "aliens" (Hebrew: *gerim;* occasionally rendered as "strangers" or "sojourners"; better: "vulnerable outsiders"), who are inherently "othered" (even in the nomenclature assigned to them) by the dominant community, are often landless and financially insecure; tenants may have access to land but remain dependent upon landlords.[19] The God of the exodus provides the very land these "aliens and tenants" have been largely unable to access themselves. The Jubilee legislation makes it imperative that God's people not "alienate" others by allowing landless poverty to endure for more than fifty years.[20]

Fourth, in the Jubilee legislation—as in the biblical corpus, generally—what we might think of as social justice is consistently assessed from below, from the lowest strata of the community's social hierarchies, where the widows, orphans, and *gerim* ("vulnerable outsiders") are found. The situation in which the weakest, most needy, and least influential find themselves in the present is the metric for measuring whether the community is functioning in a manner faithful to the character and purposes of the God of justice.[21] Contrary to the contemporary utilitarian tendency to reason in terms of potential outcomes for the powerful and influential—for the benefit of what we might consider the "functional majority" (even if it remains, in reality, a numerical minority)—or in terms of a libertarian defense of individual autonomy, one of the most overlooked and underappreciated of biblical criteria for moral reasoning, across the Bible, is the basic datum of unmet need. Moral reasoning that is entirely predicated and focused on meeting human need may seem strange and radical in a context shaped by utilitarian and libertarian logics, but human need functions as a fundamental and unavoidable criterion for biblical morality.[22] Ultimately, the present and future well-being of the community requires justice for those most marginalized and vulnerable.[23]

Fifth, the covenantal context of the Jubilee legislation is a critical component of the moral reasoning it seeks to engender. Biblical laws are not narrowly concerned with individual morality; rather, covenantal texts seek to form a community whose members understand themselves to be inextricably connected to one another. Israel's legal materials form readers such that relationships with God and with one another will be characterized by *shalom,* in which all may experience wholeness and, ultimately, flourish to their fullest human capacity. *Shalom* cannot be reduced to an "absence of conflict," as "peace" is so often understood in our contemporary society. True peace—which presupposes just economic relations (see, e.g., Jeremiah 6:13–14; 8:10–11)—requires something of every member of the community. Jubilee legislation shoulders the entire community with *proactive* responsibility for the social and material well-being—past, present, and future—of each of its members. Passive avoidance of harm, emphasized in contemporary moral logics, is insufficient. In contrast with libertarian reasoning, no one is an island from this perspective. Everyone in the community is called to mutuality and implicated in what takes place.

The "limited good" context of biblical reasoning is instructive here. Resources in the ancient Near East were understood to be available in limited supply; goods such as economic capital were scarce, with only so much to go around.[24] A surplus held by one individual meant concomitant scarcity for others. Wealth controlled by elites directly and precisely reduced what was available for the rest of the community. Everyone, by nature and necessity, lived within this inherently interconnected network of inequitable resource allocation. Thus inequality was, to a significant extent, not as impersonal and circumstantial as our contemporary economic logics tend to envision it; rather, because everyone had to draw from the same, limited pot of resources, inequality was fundamentally personal, communal, and structural. Ultimately, the well-being of the poor was intimately bound up with the behavior of societal elites. Those who bought up ancestral lands, for example, benefited from past and present inequities—as did others only indirectly involved in such economic dynamics. Jubilee legislation seeks to prevent inequitable resource allocation from getting so out of hand that those at the bottom of the social hierarchy are permanently enslaved by and through economic deprivation.

Today, with some justification, we insist that wealth and many other resources can be increased in a capitalist system.[25] As a result, we may have difficulty seeing direct links between the haves and the have-nots in our communities. But contemporary inequality is not entirely accidental and incidental. At least in part, it is rooted in the control of resources by the few at the expense of the many—quite often with readily traceable links to past and present injustices. Beneficiaries of our contemporary economic system and structures are inextricably connected to those who suffer at the hands of that system and structures.[26] No one can legitimately claim to be uninvolved and beyond responsibility.

Finally, Jubilee legislation highlights the need to deal directly with the past. Those who lost access in the past to their ancestral lands continue to suffer in the present, which portends a problematic future for the community as a whole. Addressing the past adequately is a prerequisite for a just future.

Unlike contemporary moral logics, Jubilee imagery does not discriminate among possible reasons for the loss of ancestral land. Those without land do not "deserve" to be poor in the present, regardless of what may have happened in the past. The onus for change is on those with means, not upon the poor. Again, need is need. Unmet need stands as an indictment on the community, rather than on the needy themselves. The future is not open for all until the past is addressed for all.

The Jubilee texts in Leviticus 25 raise tricky historical questions because evidence of Jubilee observance is quite limited. Whatever may or may not have happened, the fundamental interpretive dynamic concerning the Jubilee is not a historical one; rather, the critical question is one of moral logic. The Jubilee commands are best understood as communal formation for moral reasoning. The hermeneutical import of these texts is less about their historicity than about what the text communicates about God and God's people—ancient and contemporary. As I have argued elsewhere, "this text functions as something akin to an economic parable . . . a vision of what God intends."[27] The legislation was included in the text as a constant and formative reminder of the character and purposes of the God with whom the people claimed to be in a covenant relationship. Jubilee imagery reflects a biblical vision of abundance for all, which stands in stark contrast to utilitarian and libertarian rationalities rooted in contemporary assumptions of scarcity. The Jubilee points to a set of convictions or values—indeed, a moral logic. That logic suggests that it is entirely insufficient to lament contemporary inequities and the ongoing effects of past problems without serious and socially transformative, revolutionary redressing of the past in the present.

We have highlighted the assumptions and logic of biblical moral reasoning relative to the Jubilee in order to challenge, at least within the Christian community, attempts to avoid discussion of or reject reparations on the basis of other moral logics. The Jubilee highlights how movement toward a more just future is predicated upon and inextricably linked to an adequate dealing with the past. How might "Leviticus 25 . . . help to form and even transform our contemporary . . . reasoning, just as it served as an enduring, if unrealized, vision of justice for the Israelites[?] What would it look like . . . to live, as it were, according to a 'Jubilee economy'?"[28] Presumably, life in a "Jubilee economy" would reflect a radical openness and commitment to discussing, advocating for, and, indeed, participating in the enactment of a process of reparations for historical injustice as a missional imperative for the Christian community.

JUBILEE FORMATION IN ACTION: JESUS AND ZACCHAEUS

Although numerous biblical texts and traditions could be brought into this discussion, we will close briefly with two. In Luke 4, Jesus draws from the prophet Isaiah to articulate his own mission statement (vv. 18–21), indicating that radical, upside-down changes to the social status quo are part and parcel of what he—and the gospel he announces—is all about. Good news comes to the poor, captives are released, the blind see, and the oppressed are emancipated (v. 18). There is widespread agreement among scholars that "the year of the Lord's favor" (v. 19) refers to the Jubilee. In effect, Jesus claims here that his ministry inaugurates and embodies what the Jubilee involves. All of this is consistent with the reality and character of what Jesus calls "the reign of God." Addressing past and present pain and injustice for the sake of a better future is, in fact, what Jesus is up to. For Jesus, major change and hope go hand in hand.

If the Lukan Jesus supports such redress, how can his followers refuse to engage in those dynamics in their own times and places? Given widespread American opposition to institutionalized forms of wealth redistribution that benefit poorer members of society, perhaps we should not be surprised that when Jesus reminded those in his hometown that God does not meet needs in alignment with human assumptions (vv. 23–27), he almost got thrown off a cliff (vv. 28–29)! Turning entrenched structures and logics upside-down is never easy.

Finally, the story of Zacchaeus (Luke 19:1–10) provides a vivid illustration of how the moral logic of the Jubilee can and should function in contexts beyond the specifics of land redistribution in Leviticus 25. When Zacchaeus declares that he is committed to making restitution for past injustices and present inequities, Jesus announces his salvation as a member of God's people.[29] In short, Zacchaeus recognizes the need to address the effects of the past on the present—and of both past and present on the future. While Jesus does not explicitly demand that Zacchaeus participate personally in a deliberate and dramatic process of socioeconomic repair by offering "half of [his] possessions . . . to the poor" and repaying any ill-gotten gain "four times" over (v. 8),[30] the tax collector himself recognizes and chooses voluntarily to engage in the process of social reversal that Jesus announces at the outset of his activity (Luke 4:16–21) and embodies throughout the Gospel narrative. Strikingly, Zacchaeus finds his own freedom in making things right, in helping to meet the concrete, contemporary economic needs of his fellow human beings. There is a crucial, formative lesson in this story for our own moral reasoning. Unlike the rich ruler described in Luke 18:18–30, who is paralyzed by grief when confronted with the opportunity to meet the needs of the poor, Zacchaeus chooses to act and finds salvation. Luke is the only Synoptic Gospel author who does not describe the rich man departing when Jesus articulates what he, with his vast socioeconomic power and privilege, lacks and must do (see 18:18–30; cf. Mark 10:17–31; Matthew 19:16–30). In Matthew and Mark, the man leaves, but in Luke's account, he never walks away. His own liberation and a more just future for those around him remain distinct possibilities. The rich man can still choose to act in a Zacchaeus-like manner. Perhaps, in that sense, he is us.

Formed, as Zacchaeus was, by Jubilee-shaped moral reasoning, White Christians in the United States would do well to follow the tax collector's lead, eagerly making restitution for the past and addressing inequalities in the present as if our own liberation depends on doing so. Biblical imagery seeks to form a people who recognizes that in fact it does.

CONCLUSION

In conclusion, we must remember that the Israelite covenantal community did not find Jubilee provisions to be straightforward, practical, or convenient. The legislation corrects for what they would *not* have done naturally of their own accord—aiming to prevent present and future exacerbation of past inequities and exploitation by forming their readers accordingly. Though American Christians do not share ancient Israel's theocratic, covenantal context, biblical economic and social reasoning can and should form our moral imaginations and inform how we participate in a radically different context, including how we vote. Shamefully and unfaithfully, the church has too often been near the forefront of fostering racial and economic injustice in the United States, and now it often embodies the worst of the complicit bystander phenomenon.[31] The faith community must face and make restitution for the past not because doing so is straightforward, convenient, or even readily practical, but because doing so reflects the character, values, and actions of the economically and socially just biblical God.

Jubilee legislation functions to form readers to seek a better future for all people—specifically, through intentional, regular, and sweepingly reparative efforts to face the past honestly—despite all the potential difficulties that may await.[32] Biblically formed Christians and their communities are to be missionally located as allies and accomplices among those willing to face our collective wrongdoing and make restitution. Let us squarely face our past—and the ongoing realities of our present—by actively advocating and participating in the hard work of making restitution for racial injustice. Our present and future liberation, no matter who we are, depends upon it.

NOTES

1. Ta-Nehisi Coates, "The Case for Reparations," *The Atlantic*, 2014, accessed November 16, 2020, https://www.theatlantic.com/magazine/archive/2014/06/the-case-for-reparations/361631/. The article was republished with other works and extended reflections by the author, in *We Were Eight Years in Power: An American Tragedy* (New York: One World Publishing, 2017), 151–207. Among numerous recent titles, see *From Here to Equality: Reparations for Black Americans in the Twenty-First Century,* by William A. Darity Jr., and A. Kirsten Mullen (Chapel Hill: The University of North Carolina Press, 2020); and, from a Christian perspective, *Reparations: A Christian Call for Repentance and Repair,* by Duke L. Kwon and Gregory Thompson (Grand Rapids: Brazos, 2021).

An earlier version of the present essay was published in *Word & World* (Vol. 42 [2022]: 77–86) as "Economic and Social Reparations: The Jubilee as Biblical Formation for a More Just Future." Both publications grew out of a paper delivered (with financial support from the Office of Faculty Development at Saint Mary's College of California) in a session on reparations co-sponsored by the Forum on Missional Hermeneutics and the Ethics and Biblical Interpretation Section during the 2020 Annual Meetings of the Society of Biblical Literature.

2. Further, I identify as, among other things, a mid-fifties, cis-gendered, heterosexual, able-bodied, married, home-owning, Protestant (Presbyterian) Christian, highly educated, tenured college professor.

3. All forms of reparations are, of course, inherently economic and social at the same time. Money and financial concerns are always at issue, whether in reference to stolen bodies, labor, land, wealth, and opportunities, or redress for these and other forms of theft.

4. While I do not attempt to address precisely "how" reparations should be carried out, I aim to demonstrate that biblical moral logics suggest the theological necessity of contemporary Christian participation in advocating for and actively enacting reparations. An appropriate reparational response to past and present injustices must be multi-faceted and systemic. The deep-seated complexities of our racist social structures will undoubtedly require a wide diversity of reparational remedies.

5. See, for example, the 2001 ad, "Ten Reasons Why Reparations for Slavery is a Bad Idea for Blacks—and Racist Too," written by David Horowitz, one of the most well-known and long-standing opponents of reparations for Black Americans. At least several of his ten points are rooted in utilitarian and/or libertarian reasoning. (Published in *The Black Scholar: Journal of Studies and Research* 31 (2001): 48; published online in 2015; accessed online December 3, 2020 at https://www.tandfonline.com/doi/abs/10.1080/00064246.2001.11431145.)

6. For an accessible and helpful introduction to utilitarian reasoning, see Michael J. Sandel's *Justice: What's the Right Thing to Do?* (New York: Farrar, Straus, and Giroux, 2009), 31–57.

7. Among the practical problems cited in David Horowitz's "Ten Reasons" (2001), he claims that "there is no single group clearly responsible for the crime of slavery"; "there is no one group that benefited exclusively from its fruits"; "American today is

a multi-ethnic nation and most Americans have no connection (direct or indirect) to slavery"; "the historical precedents used to justify the reparations claim do not apply, and the claim itself is based on race not injury"; "the reparations argument is based on the unfounded claim that all African-American descendants of slavery suffer from the economic consequences of slavery and discrimination." From Horowitz's perspective, therefore, reparations are both impractical and unjustifiable.

8. Sandel notes that, in general, one of the primary drawbacks of utilitarian reasoning is the way in which it allows the will of the majority to override legitimate minority concerns. He cites polling data indicating "that while a majority of African Americans favor reparations, only 4 percent of whites do" (*Justice*, 2009), 210. He also reminds readers that Representative John Conyers, who died in 2019, sponsored legislation (House Resolution 40) to study reparations for slavery every year since 1989. In 2021, HR 40 was finally passed out of committee, paving the way for its consideration by the entire House of Representatives.

9. As Sandel (*Justice*, 211) notes, some utilitarian objections to reparations do run along these lines: "In some cases, attempts to bring about public apologies or reparations may do more harm than good—by inflaming old animosities, hardening historic enmities, entrenching a sense of victimhood, or generating resentment. Opponents of public apologies often voice worries such as these." These objections are powerful, not because they are insurmountable, but because as potentialities they are difficult to falsify in the present.

10. See Sandel's accessible introduction to libertarian reasoning (*Justice*, 58–74).

11. In this connection, we could highlight, among other things, slavery, Jim Crow legislation, redlining, subprime lending, racialized wealth gaps, educational inequities, disproportionate rates of officer-involved shooting deaths and incarceration, and workplace and gender discrimination.

12. See Sandel, *Justice*, 63.

13. As with utilitarian reasoning, libertarian moral logics within the United States operate within an enduring, systemic context characterized by racial injustice. To the extent that libertarian reasoning functions, intentionally or otherwise, in the reification and justification of racial injustice, it can and must be interrogated and challenged.

14. Horowitz's "Ten Reasons" document reflects this phenomenon. Temporal distance from the era of slavery problematizes reparations by sharpening the question about who should benefit in a time far removed from the original offense. It also enables opponents such as Horowitz to isolate situations in the past (or present) in ways that fail to take adequate account of the connectedness between earlier and later circumstances.

15. In any case, I suspect that many American Christians would be surprised to discover how seldom moral reasoning in biblical texts reflects ends justifying means or a foundational commitment to personal autonomy and individual rights.

16. Michael Barram, *Missional Economics: Biblical Justice and Christian Formation* (Grand Rapids: Eerdmans, 2018), 112.

17. Barram, *Missional Economics*, 116. Here and elsewhere, the Bible would seem to be far more comfortable than many Americans with institutionalized wealth redistribution.

18. Unless noted otherwise, all biblical translations are from the NRSVue.

19. Relevant here are numerous biblical affirmations of divine care and advocacy for widows, orphans, and the *gerim* (NRSV: "aliens"). See, e.g., Ex 22:21–24; 23:9; Lev 19:33–34; 24:22; Deut 10:16–19; 24:19–21; 27:19.

20. In this connection, it would be worthwhile to reflect seriously on contemporary notions of inalienable property rights.

21. See Barram, *Missional Economics*, 118.

22. Examples are legion. See, e.g., the discussion of Matthew 25:31–46 in Barram, *Missional Economics*, 185–195. See also Michael Barram, "Moral Reasoning and Embodied Love in Luke 10:25–37," in *Engaging the Bible*, ed. Mark Roncace (Point of View Publishing, 2020), 293–296.

23. Of course, the Jubilee legislation (see Leviticus 25:39–55)—as with biblical literature, more generally—falls short of condemning slavery itself (which, by contrast, readers of the Bible today universally do *despite* what we find in the Bible). While Leviticus 25 seeks to mitigate some of the worst effects of economic bondage (at least for those within the covenantal community), it does not seem to recognize or follow, as it were, the liberative potential of its own trajectory with regard to those from outside of the community. In part, at least, this is probably because of how widespread slavery (rooted primarily in debt and warfare) was in the ancient world. For readers today, it is worth noting that if we now readily go *beyond* the demands of the Jubilee expectations with regard to slavery, surely Christians can and should consider seriously the Jubilee implications for moral reasoning that we have not yet adequately wrestled with—including reparations. As communal formation, the Jubilee legislation serves at least to inspire a kind of moral imagination that can reason even beyond what the text itself could have envisioned in its own time.

24. The capitalist notion that wealth (and other resources) can grow and expand would not develop until centuries later.

25. Unfortunately, though, we have not adequately reckoned with the fact that many resources exist, in fact, in short, non-renewable, and dwindling supply.

26. For excellent explorations and analyses of these dynamics, see, e.g., Matthew Desmond, *Evicted: Poverty and Profit in the American City* (New York: Broadway, 2016); *Poverty, By America* (New York: Crown, 2023); and Edward Royce, *Poverty and Power: The Problem of Structural Inequality*, 4th ed. (Lanham, MD: Rowman & Littlefield, 2023).

27. Barram, *Missional Economics*, 115. The Jubilee was understood to be "a return to the original, perfected state in which God created the world and intended it to exist" (*Dictionary of Judaism in the Biblical Period: 450 B.C.E. to 600 C.E.*, ed. Jacob Neusner [Peabody, MA: Hendrickson, 1996]), 344.

28. Barram, *Missional Economics*, 116.

29. In verse 8, the NRSVue reads: "Look, half of my possessions, Lord, I will give to the poor; and if I have defrauded anyone of anything, I will pay back four times as much." There is debate, though, based primarily on the present-tense verbs in 19:8, concerning whether we are to understand Zacchaeus's efforts at reparation as a regularized, ongoing behavior (i.e., "I give . . . " and "I repay . . . " [iteratively]; *author's translation*) or whether the tax collector is stating a resolution to do so going

forward (i.e., "I *will* give . . . " and "I *will* pay back . . . " [so NRSVue: reading the verbs as futuristically oriented presents]). According to the former option, Zacchaeus would be articulating—and perhaps defending—his behavior in view of his critics; he would not be confessing wrongdoing, and Jesus's declaration of salvation (v. 9) would provide vindication. The latter option, by contrast, taken together with Jesus's reference to "today," would suggest that a change in the Zacchaeus's regular conduct was necessary. On the options, see, e.g., John T. Carroll (*Luke: A Commentary* [Louisville: Westminster John Knox, 2012], 371–74), who notes that "on either reading, Jesus defends the public honor of a man held in contempt by the Jewish community at Jericho" (p. 372). While both readings have been advocated and reflect a clear intention to address wrongs that have been done (whether, according to the first option, through ongoing social structures and/or unintentionally [v. 8: "if"]; see, e.g., Joseph A. Fitzmyer, *The Gospel According to Luke X–XXIV*, Anchor Bible {New York: Doubleday, 1985}, 1225] or, according to the second, interpersonally, by Zacchaeus himself), the word "today" in v. 9 arguably tips the scale toward the futuristic present.

30. The references to "half of my possessions" and "four times as much" seem to reflect voluntary choices on Zacchaeus's part. Cf., e.g., Luke 18:18–30 and references in, e.g., Fitzmyer (*Luke,* 1225).

31. See, e.g., Jemar Tisby, *The Color of Compromise* (Grand Rapids: Zondervan, 2019); Robert P. Jones, *White Too Long: The Legacy of White Supremacy in American Christianity* (New York: Simon & Schuster, 2020).

32. See Coates, "The Case for Reparations," 49, accessed November, 16, 2020, https://www.theatlantic.com/magazine/archive/2014/06/the-case-for-reparations/361631/:

> Won't reparations divide us? Not any more than we are already divided. The wealth gap merely puts a number on something we feel but cannot say—that American prosperity was ill-gotten and selective in its distribution. What is needed is an airing of family secrets, a settling with old ghosts. What is needed is a healing of the American psyche and the banishment of white guilt. What I'm talking about is more than recompense for past injustices—more than a handout, a payoff, hush money, or a reluctant bribe. What I'm talking about is a national reckoning that would lead to spiritual renewal.

BIBLIOGRAPHY

Barram, "Economic and Social Reparations: The Jubilee as Biblical Formation for a More Just Future." *Word & World* 42 (2022): 77–86.

———. *Missional Economics: Biblical Justice and Christian Formation.* Grand Rapids: Eerdmans, 2018.

———. "Moral Reasoning and Embodied Love in Luke 10:25–37." In *Engaging the Bible,* edited by Mark Roncace, 293–296. Point of View Publishing, 2020.

Carroll, John T. *Luke: A Commentary.* Louisville: Westminster John Knox, 2012.

Coates, Ta-Nehisi. "The Case for Reparations," *The Atlantic*. June 2014. Accessed November 16, 2020. https://www.theatlantic.com/magazine/archive/2014/06/the-case-for-reparations/361631/.

———. *We Were Eight Years in Power: An American Tragedy*. New York: One World, 2017.

Darity, William A., Jr., and A. Kirsten Mullen, *From Here to Equality: Reparations for Black Americans in the Twenty-First Century*. Chapel Hill: The University of North Carolina Press, 2020.

Desmond, Matthew. *Evicted: Poverty and Profit in the American City*. New York: Broadway, 2016.

———. *Poverty, By America*. New York: Crown, 2023.

Fitzmyer, Joseph A. *The Gospel According to Luke X–XXIV*, Anchor Bible. New York: Doubleday, 1985.

Horowitz, David. "Ten Reasons Why Reparations for Slavery is a Bad Idea for Blacks—and Racist Too." *The Black Scholar: Journal of Studies and Research* 31 (2001): 48; published online in 2015. Accessed December 3, 2020. https://www.tandfonline.com/doi/abs/10.1080/00064246.2001.11431145.

Jones, Robert P. *White Too Long: The Legacy of White Supremacy in American Christianity*. New York: Simon & Schuster, 2020.

Kwon, Duke L., and Gregory Thompson. *Reparations: A Christian Call for Repentance and Repair*. Grand Rapids: Brazos, 2021.

Neusner, Jacob, ed. "Jubilee year." *Dictionary of Dictionary of Judaism in the Biblical Period: 450 B.C.E. to 600 C.E.* Peabody, MA: Hendrickson, 1996, 344.

Royce, Edward. *Poverty and Power: The Problem of Structural Inequality*, 4th ed. Lanham, MD: Rowman & Littlefield, 2023.

Sandel, Michael J. *Justice: What's the Right Thing to Do?* New York: Farrar, Straus, and Giroux, 2009.

Tisby, Jemar. *The Color of Compromise*. Grand Rapids: Zondervan, 2019.

Chapter Six

Witness: Zacchaeus and the Call to Repair

A Sermon on Luke 19:1–10

Duke L. Kwon

If you were to stroll down 9th Street through the Shaw neighborhood, you'd eventually come across a modest but noteworthy memorial. There at the center, a large bronze sculpture of Carter G. Woodson sits atop a circular stone platform. And to the right, for those who are unfamiliar with Dr. Woodson's life and work, a large inscription reads: FATHER OF BLACK HISTORY. Woodson was a historian, author, and educator. He taught here in the District of Columbia for many years at M Street High School, Armstrong High School, and Howard University. But he's best known as the founder of Negro History Week, the precursor to Black History Month, which, as you know, begins this week. Deeply concerned about the erasure of Black history in America, Woodson labored to ignite what he described as a Black history "mass education movement." In 1922, he explained his goals for that movement with these words:

> We are going back to that beautiful history, and it is going to inspire us to greater achievements. It is not going to be long before we can so sing the story to the outside world as to convince it of the value of our history and our traditions, and then we are going to be recognized as men.[1]

I wonder what you heard in that quote. Two things stand out to me. The first is that the focus of this movement is beauty. Beautiful history. Beautiful ancestry. Beautiful traditions. Beautiful community. Black History Month isn't centrally about lamenting the ugliness of racism. It's about "singing the story" of Black image-bearing excellence and glory. It's about beauty. Well-meaning non-Black folks, in particular, need to keep this in mind. A second observation about Dr. Woodson's vision: Black History Month is a conscious response to a deficit—the absence of Black recognition. A nation must be reeducated. Lies must be confronted. True stories must be retold. In fact, rightly understood, Black History Month is itself a form of reparations—the repair of collective memory. A line from the HBO miniseries *Chernobyl* comes to mind: "Every lie we tell incurs a debt to truth." Beloved, a generational debt to truth—the truth about Black life in America—still remains to be repaid.

So, we've taken a stroll down 9th Street and arrived at a fork in the road called reparations. This morning I'd like to examine this important subject with you, and I'd like to do that through the lens of the story of Zacchaeus from Luke 19. Whether you're skeptical of reparations or fully on board, I pray you will come to see that the basic moral logic of reparations is firmly rooted in scripture. What I mean is this. Reparations is, in some ways, a complex topic. Questions abound: who, what, when, where, how? But lying at the heart of reparations is a surprisingly simple idea, an imperative that the Bible clearly teaches: When you steal something, repentance and love require you to return it. We expect even our dear, petty-thieving, preschool-aged children to understand this simple principle, do we not? *Give it back,* we tell them. *If you took something that doesn't belong to you, you have to give it back.* What, then, is the right moral response to the racist generational robbery of African Americans? Again, I ask, how should Christians, in particular, respond to the systematic theft of the identities, agency, and prosperity of our Black siblings and neighbors? *Give it back.* Repair. Reparations.

To unpack this further, we turn to Luke 19:1–10.[2] At the heart of this narrative is the life-changing kindness of Jesus. The king of grace once again shows off his wonderful habit of befriending all the "wrong" people. In this case, it's a tax collector. In every case, it's people like you and me, people desperate for God's better-than-we-deserve, superlative favor. By including this story, Luke seems especially intent on demonstrating that the rich and the socially marginal (as a tax-collector, Zacchaeus represents both) can enter the kingdom of God. Like the blind beggar in the previous chapter, they too can come to *"see"* Jesus and the wonder of his love (18:41, 42, 43; 19:3, 4). Poor house, rich house, frat house, drug house, your house, my house—salvation can come to *any* house. Hallelujah! And as we read about Zacchaeus's response to the saving-kindness of Jesus, we learn a few things about repairing past wrongs. Three lessons about the work of repair: its *premise,* its *practice,* and its *power.* Let's examine each of these in turn, beginning with the premise of repair.

THE PREMISE OF REPAIR

What is the work of repair a response to? What makes reparations necessary in the first place? It's theft. The call to repair presupposes that something has been sinfully taken. What career-long sin does Zacchaeus confess in verse 8? *Sykophanteō*. Extortion. Zacchaeus was a thief. All Jewish tax collectors in ancient Palestine were. It's the reason why they were so "wealthy" (v. 2). And it's why they were so viscerally despised and condemned as "sinners" (v. 7). It was bad enough that tax collectors like Zacchaeus allied themselves with the occupying Roman regime—*traitors!* But it was worse still that they regularly overcharged the people in order to line their own pockets—*thieves!* And they often did so with physical force, violence, and insatiable greed. That's why Philo of Alexandria in the first century described tax collectors as "the most ruthless of men, brimful of inhumanity."[3] Never mind what that old Sunday school song seems to suggest: Zacchaeus wasn't just an innocent, bumbling, "wee little man." He was a pitiless agent of an extractive imperial system. He was a plundering predator.

Theft. Robbery. Extraction. Greed. Plunder. This is the vocabulary we should use when talking about the evils of racism and white supremacy in America. Why? Many people act as if racism is little more than a problem of hurt feelings and strained relationships. So, they'll speak of people being "offended," and they'll casually gesture toward the vice of "division." But, no: White supremacy *extorts*. Racism *robs*. These are gross violations of the Eighth Commandment: *You shall not*—what? *Steal* (Ex 20:15; Luke 18:20). Journalist and author Ta-Nehisi Coates has said it well: "When we think of white supremacy, we picture COLORED ONLY signs, but we should picture pirate flags."[4] Racism isn't just about hateful ideas that need to be renounced, or divided neighbors that need to be reconciled, or corrupt institutions that need to be reformed, but robbed communities that need to be repaid.

Beloved, we must reckon with a haunting fact of history: The four-hundred-year story of Black people in America is a story of systematic plunder on repeat.

Bodies—*stolen.*
Agency—*stolen.*
Wages—*stolen.*
Public image—*stolen.*
Sexual sanctity—*stolen.*
Land—*stolen.*
Education—*stolen.*
Membership in Christ's church—yes, *stolen.*

Home ownership—*stolen*.
Voting rights—*stolen*.
Generational wealth—*stolen*.
Freedom to drive, jog, sleep, or even pray without fear of being lynched—*stolen*.

Stolen all! God have mercy. How should we react to this catalog of horrors? Don't just acknowledge the facts of it. Weep over it. Weep over it! Not only because we are speaking about the pillaging of real people, real flesh and blood, but also because it's impossible to see the moral necessity, urgency, and beauty of reparations except through tears.

I suspect that reframing racism as a kind of theft may be new for some of you. But this is, in fact, an old point of view, one that Black Christians have voiced for hundreds of years. Bishop Richard Allen declared, "We were stolen from our mother country." Frederick Douglass condemned enslavers as "a band of successful robbers." Maria Stewart said of consumers of slave labor, "we have planted the vines, they have eaten the fruit of them." Martin Luther King Jr. preached that Jim Crow segregation was "stripping millions of Negro people of their sense of dignity and robbing them of their birthright of freedom." What's more, these witnesses declared that these thefts were animated not finally by hate but by avarice and greed. Angelina Grimké condemned slavery as a "grand temple built to Mammon." Sojourner Truth thundered, "Our nerves and sinews, our tears and blood, have been sacrificed on the altar of this nation's avarice." Henry Highland Garnet denounced the chattel system, saying, "no cruelty is too great, no villainy and no robbery too abhorrent for even enlightened men to perform, when influenced by avarice and lust."[5]

Theft fueled by greed—are we learning to see what these saints saw? Not only in the pages of history but even today in the streets of our city? Beloved, look around—what do you see? The premise of reparations is that a mass, multigenerational campaign of theft has brutalized Black America. When we begin to perceive this reality, what should we then do? What, according to the Bible, is a moral response to theft? This brings us to our second lesson: the *practice* of repair.

THE PRACTICE OF REPAIR

Deeply moved by the mercy of Jesus, Zacchaeus renounces his former way of life. He stands, almost as if to make a public vow, and he declares in verse 8: "Look, Lord! Here and now I give half of my possessions to the poor, and if I have cheated anybody out of anything, I will pay back four times the amount." Zacchaeus openly acknowledges his life of theft. He admits his guilt, yes, but he doesn't stop there. He pledges to redress his wrongs. He will *pay back* all that he had stolen from his neighbors—fourfold, in fact. He will offer reparation. Will we?

Too often after wounding others, we might eek out an apology, but really what we want is to move forward and move on—and *quickly*. The sight of blood on our hands is, perhaps, too much to bear. But festering wounds must be healed, not forgotten or ignored. As Ralph Ellison wrote in his novel *Juneteenth*: "Blood spilled in violence doesn't just dry and drift away in the wind, no! It cries out for restitution, redemption."[6] Love perceives that cry, the voice of Abel's blood from the ground (Gen. 4:10). Love peels our gaze off ourselves and sees, at last, the ones we've hurt—the ones we've robbed. Love eagerly desires the undoing of wounds. (This is just what we mean by repair: the *undoing* of wounds, the *unwounding* of wounds.) Many will acknowledge the generational thefts named earlier, but they'd still rather roll a tombstone over the carnage and move on. Friends, love seeks not burial but resurrection. Healing. Repair. Zacchaeus began to understand this. Zacchaeus began to love like this. Will we?

At this point, a few questions or objections may come to people's minds. Someone might say: "Well, good for Zacchaeus. That was his choice. But I don't think I'm on the hook to copy what he did." Actually, friends, we are. In returning the things he stole, Zacchaeus wasn't being nice. He wasn't being charitable. He was being obedient to scripture. Zacchaeus was actually following the requirements of Exodus 22 and Leviticus 6 and Numbers 5, which say of those who are guilty of theft: "they must return what they have stolen or taken by extortion" and "give it all to the owner" (Lev 6:4, 5). In short, they "must make full restitution" (Num 5:7). Our Christian forbears—from Augustine to Aquinas to Calvin to Wesley—all saw this practice of restitution as a duty required by the Eighth Commandment. It was plain to them, and it should be to us (and our toddlers): if you steal something, you have to give it back. You *must*.

Another person might push back in a different way: "But isn't it enough to say you're sorry?" Don't be mistaken: Numbers 5 requires repentant thieves to "*confess* the sin they have committed" (v. 7). But these same passages *also* require them to "return" what they've stolen (Lev 6:4). Both are necessary—are they not? Suppose I stole your bike and got caught. Would it be enough for me just to confess my theft? Of course not. I'd also need to *return* the bike—*your* bike! Now imagine I said to you, "I'm sorry I took your bike. But, um, can I *keep* it?" You'd not only reply, "Are you kidding me? No!" You'd also question the sincerity of my apology, and rightly so. Listen, our nation has refused to relinquish its stolen bikes. And we rightly question the sincerity of its muffled apologies and shrugs. But look over here, something quite different: Zacchaeus. Confession, restitution—he does it all. And Jesus endorses it all: "Today *salvation* has come to this house!" (v. 9). Zacchaeus's sincere, Spirit-wrought repentance is revealed in his commitment to the obligations of repair. Is it enough to say you're sorry? Beloved, true repentance repairs what was ripped and returns what was ripped off.

Now, a third objection might sound like this: "OK, maybe African Americans have been robbed. But *I* didn't do it. I shouldn't have to repair a mistake that I didn't make." Let me respond in two ways. First, every person in this country has benefited, whether directly or indirectly, from the plunder of African American people. So it stands to reason that every person is implicated in these historical thefts, even if they are not personally to blame for them. We all, as beneficiaries of injustice, bear responsibility to repair the damage that's been done. Second, according to Numbers 5, if the party to which restitution is owed has deceased, the stolen items must still be returned. To whom? To the next of kin, a "close relative" (v. 8), whomever would have received those goods by way of inheritance. In other words, the duty of reparation doesn't magically disappear with the death of the original perpetrators; rather, *it passes on to their descendants* so long as they remain in possession of the ill-gotten goods. To modify the scenario mentioned earlier: If your grandfather gives you a bike he stole, you must return it even if you didn't steal it. Job 20 appeals to this exercise of generational responsibility when it warns the wicked man who has "oppressed the poor" and "seized houses he did not build" (v. 19). On a future day of reckoning, we're told, "his children must make amends to the poor; his own hands must give back his wealth" (v. 10). Friends, we are those children. The thefts of white supremacy are an inextricable part of our American inheritance. And today is that day of reckoning.

Let me put it another way. Those who insist, "I should have nothing to do with reparations because I never owned any slaves," or, "because I didn't personally obstruct Ruby Bridges from attending school," are missing a crucial point. Reparations is foremost a corporate, rather than individual, responsibility. This is because our racist, kleptocratic social order was constructed and sheltered over the centuries by three corporate entities primarily: the government, the academy,[7] and the church. For this reason, it is these groups that bear the greatest responsibility to ameliorate the harms of the past. And it is as constituent members of these groups that we should bear this burden of love and labor tirelessly to address those harms, regardless of our personal histories.

This morning, as members of Christ's body, we should be most concerned with the responsibility of that third group, the church. The temptation to duck that responsibility is strong. Some preach a soaring vision of the church. They require vows of membership. Exegete plural pronouns. Extol the "heritage" of their faith. Honor saints long passed as their own. But when confronted with the church's plunderous past, they abruptly become unaccountable individualists, free agents in Christ, exegetes of singular pronouns, strangers of saints long passed, hermetically sealed from responsibility for defaults not their own. But we must reject fair-weather ecclesiology. "The corporate witness of the church is our witness and the corporate default of the church is our default."[8] *All* of it is *ours,* including even this: responsibility for the terrors of institutionalized white supremacy.

Do you know that Christians in every generation have testified to this? James Birney condemned the church as the "bulwark of slavery." Stephen Foster called it "a power behind the throne greater than the throne itself." Francis Grimké rebuked the Jim Crow era church for being "the great bulwark of race prejudice in this country." The National Committee for Black Churchmen denounced it as "the moral cement of the structure of racism in this nation."[9] God have mercy! We are implicated, brothers and sisters. The shameful truth is that the Christian church has been *indispensable* to the despoilment of African Americans. The "blemished and scarred body" of Christ has served as thief, accomplice, and silent bystander across the centuries. Will members of Christ's church, those who bear Christ's name today, confess this? More than that, will we pursue the creative, determined, glad-and-grievous work of repair in every place where and in every way that white supremacy has left its deathly mark—reparations on repeat.

Stolen wages—*repay it!*
Stolen bodily integrity—*repair it!*
Stolen public image—*restore it!*
Stolen history—*rewrite it!*
Stolen generational wealth—*regenerate it!*
Stolen education—*rebuild it!*
Stolen suffrage—*reclaim it!*
Stolen land and property—*return it!*

In Jesus's name, repair it all! This work might be carried out by advocating for public programs. Or by creating collaborative church-based ministries in our local community. Or by laboring for the undoing of historical thefts in the institutions and industries we're a part of in our daily work. There are a number of possible ways we might respond. But this much we know: As members of Christ's church in America, beloved, we are called to participate in the repentant return of all that's been stolen.

But what will empower us to do this? To *do* the work of repair? This brings us to our final lesson drawn from Zacchaeus's story: the *power* of repair.

THE POWER OF REPAIR

Tell me, what changed Zacchaeus? To answer this question, we need to go back to the beginning of the story, where Zacchaeus has a life-transforming encounter with love. Jesus's every move is a complete surprise. Instead of passing by, he *stops*. Instead of averting his eyes in disgust or irritation, Jesus *looks up* at the man in the tree. While the crowd mutters about that "sinner" over there, Jesus addresses him *by name*: "Zacchaeus." And rather than shun and dodge the tax collector like everyone else, Jesus urges him to "come down" and come near. Behold this stunning display of love. It's a love that finds us, stops for us, sees us, calls us by name, and draws us close.

And as if this wasn't already enough, what Jesus does next is nothing short of jaw-dropping: he invites himself over to Zacchaeus's home. He insists on it: "I *must*." Three things are striking about this moment. First, as you may know, dining with someone was a gesture of intimacy and solidarity in the ancient world. It was an unmistakable sign of friendship—in this case, friendship with filth, a tax collector. Here is a culturally unthinkable, inadvisable display of kindness—*scandalous* kindness. Second, by inviting himself over as Zacchaeus's "guest," Jesus is identifying him as being worthy of his company. And he does so publicly for a man whose spirit lay long imprisoned by public contempt. Here is *un-shaming* grace. And third, Jesus gives Zacchaeus a chance to host him in his home. What's Jesus doing? He's rehabilitating Zacchaeus's heart. The "chief" must become a servant. The pathological taker must learn to give, even as he discovers the God who gives kindness and friendship and forgiveness and salvation and sonship and gives and gives and gives, indeed—as Zacchaeus himself would witness one day—giving even unto death on a cross. In the words of one commentator, Zacchaeus "provides hospitality to Jesus and finds in return the hospitality of God."[10]

We're told in Romans 2:4 that God's kindness leads us to repentance, and therein lies the open secret about what happened to Zacchaeus that day. The tax collector, the plundering predator, was blindsided by love, filled to the brim with the lavish, scandalous kindness poured out by Jesus. Is it any wonder that Zacchaeus's life would dramatically spill over with such a costly gesture of contrition? It's God's kindness that leads us to repentance and repair.

I'm not saying that one needs to be a follower of Christ to do the reparative work of love. In truth, professing Christians are among those most resistant to reparations in America. What I am saying is that followers of Christ—those who, like Zacchaeus, have encountered the saving-kindness of God—*should* be among the most eager, most ready for the work. What I am saying is that white supremacy is at root a *spiritual* sickness that requires the transformation of the inner life. Igniting and sustaining the reparative work of love in one's life, community, or nation requires spiritual power—it requires an incursion of divine love. Have you encountered the inestimable love of Jesus? It's a love that seeks the lost and calls us to "come down." *Descend.* Not from literal tree branches, but from the perches of supremacy in our souls. It's a love that resurrects dead hearts, that remakes rulers into servants, extractors into benefactors, takers into givers. It can do this in your life and mine. Indeed, the same reparative love that visited Jericho can visit our own cities today, just as it did in Pyongyang over one hundred years ago. Let me close by sharing this story with you.

In 1907, a "Great Revival" broke out in the city now known as the capital of North Korea. People begin to grieve over their unconfessed wrongdoing—God's kindness led to repentance. Not only this, their repentance ignited a dramatic display of reparative action. According to William Blair, a missionary to Korea, "All through the city men were going house to house, confessing to individuals they had injured, returning stolen property and money."[11] In some cases, we're told, large sums of money that were unjustly obtained years before were immediately returned, often to the astonishment of the recipients. But you need to hear these words of Blair as he reflected on what had taken place. He observed: "Repentance was by no means confined to confession and tears. Peace waited upon reparation, wherever reparation was possible."

Would we dare to dream and labor for something similar in the streets of this capital city today? Will we refuse to confine our repentance to confession and tears? Will we heed the call to repair? In our city, in our nation, we live surrounded by the restless agony of festering wounds, the peaceless aftermath of plunder and debts unpaid.

Beloved, peace waits upon reparation.

NOTES

1. Carter G. Woodson, "Some Things Negroes Need to Do," *Southern Workman*, 51 (January 1922), 33–36.

2. All biblical quotations are from NIV11.

3. Philo, *On the Special Laws* 3.158–62, in *The Works of Philo*, trans. C. D. Yonge (Peabody, MA: Hendrickson, 1993).

4. Ta-Nehisi Coates, *We Were Eight Years in Power: An American Tragedy* (New York: One World, 2017), 201.

5. Richard Allen, *Freedom's Journal* 1, no. 34 (1827), quoted in David Walker, *Walker's Appeal, in Four Articles; Together with a Preamble, to the Coloured Citizens of the World, but in Particular, and Very Expressly, to Those of the United States of America* (Boston: Published by David Walker, 1829), 64; Frederick Douglass,

Narrative of the Life of Frederick Douglass, an American Slave (Boston: Published at the Anti-Slavery Office, 1845), 40; Maria W. Stewart, "An Address Delivered at the African Masonic Hall, Boston, February 27, 1833," in *Meditations from the Pen of Mrs. Maria W. Stewart (Widow of the Late James W. Stewart), Now Matron of the Freedman's Hospital, and Presented in 1832 to the First African Baptist Church and Society of Boston, Mass.* (Washington, DC: Enterprise, 1879), 69; Martin Luther King Jr., *Strength to Love* (Philadelphia: Fortress, 1981), 37; Angelina Emily Grimké, *Appeal to Christian Women of the South* (New York: American Anti-Slavery Society, 1836), 15–16; Sojourner Truth, *Narrative of Sojourner Truth; a Bondswoman of Olden Time, Emancipated by the New York Legislature in the Early Part of the Present Century; with a History of Her Labors and Correspondence, Drawn from Her "Book of Life,"* ed. Olive Gilbert and Frances W. Titus (Boston, 1875), 197; Henry Highland Garnet, *Walker's Appeal, with a Brief Sketch of His Life. And also Garnet's Address to the Slaves of the United States of America* (New York, 1848), 94.

6. Ralph Ellison, *Juneteenth: A Novel,* ed. John F. Callaghan (New York: The Modern Library, 2021), 251.

7. See Craig Steven Wilder, *Ebony and Ivy: Race, Slavery, and the Troubled History of America's Universities* (New York: Bloomsbury Press, 2013).

8. John Murray, "Corporate Responsibility," in *Collected Writings of John Murray,* vol. 1 (Carlisle, PA: Banner of Truth Trust, 1989), 275.

9. James Gillespie Birney, *The American Churches: The Bulwarks of American Slavery* (Newburyport: Published by Charles Whipple, 1842); Stephen S. Foster, *The Brotherhood of Thieves; or, A True Picture of the American Church and Clergy: A Letter to Nathaniel Barney, of Nantucket* (Concord, NH: Parker Phillsbury, 1884), 28; Francis J. Grimké, "Christianity and Race Prejudice" (1910), in *The Works of Francis J. Grimké,* vol. 1, ed. Carter G. Woodson (Washington, DC: Associated Publishers, 1942), 461; James F. Findlay Jr., *Church People in the Struggle: The National Council of Churches and the Black Freedom Movement, 1950–1970* (New York: Oxford University Press), 207–8.

10. Brendan Byrne, *The Hospitality of God: A Reading of Luke's Gospel* (Collegeville, Minn.: Liturgical Press, 2015), 167.

11. William Newton Blair and Bruce F. Hunt, *The Korean Pentecost and the Sufferings Which Followed* (Carlisle, PA: The Banner of Truth Trust, 1977), 75. I am grateful to Rev. Moses Lee for bringing this historical moment to my attention.

BIBLIOGRAPHY

Allen, Richard. *Freedom's Journal.* 1, no. 34 (1827). Quoted in David Walker, *Walker's Appeal, in Four Articles; Together with a Preamble, to the Coloured Citizens of the World, but in Particular, and Very Expressly, to Those of the United States of America.* Boston: Published by David Walker, 1829.

Birney, James Gillespie. *The American Churches: The Bulwarks of American Slavery.* Newburyport: Published by Charles Whipple, 1842.

Blair, William Newton and Hunt, Bruce F. *The Korean Pentecost and the Sufferings Which Followed.* Carlisle, PA: The Banner of Truth Trust, 1977.

Byrne, Brendan. *The Hospitality of God: A Reading of Luke's Gospel.* Collegeville, Minn.: Liturgical Press, 2015.

Coates, Ta-Nehisi. *We Were Eight Years in Power: An American Tragedy.* New York: One World, 2017.

Douglass, Frederick. *Narrative of the Life of Frederick Douglass, an American Slave.* Boston: Published at the Anti-Slavery Office, 1845.

Ellison, Ralph. *Juneteenth: A Novel,* edited by John F. Callaghan. New York: The Modern Library, 2021.

Findlay, James F., Jr. *Church People in the Struggle: The National Council of Churches and the Black Freedom Movement, 1950–1970.* New York: Oxford University Press.

Foster, Stephen S. *The Brotherhood of Thieves; or, A True Picture of the American Church and Clergy: A Letter to Nathaniel Barney, of Nantucket.* Concord, NH: Parker Phillsbury, 1884.

Garnet, Henry Highland. *Walker's Appeal, with a Brief Sketch of His Life. And also Garnet's Address to the Slaves of the United States of America.* New York, 1848.

Grimké, Angelina Emily. *Appeal to Christian Women of the South.* New York: American Anti-Slavery Society, 1836.

Grimké, Francis J. "Christianity and Race Prejudice." In *The Works of Francis J. Grimké*, vol. 1. Edited by Carter G. Woodson. Washington, DC: Associated Publishers, 1942.

King, Martin Luther, Jr. *Strength to Love.* Philadelphia: Fortress, 1981.

Murray, John. "Corporate Responsibility." In *Collected Writings of John Murray,* vol. 1. Carlisle, PA: Banner of Truth Trust, 1989.

Stewart, Maria W. "An Address Delivered at the African Masonic Hall, Boston, February 27, 1833." In *Meditations from the Pen of Mrs. Maria W. Stewart (Widow of the Late James W. Stewart), Now Matron of the Freedman's Hospital, and Presented in 1832 to the First African Baptist Church and Society of Boston, Mass.* Washington, DC: Enterprise, 1879.

Truth, Sojourner. *Narrative of Sojourner Truth; a Bondswoman of Olden Time, Emancipated by the New York Legislature in the Early Part of the Present Century; with a History of Her Labors and Correspondence, Drawn from Her "Book of Life."* Edited by Olive Gilbert and Frances W. Titus. Boston, 1875.

Wilder, Craig Steven. *Ebony and Ivy: Race, Slavery, and the Troubled History of America's Universities.* New York: Bloomsbury Press, 2013.

Woodson, Carter G. "Some Things Negroes Need to Do." *Southern Workman,* 51 (January 1922): 33–36.

Yonge, C. D. transl. (1993) Philo: *On the Special Laws.* Peabody, MA: Hendrickson.

Chapter Seven

You Cannot Pay Back What You Have Never Owned

A Conversation on Reparations and Paul's Letter to Philemon

Angela N. Parker

The letters of the Apostle Paul are a large part of the New Testament and have been used to argue for and against issues related to slavery. Indeed, there is much to be gleaned from the Apostle's letters that prompt readers toward love and justice as we embrace the faithfulness of Jesus. I also have to reconcile the injustice behind many of his words, however. It is ironic that the Apostle's shortest letter, to Philemon, triggers the most cognitive dissonance for me. I will argue against the assumption in much of traditional interpretation that Paul's offer to repay Philemon has anything to do with Onesimus owing something to Philemon. In the vein of Katie Geneva Cannon, I read Paul with a womanist hermeneutic that "hits a straight lick with a crooked stick." Specifically, I contend that, while reading Paul, a womanist scholar must read as a "canonical boy" versed in biblical interpretation, while also standing in opposition to that reading as a "noncanonical other," since Paul was not thinking nor writing about Black women's experiences. Accordingly, this essay requires a two-pronged approach to reading Paul. First, I critique Paul as a free man who is short-sighted in his moral vision regarding Onesimus, an enslaved man. Paul's language to "pay back" Philemon is problematic. Paul's short-sightedness has ramifications both for Onesimus as an enslaved person and for the history of interpretation of Pauline literature. Particularly problematic is an interpretation of Paul that calls for the return of enslaved people in the era of American colonial slavery and the possible repayment to slaveholders. As a result I have to reimagine Paul's "pay back" language and his ideas of "love" as tools to challenge contemporary discussions of enslavement and repayment of indebtedness (reparations) in the letter of Philemon. Specifically, a nuanced interpretation of Paul's letter, reimagining interpretations of the words *apotino* and *ta splanchna*, allows for a distinct and profound conversation around reparations. Although I challenge Paul's motivations and language in Philemon, I readily embrace the implications of the love his argument presses toward—in order to demonstrate how hermeneutics feeds into the ethics and moral principles of contemporary readers, thus changing the trajectory of the history of interpretation.

Particularly important for my own reading of Paul's letter to Philemon is my social location as an African American descendant of formerly enslaved ancestors. Moreover, my identity as a womanist New Testament scholar takes seriously the lived experiences of contemporary Black women as we read the New Testament. Thus, my interpretation of Paul's letter to Philemon will combine an African American hermeneutic of suspicion that argues against certain elements of Paul's writing while also engaging a hermeneutic of faith/trust as a confessional womanist and follower of Jesus the Christ. I note at the outset that while descendants of enslaved Africans hoped and trusted that the United States of America would provide reparations, there was always suspicion that reparations would not come to pass.

Again, I come to Philemon from several personal, lived "locations." As an African American descendent of formerly enslaved ancestors, I will engage and interpret references to repayment in Philemon in dialogue with the question of reparations for African Americans—given the many years that our ancestors were enslaved in the American colonial South. As a New Testament scholar, I write from the perspective of a womanist Christian who has questioned her relationship to the biblical text as she wrestles with White supremacist interpretations that pervade readings of Philemon. Such readings prolonged the brutalization of enslaved people during that peculiar institution. In the 1840s, the two largest Protestant denominations—Methodists and Baptists—split over disagreements over biblical interpretation regarding slavery. In my reading of Philemon, I bring my own embodied identity as a womanist scholar who teaches and preaches the gospel message of Jesus as the Christ while teaching and preaching that White supremacist interpretations *must not be* the settled understanding of the biblical text.

In order to argue for my nuanced interpretation of Paul's letter to Philemon, my essay will unfold in the following manner. First, I will briefly describe the history of reparations in the context of the United States. Second, I will engage the context of Roman imperial slavery, which will inform my interpretation of Philemon as a text for use in discussing contemporary reparations. Third, I will discuss the Greek words *apotino* and *ta splanchna* in order to argue for a nuanced reading of Paul's desire to "repay" slaveholder Philemon once Onesimus is returned to him. Finally, I close by attending briefly to the emotional, social, and political ramifications of engaging conversations about reparations in contemporary society.

THE CASE FOR REPARATIONS

In *The 1619 Project*, Nikole Hannah-Jones brings together scholars, activists, and writers to engage the origin story of Africans in America. Pertinent for a discussion of reparations is Hannah-Jones's chapter entitled "Justice." Simply stated, reparations may be defined as a system of redress for egregious injustices. Hannah-Jones notes that the closest the United States ever came to delivering on reparations was in the immediate aftermath of slavery's demise.[1] When millions of Black people were released from slavery after the American Civil War, they were released with no money and no land. Desperate to take care of themselves, they desired land, monetary compensation for the years of work performed, and the right to vote.

For a fleeting moment immediately following the Civil War, White men were beginning to acknowledge Black people and their plight. At that time, Union general William Tecumseh Sherman met with Black leaders and asked them what they wanted for their people. Reverend Garrison Frazier, a sixty-seven-year-old man who had spent fifty-nine years in bondage, responded that land was the key to prosperity. Four days later, Sherman issued Special Field Order 15, which provided for the distribution of hundreds of thousands of acres of former Confederate land in forty-acre tracts to newly freed people. This land was along coastal South Carolina, Georgia, and Florida. Sherman's order became known as "forty acres and a mule."[2] Then-President Abraham Lincoln was amenable to the idea but was assassinated shortly thereafter. Subsequently, Andrew Johnson, the overtly racist pro-Southern vice president took over and immediately reneged on forty acres and a mule.[3]

As a result of this early reneging in 1865, Black people have been fighting for reparations to the present day. The quest for reparations was a constant theme in Black rhetoric for a number of years. Black Nationalist Marcus Garvey spoke on reparations in 1920:[4]

> They said we were heathens, we were pagans, we were savages and did not know how to take care of ourselves; that we did not have any religion; we did not have any culture; we did not have any civilisation for all those centuries, and that is why they had to be our guardians. But, thank God, we have them all now, and as such we are asking that you hand back to us 'our own civilisation.'

Hand back to us that which you have robbed and exploited us of in the name of God and Christianity for the last 500 years.[5]

In 1963, Malcolm X also called for reparations:[6]

This is what you should realize. The greatest contribution to this country was that which was contributed by the Black man. If I take the wages, just a moment, if I take the wages of everyone here, individually it means nothing, but collectively all of the earning power or wages that you earned in one week would make me wealthy. And if I could collect it for a year, I'd be rich beyond dreams. Now, when you see this, and then you stop and consider the wages that were kept back from millions of Black people, not for one year but for 310 years, you'll see how this country got so rich so fast. And what made the economy as strong as it is today. And all that, and all of that slave labor that was amassed in unpaid wages, is due someone today. And you're not giving us anything.[7]

In 1921, the Tulsa Race Massacre destroyed the prosperous Black neighborhood of Greenwood, killing hundreds. Twenty years later, an Oklahoma state commission recommended financial reparations, but they were never paid.[8] As recently as 2021, three survivors from the Massacre, all centenarians, testified to Congress in support of a reparations bill for the survivors and their descendants. Even with such testimony, reparations have not been made.

With regard to contemporary conversations about reparations, Black Lives Matter founder Patrise Cullors understands the connection between abolition and reparations as follows: "Abolition calls on us not only to destabilize, deconstruct, and demolish oppressive systems, institutions, and practices, but also to repair histories of harm across the board."[9] In essence, even as Cullors seeks to abolish dangerous practices found in policing in the United States of America, she is calling for reparations to be provided to those harmed by racist policing. When people limit reparations only to the idea of paying African Americans whose ancestors were enslaved, we lose touch with the complexities of reparations still required for ongoing injustices against African Americans. Cullors took to Twitter and Instagram to share that her cousin had been killed by the Los Angeles police department on January 3, 2023.[10] Harm continues to be done regularly to Black communities, and thus the issue of reparations remains pertinent and timely.

The conversation about reparations has spanned more than 158 years! Indeed, various groups *have* received reparations—White slaveholders after the American Civil War; Japanese after World War II internment camps; Native Americans; and Jewish people after World War II.[11] Black Americans, however, have not received any type of reparations. Accordingly, one must ask not only "why" but also about what is behind the vitriol concerning reparations for Black Americans.

THE CONTEXT OF ROMAN IMPERIAL SLAVERY

As I teach about Roman imperial slavery and American colonial slavery in the context of a seminary class, I often tell students that, while they are not equally comparable, the two systems share some similarities. Just as American colonial slavery was the foundation of the American South, Roman imperial slavery was the foundation of all social structures in the Greco-Roman world. In both systems, enslaved people generally had no legal rights. Enslaved people and the labor that they produced were viewed as nothing but commodities.

Recent research by classical historians has made increasingly visible the invisible work of enslaved people during the Roman imperial time period.[12] They were expected to do any task—sexual, reproductive, and otherwise—that the master, the *paterfamilias,* demanded of them. Even though slaves were granted food and shelter in the Roman imperial context, a benign and idealized "love patriarchalism"—in which the *paterfamilias* would have been obliged to provide for and protect their enslaved people just as they were to respect wives and children—was not matched by reality.[13] As scholars of the New Testament have interpreted texts such as Philemon and the household codes of Colossians and Ephesians, they have presupposed this putative but non-existent love patriarchalism, reading it back into the context of Roman imperial slavery. In short, the womanist reading of Philemon I am providing will argue against any notion of love patriarchalism.

Slaveholders in the Roman Empire were generally disturbed and irritated by slave movement.[14] In particular, the idea of a truant and fugitive slave was considered a "defect" that would often have to be disclosed by slave sellers to their buyers.[15] As we read Philemon with attention to the context of Roman imperial slavery, we should note that truant and fugitive slaves were perceived to have "wasted" time and resources the way other "bad" slaves did.

Roman imperial slavery was also similar to American colonial slavery inasmuch as enslaved persons did not even possess the agency to name (or even speak for) themselves. This phenomenon is readily visible in Philemon: Onesimus's name literally means "useful," a name common among enslaved people during the Roman imperial period.

In short, "love patriarchalism" did not mitigate the realities of being enslaved in the context of the Roman Empire, and the value of enslaved persons was almost entirely a function of how useful their enslavers considered them to be. With such an understanding of the context of Roman imperial slavery, we are prepared to consider how contemporary interpreters of Philemon should understand and engage the issue of reparations.

ENGAGING ONESIMUS AND PHILEMON

Theories abound about Paul's letter to Philemon. Many scholars believe that Philemon probably lived in Colossae of Asia Minor and that the main subject of the letter is the fate of "useful" Onesimus.[16] While the relationship between Philemon and Onesimus is not clear, scholars such as Allen Dwight Callahan argue that they may have been brothers.[17]

Traditionally, Onesimus has been presumed to be Philemon's slave, on the basis of verses 15–16, in which Paul asks Philemon to welcome Onesimus "back forever, no longer as a slave but more than a slave, a beloved brother" in Christ.[18] Scholars regularly argue that Onesimus had perhaps run away from Philemon and sought Paul's protection, since the latter would possess socio-cultural advantages as the founder of many churches. Interpreters of Philemon often read the letter in light of Pliny the Younger's letter to Sabinianus. In that document, Pliny acts as a "friend of the master" in the Roman practice of *amicus domini*.[19] In this practice, an enslaved person could ask for protection and mediation from someone considered their master's equal. In this scenario, Onesimus may have been hoping that Paul would use his status to intercede on Onesimus's behalf with Philemon. The problem in Philemon, however, is that readers never hear Onesimus's thoughts. The letter delineates only a conversation between Paul and the slave master Philemon.

UNDERSTANDING *APOTINO* AND *TA SPLANCHNA* IN PHILEMON

Traditionally interpreted, the letter functioned as a proof text for the establishment of the Fugitive Slave Act of 1850. Proof texts are passages taken out of context so as to appeal to or support a certain theological position, which inevitably has political and societal consequences. Defenders of the Fugitive Slave Act of 1850 pointed to Paul's letter to Philemon as scriptural justification for the law that required anyone who encountered an escaped enslaved person—even someone in a state where slavery was not practiced—to return that person to slavery.[20] The Act criminalized any provision of aid or sanctuary to escaped enslaved individuals. White Christians within slaveholding denominations in the 1800s read Philemon as a parallel to the scenario envisioned by the Fugitive Slave Act.[21] Biblical interpretation thus directly influenced public policy.

Recognizing that Philemon has been interpreted as offering support for theological positions underwriting the Fugitive Slave Act of 1850, I must read this letter as a womanist New Testament scholar and descendent of enslaved

Black women in order to wonder and ponder what the overarching message in this text means today. I argue that, morally speaking, Paul cannot pay back what he has never owned, and so we must explore what we can hermeneutically salvage from his vow to "repay" (*apotino*) whatever Onesimus owed to Philemon. Moreover, I find Paul's repeated use of the term *ta splanchna* to be critical to the message of the letter, as it provides an element of liberation and justice even as Paul's words, language, and attitudes are themselves unjust.

Let us begin with *apotino,* a word that occurs only one time in the Greek New Testament—here in Philemon 19. According to traditional interpretation and translations, Paul writes to Philemon that he will "repay" whatever Onesimus owes. According to a standard, scholarly Greek lexicon that only engages texts within early Christianity (ignoring non-Christian writings), the only possible definition and connotation of *apotino* is to "to make compensation" or to "pay damages."[22] Philemon 19 is thus usually translated "I will pay the damages."[23] But the question I must ask in my womanist imagination is as follows: Did Onesimus believe he owed any damages to repay?

As readers of the biblical text, oftentimes we take at face value the words that Paul has written—or the perceived experiences of the hierarchical men within the text, specifically Philemon. Interpreters must also pay attention to the ways that the text is silent. Onesimus possesses a roaring silence within the text. As identified in the last section on Roman imperial slavery, however, classic historians have begun to theorize about the tactics of the enslaved.

Slaveholders within the Roman imperial system often complained about slaves and their actions. Sandra R. Joshel and Lauren Hackworth Peterson argue that their work counters slaveholders' complaints of flight, damage, and theft, particularly since the enslaved people were often silenced within the historical record.[24] Nonetheless, Roman poet Juvenal claimed that slaves "made up charges against their owners in revenge for beatings."[25] Juvenal is writing from the point of view of the slaveholder in his poetry. What is interesting is that he points to ways that enslaved persons would be harmed in his throwaway remark regarding beatings. If enslaved people repeatedly suffer beatings for being "useless," then on what moral ground would an enslaved person owe a slaveholder anything when their own humanity is decreased repeatedly in the bondage of enslavement? In such instances, enslaved people saw opportunities to assert their own moral agency. Paul's offer to "repay" diminishes Onesimus's own moral agency. While Paul may not have been concerned with Onesimus's moral agency, classical historians are helpful in bridging such a silence within the text. Further, while readers may not know definitively if Onesimus experienced moral agency, it cannot be outside of the purview of interpretation.

Thus, within the history of interpretation, scholars interpret Onesimus's usefulness for Philemon and for Paul. On the one hand, some see Paul's use of Onesimus as part of Philemon's continued obligation of service to Paul (see "on your behalf" [author's translation] at v. 13).[26] On the other hand, however, Paul could also be referring to the service that Philemon would give Onesimus upon his return, either in the household or as a "beloved brother" (v. 16). In any case, scholars argue that Onesimus would have become a different person relative to Philemon. He would no longer be an enslaved person without agency, but more—Philemon's brother in Christ. While scholars do not argue that Paul is transforming the understanding of enslaved persons in their masters' minds, generally, I argue that Paul, perhaps unknowingly, does transform societal understandings of enslaved identity.

As is widely recognized, Paul's actual appeal to Philemon in the letter is skillfully constructed. He plays affectively on the fact of his own imprisonment (vv. 9, 10, 13) while hinting repeatedly at his own power that he could have exercised (vv. 8, 13–14, 19) in order to give maximum force to his appeals—love (vv. 9, 12, 16), personal ties (vv. 10, 13, 17), and the mutual obligations of family, which should be inherent as lovers of Jesus (vv. 10, 16, 20). At the same time, Paul takes care to go halfway toward Philemon (as some scholars argue) by offering full restoration and compensation (vv. 15, 17–19). Paul's rhetoric and manipulation are evident in his stated "unwillingness" to use the stronger arguments available to him (vv. 8–9, 14, 19). As such, Paul makes Philemon believe that he can act freely and honorably.[27]

Given his manipulative rhetoric, readers 2,000 years after Paul may have difficulty deciphering the implications of his appeal. While I have already alluded to the transformation of enslaved identity, I also argue that Paul's triple use of *ta splanchna* is crucial for solidifying what the transformation of enslaved identity actually entails.

In the letter, Paul uses *ta splanchna* as follows:

> [7] I have indeed received much joy and encouragement from your love, because the hearts (*ta splanchna*) of the saints have been refreshed through you, my brother.

> [11] Formerly he was useless to you, but now he is indeed useful both to you and to me. [12] I am sending him, that is, my own heart (*ta splanchna*), back to you.

> [19] I, Paul, am writing this with my own hand: I will repay (*apotino*) it. I say nothing about your owing me even your own self. [20] Yes, brother, let me have this benefit from you in the Lord! Refresh my heart (*ta splanchna*) in Christ.

As a phrase, *ta splanchna* only appears in the plural in ancient writings, referring to the heart, lungs, liver, and kidneys of an animal that is sacrificed.[28] For example, in the Septuagint, specifically in a Maccabean context, the word represents a feeding on the innards of a sacrifice. In general, when sacrifices were eaten by the sacrificers at the beginning of their feast, they ate the heart, lungs, liver, and kidneys at the beginning of their feasts.

The meaning of *ta splanchna* is not limited to the heart, lungs, liver, and kidneys, however. Metaphorically, *ta splanchna* also connotes "the seat of the feelings, affections, esp. of anger, anxiety, love, and pity."[29] Most translations depict *ta splanchna* as "heart," a rendering that is woefully lacking in texture. It is generally recognized that "heart" does not adequately tap into the highly emotive character of *ta splanchna*.

Contemporary readers of Paul's letter to Philemon must ask what the complexity of *ta splanchna* actually means for us, morally and ethically. Why does Paul keep referring to *ta splanchna* while he states that he will repay anything that Onesimus owes? It would appear that Onesimus had won a special place in the depths of Paul's "guts"—a better rendering of the sense of *ta splanchna*. By implication, Philemon would find it difficult to treat Paul's *ta splanchna* with anything but consideration and care. In effect, Paul has transformed the identity of an enslaved person from property to humanity.

As I read traditional interpreters' discussion of *ta splanchna*, I note that these scholars argue that Paul has insinuated himself within a legal relationship between master and slave. Scholars are often quick to argue that the slave was legally in the wrong and liable to serious punishment as a result of running away.[30] It always amazes me that White American interpreters of Paul place so much blame on Onesimus for seeking his own freedom. Readers of Philemon argue that Paul is sending Onesimus back not because of legal obligations, but because of Onesimus's new status: wrongs done among fellow believers had to be sorted out as among fellow believers (v. 16; cf. 1 Cor. 6:1–8). I suggest, however, that such a reading—concentrating on the status of believers alone—misses the point of transformation from enslaved status to fully human status.

At this point, I must ask if Paul's readers and interpreters actually need him to argue explicitly for that transformation? Is there not something inherent within all of us that fights for our humanity? Isn't there something inherent within all of us that resists the ways that people in power attempt to name and define others? These questions lead me to engage with the story of Margaret Garner.

In 1856, Margaret Garner was an African woman born into slavery and was the mother of three children also born into slavery. During the 1850s, when the Underground Railroad was at its peak, Garner and her husband decided to take advantage of an opportunity to escape enslavement and travel to Canada. While in Cincinnati and awaiting their next guide, the Garners' master, A. K. Gaines, stormed the Cincinnati house with warrants for the

Garners. Determined not return to slavery, Margaret Garner slit the necks of her children, succeeding in killing her two-year-old daughter. When the marshals arrived, she was about to take her own life as her other two children lay on the floor still alive.

The trial that followed was one of the longest fugitive slave trials in history. In the end, the judge denied the Garners' pleas for freedom and returned them to the Gaines family. While Margaret Garner was still trying to secure her freedom, her attorney attempted to have Garner tried for murder. Since the Gaines family moved her from planation to plantation, however, she was never served a warrant for the murder trial. It is interesting to note that a potential murder trial would have raised the question whether enslaved women and their children are actually human beings or property.

Reflecting on Margaret Garner's situation in light of what the letter of Philemon says about Onesimus, I wonder about the "wrongness" of Garner killing her children so that they would not be returned to slavery. As I consider Garner's anxiety, I ponder what anxiety Onesimus would have experienced as he was returned to Philemon. Placing Garner's story in conversation with Onesimus, I wonder how Onesimus thought of his own situation. Again, as readers we never hear Onesimus's thoughts or arguments. For me, this is where the language of *ta splanchna* becomes important.

There are two important factors to consider as we engage Garner, Onesimus, and *ta splanchna* together. First, Paul rarely, if ever, centers women and women's experiences as he writes his letters. I thus find it difficult to read Paul as a moral and ethical authority when he has such blind spots (as do the other New Testament writers). Paul cannot serve as the final arbiter of enslaved Black women's experiences and ethics when such matters are not within his purview. I do believe, however, that an expanded understanding of *ta splanchna* may relieve some of my own anxieties as I read and interpret Paul through a womanist lens. As an interpreter, I have liberty to argue against Pauline language—seemingly understood by many interpreters to emphasize what might be owed to Philemon rather than to Onesimus—that would continue injustices in contemporary society (including the fact that the Apostle doesn't argue for the abolition of first-century slavery)—even as I think of Pauline literature and the entirety of the New Testament as authoritative scripture. Therefore, *ta splanchna* becomes representative of what Black women experience in their "guts" when they have to make difficult decisions in a world that does not value their humanity. That was Margaret Garner's situation.

Second, I often say to my students, "I cannot teach you *ta splanchna,* but I can point it out in the biblical text." I do try to articulate to students that there is something intensely emotive about the term. As I read Philemon, the emotive nature of *ta splanchna* pushes me to question what repayment for

Paul actually looks like, given that Onesimus is Paul's *ta splanchna* (v. 12). I think that answer lies in how Paul "flips the script" on Philemon and lets him know that Philemon actually owes the Apostle. After Paul says that he will repay whatever Onesimus's debt may be to Philemon, he goes on to state that Philemon owes Paul his own life (v. 19b: "I say nothing about your owing me even your own self").

If we take seriously Paul's language that Philemon owes Paul his life, then we must take seriously the conversation about the United States being built upon the labor of enslaved people. The Greek word that Paul uses for Philemon owing Paul is *prosopheilo*. This word is a *hapax legomenon*, meaning that Paul's use is the only time that it occurs in the Greek New Testament. Rhetorically, Paul seems to be emphasizing that Philemon has benefited from both Onesimus and Paul.

As stated previously, classical historians have attempted to make visible the "invisible" labor of the Roman enslaved populations. This is similar to what contemporary conversations concerning reparations seek to do. Just as Philemon benefited from the "invisible" labor of Onesimus, the United States of America benefited from the highly visible labor of enslaved Africans. For example, both Brown University and the University of North Carolina have constructed memorials that recognize the role of slave labor in the creation of their campuses.[31] In 2019, Princeton Theological Seminary pledged to pay $27.6 million in reparations as an "act of repentance," because the school benefited from the slave economy.[32]

As a recipient of enslaved labor, Philemon owes Paul and Onesimus just as the United States and its various entities owe African Americans for their labor. Paul's offer to repay Philemon would be akin to a slave master or the United States government paying reparations to Confederate states who formerly owned slaves while ignoring the plight of the formerly enslaved people. Even when such an occurrence happened after the Civil War, formerly enslaved citizens recognized the reparations to former enslavers to be a grave injustice. Both Paul's language and its implications for today are problematic.

When Paul indicates that Philemon actually owes him, the apostle effectively supports an argument that reparations can come to Onesimus—but through the medium of Paul. Whatever Paul receives from Philemon would be given to his *ta splanchna*, Onesimus. Accordingly, Onesimus, in fact, would receive some reparations from Philemon.

CONCLUDING THOUGHTS

Let me reiterate that I cannot teach students to embody *ta splanchna,* but I can point it out in the scripture. Additionally, I can point out and describe what *ta splanchna* feels like. In American parlance, we often refer to "feeling something in our guts." When a crush walks by, we may talk about having butterflies in our stomach. When we experience bad news, we may talk about a "gut punch." The guts help us identify and understand feelings and emotions that, oftentimes, we may try to hide.

Conversations around reparations may cause uneasy feelings in our guts. One of my favorite t-shirts to wear has a quote by James Baldwin: "Nothing can be changed unless it is faced." We must face these hard conversations even as a majority of White-identifying people in the United States of America have difficulties engaging such conversations.

Historians do not provide us with the inner feelings of Margaret Garner, but I wholeheartedly believe that she knew in her guts that she could not stomach her children returning to slavery. Likewise, Paul did not voice Onesimus's feelings and words, but we can assume that Paul's connection of Onesimus as his *ta splanchna*—as his own "guts" (v. 12)—definitely evokes unspoken feelings of someone being returned to a precarious situation.

I have to believe that many Americans know within their "guts" that formerly enslaved Africans, whose descendants are now contemporary African Americans in society, were released into a society that was fraught with precarious situations. The Jim/Jane Crow era of the United States impeded the progress of African Americans. The systematic incarceration rates of Black women and men continue to obstruct economic progress. Further, the continued militaristic police violence that slaughters Black men and women has cut down many lives and brought about the emergence of the Black Lives Matter movement. In the guts of America, we know that something has to be done.

Further, in our guts we know that American society is siloed and segregated. Studies show that many White people live and work in predominantly White spaces and do not have significant social relationships with people of color.[33] As I write these sentences, I am currently sitting in a restaurant in Princeton, New Jersey, home to one of the most prestigious Ivy League universities in the world, and I have been surrounded by White-presenting folks for the past two hours. I have been the only African American woman in the restaurant for a significant amount of time. Socially, many White people do not understand African American experiences, values, culture, desires—and vice versa. We need to talk more to one another instead of ignoring one another. In our collective guts, I imagine that Americans know that we are more alike than different. In our collective guts, we know that we are all humans who want to live in less precarious situations. Can we tap into our *ta splanchna* to make reparations happen?

NOTES

1. Nikole Hannah-Jones, Caitlin Roper, Ilena Silverman, and Jake Silverstein. *The 1619 Project: A New Origin Story*. Edited by Caitlin Roper, Ilena Silverman, and Jake Silverstein. First edition (New York: One World, 2021), 459.
2. Hannah-Jones, *The 1619 Project*, 460–461.
3. Hannah-Jones, *The 1619 Project*, 461.
4. Hannah-Jones, *The 1619 Project*, 463.
5. See Don Rojas's 2017 speech at the Charles H. Wright Museum of African-American History in Detroit, Michigan: "Reparations and the Legacy of Marcus Mosiah Garvey," accessed March 11, 2023, https://ibw21.org/commentary/reparations-legacy-marcus-mosiah-garvey/.
6. Hannah-Jones, *The 1619 Project*, 463.
7. Malcolm X, "The Race Problem." Speech to the African Students Association and NAACP Campus Chapter. Michigan State University, East Lansing, Michigan. January 23, 1963.
8. Hannah-Jones, *The 1619 Project*, 464.
9. Patrisse Cullors, "Abolition and Reparations: Histories of Resistance, Transformative Justice, and Accountability," *Harvard Law Review* 132, no. 6 (2019): 1684–94; 1686.
10. Tomas Kassahun, "BLM Co-Founder Patrisse Cullors Claims LAPD Killed Her 31-Year-Old Cousin, English Teacher Keenan Anderson, *Yahoo!News*, January 11, 2023. Accessed May 15, 2023 (https://news.yahoo.com/blm-co-founder-patrisse-cullors-171500485.html).
11. See National African-American Reparations Commission, "U.S. moves closer to compensating Blacks for generations of racism," April 3, 2022. Accessed March 10, 2023, https://reparationscomm.org/reparations-news/reality-of-reparations/#:~:text=He%20says%2C%20%E2%80%9CThe%20only%20victimized,community%20received%20reparations%20after%20WWII.
12 Sandra R. Joshel and Lauren Hackworth Petersen. *The Material Life of Roman Slaves* (New York: Cambridge University Press, 2014).
13. Love patriarchalism is the is idea that hierarchical relationships such as man over wife, parent over child, and master over slave were maintained as normative and reduced the frictions of status inequality through the love that the *paterfamilias* showed to all subordinates. See K. Syreeni, "Paul and Love Patriarchalism: Problems and Prospects," *Die Skriflig: Tydskrif van Die Gereformeerde Teologiese Vereniging* 37, no. 3 (2003): 395–422, accessed May 19, 2023, https://doi.org/10.4102/ids.v37i3.475.
14. See Joshel and Petersen, *The Material Life of Roman Slaves*, 95.
15. Joshel and Petersen, *The Material Life of Roman Slaves*, 95.

16. Eric C. Smith, *Paul the Progressive?: The Compassionate Christian's Guide to Reclaiming the Apostle as an Ally* (Saint Louis, MO: Chalice Press, 2019), 97.

17. Allen Dwight Callahan, *Embassy of Onesimus: The Letter of Paul to Philemon* (Valley Forge: Trinity, 1997).

18. Unless note otherwise, all biblical quotations are from the NRSV.

19. Todd D. Still, *Philippians & Philemon* (Macon, GA: Smyth & Helwys, 2011), 170.

20. Smith, *Paul the Progressive?*, 98.

21. Smith, *Paul the Progressive?*, 99.

22. William Arndt et al. eds., *A Greek-English Lexicon of the New Testament and Other Early Christian Literature* (Chicago: University of Chicago Press, 2000), 124.

23. Arndt et al., *Lexicon,* 124.

24. See Joshel and Petersen, *The Material Life of Roman Slaves,* 13.

25. See Joshel and Petersen, *The Material Life of Roman Slaves,* 14.

26. James D. G. Dunn, *The Epistles to the Colossians and to Philemon* (Grand Rapids, MI: Eerdmans, 1996), 329.

27. While I appreciate Dunn's work in thinking through Philemon, I would argue that Paul acts more manipulatively than honorably. See Dunn, Colossians, and Philemon, 323.

28. H. G. Liddell, H. G., R. Scott, H. S. Jones, and R. McKenzie, *A Greek-English Lexicon* (Oxford: Clarendon Press, 1996), 1628.

29. Liddell et al., *Greek-English Lexicon*, 1628.

30. Dunn, *Colossians and Philemon,* 329–330.

31. Ashley V. Reichelmann and Matthew O. Hunt, "White Americans' Attitudes Toward Reparations for Slavery: Definitions and Determinants," *Race and Social Problems* 14, no. 3 (2022): 269–81, accessed May 18, 2023, https://doi.org/10.1007/s12552-021-09348-x.

32. Reichelmann and Hunt, "White Americans' Attitudes," 270.

33. See Elijah Anderson, *Black in White Space: The Enduring Impact of Color in Everyday Life* (Chicago: University of Chicago Press, 2022). Drawing on his forty years of qualitative fieldwork, Anderson documents the phenomena that White people typically avoid Black space while Black people are required to enter and navigate White space.

BIBLIOGRAPHY

Anderson, Elijah. *Black in White Space: The Enduring Impact of Color in Everyday Life.* Chicago: University of Chicago Press, 2022.

Arndt, William, et al., eds. *A Greek-English Lexicon of the New Testament and Other Early Christian Literature.* Chicago: University of Chicago Press, 2000.

Callahan, Allen Dwight. *Embassy of Onesimus: The Letter of Paul to Philemon.* Valley Forge: Trinity, 1997.

Cullors, Patrisse. "Abolition and Reparations: Histories of Resistance, Transformative Justice, and Accountability." *Harvard Law Review* 132, no. 6 (2019): 1684–94.

Dunn, James D. G. *The Epistles to the Colossians and to Philemon.* Grand Rapids, MI: Eerdmans, 1996.

Hannah-Jones, Nikole, Caitlin Roper, Ilena Silverman, and Jake Silverstein. *The 1619 Project: A New Origin Story.* First edition. New York: One World, 2021.

Joshel, Sandra R., and Lauren Hackworth Petersen. *The Material Life of Roman Slaves.* New York: Cambridge University Press, 2014.

Tomas Kassahun. "BLM Co-Founder Patrisse Cullors Claims LAPD Killed Her 31-Year-Old Cousin, English Teacher Keenan Anderson," *Yahoo!News,* January 11, 2023. Accessed May 15, 2023. https://news.yahoo.com/blm-co-founder-patrisse-cullors-171500485.html.

Liddell, H. G., R. Scott, H. S. Jones, and R. McKenzie. *A Greek-English Lexicon.* Oxford: Clarendon Press, 1996.

National African-American Reparations Commission. "U.S. moves closer to compensating Blacks for generations of racism." April 3, 2022. Accessed March 10, 2023. https://reparationscomm.org/reparations-news/reality-of-reparations/#:~:text=He%20says%2C%20%E2%80%9CThe%20only%20victimized,community%20received%20reparations%20after%20WWII.

Reichelmann, Ashley V., and Matthew O. Hunt. "White Americans' Attitudes Toward Reparations for Slavery: Definitions and Determinants." *Race and Social Problems* 14, no. 3 (2022): 269–81. Accessed May 18, 2023. https://doi.org/10.1007/s12552-021-09348-x.

Rojas, Don. "Reparations and the Legacy of Marcus Mosiah Garvey." 2017 speech at the Charles H. Wright Museum of African-American History in Detroit, Michigan. Accessed March 11, 2023. https://ibw21.org/commentary/reparations-legacy-marcus-mosiah-garvey/.

Smith, Eric C. *Paul the Progressive?: The Compassionate Christian's Guide to Reclaiming the Apostle as an Ally.* Saint Louis, MO: Chalice Press, 2019.

Still, Todd D. *Philippians & Philemon.* Macon, GA: Smyth & Helwys, 2011.

Syreeni, K. "Paul and Love Patriarchalism: Problems and Prospects." *Die Skriflig: Tydskrif van Die Gereformeerde Teologiese Vereniging* 37, no. 3 (2003): 395–422.

X, Malcolm. "The Race Problem." Speech to the African Students Association and NAACP Campus Chapter. Michigan State University, East Lansing, Michigan. January 23, 1963.

Chapter Eight

Philemon as a Plea for Reparations Then and Now

Michael J. Gorman

Paul's short but dramatic letter to Philemon and the church in his house is often interpreted as a document that reflects a situation involving a runaway slave, Onesimus, who has done harm to his owner, Philemon. (This has been the main opinion since Chrysostom, perhaps earlier.) In the hands of slave-owners, this interpretation led to widespread abuse of slaves with allegedly biblical support.[1] Although other interpretations of the historical setting have emerged in recent years, many interpreters would agree that Paul's main goal is to effect reconciliation between Onesimus and Philemon. It also appears to many that one of Paul's strategies for achieving this goal was to offer to make reparations for the damage Philemon had suffered. The letter even seems to contain Paul's I.O.U. to address this damage: "If he [Onesimus] has wronged you [Philemon] in any way or owes you anything, charge that to me. I, Paul, am writing this with my own hand: I will repay it" (Phlm 18–19a).[2]

This essay, however, will argue otherwise: a primary aim of the letter is to effect reparations—that is, tangible compensation for injustice, with the goals of increasing justice, repairing relationships, and working toward a better future—for the harm *Onesimus* has endured. Just as there are various interpretations of the letter's historical situation, there are also multiple understandings of Paul's objectives. I see no evidence that Onesimus was a runaway slave or thief, even if he owes Philemon something. I will argue that Paul's goals for Philemon are encapsulated in the phrase "no longer as a slave but more than a slave, a beloved brother" (v. 16),[3] and that this phrase implies specific practical, costly consequences, with the focus not on reconciliation, but on liberation and new beginnings both in the church and in the world.

If Philemon complies, he will essentially be making reparations for treating a human being as property, even if it takes Onesimus's Christian conversion for that to be made clear. While there are many differences between this scenario (and the interpretation of it to be offered) and the current context in the United States, there are sufficient parallels to be stimulating for Christian praxis regarding reparations—which will similarly be both costly and public.

THE LETTER'S DRAMA

At just 335 Greek words, the letter of prisoner-Paul and Timothy to Philemon and his house-church is the apostle's shortest, but arguably most dramatic, letter.[4] In fact, it resembles a drama in five acts:[5]

1. *the relatively distant past*, in which Philemon becomes a Christian under Paul's influence (v. 19b), and an *ekklēsia* begins to meet in Philemon's house (v. 2);
2. *the immediate past*, in which Paul (vv. 1, 9–10, 13) and Epaphras (v. 23) are imprisoned; Onesimus leaves Philemon and encounters Paul in his imprisonment, where he also becomes a Christian thanks to Paul (v. 10); and Onesimus assists Paul in some capacity, functioning as a surrogate for Philemon (v. 13) and also reporting on Philemon's faithfulness and love (vv. 5, 7);
3. *the present*, in which Paul writes to Philemon, sending the letter (and Onesimus, v. 12), to Philemon and the church (vv. 1–2), with requests of Philemon (vv. 8–10, 13–17, 20–21) and a promise of repayment for any debt or damages (vv. 18–19a);
4. *the immediate future*, in which the letter is read aloud in the assembly and Philemon is faced with a decision to make (vv. 9, 14, 21); and
5. *the (relatively) distant future*, in which Paul pays Philemon a visit (v. 22) and in which Philemon's decisions are embodied.

THE CHANGED SITUATION

As we consider this drama and its possible consequences for the question of reparations, we must keep in mind the revolution in the relationships among Paul, Philemon, and Onesimus that Onesimus's conversion to Christ has effected.[6]

As the sons of one spiritual father, Philemon and Onesimus are now brothers, and they are missional colleagues as Paul's helpers (vv. 1, 7, 11, 13):

Philemon as a Plea for Reparations Then and Now

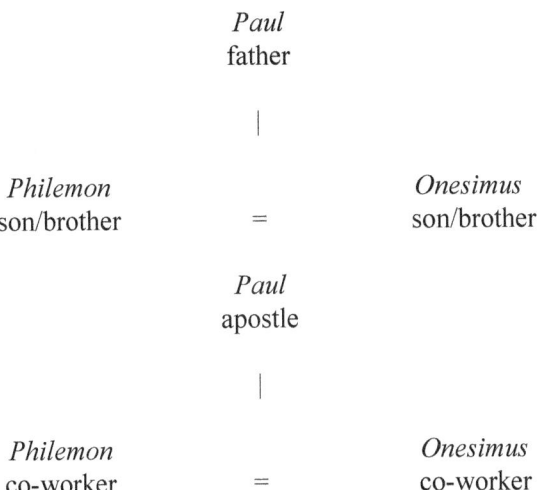

Furthermore, Onesimus functions both as Paul ("my own heart" [more literally, "my gut"] in v. 12 and "as . . . me" in v. 17) and as Philemon ("in your place"; 1:13):

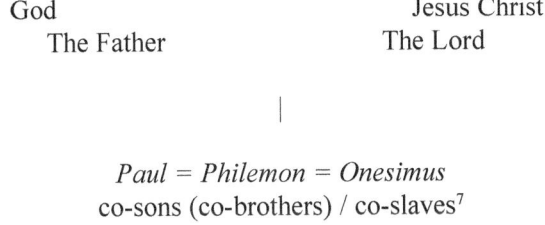

And, finally, all three Christian men are co-sons of one Father, and thus co-brothers, and co-slaves of one Lord:

        God   Jesus Christ
       The Father   The Lord

|

Paul = Philemon = Onesimus
co-sons (co-brothers) / co-slaves[7]

Into this changed situation Paul inscribes, or "positions," not only Onesimus, but also both himself and Philemon.[8] He does so with theological conviction and rhetorical power. And yet, while Paul is clear about the nature of this new situation, this new creation, and (I will argue) equally clear about its consequences, he does not force Philemon to do anything (vv. 8–9, 14).

Rather, Paul assumes a Christlike, cruciform posture of apostolic example—indeed, of love. Alluding to the opening of the Christ-poem in Philippians (Phil 2:6–8) and his own practice of that poem (e.g., 1 Thess 2:5–8; 1 Cor 9, esp. vv. 12–19), Paul says, "though I am more than bold enough in Christ to command you to do the right thing, yet I would rather appeal to you on the basis of love" (vv. 8–9a). Rather than exercise his apostolic right, he acts in love and (as apostolic model) implicitly expects the same kind of cruciform, costly, other's-centered love from Philemon.

PAUL'S CRUCIFORM OBJECTIVES FOR PHILEMON

Paul, then, invites Philemon to "do the right thing." This will be costly, but more importantly it will be Christlike and thus truly Christian. I contend that Paul wants Onesimus to perform five interrelated acts of cruciform love—which are also, as public deeds, acts of justice—to embody the truth of the changed situation:

1. *recognition*: acknowledge Onesimus's status as his new Christian brother;
2. *liberation*: manumit Onesimus;
3. *equalization*: treat Onesimus as a Christian brother and an equal—with all the social, practical, and economic implications—both in the context of the Christian assembly that meets in his (Philemon's) house and in the public square;
4. *forgiveness*: as an act of Christian love, and in recognition of his own debt to Paul, forgive any debt owed by Onesimus; and
5. *return*: send Onesimus back to Paul.

Recognition: No Longer a Slave, but a Beloved Brother

Onesimus the convert is now his master's brother. What happens next? Some interpreters, such as N. T. Wright, have argued that v. 17 is the key to Paul's request of Philemon: "So if you consider me your partner, welcome him as you would welcome me."[9] Wright thinks that v. 21 ("knowing that you will do even more than I ask") implies manumission as part of a threefold request: (1) accept Onesimus as a reconciled brother, without punishing him; (2) send him back to me to help me; and (3) perhaps grant him freedom.[10] But according to Wright the letter's "main thrust" is not manumission; it is reconciliation and its resulting *koinōnia*.[11]

Reconciliation is of course a critical Pauline theme, but to make that central to this letter's interpretation requires accepting the traditional understanding that Onesimus has done something wrong. Since that understanding has been justly questioned, I suggest that the key to Paul's request is in vv. 15b–16, with other texts supporting or amplifying that appeal, and that therefore *koinōnia* is highly significant, but not as a result of reconciliation. Rather, it is a result of a two-part equality, as siblings in Christ and as equal free people in the public sphere.

The words "have him back for the long term, no longer as a slave but more than a slave, a beloved brother (*ouketi hōs doulon all' hyper doulon, adelphon agapēton*)" in vv. 15b–16 are open to two possible interpretations: *supplemental* and *replacement*. The *supplemental* interpretation argues that Onesimus will remain a slave but should also be considered as a (Christian) brother. This view may stress the words "as" and "more than" and contend that terms related to manumission are missing from the letter. The *replacement* interpretation argues that Onesimus is no longer to be seen as a slave, but only as a brother, and is thus to be manumitted. It may stress the word "no longer" and contend that Paul's liberative rhetoric throughout the letter is deliberately subtle.

Some scholars have argued that the letter provides insufficient evidence to decide between these two positions. I contend that the replacement interpretation is the correct one and offer here a brief overview of the reasons for that claim.

Liberation: Manumission

There are two main reasons for supporting manumission as Paul's fundamental objective.

First, the Greek word translated "no longer" (*ouketi*) in v. 16 implies the cessation of one status and the start of another. There are no qualifying words such as "only" and "also," as if Paul had written "take him back no longer *only* as a slave but *also* as more than a slave—as a brother." That is not what Paul wrote, though he could have done so.[12]

One might counter, with Scot McKnight, that Paul uses "no longer" language as an expression of his theology about the radical change brought about by God in Christ, and consequently in those who believe, without requiring a concrete change in the social arrangement.[13] While it is true that Paul's "no longer" language does express deep theological convictions, some uses of it clearly imply the termination of a person's original status. A close parallel to Philemon 16 is Galatians 4:7 (suggested by McKnight himself): "So you are no longer (*ouketi*) a slave (*doulos*) but a child, and if a child then also an heir through God." Here slavery is not to a person but to "the elemental principles of the world" (Gal 4:3), yet the fundamental point remains the same. "No longer" means precisely that: one was once a slave but is henceforth no longer a slave, but a child of God and heir (so Galatians) or brother (so Philemon). Neither text states nor implies "also," as if the original condition persists.

Second, although the words "both in the flesh and in the Lord (*kai en sarki kai en kyriō*)" in v. 16 have sparked many interpretations, they are best understood as references to two different spheres of Philemon's (and Onesimus's) life: public and ecclesial, with special emphasis on the public dimension. The phrase *en sarki* is the antithesis of *en kyriō*, indicating life "outside" the Lord and outside the *ekklēsia*: life in the public sphere of the unbaptized.[14] To have Onesimus as a brother in that public sphere means to view and treat him differently than one would normally view and treat a slave, and not just on Sunday evening in the house-church meeting. Onesimus's change in status from slave to brother has no social or spatial boundaries; it must be recognized and embodied everywhere and at all times. *The change from slave to brother is also a change from property to person.*

One might counter that slaves were sometimes referred to with familial language (which is true), but that such language did not make them anything other than slaves in terms of social realities. McKnight, for example, takes that view, limiting Paul's concern to "liberation in the context of the household and church," and claiming that positing legal manumission "is both to impose modern sensibilities on Paul and to avoid what Paul does emphasize: reconciliation in Christ."[15] The problem of imposing modern sensibilities, however, manifests itself especially in the limitation of radical change to the realm of attitudes and personal and domestic relations, without sufficient attention to broader social realities.

In conclusion, although there is no precise, explicit request for manumission in the letter, the language of "no longer" and "both in the flesh and in the Lord" make the most sense as pointing toward manumission, with all of its attendant internal and external consequences—not all of which can be known to Philemon, to Onesimus, or to us. Moreover, as Stephen Young argues, although Paul does not "technically" ask Philemon to manumit Onesimus, he is "positioning Philemon within a local moral context in which this is the only morally acceptable course of action," for "sibling love implies that brothers do not enslave brothers."[16]

Equalization: Implications in the Church and in the Public Square

We have just seen that Paul names two spheres of existence in which Philemon, Onesimus, and all Christians operate: "in the flesh," meaning "outside" the Lord, or in the "world"; and "in the Lord," meaning in the body of Christ, the *ekklēsia*. Paul insists that Onesimus be treated as a brother, not a slave—or even ex-slave—in both the church and the world. What does this mean on the ground? We will reverse Paul's order and begin with the church.

In the Lord (In the Assembly)

It is fairly easy to determine with some certainty what it would mean in the church, practically speaking, for both Philemon and Onesimus for Philemon to welcome Onesimus as a brother and not a slave. We learn from various texts what mutual expectations existed among the members of the Pauline assemblies. Philemon would have been expected to be guided by the following sorts of values and practices:

> [10][L]ove one another with mutual affection; outdo one another in showing honor.... [13]Contribute to the needs of the saints; pursue hospitality to strangers.... [15]Rejoice with those who rejoice; weep with those who weep. [16]Live in harmony with one another; do not be arrogant, but associate with the lowly; do not claim to be wiser than you are. (Rom 12:10, 13, 15, 16)
>
> [1]If, then, there is any comfort in Christ, any consolation from love, any partnership in the Spirit, any tender affection and sympathy, [2]make my joy complete: be of the same mind, having the same love, being in full accord and of one mind. [3]Do nothing from selfish ambition or empty conceit, but in humility regard others as better than yourselves. [4]Let each of you look not to your own interests but to the interests of others. (Phil 2:1–4)

In other words, however Philemon had treated Onesimus as his slave, his possession, he must now do things that would not be normal in the slave-master relationship. "Enslaved people had no physical integrity and honor."[17] Philemon must now give more honor to Onesimus than he receives from him; he must regard, and therefore treat, Onesimus as better than himself. He must look out for Onesimus's interests rather than his own, including even Onesimus's financial needs. Lest these exhortations be understood as vague practices of being nice, we should consider one concrete activity: the assembly's meals together. As McKnight says, "The language [of v. 16] elevates a slave from the margins of the family to the family table."[18] This is literally true for Onesimus.

In the Greco-Roman world, meals expressed and created social boundaries.[19] As a non-Christian slave, Onesimus would not normally have participated, or participated fully, in any banquet held in Philemon's house, including the meals of the *ekklēsia*—the Lord's Supper. If slaves, women, and children were present at banquets in that world, they did not recline with the host's honored guests—his free male peers—but would be seated.[20] If Onesimus had been a Christian slave, he should have been, and perhaps would have been, treated as a peer at the Lord's Supper; such was the implication of Paul's theology of "no longer slave or free" (Gal 3:28). But Paul does not now want Onesimus's participation to be in question, for he is to be welcomed, not as a (non-Christian) slave, and not even as a Christian slave, but only and fully as a brother, an equal, a peer. The meal is about social equality,[21] and Onesimus is now an equal. This would certainly, at the very least, mean that Onesimus now eats both *with* and *like* everyone else in the *ekklēsia*, making up for years of second-class treatment, at best. Moreover, if he is ever in need of any kind of assistance, including financial, he is now a full participant in a community whose members have covenanted to care for one another (e.g., Rom 12:10, 16; 1 Cor 12:25) and "be enslaved to" one another in love: "through love become slaves [*douleuete*] to one another" (Gal 5:13). That is, in a stunning reversal of fortunes with real, if not fully defined, consequences, Philemon has become Onesimus's slave, and that is certainly a form of reparations.

We do not know what Onesimus had done in general as Philemon's slave, or what specifically he would have done when the Christian assembly convened at Philemon's house. Perhaps he shopped for the banquet's food and then helped prepare the meal. Perhaps he washed the feet of the guests, carried the food into the triclinium, and served the participants. If Philemon did at one time expect Onesimus to serve him and others, now one way Philemon could associate with the "lowly" and give honor instead of receiving it would be to serve the slave-turned-brother his food at the meal, or perhaps even wash his feet as—yes—his slave in Christ.

Such counterintuitive, cruciform conduct would not be easy for anyone. Fortunately, Philemon is not alone in his decision making and its consequences. The letter's addressees—the community—"would provide a matrix for Philemon to fulfill his new obligations toward Onesimus. . . . The church as a family with its resetting of social relations will provide a local moral context with the potential to reshape Philemon's self-concept if he chooses to count himself as an insider and abide by its norms and values."[22]

In the "Flesh"

Manumission, writes Sandra Joshel, "was a sort of social 'rebirth' (although not a complete one)."[23] A freed slave was no longer someone's property, and as such gained new or expanded legal rights (regarding marriage, property ownership, contracts, etc.). In fact, if the former owner was a citizen, the manumitted slave became a citizen too.[24] At the same time, ex-slaves were plagued with "legal and social disabilities"; the "servile past" of freed slaves "was a social stigma, and a continued relationship with their former owners placed limitations on ex-slaves' actions and behavior."[25] Freedmen were generally thought of as aliens from other cultures (since they often actually were from elsewhere) and as illegitimate children without a socially recognized father.[26]

The ongoing relationship between ex-slave and ex-master normally—but not always—took the form of a patron-client arrangement that had both social and legal dimensions.[27] The grace of manumission carried with it the expectation of the ex-slave's ongoing compliance, even if the patron could not control or abuse the client as one could a slave. "In effect, freed slaves gained the physical integrity that slaves lacked in relation to others, but apparently they could never fully claim it in relation to the ex-owner who once claimed their bodies."[28] Both socially and legally, patrons could oblige their ex-slaves to work, often to excess; they could still engage in certain forms of punishment, even without the right to life and death; and they could lay claim to the ex-slave's estate.[29] The ex-slave might end up as a household servant living in the same household.[30] Whatever the precise arrangement, the ex-master was still in a position of power over the ex-slave, both in the household or family business and in the eyes of others in society.

I would suggest that all of these normal attitudes and behaviors are challenged by Paul with the little phrase "in the flesh." And the changes will likely be costly in various ways.

As Philemon interacts with his peers in the world, he now has an obligation to treat Onesimus as his brother, and even to refer to him that way. This would be an appropriate way of honoring his new sibling, but it would likely come at a significant cost to Philemon's own honor among his peers. Moreover, since he and Onesimus are now brothers with a common Father—in fact, two common fathers, one divine and one human (Paul)—Onesimus is relieved from the stigma of illegitimacy by virtue of his association with his brother, his ex-owner Philemon. But it is only Philemon, the more powerful and the already recognized sibling, who can make that legitimate sonship known outside the church. Once again, this would likely come at some cost, at least in social capital and perhaps in other forms, unless and until Onesimus returns to Paul. Furthermore, as we will see below, the return to Paul may be costly for Philemon too.

Forgiveness: Relief from Any Debt

Much of the rationale for the most common interpretations of this letter can be found in the alleged I.O.U. Paul offers in vv. 18–19. Paul, it is argued, is willing to absorb the moral and financial debt Onesimus owes Philemon in order to bring about justice, stop any threat of punishment, and contribute to the process of reconciliation.

We do not know if there actually is any damage or debt, for Paul begins v. 18 with the word "If." Furthermore, we do not know the reason for any possible debt;[31] perhaps, as Mary Ann Beavis suggests, Paul is offering to pay for anything Onesimus owes toward his manumission.[32] Or perhaps Paul is offering to help with the financial loss to Philemon that manumission will effect. More importantly, the typical interpretation of the situation underestimates the content and rhetorical power of the last words of v. 19: "I say nothing about your owing me even your own self." Paul is saying that there can be no debt owed to Philemon that even approximates the debt Philemon owes to Paul.[33] Cruciform love and gratitude—the circle of grace—will require Philemon to forgive any debt that might exist.

Return: Even More

If the foregoing four points are valid, then we must finally interpret v. 21, "Confident of your obedience, I am writing to you, knowing that you will do even more than I ask." Since Paul is not commanding Philemon, the obedience he has in mind must be a cruciform, Christlike obedience to God the Father (cf. Phil 2:8). And what could be "more" than these four costly requests?

It is likely that Paul is asking Philemon to send Onesimus back to Paul for continued mission work. This would also be a form of reparations, or payment. By losing Onesimus not only as his slave but also as his ex-slave and client, Philemon is again taking another loss and simultaneously making a double-gift (i.e., to Paul and to Onesimus), especially if he takes the hint and drops all interest in financial recuperation. In fact, it is likely that Philemon would incur certain direct costs in the process of manumission, and the "even more" could well be a subtle request to provide financially for Onesimus in his new missional life with Paul. Both are acts of cruciform love and justice, the latter more obviously a form of reparations.

There is much in the narrative of this letter that resembles the instructions for slave manumission in Deuteronomy 15.[34] We cannot say with certainty that Paul had that text in mind, but several commonalities exist, especially the language and theology of "brother" (Deut 15:2, 3, 12; not "member of your community" as in the NRSV) and the stipulation to provide materially for freed slaves at their manumission (Deut 15:12–18). In the case of Onesimus, that provision could very well include support for his work with Paul.

CONCLUSION

We have summarized Paul's plea for reparations issued to Philemon as five acts of cruciform love: recognition, liberation, equalization (ecclesial and public), forgiveness, and return to Paul (with financial obligations). We turn now to the question of generalizability.

From Specific Instance to General Principle?

Even if one accepts the argument that Paul desired Onesimus's manumission, there are possible roadblocks to moving from that conclusion to any general principle about slavery and liberation, even before considering reparations. One potential roadblock would be the possibility that Paul's desire for Onesimus's liberation is not generalizable because his concern was for one individual (a concern that was possibly self-serving) and not for all slaves or for slavery as a system. (We have already seen, however, that even liberation for mission work with Paul could provide a model of costly reparations.) Another, related potential roadblock would be that Paul's concern was only for slaves who are in Christ, whose liberation is dependent on their being a Christian brother or sister, not simply on their being a human being. Yet a third possible roadblock would be the canonical question about letters bearing Paul's name—Colossians and Ephesians—and possibly actually authored by him, as I would argue, that do not appear to challenge slavery one iota.

At one level, these possible roadblocks are irrelevant because the argument of this essay is not that Paul sought to dismantle slavery, or that he grounded his plea in a philosophical conviction about all humans apart from his "in-Christ" approach, or that this one appeal became Paul's (or the early church's) fundamental attitude toward slaves and slavery. Rather, the argument of this essay, to be continued below, is that this one particular situation involving the triadic Paul-Philemon-Onesimus relationship can be interpreted analogically as a plea for reparations for African Americans. At the same time, I want to say something about the second and third concerns.

In contrast to many interpreters, I have argued elsewhere that the household codes of Colossians and Ephesians, read carefully in their specifics and in their larger context of early Christian ethics in those letters, do not merely *underwrite* ancient patriarchy; rather, in a profound way, they *undermine* key aspects of it.[35] Members of a Christian household are in some sense equals, accountable to the same Lord. If equality and mutuality constitute at least one dimension of reparations, even the household codes convey a basic sense of reparations (as defined above and by Olúfẹ́mi O. Táíwò below) that replaces a structure of hierarchical domination and abuse. And of course a robust sense of mutuality and equality permeates the letter to Philemon itself.

As for the question of whether liberation (and implicitly reparations), or even simply just treatment, is dependent on a shared Christian identity, two things can be said. First, the implication of Col 4:1—"Masters, treat your slaves justly and fairly, for you know that you also have a Master in heaven"—is that Christian masters must treat even non-Christian slaves justly and fairly. Second, in the undisputed Pauline letters there is an ethical theme that Christians' treatment of outsiders must, in critical ways, be comparable to their treatment of fellow believers. Paul himself tells the Galatians, "let us work for the good of all and especially for those of the family [lit. 'households'] of faith" (Gal 6:10), and he says to the Thessalonians, "always seek to do good to one another and to all" (1 Thess 5:15; cf. Rom 12:17).

The implication of this moral motif of centrifugal as well as centripetal activity—that is, action directed outside as well as inside the community—is that an analogy suggesting reparations for *Christians* on the basis of *shared identity* can also provide the grounds for reparations for *others* on the basis of a *fundamental biblical ethical mandate*: the call to love one's neighbor, understood to include those outside the community. So what might this mean, by way of analogy, for the contemporary issue of reparations?

Reparations

For many people, there will no doubt be such a wide gap between the Paul-Philemon-Onesimus situation and the question of reparations for African Americans in our context that no connection can be made and no moral consequences discerned. I would suggest, however, that the approach of what Love Lazarus Sechrest calls "associative hermeneutics" can be helpful for us.[36] Associative hermeneutics does not say there is a one-to-one correspondence between a biblical moral matter and a contemporary one. Rather, an associative hermeneutic seeks to take both the ancient and the current context seriously, acknowledging both similarities and differences. Its goal is to bridge the gap between the two worlds while also recognizing the limits of all analogies—to hear the way the two situations "rhyme" without underestimating their differences, much less conflating them.

"Reparations" is a term with multiple interpretations. According to philosopher Olúfẹ́mi O. Táíwò, most understandings of reparations focus on the past or the present ("harm-repair" and "relationship-repair" perspectives), and the debate stalls for various reasons. Táíwò argues that the discussion should be future-oriented, concerned less about ancestors than about descendants. He calls reparations a "construction project," drawing on Martin Luther King Jr., among others, to argue for this constructive view of reparations.[37] "What if" he asks, "building the just world *was* reparations?"[38] And Táíwò looks beyond America to a global vision of justice, with a special focus on addressing climate change within our "global racial empire."

Táíwò's future orientation rhymes in a certain way with Paul's approach to the Philemon-Onesimus situation. Paul seeks a new beginning as he "re-positions" (to use Young's language) the characters in the drama that is unfolding. Paul does not focus on past injustices committed by Philemon but instead on the future implications of the "no longer" that has been effected by God's grace manifested in Onesimus's conversion. This way of framing the reparations question also means that we can see the larger revolution implied by Paul's letter as inevitably leading to a future in which institutions of slavery are challenged (especially, but not only, by Christians), brought down, and replaced with systems of justice and equality in which people are never property.

At the same time, Táíwò's future orientation needs to be supplemented by the concerns about the past and the present (concerns he does not deny) emphasized by other approaches to reparations, most notably the influential work of William Darity and Kirsten Mullen.[39] As we have seen, Paul's multivalent plea to Philemon would be both public and costly in multiple, practical ways, were he to follow through on Paul's requests. I would suggest that the proposal of Darity and Mullen also rhymes, though of course not precisely, with Paul's letter. The aim of reparations, in their view, is to end black–white disparity, especially economic disparity, and to "open the door" to a "new tomorrow."[40] Their understanding of reparations includes three primary elements: *acknowledgment* of the injustice, with apology; *redress*, either by restitution (preferred) or atonement; and *closure*, meaning "conciliation," or agreement to work together for equality in the future (all summarized with the acronym ARC).[41] This is a costly endeavor to be paid by the offending party—the government that legalized slavery and has permitted segregation and discrimination.

Paul's requests of Philemon bear some substantive resemblance to ARC:

- A: Although Paul, unlike Darity and Mullen, does not (explicitly) look back at past injustice, his objectives include Philemon's acknowledgment that Onesimus is a brother and that his continued enslavement would be unchristian and wrong.
- R: Paul also makes requests that are costly to Philemon; he is to make redress through liberation and its associated costs to him and benefits to Onesimus discussed above, including the likelihood of ongoing financial support. Together, these costs constitute a form of restitution. Furthermore, Philemon is to do so in a loving, cruciform manner—behavior similar to atonement.
- C: Finally, the changed situation of Christian brotherhood and missional collegiality is certainly a sign of closure, conciliation, and future cooperation that all must embrace.

Anything even approximating Darity and Mullen's multifaceted "Program of Black Reparations" of $14 trillion paid by the federal government—about $350,000 for each of the 40 million eligible recipients[42]—would be in an absolute way completely unrelated to the cost to one person named Philemon. But the differences do not invalidate the principle: a future that is just (or, that reflects the will of God) is dependent on correcting the past in a way that will necessarily be costly to some—those who have profited either directly or indirectly from the enslavement of others (the majority of American taxpayers; Philemon)—for the benefit of others, namely, those affected by slavery and its aftermath.

If Philemon complies with Paul's multifaceted request, he will not only be recognizing Onesimus's equal worth and giving Onesimus what he is due, but he will also be suffering an economic loss (i.e., his slave—Onesimus), with all that such a loss could entail. Moreover, he will experience both social costs and (most likely) financial costs after manumission. In essence, Philemon will be making reparations for treating a human being as property, even if it takes Onesimus's Christian conversion for that to be made absolutely clear. Because the letter is addressed to Philemon and the church that meets in his house, and because Philemon's decision must also be embodied "in the flesh" (publicly), this form of reparations will be a public matter.

On the Pauline principle of doing good both to the Christian household and to outsiders, Paul's plea to Onesimus can be legitimately understood, in our context, as an implicit call to treat all people with costly forms of justice that promote equality and mutuality. While there are many differences between the Onesimus-Philemon-Paul situation and the current context in the United States, there are sufficient parallels, or rhymes, to be stimulating for Christian praxis and advocacy regarding reparations.

At the same time, Christians cannot pretend that human beings can "remake the world" (Táíwò') or create a "new tomorrow" (Darity and Mullen). God has done that, and is doing that, in Christ by the power of the Spirit. Humans can at best bear witness to, and participate in, that aspect of the *missio Dei*.[43]

NOTES

1. This has been well documented. For interpretations of the letter by the White Rev. Charles Colcock Jones and by African Americans, especially Frederick Douglass, see Lisa M. Bowens, *African American Readings of Paul: Reception, Resistance, and Transformation* (Grand Rapids: Eerdmans, 2020), 114–17, 297.

2. All biblical quotes, unless otherwise indicated, are from the NRSVue.

3. Space permits interaction with very little of the scholarship on the letter and prevents me from making a full defense of my argument. My overall interpretation of the letter—arrived at independently—bears significant similarities (apart from his use of Positioning Theory) to Stephen E. Young, *Our Brother Beloved: Purpose and Community in Paul's Letter to Philemon* (Waco: Baylor University Press, 2021).

4. As co-author, Timothy is possibly Paul's scribe, but apart from the first verse, the letter is written in the first-person singular.

5. Expanded from Michael J. Gorman, *Apostle of the Crucified Lord: A Theological Introduction to Paul and His Letters*, 2nd ed. (Grand Rapids: Eerdmans, 2017), 530.

6. The following is adapted from Gorman, *Apostle*, 533–34.

7. That Paul, Onesimus, and Philemon (and all members of Christ's body) are slaves of the Lord Jesus is implicit in the honorific "Lord" and explicit elsewhere in the Pauline corpus (e.g., 1 Cor 7:22; Eph 6:6; cf. Rom 6:22).

8. "Positioning" is the term of Young, *Our Brother Beloved*.

9. N. T. Wright, *Paul and the Faithfulness of God* (Minneapolis: Fortress, 2013), 10–15.

10. Wright, *Paul and the Faithfulness of God*, 15.

11. Wright, *Paul and the Faithfulness of God*, 12 (see also 3–22). Young (*Our Beloved Brother*, esp. 140–47) also sees v. 17 as the key request but argues that it implies manumission.

12. See further Young, *Our Brother Beloved*, 123–40.

13. Scot McKnight, *The Letter to Philemon*, NICNT (Grand Rapids: Eerdmans, 2017), 96.

14. There are close parallels in Rom 7:5 ("living in the flesh") and 8:9: "But you are not in the flesh; you are in the Spirit" (8:9a). For Paul, being "in the flesh" is the antithesis of being "in the Spirit" or "in Christ."

15. McKnight, *Letter to Philemon*, 97. Surprisingly, Young (*Our Brother Beloved*, 139) also reads the phrase as referring to church and household.

16. Young, *Our Brother Beloved*, 181.

17. Sandra R. Joshel, *Slavery in the Roman World* (Cambridge: Cambridge University Press, 2020), 41.

18. McKnight, *Letter to Philemon*, 95.

19. Dennis E. Smith, *From Symposium to Banquet: The Banquet in the Early Christian World* (Minneapolis: Augsburg Fortress, 2003), 174–75 (with the Pauline churches specifically in mind).

20. Smith, *From Symposium to Banquet*, 11, 42, though there were some exceptions for women (see 43–44; 208–9). Referring to 1 Cor 14 (i.e., 14:30), Smith suggests that, like other larger banquets, early Christian meals may have involved sitting to accommodate more people (178).

21. Smith, *From Symposium to Banquet*, 175.

22. Young, *Our Brother Beloved*, 182.

23. Joshel, *Slavery*, 42.

24. Joshel, *Slavery*, 42.

25. Joshel, *Slavery*, 42.

26. Joshel, *Slavery*, 43–44,

27. Joshel, *Slavery*, 44–47. For exceptions, see 47.

28. Joshel, *Slavery*, 44.

29. Joshel, *Slavery*, 46.

30. Joshel, *Slavery*, 47.

31. For options, see, e.g., Young, *Our Brother Beloved*, 152–54.

32. Mary Ann Beavis, *The First Christian Slave: Onesimus in Context* (Eugene, OR: Cascade, 2021), 51. See also Young, *Our Brother Beloved*, 153–54.

33. This is reminiscent of Jesus's parable recorded in Matt 18:21–35.
34. I owe this suggestion to Michael Rhodes.
35. See my *Apostle*, 565–67; 603–6.
36. Love Lazarus Sechrest, *Race and Rhyme: Reading the New Testament* (Grand Rapids: Eerdmans, 2022). Sechrest sketches her basic approach in the book's first chapter. There are aspects of Sechrest's approach, when executed, with which I disagree. Nonetheless, I find the "associative" language and basic approach helpful, especially with respect to matters that at first appear so different from each other.
37. Olúfẹ́mi O. Táíwò, *Reconsidering Reparations* (New York: Oxford University Press, 2022); see esp. 69–103 for his basic view and 104–46 for his response to others.
38. Táíwò, *Reconsidering Reparations*, 3.
39. William A. Darity Jr. and A. Kirsten Mullen, *From Here to Equality: Reparations for Black Americans in the Twenty-First Century*, 2nd ed. (Chapel Hill: The University of North Carolina Press, 2022). Táíwò calls their work an example of harm repair (*Reconsidering Reparations*, 124–27, 131–32).
40. Darity and Mullen, *From Here to Equality*, 270; cf. xi–xii, 47, 219–36.
41. Darity and Mullen, *From Here to Equality*, 2–3.
42. Darity and Mullen, *From Here to Equality*, 256–70; cf. xi–xii.
43. I am grateful to Andy Johnson and Michael Rhodes for their feedback on a draft of this essay.

BIBLIOGRAPHY

Beavis, Mary Ann. *The First Christian Slave: Onesimus in Context*. Eugene, OR: Cascade, 2021.

Bowens, Lisa M. *African American Readings of Paul: Reception, Resistance, and Transformation*. Grand Rapids: Eerdmans, 2020.

Darity, William A., Jr., and A. Kirsten Mullen. *From Here to Equality: Reparations for Black Americans in the Twenty-First Century*. 2nd ed. Chapel Hill: The University of North Carolina Press, 2022.

Gorman, Michael J. *Apostle of the Crucified Lord: A Theological Introduction to Paul and His Letters*. 2nd ed. Grand Rapids: Eerdmans, 2017.

Joshel, Sandra R. *Slavery in the Roman World*. Cambridge: Cambridge University Press, 2020.

McKnight, Scot. *The Letter to Philemon*. NICNT. Grand Rapids: Eerdmans, 2017.

Smith, Dennis E. *From Symposium to Banquet: The Banquet in the Early Christian World*. Minneapolis: Augsburg Fortress, 2003.

Táíwò, Olúfẹ́mi O. *Reconsidering Reparations*. New York: Oxford University Press, 2022.

Wright, N. T. *Paul and the Faithfulness of God*. Minneapolis: Fortress, 2013.

Young, Stephen E. *Our Brother Beloved: Purpose and Community in Paul's Letter to Philemon*. Waco: Baylor University Press, 2021.

PART TWO

Reparations and Christian Theology

Chapter Nine

The Reparational God

Mark Labberton

THE CONVICTION AND CONTEXT

The conviction of this essay is that the theological question of reparations centers neither on the need for nor the possible legal, social, political, or economic legitimacy of reparations, but on the character and actions of the God depicted in the Bible. The theological case for reparations reflects the moral, ethical, and gracious character of God. People of Christian faith come to the issues of reparations because of who God is and how God acts. God is the most determinative and motivational center for the rationale for Christians to act and lead in reparation efforts.

By contrast, reparation debates in the United States typically center first and foremost on the context and nature of colonization and enslavement, and their historical and contemporary aftermath. While this essay argues that Christians ought to engage reparations based on their convictions about God, this American context remains essential for our wrestling with how to live out those convictions about God. Whether viewed in micro or macro detail, the horrors of colonization and enslavement still stir some of the deepest feelings of moral injustice and outrage in the history of the United States. For contemporary descendants of victims, who are often still victims themselves, the brutal wounds of colonization and enslavement are always current, never only past. To ask a White American if they would be willing to swap their social location for that of a Native American or an African American produces only one answer. That reaction alone speaks volumes about the existential burden carried today by the heirs of such historic wrongs.

Despite the burden of this daily reality, these horrific American narratives have been (and still are) buried, ignored, diminished, or rejected by government, institutions, schools, cultural practices, and public ritual. No surprise then that *The 1619 Report*, a study published by the *New York Times* in 2019, revealed how many Americans reject or deny the moral violations of slavery,[1] often partitioning them into the past, escaping, and refusing any contemporary implications at all. Some say, "That was that. Then was then. It doesn't help anybody to keep bringing up things that happened a long time ago." Others would end up in the same place but add that the Civil Rights Act of 1967 addressed "all that. Now it's time to get on with what is, not keep fighting over what was."

The ongoing, daily impact of injustice experienced by Indigenous people and African Americans today cannot be recounted enough, not because those impacts and injustices have failed to be reported, but because they have yet to be truly heard and believed by many in the dominant culture. There is a privileged audacity in any suggestion that four hundred years of cruel abuse and suffering in one's family can be lodged neatly "in the past." Such an assertion is another part of the extended, daily moral insult meted out personally and communally against the millions of victims' heirs in our nation.

"Reparations" in response to this context refers to a range of personal, institutional, or governmental acts that seek to redress, repair, and compensate victims and heirs for the unjust taking of life, family, dignity, time, labor, property, and hope—primarily in relation to the colonizing degradation and abuse of Indigenous people and of enslaved Africans in the United States. Debates about reparations grapple with questions like: In what ways are such matters still current? In what ways have they been addressed and/or "finished"? In what ways and for what reasons are these matters still open and needed? Who should respond and what responses are possible, appropriate, required? Why? These are vital issues.

A few steps of reappraisal and redress, apologies and payments, have been made by local, state, and federal bodies.[2] Given the mortal and moral violations involved, however, such responses can be seen, even at their best, as woefully lacking. The compound wounds of slavery continue to bleed. Individuals, institutions, and society in the United States have by no means reached any true "resolution." Why they might do so from a theological perspective is the burden of this book and this piece.

This essay focuses on the relationship between the nature of God as revealed in the Bible and the colonization of Indigenous peoples and the enslavement of African people, and the related contemporary consequences of such injustices. What we will find in the Bible will lead us to see God's reparational actions to be both: (a) material (in relation to specific wrongs done and corresponding reparations of persons and property); and (b) spiritual (in relation to the personal and corporate redemption, healing, restoration, and new life needed in light of the material wrongs). God's reparational embodiment of both are manifestations of God's character, grace, and justice.

A THEOLOGICAL FRAMEWORK

The primary assertion of this essay is not that the God of the Bible explicitly commands reparations in ways that would directly apply to the US context we are considering. Rather, the argument is a theological one: that the God made known through the scriptures—in relationship to Israel, and in the incarnation, death, and resurrection of Jesus Christ—reveals a God of reparational love, mercy, and justice. For Christians, this view of God thereby makes the reparations we are discussing a reflection of the God we worship, and Christian advocacy and support for reparations consistent with God's character of justice and mercy.

I am writing this at a time when reparations are under renewed discussion, animated for many by their Christian faith. In the minds and hearts of many of those who are stirred up by this engagement, there is no doubt a desire, maybe an assumption, that the God of Scripture, made known in Jesus Christ, is or should be reparational. The horrific injustices perpetrated against Indigenous people and enslaved Africans are so extreme, so public, and so multigenerational in their devastation, that reparations seem to be closer to a minimum, not a maximum, response within God's redemptive justice and healing. We are examining here whether such a view of God is actually found in the Bible.

The scriptures indicate that what is needed in the depths of all human sin, suffering, and injustice, including the ravages of slavery and colonialism, is redemption both from "sin" and "sins." To define this distinction, "sin" is the *pervasive condition* of human beings reflected in assumptions, attitudes, and structures of disobedience, disaffection, and distance toward God, i.e., a pervasive part of our human existence. "Sins" are *particular acts* or instantiations of "sin"—personal, communal, and structural (Rom 1–8). The latter is an outgrowth of the former.

What human beings need involves the deepest and most profound kind of deliverance or rescue, the gathering up of the diabolical and violating realities perpetrated against the innocent. Based on the varying voices and narratives within the Bible, God's redemption alone fully sees and names that there is no person, no family, no beauty, no love, no intimacy, no vulnerability, no sorrow that is crushed and destroyed by the evils of colonization and slavery which is unknown or outside God's grieving and redeeming love (Rom 8:31–39).

God's own pathos—loving anguish and suffering participation—with the embodied realities of humanity and of human beings is the seedbed from which potentialities of human communion with God and with one another arise. The narrative witness of the Hebrew scriptures and of the New Testament portray a picture of God's own character and being as one for whom there is no apparent limit of truth, compassion, or persistence in the work of re-creation. Again, this is the material and the spiritual redemption and reparation of God's love. Let's examine how this unfolds.

The relentlessness of God's pursuit of re-creation is what drives the theological arc of the Bible's story from Genesis through Revelation. The scriptures begin with the Creator speaking various realities into their existence and declaring each element "good" (Gen 1).[3] The Creator oversees and intends the well-being of the created order, and, on "the sixth day," calls into existence human beings, made after God's image for communion with God and with one another (Gen 1:26–2:9; 2:18–25). God declares the work of this sixth day to be "very good." God entrusts to these divine image-bearers—human beings—the stewardship needed for the well-being and thriving of all of creation (Gen 1:26).

Even when fallen human beings hide and are held accountable by God for their wrong-doing (Gen 3), God does not end human existence, nor sever God's relationship with humanity. Rather, in honor and dignity, God pursues Adam and Eve, calling to them, and rhetorically asking, "Where are you?" Adam names the couples' fear and nakedness, and the LORD confronts their disobedience and vehemently pronounces the consequences of their actions. Even judgment like this is an expression of the value and dignity of human beings, not a repudiation of their existence but of their behavior. Even as God decisively expels them from the garden, "the LORD God [nevertheless] made garments of skins for [Adam] and for his wife and clothed them" (Gen 3:21). We see here both material and the spiritual reparational aspects to God's actions.

The mounting crisis of human sin is relentless (Gen 4–5), as is God's sustaining grace. Even in the LORD's staggering judgment in the flood, God maintains a commitment to human freedom with protection and provision for Noah, his family, and the animals in and following the devastation (Gen 6–9). Following this tragedy, God makes a promise never to bring such cataclysm again, and seals that promise with the sign of the rainbow. In full view of this tragedy and horror, God promises never to repeat it. God then sets divine boundaries on the limits of punishment and consequences for wrong.

God provides a new human beginning in the new covenant with Abram and Sarai as the LORD promises to them, and to their heirs more numerous than all the stars in the sky, to make a people for himself, blessing them in order that they might be a redemptive blessing to the nations (Gen 12; 15). This is the next juncture of God's relentless love and mercy, the cornerstone that leads to God's highly consequential covenant with Moses (Ex 3) and Israel's deliverance from Egypt.

This next chapter of Yahweh's relentless love of Israel turns around Israel's multi-century enslavement in Egypt (Ex 1–14). God promises an end to this injustice and suffering and appoints Moses to confront Pharoah and to lead the liberation of God's people. With the LORD's liberation, after four hundred years of enslavement that enriched Egypt in countless ways, comes not only Israel's freedom from such oppression, but Yahweh's anticipation and admonition for Israel to ask for and receive gifts or reparations from their Egyptian oppressors (Ex 12:35–36). With such reparations, Israel receives riches from the Egyptians' hands as divine provision in recompense for the riches created by the slavery of the Israelites themselves (Ex 12:21–51). Still further, God's "promised land" provides gifts and blessings, which are in part meant to help Israel remember forever the suffering slavery from which Israel was delivered, as well as God's persistent provision and blessing. These reparational gifts reset Israel for its future in the promised land.

While this divine pathos is extended to all of Israel in the Exodus, it is also and specially attuned to the needs of Israel's widows, orphans, and poor. God's sensitivity and bias toward the most vulnerable shows up in the narrative of God's story with Israel, including the Law that orders the common life of Israel in intentional, preventative, and protective ways. The command and rhythm of weekly sabbath, the seven-year return of the land and property, and the fifty-year Jubilee, all presuppose that for Israel, ownership is God's alone, and that human stewardship and compassion limits human agency and ownership for the sake of those who suffer (Ex 21–24; Lev 25:20–22; Deut 15:1–3).

The Bible's portrait of human stewardship is not to be confused with ownership: "the land is mine," says the LORD (Lev 25:23). This subverts any human claims of ultimate dominance or control. If even the LORD embraces and practices sabbath, a suspension of the necessity of human labor for the sake of rest and well-being of all, so should Israel (cf. Deut 5:12–15). God's people are to live in God's reality, distinctive from the surrounding habits and practices of nations and tribes. Worship that acknowledges and embodies such distinct reality will reflect God's relentless love for the vulnerable, not our human proclivity for self-interest. This is why God sends prophets that excoriate Israel for practicing "as if" worship, that is, worship for their own benefit rather than worship that reflects the just and merciful *hesed* of the LORD (Is 58:2). All forms of sabbath are meant to check the limits of human greed and power, and to restore human relationships and practices of social and economic power and equity. In other words, Israel is to embody God's justice (Is 58:6–14).

Beyond Yahweh's covenant community, this portrait of the God of justice and mercy extends to surrounding people, tribes, and nations. While Yahweh is Israel's God, this never implies that the God of Israel is only God to and for Israel. Even in God's covenantal promise to Abraham, the blessings for Israel intend a far greater trajectory and impact—blessed to be a blessing (Gen 12:3). Faithful Israel is a divine instrument of blessing for the wider world affected by the example of God's blessings to Israel, and in turn, Israel's blessings beyond itself. In that sense, the Giver of the promises to Israel also remembers and cares about those beyond God's own community. To take but one example, in Leviticus 19:33–34, the LORD declares:

> When a foreigner resides among you in your land, do not mistreat them. The foreigner residing among you must be treated as your native-born. Love them as yourself, for you were foreigners in Egypt. I am the LORD your God (NIV11).

The Israelites are called to remember their suffering and deliverance when looking upon the extreme needs and vulnerabilities of others, even beyond Israel itself.

Israel typically but wrongly understands God's judgment to fall exclusively upon the enemies of Israel and not upon themselves. Those outside Israel who claim power, authority, or ownership over the people, the land, or the things of God are indeed those whom God judges most harshly. At the same time, however, when God's people are guilty of internal acts of over-reaching power and injustice against the most vulnerable within Israel (e.g., Is 58; Hos 1; Jer 1), God's judgment is emphatic here, as well (Mic 3).

God continues to redeem God's unjust people and wants them to make that work tangible and visible—both within Israel, and beyond. Israel is to be the embodiment of God's justice and shalom. God's vision is for the "mountain of the Lord" to be raised to the highest level, from which the reverberations of Israel's faithful life will even draw surrounding nations to it for its exemplary wisdom and justice (Mic 4). Again, we see the material and spiritual dimensions of God's reparational character and actions.

Israel displays the spiritual bankruptcy of professed worship that fails to live out its true worship in material ways—where Yahweh's Name, righteousness, justice, and faithfulness are violated—and this betrayal forms the core of the repeated scandal and tragedy pronounced by the prophets. The expectation of serious, even sacrificial efforts to serve the vulnerable and those who suffer from injustice is meant to be Israel's enactment of Yahweh's righteousness and justice. When instead Israel offers up festivals and façades of worship in place of showing justice to the vulnerable, Yahweh declares his hatred of the very things in which Israel takes pride. While the entirety of Isaiah 1 enunciates these themes, consider just verses 21–23:

> How the faithful city has become a whore!
> She that was full of justice, righteousness lodged in her—but now murderers!

Your silver has become dross, your wine is mixed with water.
Your princes are rebels and companions of thieves.
Everyone loves a bribe and runs after gifts.
They do not defend the orphan, and the widow's cause does not come before them.

In the New Testament witness, the God of Israel's redemption and reparations from Egypt is incarnate in Jesus Christ (Jn 1:1–18). On humanity's behalf, and without sin or obligation, Christ's self-offering brings God's redemption and reparations "to the Jew first and also the Greek" (Rom 1:16): spiritual and material reparations. This is a broadening and deepening enactment of reparations. Unlike perpetrators who may "owe" reparations, reparation and restoration comes from Jesus, a non-perpetrator, as free gifts, freely given. The Gospel texts are replete with stories of Jesus offering mercy, healing, forgiveness, restoration, and communion to those enslaved to circumstances and powers of many kinds (powers, spirits, diseases, fears, sins). The ontological, existential, and pragmatic powers of sin, of self, of families, of communities, of secular and religious power structures, and of spiritual forces pervasively dominate and destroy human lives. The exodus of Israel becomes the prototype for New Testament liberation and shalom—from bondage to freedom, from oppression to hope, from deprivation to reparation.

In a world of disordered power, the crisis of injustice by some of God's image-bearers against other image-bearers is pervasively present despite time or context. This injustice is intra-personal, inter-personal, and structural—sin and sins. Working out the complex and difficult implications of re-ordering power has always been among the most challenging aspects of living as God's people—for the welfare of Israel, for the Christian community, as well as for the welfare of life and cultures more broadly. The vocation of Israel in exile to "seek the welfare of the city (Babylon) where I have sent you into exile . . . for in its welfare, [Israel] will find [its] welfare" (Jer 29:7), is a radical vocation. When Jesus calls those in the reign of God to live out love toward "the other," the "offenders," and specially the "enemies" (Matt. 5:43–47), this message of extravagant, unexpectant, and undeserved love is set forth as the norm for life in the reign of God. Followers of Jesus follow an enemy-loving God and are called to do likewise.

No biblical text explicitly orders God's people to provide reparations. But the magnanimous narrative of God rescuing, redeeming, and abundantly providing "the land of milk and honey," witnesses to God's reparational character and purposes. This magnanimity on God's part is meant to be the defining grace that Israel receives and imitates. Though God's provision addresses the suffering and injustice of Israel's enslavement in Egypt, Israel does not itself remember or imitate such actions toward one another or toward the surrounding peoples. Israel's very costly failure to live God's life toward others, not least toward the most vulnerable, violates God's expectations of what God's reparational grace is meant to produce in the lives of those who have first received it (Isa 5:1–7; Matt 5:16). God's people are to love "because [God] first loved us" (1 Jn 4:19).

This seems to be the backdrop to the many times in Jesus's ministry when stinginess of heart and action causes Jesus to speak as sternly as he does. To receive great blessing but then fail to extend blessing to others eviscerates the meaning of grace (e.g., Matt 18:21–35; Lk 10:25–37). To receive generously and then fail to do likewise toward others scandalizes Jesus because it is that very problem that demonstrates the crisis within Israel, and potentially the crisis that the disciples may disappointingly reproduce.

God's character and actions call God's people to act reparationally toward others. It is not the explicit directive of scripture that calls God's people to do so, but the Spirit of the life of God. In the broader sense, the profound and pervasive ways and works of God, most tangibly in Jesus Christ, are the beacon for those seeking to live within the reign of God. God's incarnational redemption and reparation resolves our spiritual crisis and recreates our lives as the people of God, making it possible for the people of God to embody the fruit of God. In the midst of human and covenantal sin and brokenness, God came to recreate and restore, to repair and make whole, out of an abundance of loving grace. Grace is the theological, character-logical underpinning of reparations. Yes, in the context of injustices and inequities; yes, in empathy for the cost of undeserved suffering and pain; yes, for the benefit of the most violated and mistreated. But "for the sake of the joy that was set before him," Jesus "endured the cross" (Heb 12:2). In short, God's people are called to follow and imitate God's reparational love and mercy.

This approach, then, is not a claim that, as a theological matter, reparations ought to be understood primarily as a legal requirement, not least in a fallen world guided by secular requirements. Of course, a legal appeal has been, can, and should be presented on the grounds of and in response to immoral laws and practices that allowed the human slave trade to continue for four hundred years. It was violently wrong and those who suffered—and their heirs—are entitled to recompense. On the material and spiritual grounds of the human dignity of millions of abused and enslaved Africans—and tens of millions of their heirs—as well as the millions of Indigenous people, all of whom were violated over generations up to today, injustice can and must be addressed.

These brutalities, carried out for the sake of dramatic economic gain and the indulgence of others, catalyzed the wealth engine of the United States for centuries. While doing so, these practices meant Indigenous people and slaves incurred individual, familial, and collective suffering and loss. In addition, this meant not receiving anything in return for contributing to the economic engine they were making possible through their agonizing losses. The severe price was extracted from Indigenous people and African slaves on the front, the middle, and the back end of the brutalities against them.

Reparations to Israel were assumed and affirmed by God before, during, and after the Exodus—in the texts that recount the release of Israel from slavery, and in those texts that were to inform its ongoing life. These assumptions and affirmations underscore that the God of liberation is also the God of justice. God's character defines mercy and justice. The bounty of grace testifies to the unexpected generosity of God's vision that is not only about an "equalizing of debts," but an excessive provision. Israel is to live God's life in public, and therefore, Israel is commanded to remember continuously that just as God has liberated Israel from its slavery and provided reparations from Egypt, so Israel should order its own life and practices (see Deut 15:12–15).

As with Israel, the life, ministry, death, resurrection, ascension, and rule of Jesus Christ is not a mere "equalizing of debts" between humanity and God, but the supreme example of God's reparational abundance, far beyond the requirements of justice or mercy. Jesus's death is not a mere covering for humanity's sinful debt, but the gift of abundant life.

This theological argument for reparations is grounded in who we understand God to be in terms of both love and justice. This leads us to a strong theological defense of the legitimacy and urgency of reparations to mark the life of the people of God. For out of our human, economic, racial, and spiritual slavery to sinfulness, we have been rescued to manifest and demonstrate the reparational character of God in the world. God's Spirit dwells in us by grace as the living presence of God's reparational love in and for God's people, and through us to the world.

The theological argument is sustainable across generations of obligation, as the long arc of biblical redemption portrays. As long as the obligation of reparations has not been satisfied, the claim continues to be legitimate. Reparations are not an attempt to rewrite or deny history and its abuses, but to manifest a fundamental readiness to respond reparationally and sufficiently to peoples who have been and are abused by a society or nation. To be sure, the reality of abuse and injustice will linger both in exhaustion and in-exhaustibility. Reparations cannot ever fully heal and remove the devastating trail of abuse and injustice, whether psychologically, socially, economically, or otherwise.

What reparations would provide to Indigenous people and slave ancestors is the acknowledgment of true, consequential, tragic, and sustained wrong having been perpetrated unjustly; and a generous recompense by the government for the economic dimension of the tragic and profound losses entailed by those abuses, which resulted in wealth production that benefitted society while utterly excluding the laborers who made it possible.

These reparations would be an ethical response by a moral and just society. This essay, however, is a theological reflection on the reparational character and actions of the God of Scripture. Therefore, the argument here is that the ethical response for these reparations would be an expression of the consciences of people of Christian faith. Everything about God's people "being made new" would be needed for such a conscientious response to emerge from most Christians.

For many in US congregations, now is a time to consider the competing values in their lives, including what it means to let one's life be primarily ordered in light of the reign of Jesus Christ as Lord. In light of the reign of God, justice is not brought about only or even primarily by law and the rule of law, but by the God of grace and reparations. The theological case for reparations is not ultimately based on the law of God but on the moral, ethical, and gracious character of God. People of Christian faith come to the issues of reparations because of who God is. God's reparational character and actions are the most determinative and motivational center for the rationale and motivation for Christians to act and lead in reparation efforts.

Many writers and readers of this volume come to these issues because we are part of a society and nation that meted out intergenerational injustice, and therefore, we are beneficiaries of a nation built on that abuse. More broadly, life in the United States has been created by underlying abuse, and the residue is plainly evident in the lives of Indigenous people and in the descendants of chattel slaves. This reality has been obscured by a positive or neutral national narrative that extends the implications of the historic abuse by burying the reality of these horrific realities of conquest and slavery. What protracts so much of the racial injustice of our society is the lack of the scale of reckoning that appropriate reparations could address. Of course, whatever the sum would never be enough. Given all things. But appropriate reparations could be a serious turning point.

But again, I am arguing that it is God's character rather than our context that most fundamentally shapes a Christian approach to reparations. In a time when secularism in and outside the Christian community rejects and evacuates theological moral claims, the God-centeredness of this argument for reparations may make little or no sense. Neither does the life and ministry of Jesus. A theological logic, motivation, and frame undergirds an otherwise unlikely commitment to reparations. Jesus's reflection on his own ministry describes the primacy of this theological lens: "Very truly, I tell you, the Son can do nothing on his own, but only what he sees the Father doing; for whatever the Father does, the Son does likewise" (Jn 5:19).

Jesus, ever the social and spiritual realist, says at the end of the Sermon on the Mount, that actually doing the truth—rather than merely affirming or believing it—is what places our lives on the rock. Christians are called not only to believe that God is good and gracious but to show by our actions that God is good and gracious (Matt 7:24–27). That is the challenge that followers of Jesus in the United States need to grapple with, not least in relation to reparations. May Christians in the United States then receive and pass on God's generous and consequential blessing with lament, repentance, and hope.

NOTES

1. Adam Serwer, "The Fight Over the 1619 Project is Not About the Facts," *The Atlantic*, December 23, 2019, accessed May 18, 2023, https://www.theatlantic.com/ideas/archive/2019/12/historians-clash-1619-project/604093/

2. Adeel Hassan and Jack Healy, "America Has Tried Reparations Before. Here is How It Went," *New York Times,* June 19, 2019.

3. Unless noted otherwise, all biblical quotations are from the NRSV.

BIBLIOGRAPHY

Hassan, Adeel, and Jack Healy. "America Has Tried Reparations Before. Here is How It Went." *New York Times.* June 19, 2019.

Serwer, Adam, "The Fight Over the 1619 Project is Not About the Facts." *The Atlantic.* December 23, 2019. Accessed May 18, 2023. https://www.theatlantic.com/ideas/archive/2019/12/historians-clash-1619-project/604093/.

Chapter Ten

Myth, Belonging, and Reparative Ethics

A Theological and Pedagogical Account

Drew G. I. Hart

The stories we choose to prioritize through memory—and the habitus formed by our racialized identities—have already opened or restricted our ethical imagination regarding reparations for Black Americans. Faithfully remembering one particular Jewish body while learning about the bodily stories of those most harmed in our own society can transform ethical reasoning concerning the need for healing justice. If more of the church beyond Black people are going to awaken to the need for repair in response to the ongoing centuries of oppression African Americans have endured, telling truthful history and cultivating belonging will be necessary. So what follows is less of a direct argument for reparations, as it is a theo-ethical argument for the kind of knowing that is necessary to have conversations on reparations that move beyond our typical gridlocked positions.

The need to transfigure our ways of knowing when discussing reparations became especially evident to me while teaching a First Year Seminar course entitled "The Politics of Blackness" at Messiah University. The course explored Black history, theology, and other forms of intellectual thought, designed to introduce students to important themes in African American history, theology, and lived experience. A few years ago, students in this course read Ta-Nehisi Coates's *We Were Eight Years in Power*, and then *The Color of Money: Black Banks and the Racial Wealth Gap* by Mehrsa Baradaran.[1] Then they read my book, *Trouble I've Seen: Changing the Way the Church Views Racism*.[2] Students were exposed to the great writing prose of Coates, the history of the racial wealth gap in the United States, and anti-racist theology, along with other smaller readings, documentaries, and pursuing their own academic research.

Reading *The Color of Money* thoroughly unveiled the power of the students' inherited myths and sense of racial belonging to shape their ethical reasoning on reparations. When students began the book, even many of the students of color were a bit hesitant and tentative about the subject of reparations. But we moved through the history and its arguments, reading chapter by chapter. The book explores the racial wealth gap from the beginning of African enslavement up through the twenty-first century, exposing how a racially segregated economy, Jim Crow laws, housing policies, and a variety of other racist systems advantaged white people and excluded Black people, making it impossible for African Americans as a community to participate fully in the thriving economy. The central thread of the book follows the optimistic myth that Black banking, even under the conditions of discrimination described through African American history, could somehow generate wealth *ex nihilo*. Not so. *The Color of Money* offers a compelling historical account of the designed obstacles that prevent racial equity in regard to wealth. Students comprehended the main arguments and ideas as we moved through the text.

The end of *The Color of Money* organically ignites a conversation on reparations. The class spent the last day on the book discussing that very topic. After walking through a historical narrative of the racial wealth gap from slavery to our present day, there was a radical shift among the students. They could articulate (orally and in writing) a more nuanced history of how we got to where we are today, and this included their capacity to name various forms of economic oppression, discrimination, and exclusion that African Americans survived, and how they have never fully ended. Almost all of the students had changed their perspective on reparations by the end of the book. By filling in gaps in their understanding of our history (which many repeatedly mentioned they were never taught), *The Color of Money* provided a very different vantage point from which they reasoned through the ethics of reparations. Clearly the narratives we inherit and tell directly shape our ethical imagination.[3]

The one white male student in my class, however, had a different initial response to the call for reparations on the last day of discussing the book. When I first raised the question to the group, this student spoke up first. And he responded with his own follow-up question. He understood the harm that African Americans had undergone but wanted to know what impact reparations would have on white people, concerned that it would be unfair. The thrust of the question was, "How will reparations hurt white people today?" My heart sank as he posed his question. The particularly difficult part was that this was a student who had adequately articulated the history of oppression and economic exclusion Black people endured, and he demonstrated his comprehension in written assignments about how the past and ongoing obstacles continue to shape our present. And yet, his immediate and instinctive response to the question of reparations centered, first and foremost, around white people—while moving those whom he recognized as most harmed (Black people) to the margins of his concern. This (self-identifying Christian) student failed to love Black people concretely, prioritizing the minor discomforts of those who benefited from racial exploitation and exclusionary practices over the healing and repair of "those faces at the bottom of the well." To be fair, by the end of the class—after more robust conversation—he had mostly shifted his view on reparations. What I am highlighting at this moment is the impulse to prioritize, value, and identify with white people even when a more truthful story has begun to be understood. Narrative made new conversations possible, and yet, racial belonging can still restrict a person's ethical responsibility to love and seek healing for those who have been harmed.

With that observation, the impact of truthful narratives and racial belonging is especially noteworthy. On one hand, this teaching experience exposes the power of the inherited narratives that we live by. They help people make sense of the world, from their ethical reasoning to their response to present day challenges. On the other hand, telling more truthful stories must be accompanied with radical belonging that breaks the captivity of white identity. This radical belonging must be capable of cultivating a genuine, non-sentimental, love with and for others, leading to compassionate solidarity.[4]

This essay will briefly underline the importance of telling truthful stories about how we arrived at our present moment, it will reflect theologically on the significance of Christ's body broken and its potential to transfigure our ways of knowing, and it will encourage us to gesture one another toward a new belonging no longer bound by the apathy and white-centered imagination that white identity imposes. There will also be practical and pedagogical implications embedded throughout the essay. The argument will first explore a theology of story (gesturing toward new ways of belonging). Next, it will provide a brief sketch of some of the history (highlighting specific resources) that must be remembered to engage in ethical reasoning on reparations. While not comprehensive, these resources have assisted actual, self-identified (many white) Christian students in changing their perspectives. The essay will conclude by sharing some pedagogical tools that invite participants to vulnerably tell more truthful stories that subvert racial belonging bounded by whiteness—fostering the capability to love Black people through compassionate solidarity. Whether for disciples of Christ in a congregation or students in the classroom, the need to think theologically, pedagogically, and practically about historical harm and the ways racial belonging restricts and guides us are necessary when engaging in the ethical work of reparations.

A THEOLOGY OF STORY (AND BELONGING)

Myths are meaning-making stories that we live by. It is the church's responsibility to remember and interrogate our past and its relationship to the present faithfully. Scholars utilize the word *myth* differently than the way the word is used in everyday speech in English. Richard Hughes explains that "The English word *myth* derives from the Greek word *mythos*, which literally means 'story.' Contrary to colloquial usage, a myth is not a story that is patently untrue. Rather, a myth is a story that, whether true or false, helps us discern the meaning and purpose of our lives and, for that reason, speaks truth to those who embrace it."[5] Therefore, in that academic sense, the myths that we live by are important to the church because they enter into the domain of theology, which is concerned with providing a faithful lens for making sense of our world and realities of ultimate significance. Myths also intersect with our everyday and ordinary, concretely embodied lives, which is the terrain of discipleship. Through storytelling, selective forgetting and remembering, and sometimes outright nostalgia, denial, and propaganda, we inhabit myths that provide a basis for our moral imagination. Part of the church's vocation is to remember the story of the body of an executed and humiliated first-century Palestinian Jew, who lived under the control and domination of the Roman Empire, and, from that vantage point, to see all of life and our moral imagination anew.

No one is an empty slate as far as myths go. People are already living into powerful stories that make meaning for their lives and the world they inhabit. One of the most powerful forces that shapes meaning for others, even if subtly, is the myth of white supremacy. We are enveloped in the inertia of centuries of white supremacist mythmaking and ideology, which, in fact, has organized our society, our *a priori* moral sensibilities, and the stories we live by. Religious historian Richard Hughes discovered this as he studied the foundational national stories that orient the United States. While writing his first edition of *Myths America Lives By*, Hughes initially only identified the myths of a chosen nation, nature's nation, a Christian nation, a millennial nation, American capitalism, and an innocent nation. Through ongoing conversation and deeper research, however, he saw white supremacy as the overarching myth that the other myths seek to bolster and conceal.[6] He explains how pervasively the myth of white supremacy has shaped our society:

Assumptions of white supremacy are like the very air we breathe: they surround us, envelop us, and shape us, but do so in ways we seldom discern. Put another way, notions of white supremacy are so embedded into our common culture that most whites take them for granted, seldom reflecting on their pervasive presence or assessing them for what they are.[7]

As the church, we need a theology of myth and truth-telling capable of disrupting large segments of the body of Christ that are practicing selective memory and the erasure of the particular stories and experiences of the bodies crucified by the American imperial project. In remembering Christ crucified, we are invited to repent and yield our lives to God and love our neighbors, especially those on the underside of our willful forgetfulness. The church will not own its responsibility to seek repair and healing for centuries of harm unless it fixes its eyes at the "remainders of the property regime of racial slavery." This transformed optics must be done through the vantage point of the subjugated and executed body of Jesus with the goal of vulnerable remembering.[8] The renowned Catholic and womanist theologian, M. Shawn Copeland underscores that Jesus's crucifixion clashes with the desire to forget or respond in apathy: "For the Christian theologian, the suffering and death of the Jewish Jesus of Nazareth rebukes our amnesia, our forgetfulness of enslaved bodies, and our indifference to living black children, women, and men."[9] The church has been called to remember rather than forget Jesus's state-sanctioned execution under the power and authority of the Roman empire, and thereby we are called to remember all people throughout human history and in our present that have experienced similar subjugation and oppression.

One of the issues for Copeland is that our nation has intentionally and willfully repressed and erased from our nation's story the particular memories of African enslavement and subsequent forms of anti-Black oppression like Jim Crow and our current system of mass incarceration. Our capacity for faithful ethical reasoning and moral action is tied directly to the way we remember. Likewise, we lose the capacity to do justice and love mercy when forgetting atrocities against the most vulnerable is the foundation of our knowing. As Copeland explains, "By *forgetting* its past, a community or a nation relinquishes social and moral integrity and risks its cohesion and moral existence."[10]

Of course, no one remembers everything. Forgetting in general is a normal and necessary part of life. The church itself must forget or minimize some memories as part of course correcting and charting new directions toward faithful journeying with God. As Copeland suggests, however, "forgetting something as profoundly detrimental to humanity, to the body of Christ, as chattel slavery can wound the church."[11] Sometimes it is forgotten that memory itself undergoes a process of intentional selection. We don't remember everything, so certain events are prioritized and others are marginalized, consciously and unconsciously. And the opposite is true as well: forgetting involves willful deletion as well as "unintentional failures to notice" or prioritize some memories.[12] So the stories we tell and live by are a mirror of people's priorities and values.

"DO THIS TO REMEMBER ME"

Early Christians, including Paul, understood how significant careful and intentional remembering was for cultivating the ethics of the Church in the upside-down reign of Christ. For example, Paul selects and prioritizes the Eucharist around the Lord's table as essential for Christian memory:

> I received a tradition from the Lord, which I also handed on to you: on the night on which he was betrayed, the Lord Jesus took bread. After giving thanks, he broke it and said, "This is my body, which is for you; do this to remember me." He did the same thing with the cup, after they had eaten, saying, "This cup is the new covenant in my blood. Every time you drink it, do this to remember me." Every time you eat this bread and drink this cup, you broadcast the death of the Lord until he comes (1 Corinthians 11:24–26).[13]

For Paul, our capacity to reason is grounded in our remembering. Therefore, to address the harms and divisions of the Corinthian church, Paul reminds the gathered disciples of Jesus about the tradition of remembering Jesus's broken body and shed blood. The assumption is that the community will find new life while remembering the bodily experience of Jesus. Both bodies (the body of Jesus and the church) are to be Christ taking on flesh in the world. And the remembering ought to result in a reorganizing of the church's life, leading ultimately to the redistribution of food and resources for the poorer members being neglected by the wealthier members. It might be helpful to note that 1 Corinthians 1 rehearses the vital importance of preaching Christ crucified. And the reason isn't to undergird an atonement theology but to remind us of God's "power" and "wisdom" that is revealed through the vulnerable and weak body of Jesus. And in doing so disciples could learn to understand God's presence and activity from a different vantage point, because "God chose what the world considers weak to shame the strong. And God chose what the world considers low-class and low-life—what is considered to be nothing—to reduce what is considered to be something to nothing" (1 Cor. 1:27b-28). Remembering Jesus's crucified body ought to change how we view those erased from memory and considered to be nothing.

Copeland underscores that we must "situate a broken body at the center of Christian reality." For her, this is the meaning of "This is my body, which is given for you . . . This is my blood . . . which is shed for you."[14] The point is not that we become obsessed with death itself, which the church has too often been inclined to do, but that we understand all of creation anew from the social standpoint of the executed Messiah, along with all those whose "backs are against the wall" and whom the world considers socially, economically, and politically weak. Copeland rightly highlights the epistemological overlap of remembering Jesus and Black bodies simultaneously: "the memory of the Jewish Jesus and the memory of the black (chattel) body coalesce as memories of a past that is not over, that must be encountered and confronted in the here and now even as they open onto hope and future life."[15] This coalescing of memories undergirds a transfigured ethical imagination.

Womanist theologian Kelly Brown Douglas also calls us to the work of "anamnesis remembering" grounded in Jesus's command during the Last Supper. Douglas notes that the Greek word for remembrance being used is *anamnesis*, which "is about bringing the past together with the present. Jesus is calling his disciples to bring a memory of him into their present. Furthermore, this is to be an incarnate memory . . . 'This is my body.'" Douglas continues, "Jesus is symbolically connecting his incarnate reality to the call to remember. He is asking the disciples to re-embody him, that is his ministry, in their present. Simply put, Jesus's call is a charge to his disciples to embody in their present their memory of him. Such a remembering would reflect a movement from crucifying realities toward God's promised future," explains Douglas. This anamnesis remembering is vital if we are to transform our social memory and myths toward a knowing that is healing, reparative, and resurrecting.[16]

For Douglas, there are two dynamics to anamnesis remembering that are especially vital. First, anamnesis remembering breaks the cycle of knowing history primarily through prioritizing white narratives. And this concern moves beyond recounting the blatantly distorted memories and willful erasure of one community's participation and complicity in injustice. Just telling the truth of one's family and communal sins is not enough and doesn't lead to repentance and repair. A different standpoint is needed for telling our stories. Douglas contends that "Essentially, this kind of truth in retrieving uncomfortable parts of history, it reflects white telling. It is a white knowing of a white history."[17] In one way or another, white innocence is still maintained through these safe confessions, and no new way of comprehending our world is inaugurated. Anamnesis remembering is designed to change our lens for interpreting history. This happens by seeing the world from "the perspective of the crucified."[18] More explicitly, Douglas argues that "Anamnesis remembering must resurrect the subjugated knowledge of the Black oppressed. The knowledge they have imparted through narratives, testimony, song, prayers, poetry, and other artifacts of knowing needs to provide the prism, the very starting point, through which history is to be interrogated."[19] And we can extend this point to connect with Douglas's earlier concern about white stories. Speaking truthfully about white stories of participation and complicity in racial oppression, without trying to maintain white innocence, and seeking repair and restorative justice will have to be done through the interrogative lens of Black lived experience and knowing. So, the prioritized vantage point must be that of the crucified of the world because merely confessing the crucifiers' sins does not break ways of knowing grounded in racial belonging. White people are capable of entering into, and empathizing with, the stories of disproportionate suffering and resistance of Black people and allowing that to transfigure how they comprehend the world.

Anamnesis remembering, a second way of knowing, not only turns us to knowing through Black experience as we view and scrutinize our stories from the underside, but such transformed epistemological standpoints turn our attention to the agency of the oppressed. The dominant white view narrates Black people as passively and compliantly suffering under white oppression. The truth is that Black people "were in fact active agents in the fight for their freedom."[20] Black people could not restrict their moral imaginaries and myths to white ones which were incapable of producing faithful resistance. Rather, they strive toward freedom and justice with stories that have a trajectory and culmination in "a future in which the sacred humanity of each person is honored and respected."[21] History flowing from Black knowing and a transcendent vision of God's future created a Black imagination of a just society, which converted a story of a crucified people into "a resurrecting story" where white supremacy did not hold the final claim over their lives.[22] This is why it is essential to break from white epistemologies and myths, and enter Black ways of knowing from below. And it is also vital to narrate the resurrecting story of struggle for justice and dignity as a vital part of seeing our past and present when remembering Christ's own crucified body.

White supremacist myth and racial belonging are transfigured when we immerse our understanding of our stories in the baptismal waters, putting to death the viewpoint born from dominance and resurrecting a remembering that understands our past, present, and future through the prism of the crucified and resurrected Christ. A theology of remembering Christ crucified provides an ethic that is liberated from death-dealing myths and distorted boundaries of belonging. Christ's resurrected presence with oppressed people in their active fight for "justice" to "roll down like waters" (Amos 5:24) deepens our storytelling into the present and the future. This is why matters of memory and forgetting are not neutral concerns for the church but are vital practices that must yield to Christian discipleship. This is why

Copeland makes the point that "the memory of the suffering Jewish Jesus opens the church over and over again to other crucified victims in the past and present."[23] And that knowing is not just for the sake of knowing per se, but it provides the contours for our Christian responsibility to others. Just before making that point, Copeland suggests that "Restorative justice may be found only in taking up the ethical responsibility of memory and the ethical impossibility of forgetting."[24] The church must think theologically about the stories we tell and inhabit when exploring reparations. We won't have the epistemological standpoint from which we can discern our ethical responsibility without Christian ways of prioritizing our memory selection. Copeland also believes we must take responsibility for remembering slavery, rather than allowing denial and trivialization to define willful white forgetting. Unethical efforts to willfully forget the memory of those who suffer are visible in contemporary efforts to distort and then ban Critical Race Theory, while lumping every anti-racist effort under that umbrella to secure willful ignorance of Black narratives, viewpoints, and experiences for future generations.[25]

Remembering Christ Crucified in our present, while looking toward our future helps us not trivialize the past as is fashionable to do when people desire to skirt ethical responsibility for our present. This is all the more vital since our entire faith is grounded by immersing ourselves in the stories of Israel. For Copeland, "To trivialize chattel slavery is to fix it in the past as if the past is really past and, thus, bears no relation to the present or to the future."[26]

Of course, the past is not past but provides the floor on which the present stands. This is an essential part of our faith as well as a matter of fact for all human history. The stories we tell and the way they construct our racial belonging are matters of ultimate significance as we seek to understand our lives and the society we inhabit. And so, Douglas compels us to practice moral memory:

> Moral memory is nothing less than telling the truth about the past and one's relationship to it. Moral memory is not about exonerating ourselves for the past. Rather, it is taking responsibility for it. To have a moral memory is to recognize the past we carry within us, the past we want to carry within us, and the past we need to make right. Righting the past is about more than facile apologies or even guilty verdicts for killers of innocent black children. Rather, to right the past is to acknowledge the ways in which our systems, structures, and ways of being in society are a continuation of the myths, the narratives, the ideologies of the past and then to transform these present realities.[27]

FILLING IN THE GAPS OF OUR HISTORICAL ACCOUNTS

Most Americans have been miseducated about the history of the United States. Clearly, the era of racialized chattel slavery has been trivialized, domesticated, and marginalized in mainstream white ways of remembering our past. When it comes to challenging the dominant myths that skirt social responsibility for Black Americans, helping people better understand our post-slavery world, especially our twentieth century, is just as vital (if not more so). A tremendous gap exists in the prevailing historical narratives of most Americans for comprehending the role the twentieth century played in sustaining the racial wealth gap and other inequities. In the classroom, my students enter conversations under the impression that the twentieth century was solely about Black people sitting at the back of buses or drinking from segregated water fountains (primarily because that is how they are taught to understand that era). They then believe that Black people only started to resist under the leadership of Dr. King in the 1950s. Most know nothing of the major ways white supremacy and anti-Black racism organized society, providing ongoing advantages for white people while intentionally discriminating, excluding, and disadvantaging most Black people, resulting in their socio-economic deprivation. Furthermore, most Americans socialized by white epistemologies are clueless about the ongoing, contemporary manifestations of economic exclusion and disadvantage built into our twenty-first century society. For this reason, speaking truthfully about our history and present will require an open, curious, and vulnerable investigation into our national, regional, and local past, one that will question the prevalent narratives within which we operate by filling in the gaps and silences our myths seek to conceal.

There are plenty of books and documentaries available to help accomplish this goal. The following are non-theological resources that have helped students tell better stories that prioritize the Black lived experience in American history. Two powerful resources on the enslavement of African Americans are *The Half Has Never Been Told* by Edward Baptiste, which provides a closer look at the economics of American slavery and its direct implications for Black experience,[28] and *There Is a River* by Vincent Harding, which is a classic must-read that centers Black American resistance to slavery from the shores of Africa until the end of the Civil War.[29] Books such as *The Color of Law: A Forgotten History of How Our Government Segregated America* by Richard Rothstein,[30] and *The Condemnation of Blackness* by Khalil Gibran Muhammad,[31] aid in filling in some of the gaps of our post-Civil War society, especially beyond the South alone, which tends to function like a scapegoat for the rest of the nation that maintains white innocence. *The Color of Money: Black Banks and the Racial Wealth Gap*, by Mehrsa Baradaran, mentioned previously, and *From Here to Equality: Reparations for Black Americans in the Twenty-First Century*, by William A. Darity and A. Kirsten Mullen both provide powerful accounts from slavery to our present that can organically lead to conversations on economic reparations for Black Americans.[32] If someone were only reading one book (which is not recommended), I'd have them read one of these. Also noteworthy is Ta-Nehisi Coates's *We Were Eight Years in Power*, which includes "The Case for Reparations," a popular essay that helped elevate and bring more visibility to reparations movements in recent years.[33] There are also plenty of documentaries that aid in transfiguring our distorted national narratives. For example, *Slavery by Another Name* by Douglas Blackmon,[34] is not only an important book but also a provocative video documentary on racialized neo-slavery and Black codes (especially focusing on the convict leasing system) post-Civil War.

The distorted myths we live by that inevitably lead to apathy and disregard of Black people's well-being must be disrupted. This is done by immersing ourselves in conversations in which Black ways of perceiving our history can be received as a gift that transforms dominant perspectives. And dominant streams of theological reflection must be disrupted so we view Jesus's crucified body in such ways that it transfigures our lens of Black experiences. And we must also intentionally disrupt our myths through historical exploration via credible and responsibly researched resources that are courageous enough to investigate our silences, gaps, misconceptions, and nostalgia.

For many white—and some other non-Black—people, in particular, these truth-seeking narratives will re-narrate their relationships to the white dominant culture as a whole and foster an ethical dilemma where the option of reparations must be taken seriously and critically reflected upon. While people have inherited a narrative claiming that they thrive in the present because of the hard work of their grandparents, parents, as well as their own efforts, more truthful accounts will expose that their family's "hard work" was often supplemented by the exploitation of Black people's labor that built and bolstered the entire American economy at the cost of Black people. When people have inherited stories of Black people taking advantage of the welfare system, more truthful accounts expose that the early twentieth-century progressive era was a massive white welfare program (through Housing, Social Security, GI Bills, Credit systems, etc.) that helped to create the white middle class (which was practically non-existent before government intervention). At the same time, the government intentionally excluded Black people from these programs and further discriminated and oppressed entire Black neighborhoods through economic exclusion, redlining, education inequality, and political disenfranchisement, among other oppressive laws and policies. When people today inherit the myth that our present society has created an equal playing field, they must confront education funding inequities, mass incarceration systems, inadequate access to quality healthcare, housing, and food for disproportionate segments of the Black community, and ongoing evidence of steep racial bias and discrimination in access to capital, employment processes and wages, and a staggering racial wealth gap in our present that hasn't budged much in percentage since right after legalized chattel slavery ended in 1865.

Practically, whether in congregations, classrooms, or community groups, people will need to practice different ways of cultivating our stories and identities before, during, and after exploring or seeking reparations for Black Americans. There is a practical pedagogical tool I've used to disrupt white myths, white knowledge, and white belonging—which led to white resentment in response to the mere suggestion of Black American reparations. It is a collective communal history exercise that I've adapted after observing others do similar pedagogical exercises. The goal is for students to collectively narrate a "macro" look at the history of colonialism and white supremacy by recalling and attending to many particular historical events and figures (narrating oppression and resistance in the process). Beginning in January of 2022, I shifted from using a blackboard and instead assigned the four walls of the room to different eras, following the example I observed Regina Shand Stoltzfus and Tobin Miller Shearer use during a day long anti-racism seminar I hired them to lead.

Typically, I begin with the fifteenth century (which allows for a more global look at colonial conquest). For our sake, here, let's say we stipulate the following eras: 1400–1600; 1600–1865; 1865–1970; and the 1970s to the present. Each of the four walls in the room symbolize a time period. We discuss one period at a time. Students huddle in small groups and recall all the significant racial events they are aware of in that particular era. They are allowed to cheat and use Google, if they know nothing. After about ten minutes of group discussion, we come back together and imaginatively plot events along the wall. This is an oral exercise, so nothing needs to actually be written down. Then, we rinse and repeat with the next era, until we arrive at the present. (If we have less time, I assign each group an era and they work simultaneously on different time periods, before they write down their events on the board in timeline format.) The facilitator guides conversation of the group's takeaways between each era, and for the overall narrative of history shared at the end. The facilitator needs to be knowledgeable about Black history and capable of carefully guiding conversation and interjecting as needed without dominating the experience. This has worked in various settings to create cognitive dissonance with white myths and perspectives, and to open people up to curiosity about Black and other colonized experiences and stories that have been suppressed in mainstream education.

There are also two pedagogical frameworks that can supplement the work of transfiguring white myths and memory while also addressing white belonging. First, Elain Enns and Ched Myers have developed a Landlines, Bloodlines, and Songlines (LBS) framework. It is important to mention that their book, *Healing Haunted Histories,* is designed to address white settler/Indigenous stories and not explicitly white/Black stories. Still, it takes very little imagination to incorporate Black experience into the framework. *Healing Haunted Histories* invites readers to enfold their family and communal stories alongside and within the stories and experiences of the Indigenous, and the lands upon which white settlers now live. Telling family *landlines* (landed stories), *bloodlines* (intergenerational stories), and *songlines* (resistance stories and cultural resources) provides a multifaceted approach to seeking more truthful narratives, while transfiguring them as they become accountable to the stories of others.[35]

Second, David Evans and Tobin Miller Shearer have developed three pedagogical principles explicitly designed for confronting white identity.[36] For them, "Principled Dislocation" is about intentionally creating cognitive dissonance for students. "Supportive Relocation" encourages teachers to provide new pathways forward and new positive examples to be inspired by. Finally, there is "Sustained Cultivation," which takes seriously the ongoing community beyond the classroom that white students must be encouraged to seek out—so they do not "backslide" into white supremacist logics. These three pedagogical principles are worth exploring and reflecting on when engaging white people on the subject of reparations. The pedagogical principles take seriously the power of white racial identity and the restrictive social and moral imagination it cultivates, which make conversations on reparations difficult.

My pedagogical goal is not merely to engage students in any and every kind of generic theological discourse. Rather, we must discipline our memory and reasoning through the contours of the Jesus event as we learn about the harms of the past, and what the vocation of the church is in our present, so we can participate in the reparative justice of God.

CONCLUSION: A FRAMEWORK FOR STORYTELLING (AND BELONGING)

The goal of participating in God's reparative and restorative love and justice in the midst of ongoing global oppression and cycles of violence is that our penultimate efforts (present healing and liberation) are drawn into divine usefulness in ushering in God's dream for all creation. The history of the United States is inseparable from the forcible removal of Indigenous people from their ancestral lands, legacies of ongoing conquest and targeted colonization, and mass genocide and social erasure. And it is also directly tied to the legacies of stealing African people from their homeland, constructing a society of racial chattel enslavement to exploit labor, and organizing and embedding anti-Black oppression into the social, economic, political, and geographic fabric of our social systems. This essay adds to the chorus of voices calling for Black reparations by addressing how myth, memory, and racial belonging influence ethical reasoning when addressing reparations for Black people.

When one's habitus is formed around Lord's table sharing in the Eucharist, ingroup and outgroup boundaries of "us" and "them" are broken down, along with the myths that sustain those identities. At the heart of white identity is this problem of "us" and "them." White narratives and white ways of knowing coupled with white belonging will never cultivate a concrete love for Black people that transfigures our optics to see "us" and "them" blur. Subverting racial identity and belonging is necessary to practice radical compassion, solidarity, and reparative action.

Thinking theologically about Christ's broken body as the lens through which to understand Black experience—yielding every thought captive to the God that has chosen the things that are considered socially weak and disposable—is a necessary intervention that can disrupt cyclical white arguments rooted in the desire to maintain white innocence or reactively bolster white resentment because of perceived social status threats. Only in remembering Jesus as one who had his "back against the wall" under Roman imperial domination and who turns our orientation toward all the crucified of the world, and their sacred stories and perspectives, can we clear the table of white apathy and resentment. After this radical remembering from the underside, we can begin again with vulnerable, truth-seeking, healing-justice shaped conversations on reparations that reflect the ethical vocation found in Jesus Christ.

Myth and memory are often not explicitly addressed when talking about reparations for Black Americans. This must change. Critical theological reflections from the underside, especially ones that help us see our entire reality anew through Christ's broken body, are capable of unveiling broken Black bodies and the need for repair. Transfigured myths, memories, and belonging—drawn into God's dream for all of creation—inherently work to make right historic and ongoing wrongs, and to heal the wounds of our body politic. We need theological and biblical interventions, but we must couple them with historical resources and pedagogical best practices that lead to moral responsibility for historic wrongs that treat people made in the image of God as nonhuman commodities. Stories are powerful. In the United States and around the world, those who control myths shape society. New stories and memories are necessary. Only then will those who suppress, trivialize, or forget the lived stories from the underside ever transfigure their selective memory according to the priorities of God as revealed in Jesus Christ. Reparations requires remembering our past, present, and future through the lens of the body of the crucified and resurrected one so that crucifying forces are overcome with Jesus's present resurrecting power. Only people who engage in ethical reasoning emerging out of transfigured stories and expanded belonging can discern what to do in the aftermath of centuries of harm, disparities, and the disproportionate suffering caused by slavery, Jim Crow, and ongoing systemic advantaging and disadvantaging. To pursue reparations for Black Americans requires that we remember the story of one broken body, which makes us attentive to the need for healing the stories of all broken bodies.

NOTES

1. Ta-Nehisi Coates, Barbara M. Bachman, and Ben Grandgenett, *We Were Eight Years in Power: An American Tragedy* (New York: One World, 2018); Mehrsa Baradaran, *The Color of Money: Black Banks and the Racial Wealth Gap* (Cambridge, MA: The Belknap Press of Harvard University Press, 2017).

2. Drew G. I. Hart, *Trouble I've Seen: Changing the Way the Church Views Racism* (Harrisonburg, PA: Herald Press, 2016).

3. Baradaran, *The Color of Money.*

4. Richard T. Hughes, Robert N. Bellah, and Molefi Kete Asante, *Myths America Lives By: White Supremacy and the Stories That Give Us Meaning*, 2nd ed. (Urbana, IL: University of Illinois Press, 2018), 10.

5. Hughes, Bellah, and Asante, *Myths,* 10.

6. Hughes, Bellah, and Asante, *Myths.*

7. Hughes, Bellah, and Asante, *Myths,* 3.

8. M. Shawn Copeland, *Knowing Christ Crucified: The Witness of African American Religious Experience* (Maryknoll, NY: Orbis Books, 2018), 83.

9. Copeland, *Knowing Christ Crucified,* 84.

10. Copeland, *Knowing Christ Crucified,* 87.

11. Copeland, *Knowing Christ Crucified,* 88.

12. Copeland, *Knowing Christ Crucified,* 95–96.

13. All biblical citations are from the Common English Bible.

14. Copeland, *Knowing Christ Crucified,* 96–97.

15. Copeland, *Knowing Christ Crucified,* 97.

16. Kelly Brown Douglas, *Resurrection Hope: A Future Where Black Lives Matter* (Maryknoll, NY: Orbis Books, 2021), 150–51.

17. Douglas, *Resurrection Hope,* 151.

18. Douglas, *Resurrection Hope,* 152.

19. Douglas, *Resurrection Hope*, 153.
20. Douglas, *Resurrection Hope*, 155.
21. Douglas, *Resurrection Hope*, 157.
22. Douglas, *Resurrection Hope*, 158.
23. Copeland, *Knowing Christ Crucified*, 98.
24. Copeland, *Knowing Christ Crucified*, 97.
25. Copeland, *Knowing Christ Crucified*, 98.
26. Copeland, *Knowing Christ Crucified*, 98.
27. Kelly Brown Douglas, *Stand Your Ground: Black Bodies and the Justice of God* (Maryknoll, NY: Orbis Books, 2015), 221–22.
28. Edward E. Baptist, *The Half Has Never Been Told: Slavery and the Making of American Capitalism* (New York: Basic Books, 2014).
29. Vincent Harding, *There Is a River: The Black Struggle for Freedom in America* (New York: Harcourt Brace Jovanovich, 1981).
30. Richard Rothstein, *The Color of Law: A Forgotten History of How Our Government Segregated America*, First edition (New York: Liveright Publishing Corporation, a division of W.W. Norton & Company, 2017).
31. Khalil Gibran Muhammad, *The Condemnation of Blackness: Race, Crime, and the Making of Modern Urban America* (Cambridge, MA: Harvard University Press, 2010).
32. Baradaran, *The Color of Money*; William A. Darity Jr., and A. Kirsten Mullen, *From Here to Equality: Reparations for Black Americans in the Twenty-First Century* (Chapel Hill: The University of North Carolina Press, 2020).
33. Coates, Bachman, and Grandgenett, *We Were Eight Years in Power*.
34. Douglas A. Blackmon, *Slavery by Another Name: The Re-Enslavement of Black Americans from the Civil War to World War II* (New York: Doubleday, 2008).
35. Elaine Enns et al., *Healing Haunted Histories: A Settler Discipleship of Decolonization*, Center and Library for the Bible and Social Justice Series (Eugene, OR: Cascade Books, 2021).
36. David Evans and Tobin Miller Shearer, "A Principled Pedagogy for Religious Educators," *Religious Education* 112 (2017): 7–18.

BIBLIOGRAPHY

Alexander, Michelle. *The New Jim Crow: Mass Incarceration in the Age of Colorblindness*. New York, N.Y.; Jackson, TN.: New Press; Distributed by Perseus Distribution, 2012.

Allen, James. *Without Sanctuary: Lynching Photography in America*. Santa Fe, N.M.: Twin Palms, 2000.

Baptist, Edward E. *The Half Has Never Been Told: Slavery and the Making of American Capitalism*. New York: Basic Books, 2014.

Baradaran, Mehrsa. *The Color of Money: Black Banks and the Racial Wealth Gap*. Cambridge, MA: The Belknap Press of Harvard University Press, 2017.

Blackmon, Douglas A. *Slavery by Another Name: The Re-Enslavement of Black Americans from the Civil War to World War II.* New York: Doubleday, 2008.

Brown, Pete. *The Rise of Western Christendom: Triumph and Diversity, A.D. 200–1000.* Malden, MA: Blackwell Publishers, 2003.

———. *Through the Eye of a Needle: Wealth, the Fall of Rome, and the Making of Christianity in the West, 350–550 AD.* Princeton: Princeton University Press, 2012.

Coates, Ta-Nehisi, Barbara M. Bachman, and Ben Grandgenett. *We Were Eight Years in Power: An American Tragedy.* New York: One World, 2018.

Cone, James. *A Black Theology of Liberation.* Philadelphia: Lippincott, 1970.

———. *Black Theology and Black Power.* New York: Seabury Press, 1969.

———. *God of the Oppressed.* New York: Seabury Press, 1975.

———. *The Cross and the Lynching Tree.* Maryknoll, NY: Orbis Books, 2011.

Copeland, M. Shawn. *Knowing Christ Crucified: The Witness of African American Religious Experience.* Maryknoll, NY: Orbis Books, 2018.

Darity, William A., Jr., and A. Kirsten Mullen. *From Here to Equality: Reparations for Black Americans in the Twenty-First Century.* Chapel Hill: The University of North Carolina Press, 2020.

Douglas, Kelly Brown. *Resurrection Hope: A Future Where Black Lives Matter.* Maryknoll, NY: Orbis Books, 2021.

———. *Stand Your Ground: Black Bodies and the Justice of God.* Maryknoll, NY: Orbis Books, 2015.

———. *The Black Christ.* Maryknoll, N.Y.: Orbis, 1994.

Enns, Elaine, Ched Myers, June L. Lorenzo, and Harry Lafond. *Healing Haunted Histories: A Settler Discipleship of Decolonization.* Center and Library for the Bible and Social Justice Series. Eugene, OR: Cascade Books, 2021.

Evans, David, and Tobin Miller Shearer. "A Principled Pedagogy for Religious Educators," *Religious Education* 112 (2017): 7–18.

Floyd-Thomas, Stacey, Nancy Lynne Westfield, Juan M. Floyd-Thomas, Carol B. Duncan, and Stephen G. Ray. *Black Church Studies: An Introduction.* Nashville, TN: Abingdon Press, 2007.

Gonzalez, Antonio. *God's Reign and the End of Empires.* Miami: Convivium Press, 2012.

Gonzalez, Justo. *The Story of Christianity: Reformation to the Present Day.* San Francisco: Harper & Row, 1985.

———. *The Story of Christianity: The Early Church to the Dawn of the Reformation.* San Francisco: Harper & Row, 1984.

Harding, Vincent. *There Is a River: The Black Struggle for Freedom in America.* New York: Harcourt Brace Jovanovich, 1981.

Hart, Drew G. I. *Trouble I've Seen: Changing the Way the Church Views Racism.* Harrisonburg, PA: Herald Press, 2016.

Harvey, Paul. *Through the Storm, Through the Night: A History of African American Christianity.* Lanham, MD: Rowman & Littlefield Publishers, 2011.

Hughes, Richard T., Robert N. Bellah, and Molefi Kete Asante. *Myths America Lives by: White Supremacy and the Stories That Give Us Meaning.* 2nd ed. Urbana, IL: University of Illinois Press, 2018.

Johnson, Paul E. *African-American Christianity Essays in History*. Berkeley, CA: University of California Press, 1994.

Lui, Meizhu and United for a Fair Economy. *The Color of Wealth: The Story Behind the U.S. Racial Wealth Divide*. New York: New Press: Distributed by W.W. Norton, 2006.

Muhammad, Khalil Gibran. *The Condemnation of Blackness: Race, Crime, and the Making of Modern Urban America*. Cambridge, MA: Harvard University Press, 2010.

Rediker, Marcus. *The Slave Ship: A Human History*. Reprint. Penguin Books, 2008.

Rothstein, Richard. *The Color of Law: A Forgotten History of How Our Government Segregated America*. First edition. New York: Liveright Publishing Corporation, a division of W.W. Norton & Company, 2017.

Weaver, J. Denny. *The Nonviolent Atonement,* 2nd ed. Grand Rapids, MI: Eerdmans, 2011.

Chapter Eleven

"Don't Make Me Feel Guilty"

Why Penal Substitution Interferes with Reparations and Reconciliation

Mako A. Nagasawa

THE STARTING POINT: THABITI ANYABWILE'S CONCERN FOR WHITE SUPREMACY

On April 4, 2018, Thabiti Anyabwile, an African American pastor, posted on *The Gospel Coalition* website an article entitled, "We Await Repentance for Assassinating Dr. King."[1] April 4, 1968 was the day James Earl Ray assassinated Dr. King, which prompted Anyabwile to reflect on how a young white man could take cues from America's political leaders like George Wallace (whose presidential campaign Ray supported), the anti-Civil Rights movement, the FBI's anti-Civil Rights program COINTELPRO, local police brutality, and housing and schooling segregation. In October of 2019, Anyabwile argued that reparations are biblical and due to African Americans. But already, in his earlier article, Anyabwile had explicitly addressed the emotion of guilt, as if to head off a concern:

> I don't need all white people to feel guilty about the 1950s and 60s—especially those who weren't even alive. But I do need all of us to suspect that sin isn't done working its way through society. . . .
> My white neighbors and Christian brethren can start by at least saying their parents and grandparents and this country are complicit in *murdering* a man who *only preached love and justice.*
> If we're serious, then we can go on to commit ourselves to laying down our lives for others as Dr. King did. After all, the King of Kings said, "Greater

love has no one than this, that someone lay down his life for his friends" (John 15:13).[2]

Many white evangelical advocates of the theological doctrine of penal substitutionary atonement (PSA); however, read Anyabwile as if he were saying that they should "feel guilty" and be motivated by that guilt. They accused him of betraying a commitment to PSA, a specific and particular perspective regarding human redemption (to be unpacked below) that Anyabwile's critics understand as inseparable from the gospel itself. I found many reactions online to Anyabwile and will sample from them to show this consistent pattern.

On April 5, one day after Anyabwile posted his article, *Pulpit and Pen* tersely and acerbically rejected it, doing so *first and foremost* by waving the banner of penal substitutionary atonement. They called his article "anti-Gospel." They asserted that "he refused to acknowledge or apply the concepts of Christ's atoning death."[3]

That same day, Philip R. Johnson, Executive Director of Grace To You (a ministry featuring the teaching of John MacArthur), and founder and curator of The Spurgeon Archive online, tweeted a critical response.[4] Later, Johnson, a collegial acquaintance of Anyabwile, said, "If you want racial reconciliation, you have to start with forgiveness. Forgiveness is not the pinnacle we [are] appointed to climb. Forgiveness has to be the foundation we build from. If you want men and women to reconcile their long grievances with each other, you have to begin with forgiveness, you have to start with pardon."[5]

On April 13, Debbie Lynn Kespert at *The Outspoken TULIP* replied to Anyabwile in a post titled, "Are White Evangelicals Guilty of Assassinating Martin Luther King, Jr?"[6] Kespert assumed that she and Anyabwile shared in common a rootedness in penal substitutionary atonement. While polite, Kespert suggested that Thabiti Anyabwile had not truly repented, and was not truly an evangelical. By the logic of her PSA framing, Kespert suggested that Anyabwile could not be among "those evangelicals who are truly saved." Why? Because he "seems to ignore basic Gospel teaching." Anyabwile's demand was "unbiblical and unnecessarily divisive." His teaching was "opposed to the foundations of the Protestant Reformation." He did not seem to have "experienced complete forgiveness at the cross." How would that be evident to her? Because in Kespert's opinion, Anyabwile did not extend "complete forgiveness at the cross" to white evangelicals.

Ed Dingess, a former pastor with a doctorate in systematic theology,[7] has authored an extensive amount online adult Christian education content at Reformed Reasons. In March of 2019, Dingess wrote an article in *Reformation Charlotte* entitled "Thabiti Anyabwile, The Heretic."[8] Like the others, Dingess's argument proceeded straight from the perspective of penal substitutionary atonement:

> When we make demands on people and attach those demands to genuine faith, divine grace, and forgiveness in Christ, we corrupt and pervert the gospel. When we talk about past guilt to those who have genuine faith in Christ, we speak about something that does not actually exist if in fact the gospel is true. When you place guilt upon the forgiven, you arrogantly claim to undo what Christ has done. And to claim that the work of Christ can be undone is to reject the true essence of the gospel.

DEFINING TERMS

Many adherents of PSA demonstrate a reluctance, even inability, to process the emotion of guilt. Thus, they lack the posture necessary for reparations and restitution. I believe that this is not coincidental, but rather a deep emotional characteristic of spiritual formation under the penal substitution theory of atonement.[9]

The debate between Thabiti Anyabwile and his critics is noteworthy because all of the participants hold to PSA. Anyabwile pastors Anacostia River Church in Washington, DC. He is a member of, and frequent contributor at, The Gospel Coalition, which is a self-described

> fellowship of evangelical churches in the Reformed tradition deeply committed to renewing our faith in the gospel of Christ and to reforming our ministry practices to conform fully to the Scriptures . . .[10]

By referring to "the gospel of Christ," The Gospel Coalition means this:

> on the cross he canceled sin, propitiated God, and, by bearing the full penalty of our sins, reconciled to God all those who believe. . . . By his sacrifice, he bore in our stead the punishment due us for our sins, making a proper, real, and full satisfaction to God's justice on our behalf.[11]

In other words, The Gospel Coalition insists that God's justice is retributive and demands satisfaction. Jesus absorbed the retributive punishment God aimed at us, producing forgiveness for us. In short, Jesus took our guilt away. This PSA theology is important to highlight at the outset because Anyabwile's critics argued that he betrayed it. How? By calling for reparations and racial justice.

Before we address the question of reparations, I wish to compare and contrast penal substitutionary atonement with the most ancient atonement theology of the Christian movement, which, in order to contrast it more strongly with PSA, I will call medical substitutionary atonement (MSA). The second century Christian writer, Irenaeus of Lyons, called it "recapitulation,"[12] because Jesus had to "re-head up" the stories of Adam, Israel, and David, by taking upon himself the same fallen human nature and retelling their stories, but without making their mistakes. Irenaeus (AD 130–202) had an impressive and weighty pedigree and was the first major Christian theologian outside the New Testament to write anything close to a "systematic theology."[13] In this understanding, Jesus shared our fallen humanity so we could share in his healed humanity—thus, MSA. At his cross, Jesus was not the victim of the retributive justice of God, because God's justice is not retributive—a major difference from PSA. Rather, Jesus was the agent of the restorative justice of God, because he killed the corruption of sin within our human nature, which was killing us, and he rose with a restored, healed, Spirit-soaked human nature in his resurrection, which he shares with us by his Spirit. Jesus restored human nature in himself, so he could restore human nature in us, and in so doing, he restored human relationships to be how he always intended them from creation. This venerable understanding from the earliest Christians meshes rather seamlessly with the need for reparations, along with other aspects of restorative justice. While in PSA, Jesus solves the problem of guilt before divine retributive justice, in MSA, he solves the problem of human evil and brokenness first in himself and then in us by his Spirit. While in PSA, Jesus separates us in some sense from God's demand that we redress the past, in MSA, Jesus shares his renewed humanity with us precisely so that we can redress the past with God's help.

DON'T MAKE ME FEEL GUILTY

One clear and common objection to Anyabwile's call for reparations involves an allergic reaction to the feeling of guilt itself. Kespert, for example, asserts that while we can feel "sorrow over sin," we cannot "wallow in guilt." Hence, she objects, "Has Anyabwile forgotten that we can't atone for our own sins, much less the sins of our parents and grandparents?" Kespert says that true repentance is an experience of "complete forgiveness at the cross." She defines "forgiveness" as "forgiveness from God for all my wrong-doing, past, present, and future." So anything less diminishes what Jesus himself endured at the cross. If Kespert were to allow herself—or induce others—to feel guilt for something, and to be moved to act because of that guilt, she could only interpret herself as being unfaithful to PSA.

Anyabwile and his critics alike share critical assumptions entangled with PSA that I believe are misguided. First, they believe that guilt and love are *motivations*—and are thus psychological and emotional. Second, they further believe guilt and love are non-overlapping motivations. Third, they believe that genuine love proceeds out of a sense of being forgiven by God and others. Anyabwile thus proposes that his Christian readers be motivated by love, but in this framework, "love" without any "guilty feelings" limited his own argument. For him, guilt and love are emotional "motivations" that exclude one another.

In my understanding of scripture, however, love is not reducible to "a motivation," and can, in fact, encompass guilt in some ways. After all, the Psalmist combined the emotion of guilt with a fervent desire for God to change him, and the hope that he would (Ps 51). Jesus, too, said, "Blessed are those who mourn" (Matt 5:4)[14]—mourn their own sin, since the eight beatitudes (Matt 5:3–12) describe not eight people, but one person, who goes through a pattern of growth distilled from Old Testament piety and hope, including *mourning Israel's exile* (Isa 57:18; 61:1–2).[15] And Jesus honored Zacchaeus's commitment to pay restitution for theft (Luke 19:1–10) according to Jewish law (Ex 22:1–14; Num 5:5–10; 2 Sam 12:6), which by any account flowed out of his awareness of guilt. Paul wrote that love is a commitment and actions consistent with that commitment (e.g., 1 Cor 13), where guilt can actually serve a limited but constructive role (2 Cor 7; Acts 2:23, 36; Gal 2:11–14). Guilt, if it is "a motivation," is not, strictly speaking, mutually exclusive with love. Guilt can be a component of love. Guilt is the sharp awareness that one has not loved another person well. In emotionally healthy people, guilt transitions into an other-centered grief, a genuine lament in love, and a desire to grow in Christ for the sake of others.

People who advocate PSA often have a difficult time even with the implication that guilt might play a positive role in our ongoing Christian spiritual formation, and a constructive role in relationships. Having studied black and white evangelical attitudes regarding race in America, sociologists Michael O. Emerson and Christian Smith point out that forgiveness means "guilt-removal" and is sometimes considered, especially by white Christians, *to be reconciliation itself.*[16] Johnson, for instance, makes an emotional equivalence. Black people and white people, he says, simply have had "long grievances with each other." But we must ask: are black people and white people, broadly speaking, responsible for the same thing? For simply having emotions? Where do these "long grievances" come from? This lack of exploration of root causes and facts suggests that Johnson and other PSA advocates define "reconciliation" as a matter of rearranging thoughts and emotions, as opposed to rearranging power and wealth.

Thus, when Anyabwile makes them feel guilty, who is at fault? They believe *he* is. For Anyabwile to suggest that there is some guilt leftover for which white evangelicals as individual people must acknowledge, grapple with, and help undo raises very troubling emotions for them *about him*.

DON'T MAKE ME REPAIR HARM I'VE DONE

Significantly, Anyabwile did not even name the very real legal category of "possession of stolen property" as the most objectively relevant moral and legal issue. If you own stolen property, then you are guilty of that sin and you must atone by returning it. This is a personal question even before it is a systemic one. White Americans possess land stolen from Native Americans under the pretext of the "Doctrine of Discovery," along with wealth and land stolen from Black Americans under various other pretexts. Yet PSA advocates seem to have a hard time considering "possession of stolen property." Why? Because PSA requires that guilt for all a person's sin—past, present, and future—be entirely shifted over to the person of Christ. When an individual person receives the atoning work of Jesus, as understood in PSA, all of that person's guilt is considered to be taken away by Jesus. All of it. Otherwise, Jesus's work was not "complete." This produces a conundrum.

Penal substitutionary atonement creates difficulties, even if the racial injustices are just one generation old. How do you call a non-Christian white supremacist son of plantation owners, or plantation bankers, to repent and believe in Jesus? Is there anything that person needs to do in addition to cognitively believing in Jesus and praying "the sinner's prayer"? In PSA, the preacher says, "Christ paid for all your sins and took all your guilt; there is nothing you can do to affect your standing before God because Christ's work alone is finished." Is there something that the inheritor of ill-gotten gains must do in order to participate in atonement? The problem with PSA is not whether personal guilt can be present from one generation to the next. One generation's sin of theft creates the next generation's sin of possession of stolen property. The sins are related, but not identical. The problem involves the emotional relevance and permissibility in Christian ministry of ongoing objective guilt, subjective guilty feelings, and whether we should undo the guilt. The PSA advocate becomes conflicted at this very point.

Indeed, Anyabwile trod lightly when he said that we must "suspect that [this] sin isn't done." Indeed, Donald Trump was president at the time Anyabwile wrote his article, having been elected despite, or perhaps because of, his prejudicial actions,[17] campaign remarks,[18] and policy proposals.[19] In August 2017, Trump could not bring himself to condemn the white supremacist rally in Charlottesville, VA, instead saying, "There were fine people on both sides." Then in March 2018, one month before Anyabwile wrote, the *New York Times* spotlighted Trump's decision not to carry out the Fair

Housing Act, which was having the effect of reinvigorating and further ensconcing "decades of racial, ethnic and income segregation."[20] In addition, the US public was becoming increasingly aware of active and passive racial bias in real estate development and housing policies,[21] in the schooling system,[22] in the militarization of the police from the "War on Drugs,"[23] in the criminal justice system as a whole,[24] in medical care and healthcare in general,[25] in the erosion of labor rights and vision for domestic manufacturing which disproportionately impacted workers of color,[26] in the repeal of the 1965 Voting Rights Act ensuring voting rights at the state level,[27] and in the Republican Party's "Southern Strategy" since the time of Richard Nixon wherein GOP leaders curried the support of white segregationist Southern Democrats.[28] All this information was publicly available when Anyabwile wrote, though none of his critics addressed these points when he brought up reparations.

Michael Rhodes has written a very thoughtful article entitled "Should We Repent of Our Grandparents' Racism? Scripture on Intergenerational Sin."[29] Rhodes reminds us that one Israelite family could have acquired the land of another unjustly (Lev 25:14, 17), and sufficient time could have passed between one Jubilee year and the following one so that the next generations of those family members would now be facing each other. Do the adult children of one family owe reparations to the children of the other? Leviticus says yes, and Rhodes concludes:

> The Year of Jubilee teaches us that to continually refuse to repair our ancestors' sins is to make them our own. Leviticus then demands that we confess our own sins and the sins of our fathers [and mothers]. In our context, I suggest this means that I must confess my own white supremacy and the white supremacy of my ancestors. Why? Because the economic injustices perpetrated by the white community against the black community still benefit white households and still harm black households.

Lest we think that the movement from Moses to Jesus annuls this responsibility, recall that Jesus pointedly removed the supposition of the near-family relation in his parable of the Good Samaritan, and replaced it with its antithesis: a strained, hostile relation. The Samaritan paid the innkeeper to care for the needs of the near-dead Jewish man, paying his debt (Lk.10:35).

Consider the expectation that I pay others' debts, in both Moses's and Jesus's teaching. If I can play a part in doing that, then God calls me to do so. The principle we see at work here is that one person's active, not passive, obedience is substituted for another's, to fulfill the obligation that person had. This same principle is affirmed in medical substitutionary atonement, where Jesus substitutes his active, not passive, obedience for Israel's under the Sinai covenant, because they could not internalize God's commandments deeply enough so as to "circumcise your heart" (Deut 10:16) and thus cut away the corruption of sin from human nature.[30] God's requirement that I pay the debts of another flies in the face of the white evangelical tendency to say that each person's debts, even guilt, is their own problem.

Curiously, Kespert and Dingess both use Ezekiel 18 as a shield against needing to repair harm done by their parents and grandparents. While in Ezekiel 18, God says that He will not make children bear the punishment for their ancestors' sin,[31] God can still hold us responsible for undoing the damage of our ancestors' sins, especially if they were committed in the name of Jesus. Consider, for example, the Christian nationalism of the Puritans who claimed the land of Native Americans, or the Christian slaveholding plantations of the US South that claimed the lives of enslaved people of African heritage, or the construction of church buildings with slave labor. Dingess apparently wants to be released from certain relational obligations and perceives them as punishment. But he is incorrect.

Undoing damage, like liberating a relative from debt in the Jubilee Year, is not a punishment. It was considered an honor, for it made a person an imitator of God and helps us grow in the likeness of God. For when God says that He brought Israel out of the land of Egypt and into the garden land (Lev 25:38, 42, 55; Deut 15:15), He explains why He brings Israelites out of indebtedness and back to their family's portion of the garden land; He also explains why those Israelites who help deliver their brethren from indebtedness are imitators of God. Or, consider lesser analogies: On the basis of patriotism, I feel and believe strongly that I am indebted to pay for veterans' care through my taxes, even though I also feel and believe strongly that Vietnam, Afghanistan, Iraq, and the "War on Terror" were morally wrong. We can inherit debts without those debts being personal punishments. Clearly, though, penal substitutionary atonement fits comfortably into a framework where one can imagine that we have no relational obligations.

BUT WHAT IS FORGIVENESS, THEN? ATONEMENT AND COLOSSIANS 1

But what does it mean to be forgiven if not released from relational obligations and past history? How should we interpret Jesus's crucifixion and death? To support her case, Debbie Kespert reads Colossians 2:13–15 from the English Standard Version. The ESV says:

> And you, who were dead in your trespasses and the uncircumcision of your flesh, God made alive together with him, having forgiven us all our trespasses,

by canceling the record of debt that stood against us with its legal demands. This he set aside, nailing it to the cross. He disarmed the rulers and authorities and put them to open shame, by triumphing over them in him.

Doesn't that support PSA? No. Let me explain.

The letter to the Colossians first speaks of "forgiveness of sins" in terms of God transferring us from one domain to another (1:13–14). That is because the Greek word "*aphesin,*" translated into English in 1:14 as "forgiveness," properly means "dismissal of, remittance of, sending away, release from."[32] So in 1:14, Paul speaks of the dismissal and remittance of sin, the sending away of sin, and the release from sin.[33] Of course he does: For Christ is the only human being who has dismissed the corruption of sin from his own humanity, sent it away from himself, and released his human nature from it. No wonder that Paul in 1:14 speaks of us being transferred from one domain to another. That new domain is "in Christ," that is, within the one human being in whom we have redemption—in effect, the dismissal and sending away of sins. The "sins" spoken of refer to Adamic fallenness and all the things we have done individually to corrupt our human nature further (cf. Eph 4:17–19; Rom 1:21–32).

Paul then introduces Jesus as the author of both creation and new creation—as "firstborn of all creation" (1:15–17) and also "firstborn from the dead" (1:18–20). Jesus brings about a new creation "in himself" by his death and resurrection, bringing about, for the original but fallen creation, reconciliation and peace with God (Col 1:20, 22).

This is critical: God did not reconcile Himself to us. In Christ, God reconciled us, and specifically, human nature, to God's self. That is a major difference between penal and medical substitutionary atonement theories. In the former, God exhausts divine retributive justice to the satisfaction of the Father, leaving God at peace with us. In the latter, Jesus exhausts the strength of the corruption of sin which had been lodged like a disease in his human nature, leaving human nature at peace with God. In PSA, the atonement is located in God, and done by God. In MSA, the atonement is located in the human, and done in a partnership between God and the human.

Notice Paul's focus in Colossians on the change in the human. We "were formerly alienated and hostile in mind, in evil deeds" (1:21). "Yet," Paul explains, "he has now reconciled you in his body of flesh through death, in order to present you before him holy and blameless and beyond reproach—if indeed you continue in the faith firmly established and steadfast, and not shifting . . ." (1:22–23). In other words, where was the "hostility"? In God, toward us? No: The "hostility" was in us, toward God.

Jesus accomplished the remarkable transformation of the human. Jesus utterly exhausted and overcame the "hostility" to God within human nature and brought about within his resurrected human nature "peace" with God in place of "hostility," reconciliation with God in place of alienation. But how? In the PSA framework, we are supposed to feel emotional gratitude for Christ's work of removing our guilt, which is supposed to be the sufficient emotional motivation to produce holy living. Isn't that what Paul is talking about here? No.

To explain how Jesus transformed the human, Paul stresses the fact that Jesus had a "fleshly body" which he took "through death." When Paul uses the term "flesh" in these contexts, as he did in Romans 7:14–25, he means "the evil which indwells me" and "the corruption of sin within human nature." He does not simply mean "physical human matter." "Fleshly" has a specific Jewish meaning, and Paul demonstrates that he is thinking about this Jewish meaning later when he uses the visceral imagery of "the circumcision of Christ" (2:11). Paul is already thinking in Colossians 1:21–23 about the surgical, medical nature of Jesus's atoning work where "flesh" is cut away. Bodily circumcision of the male penis was expressed in the language of the cutting away of flesh (Gen 17), along with the shedding of blood, physically. But already in the Pentateuch, bodily circumcision had begun to serve as the conceptual anchor point for circumcision of the heart (Deut 10:16). Israel would not be able to actively obey God faithfully enough to cut away the corruption of sin from the human heart. Therefore, God declared that He would "circumcise their hearts" (Deut 30:6) in association with returning Israel from exile back into the fullness of garden life.

ATONEMENT AND CIRCUMCISION

Lest we think Paul haphazardly joins two "salvation motifs" together in a sloppy fashion, we must observe how the book of Genesis has already joined the practice of circumcision and an example about "death-to-life" in the story of Abraham and Sarah. God brought Abraham and Sarah from old age (Gen 12) to very old age (Gen 17). Abraham may have believed that God would bring about a son from his loins as early as Genesis 15:6. But Abraham and Sarah had to become absolutely "dead" reproductively, via old age, and still believe that God would do such a supernatural thing as bring forth life out of death. Then God gave the sign of circumcision to Abraham (Gen 17). They were both reproductively dead when Abraham was 100 and Sarah was 90, when their son Isaac was supernaturally born.

Not only that, Abraham and Sarah had to volitionally "die" to other reproductive alternatives that were sinful, or at least not available to the original Adam and Eve. First, Abraham apparently suspected that God made a promise to him and not Sarah, his wife (Gen 12:10–16); God had to cut off that thought from Abraham's mind by making clear that Abraham had to honor Sarah as his wife, not his sister (Gen 12:17–20). Second, Abraham thought he could do what any patriarch of his time could: name a male heir (Gen 15:1–3); God had to cut off that thought from Abraham's mind as well (Gen 15:4–6). Third, Sarah and Abraham thought that they could do what any matriarch and patriarch of their time could: use a surrogate mother, Hagar (Gen 16:1–17:18); God had to cut off that thought from them by insisting that Sarah would be the biological, not merely the legal, mother (Gen 17:19). God also wanted Sarah's trust and faith, too, not just her womb (Gen 18:13–15).

God wanted Abraham and Sarah to be a partial restoration of Adam and Eve, living again in a garden land. God called them to embody "new creation." They had to trust God the way Adam and Eve did not and have a son-heir the way Adam and Eve would have. Abraham, in particular, had to "die" to male privileges that his culture gave him—which is another way of saying that he had to partner with God in cutting off sinful attitudes and beliefs from himself. It is no wonder that God, after cutting off male privileges from Abraham, told Abraham to cut off a piece of physical flesh from his own penis (Gen 17). It was the sign of Abraham's quite active, not passive, obedience. For Abraham and Sarah, the whole purpose of entering biological and reproductive death was to cut sinful beliefs away from themselves.

Since circumcision already supplied the inner meaning of "death to life" and "new creation," it was appropriate that circumcision would continue to be associated with those things, culminating in the story of Jesus. God and Moses related "circumcision of the heart" to Israel's partnership with God. God called Israel to internalize His commands so as to cut away the corruption of sin itself (Deut 10:16), which would be the ultimate form of returning to the garden, and becoming God's true humanity, and therefore the highest form of "death to life" and "new creation." God's call on Israel to be God's people in God's garden land was marked by circumcision, the cutting away of sinful attitudes and the source of sin in each person. The sacrificial system also represented a circumcision—a cutting away of uncleanness.

Israel would not be able to fully cut away the corruption of sin, however, so God called them to hope for the day when God would do it, in some way, in tandem with bringing Israel back from exile into their garden land (Deut 30:6). Thus, Jesus was Israel's medical and surgical substitute, through his active obedience. He was the one true Israelite who lived faithfully unto the Father—what the Sinai covenant called for and represented—and brought about "circumcision of the heart" through his own death and resurrection. This is perfectly consonant thematically with Abraham and Sarah. Therefore, it is not at all haphazard for Paul to perceive that meaning too. Paul uses "circumcision of the heart" and Jesus's active, not passive, obedience, as the way to interpret Jesus's death and resurrection (Rom 2:28–29; 6:6; 8:3–4). In other words, "circumcision of the heart" is the inner meaning of Jesus's life, death, and resurrection. This is medical substitutionary atonement: Jesus shared in our fallen humanity, so that we might share in his healed humanity.

ATONEMENT AND COLOSSIANS 2

The PSA advocate will object: But isn't divine forgiveness based on Jesus exhausting God's wrath and bearing the punishment we deserved? No. And this question allows us to recognize deeper connections between the first and second chapters of Colossians.

"Circumcision of the heart" refers to the transformation of the human, first in Jesus himself and then in us. The fact that "the circumcision of Christ" in 2:11 can be read as what Christ himself did/experienced in himself (the subjective genitive) and also the work Christ does in us (the objective genitive case) is very significant.[34] I believe the ambiguity is intentional: The phrase contains both meanings. But the former meaning is built on the latter. The "circumcision of the heart" accomplished in us is built on the "circumcision of the heart" accomplished by Jesus in himself. Or, rather, our "circumcision of the heart" is our participation in the new humanity of Jesus, which he reproduces in us through a human journey much like his.

In fact, Paul says, we die and rise with Christ. Once again, this dying and rising in union with Christ is anchored in MSA, not PSA. In PSA, Jesus died instead of us, which is supposed to produce emotions of guilt-relief and then gratitude that God will not torture us infinitely. In MSA, Jesus died ahead of us, which is supposed to produce emotions of hope that we might be transformed in accordance with God who calls us into His goodness by putting to death the evil that is in us, lest we remain addicted to the corruption of sin unto eternity. In that case, the purifying and healing love of God itself will be received as torment, as a determined alcoholic will receive loving calls to be purified and healed of alcoholism as torment, or a deluded narcissist will hear loving calls to apologize as torment.[35] A determined racist will hear loving calls to repent as torment too.

Jesus's death was a death that was open to us in principle, and we are transformed by our participation in his death and resurrection by the Spirit, "through death," as Paul said in Colossians 1:22. Paul will continue expanding on our participation in Jesus's death (2:20) and resurrection (3:1) by referring to an old self and a new self that is being renewed (3:9–10). All this is rooted in an understanding of what Jesus did to his own human nature as an advance of what he does in ours. Jesus did not die instead of us; he died ahead of us.

How we interpret Jesus's death and resurrection is controlled by a first Jewish idiom—"circumcision of the heart" (Col 2:11–13; Deut 10:16; 30:6; Jer 4:4; Rom 2:28–29)—and then a second: the taking away of "the record of debt that stood against us" (Col 2:14 ESV). Protestants often equate this "record" (ESV) or "certificate" (NASB) or "handwriting" (NRSV) with the curses of the Sinai covenant. Our cultural experience probably contributes to that tendency: In the Latin-influenced West, law operates as an adversarial system, with legal standards menacing us from the outside. But Paul sees the Sinai covenant playing a positive role as a guide and tutor (Gal 3:24).

In Romans, Paul says that God gave the Sinai covenant to Israel as a spiritual health regimen to help Israel diagnose the disease of sin (Rom 7:7), even though the corruption of sin resisted it (Rom 7:8–13). The Sinai covenant nevertheless helped the Jewish people understand their inner struggle: there is an "I myself" that was indeed made in the image of God, which still "wants to do good" in joyful agreement with God, and also a parasitic disease, "the flesh," "the sin that dwells in me," "the evil present in me" which desires otherwise (Rom 7:14–25). The Sinai covenant was meant to help Israel; the corruption of sin within us opposed it; it was "weak" in its purpose (Rom 8:3). One must understand the disease in order better to hope for the cure, and the one who would be the cure, who would share himself with us by the Spirit, since the "requirement of the law" was in fact "circumcision of the heart" (Rom 8:3–4; 2:28–29). So the Sinai covenant per se was not actually against Israel or against humanity.

What was against us? The "sinful handwriting," which Jeremiah said was on our own hearts (Jer 17:1–10). The idiom of "writing on our hearts" was another Jewish idiom that referred to our human being—human becoming. God wanted Israel to be the "scribe of the heart." He wanted them to partner with Him by overwriting the script of sin which came from the fall, and instead write His commandments there (Deut 6:4–9; Prov 3:3; 7:3). Jeremiah deployed this image when he saw that the Israelites of his generation had written sinfulness so thoroughly into their hearts, it was indelible (Jer 17:1–10). Jeremiah used the image again, however, in the great prophetic passage about the new covenant: the Lord God will write his law on people's hearts, not on stone tablets (Jer 31:31–34; Heb 8:7–13). Paul deployed the idiom positively when he said that in Christ, the Holy Spirit writes on human hearts, not tablets of stone (2 Cor 3:2–3). God does not keep a scoresheet in His mind to keep track of when we have been naughty. The scoresheet, if there is one, is within human nature. What condition is your human nature? Mine?

Irenaeus of Lyons believed the "handwriting against us" referred to the script of sin on our hearts.[36] When the apostle Paul says that Jesus "nailed it to the cross," Irenaeus reads the word "it" as meaning the particular corruption of sin embedded in Jesus's human body. Notice how well this agrees and aligns with Paul's use of "fleshly body" in Colossians 1:22, anticipating "circumcision" of that "flesh" in Colossians 2:11–12 on the level of human nature. Because we die and rise with Jesus, in union with him, we share in his healed humanity, because he shared in our fallen humanity but overcame its fallenness.

Contrary to how some evangelicals read "the handwriting which was against us" in Colossians 2:14, Jesus certainly did not nail a copy of the Pentateuch or the Sinai covenant on the cross, and it is hard to imagine how we might stretch this language to reach that understanding metaphorically. Jesus nailed his human body there, and he left for dead the corruption of sin that was in his "fleshly body." At his death, Jesus crucified "the body of sin" (Rom 6:6). In his resurrection, he "became perfect" (Heb 5:7–9), and thus the source of our salvation from the corruption of sin, because he perfected faith (Heb 12:1–2).

The ESV translation, therefore, is misleading. In English, Colossians 2:11–15 should read like this instead. (I include parenthetical notes to a combination of the NASB and Irenaeus's commentary for clarity):

> And in him you were also circumcised [of the heart] with a circumcision [of the heart] made without hands, in the removal of the body of the flesh by the circumcision of Christ, having been buried with him in baptism, in which you were also raised up with him through faith in the working of God, who raised him from the dead. And when you were dead [that is, mortal] in your trespasses and the uncircumcision of your flesh [that is, your fallen humanity], He made you alive together with him, having [sent away from us] all our wrongdoings, having canceled the [internal] handwriting [note the singular "handwriting"] of the decrees, which was [note the singular] against us [that is, against our true image-of-God selves]; and he has taken it [note the singular; that is, the sinful handwriting in human nature] out of the way, having nailed it to the cross [through his own fleshly and mortal body]. When he disarmed the rulers and authorities, he made a public display of them, by triumphing over them through him.

CONCLUSION

Because I do not share the same theology of atonement with "Pulpit and Pen," Kespert, Johnson, and Dingess, or even Anyabwile himself, we have very different understandings of how to handle conversations about reparations and our emotional formation.

In Christian MSA, Jesus can and does work with some of our feelings of guilt. That is not to say that all of our guilty feelings are correct, or that guilt automatically guides us to the right action. But guilt can be a preliminary experience of genuine love. It is a stirring—a feeling that alerts us to our lack of love for other people, or God. For Jesus saves us from human evil and the corruption of sin in our humanity. Why not support reparations, then?

In PSA, people who try to make you feel guilty and then motivate you out of guilt are in the wrong, because they are diminishing the finished work of Christ who absorbed all your reasons for feeling guilty. This leads to the startling conclusion that anyone who tries to make you feel guilty *is theologically wrong.* PSA, therefore, serves as a tool of deflection. Evangelicals who are adamant about PSA enclose themselves in an emotional barrier through which facts and analysis do not break through. Evangelicals who hold to PSA and advocate for reparations seem to do so by loosening—as many people are eclectic—or reconfiguring their understanding of the relationship between atonement and our emotional development and Christian ethics.

To prove my point more broadly, a controlled study needs to be done. I do not know of a broad survey or study that measures support for and opposition to reparations while controlling for both race and Christian denomination/theology. I suspect, however, that white American Anabaptists[37] and Catholics,[38] who have understood atonement in a non-PSA framework—non-violent, restorative, healing, or penitential—are more favorable to reparations based on their greater support for other policies, such as criminal justice reform, social welfare policies, and economic policies, which also have a corrective impact on racial disparities. This is not to say that white American Anabaptists and Catholics have not been racially prejudiced or supported policies advancing white supremacy. But to the extent that they oppose reparations in particular, I doubt they would explain their opposition based on an understanding of atonement.

When I tweeted Anyabwile a longer blog post with these observations,[39] he generously read it and tweeted back, "I suspect you place too much at the foot of PSA when a simpler explanation would be 'whiteness.'" Thanking him for reading and replying, I nevertheless disagreed: "I do think there is now a considerable amount of evidence that PSA and the notion that divine justice is retributive lie behind evangelical whiteness. Catholic and Anabaptist whites don't act that way. Different theology." Sadly, he did not write back.

NOTES

1. Anyabwile Thabite, "We Await Repentance for Assassinating Dr. King," *The Gospel Coalition*, April 4, 2018, accessed May 18, 2023, https://www.thegospelcoalition.org/blogs/thabiti-anyabwile/await-repentance-assassinating-dr-king/.

2. Thabite, "Repentance for Assassinating."

3. News Division, "Thabiti Anyabwile Says All Whites Are Complicit in Murdering Martin Luther King, Jr." *Pulpit and Pen*, April 5, 2018, accessed May 18, 2023, https://pulpitandpen.org/2018/04/05/thabiti-anyabwile-says-whites-complicit-murdering-martin-luther-king-jr/.

4. https://twitter.com/Phil_Johnson_/status/981955880185880576. See also Philip R. Johnson, "Against Mission Drift," Pyromaniacs: Setting the World on Fire, February 11, 2016, accessed May 18, 2023, http://teampyro.blogspot.com/2016/02/against-mission-drift.html. Johnson linked to an earlier 2016 post critiquing Anyabwile, adding his evaluation of the MLK article: "Thabiti's 2nd-to-last paragraph is his most succinct statement of what I find objectionable about that blogpost."

5. Philip R. Johnson, "In Which I Make Some Concessions to Thabiti Anyabwile," *Romans45.org*, accessed May 19, 2023, http://www.romans45.org/misc/Thabiti.pdf. See also Johnson, Philip R. "Against Mission Drift," *Pyromaniacs: Setting the World on Fire*, February 11, 2016, accessed May 18, 2023, http://teampyro.blogspot.com/2016/02/against-mission-drift.html displays an earlier exchange between them.

6. Debbie Lynn Kespert, "Are White Evangelicals Guilty of Assassinating Martin Luther King, Jr?" *The Outspoken TULIP: Discipling Women for Discernment Through Doctrine*, April 13, 2018, accessed May 18, 2023, https://headstickdeb.com/2018/04/13/are-white-evangelicals-guilty-of-assassinating-martin-luther-king-jr/.

7. Ed Dingess, *Reformed Reasons*, accessed May 18, 2023, https://reformedreasons.com/.

8. Ed Dingess, "Thabiti Anyabwile, The Heretic," *Reformation Charlotte*, March 24, 2019, accessed May 18, 2023, https://reformationcharlotte.org/2019/03/24/thabiti-anyabwile-heretic/.

9. This chapter is a condensed version of a longer analysis, found at Mako A. Nagasawa, "Atonement Theories & Guilt, Part 2: 'Don't Make Me Feel Guilty': How Penal Substitution Interferes with Reparations and Reconciliation," *Anastasis Center*, February 2021, accessed May 18, 2023, https://www.anastasiscenterblog.org/atonement-emotional-development/atonement-theories-and-guilt-part-2.

10. The Gospel Coalition Council, "Preamble," *The Gospel Coalition*, accessed May 18, 2023, https://www.thegospelcoalition.org/about/foundation-documents/#preamble.

11. The Gospel Coalition Council, "Confessional Statement," *The Gospel Coalition*, accessed May 18, 2023, https://www.thegospelcoalition.org/about/foundation-documents/#confessional-statement. Tim Keller and D.A. Carson wrote booklets exploring the 14 points of the Confessional Statement.

12. Irenaeus of Lyons, *Against Heresies* 2.24.2; 3.18.7

13. According to tradition, Irenaeus was taught by Polycarp, bishop of Smyrna, which was a short distance from Colossae and Ephesus, where Paul had spent three years (Acts 20:31). Polycarp had in turn been taught by John, the writer of the Gospel and the Revelation, who had invested much time in Western Asia Minor.

14. Unless noted otherwise, biblical quotations are from the NASB.

15. Thomas C. Oden, general editor, *Ancient Christian Commentary on Scripture, New Testament 1A: Matthew 1–13* (Downers Grove, IL: InterVarsity Press, 2001), 81–82. Patristic commentators almost uniformly held this view.

16. Michael O. Emerson and Christian Smith, *Divided by Faith: Evangelical Religion and the Problem of Race in America* (Oxford: Oxford University Press, 2001).

17. Trump did not rent to black tenants at his family's real estate properties in compliance with the Fair Housing Act. See Jonathan Mahler and Steve Eder, "'No Vacancies' for Blacks: How Donald Trump Got His Start, and Was First Accused of Bias," *New York Times*, August 28, 2016, accessed May 18, 2023, https://www.nytimes.com/2016/08/28/us/politics/donald-trump-housing-race.html. Mahler and Eder write that despite narrowly avoiding a DOJ suit, "an investigation by The New York Times—drawing on decades-old files from the New York City Commission on Human Rights, internal Justice Department records, court documents and interviews with tenants, civil rights activists and prosecutors—uncovered a long history of racial bias at his family's properties, in New York and beyond." Trump also called for the Parkland Five to be administered the death penalty in 2014 and 2016 despite them being exonerated in 2002. See Dareh Gregorian, "Trump Digs In On Central Park 5: 'They Admitted Their Guilt,'" *NBC News*, June 18, 2019, accessed May 18, 2023, https://www.nbcnews.com/politics/donald-trump/trump-digs-central-park-5-they-admitted-their-guilt-n1019156.

18. Trump maintained the "birther" lie about President Obama; Trump also said that Judge Gonzalo Curiel could not properly do his job because of his Mexican heritage. See Nina Totenberg, "Who Is Judge Gonzalo Curiel, The Man Trump Attacked For His Mexican Ancestry?" *NPR*, June 7, 2016, May 18, 2023, https://www.npr.org/2016/06/07/481140881/who-is-judge-gonzalo-curiel-the-man-trump-attacked-for-his-mexican-ancestry.

19. Trump campaigned on a Muslim ban. He also ran on a racial dog-whistle "law and order" policy, which was undermined by his later use of border agents against innocent children, police against peaceful protestors, and then the violent insurrection on January 6, 2021. Finally, Trump proposed a US-Mexico border wall compared to other border policies like employer restrictions.

20. Glenn Thrush, "Under Ben Carson, HUD Scales Back Fair Housing Enforcement," *New York Times*, March 28, 2018, accessed May 18, 2023, https://www.nytimes.com/2018/03/28/us/ben-carson-hud-fair-housing-discrimination.html. The activity only increased over time. See Hailey Fuchs, "Trump Moves to Roll Back Obama Program Addressing Housing Discrimination," *New York Times*, July 23, 2020, accessed May 18, 2023, https://www.nytimes.com/2020/07/23/us/politics/trump-housing-discrimination-suburbs.html.

21. Just three days after Anyabwile published his post, the *NY Times*' Editorial Board wrote an op-ed about government policies that created ghettos. The Editorial Board, "America's Federally Financed Ghettos," *New York Times*, April 7, 2018, accessed May 18, 2023, https://www.nytimes.com/2018/04/07/opinion/sunday/americas-federally-financed-ghettos.html. See also Douglas Massey and Nancy Denton, *American Apartheid: Segregation and the Making of the Underclass* (Cambridge, MA: Harvard University Press, 1993); Richard Rothstein, *The Color of Law: A Forgotten History of How Our Government Segregated America* (New York, NY: Liveright, 2017); Gene Slater, *Freedom to Discriminate: How Realtors Conspired to Segregate Housing and Divide America* (Berkeley, CA: Heydey, 2021).

22. See Gary Orfield, "St Louis, School Desegregation and Housing Policy," *HTH Video*, June 11, 2009, accessed May 19, 2023, https://www.youtube.com/watch?v=33AgYGJvY8c; Richard Rothstein, "The Racial Achievement Gap, Segregated Schools, and Segregated Neighborhoods—A Constitutional Insult," *Economic Policy Institute*, November 12, 2014, accessed May 18, 2023, https://www.epi.org/publication/the-racial-achievement-gap-segregated-schools-and-segregated-neighborhoods-a-constitutional-insult/.

23. See Michelle Alexander, *The New Jim Crow: Mass Incarceration in the Age of Color-Blindness* (New York, NY: The New Press, 2012); Tom McKay, "One Troubling Statistic Shows Just How Racist America's Police Brutality Problem Is," *Mic*, August 18, 2014, accessed May 18, 2023, http://mic.com/articles/96452/one-troubling-statistic-shows-just-how-racist-america-s-police-brutality-problem-is; Michael Daly, "Ferguson Feeds Off the Poor: Three Warrants a Year Per Household," *Daily Beast*, August 22, 2014, accessed May 18, 2023, https://www.thedailybeast.com/ferguson-feeds-off-the-poor-three-warrants-a-year-per-household; Ben Swann, "The Root of Police Militarization," *Truth in Media*. December 10, 2014, accessed May 19, 2023, https://www.sott.net/article/290512-Truth-in-Media-The-Root-of-Police-Militarization; Christopher Moraff, "Will Private Money Take the Sting Out of Obama's Police Demilitarization?" *Next City*, May 26, 2015, accessed May 18, 2023, https://nextcity.org/daily/entry/private-money-police-foundations-obama-police-demilitarization.

24. See Michelle Alexander, *The New Jim Crow: Mass Incarceration in the Age of Color-Blindness* (New York, NY: The New Press, 2012); Bonnie Kristian, "Seven Reasons Police Brutality Is Systemic, Not Anecdotal," *The American Conservative*, July 2, 2014, accessed May 18, 2023, https://www.theamericanconservative.com/seven-reasons-police-brutality-is-systematic-not-anecdotal/.

25. The *Unnatural Causes* video series was published on YouTube in 2008. See also Clarence C. Gravlee, "How Race Becomes Biology: Embodiment of Social Inequality," *American Journal of Anthropology*, February 18, 2009; Elizabeth N. Chapman et al., "Physicians and Implicit Bias: How Doctors May Unwittingly Perpetuate Health Care Disparities," *Journal of General Internal Medicine*, November 2013, accessed May 18, 2023, https://www.ncbi.nlm.nih.gov/pmc/articles/PMC3797360/.

26. Ha-Joon Chang, *Bad Samaritans: The Myth of Free Trade and the Secret History of Capitalism* (New York, NY: Bloomsbury Publishing, December 2008); The Economist, "Place-Based Economic Policies as a Response to Populism," *The Economist*, December 15, 2016, accessed May 18, 2023, http://www.economist.com/news/finance-and-economics/21711882-orthodox-economics-distressingly-unhelpful-solving-problem-regional. With helpful comparison US vs. EU; noting history of land-grant universities.

27. See Jason Zengerle, "The New Racism: This is How the Civil Rights Movement Ends," *New Republic*, August 10, 2014, accessed May 18, 2023, http://www.newrepublic.com/article/119019/civil-rights-movement-going-reverse-alabama; Jim Rutenberg, "A Dream Undone: Inside the 50 Year Campaign to Roll Back the Voting Rights Act," *New York Times*, July 29, 2015, accessed May 18, 2023, http://www.nytimes.com/2015/07/29/magazine/voting-rights-act-dream-undone.html.

28. See Earle Black and Merle Black, *The Rise of Southern Republicans* (Cambridge, MA: Harvard University Press, 2003); Tommy Christopher, "RNC Chair Michael Steele Confesses to Race-Based Southern Strategy," *Mediaite*, April 23, 2010, accessed May 18, 2023, https://www.mediaite.com/tv/rnc-chair-michael-steele-confesses-to-race-based-southern-strategy/; Lawrence Freedman, "Reagan's Southern Strategy Gave Rise to the Tea Party," *Slate*, October 27, 2013, accessed May 18, 2023, http://www.salon.com/2013/10/27/reagans_southern_strategy_gave_rise_to_the_tea_party/.

29. Michael Rhodes, "Should We Repent of Our Grandparents' Racism? Scripture on Intergenerational Sin," *The Biblical Mind*, June 19, 2020, accessed May 18, 2023, https://hebraicthought.org/repenting-intergenerational-racist-ideology-scripture-intergenerational-sin/. Rhodes also gives examples of various patterns in scripture that are relevant to our discussion about Anyabwile's article:

Examples of intergenerational confession in scripture, where the present generation confesses their own sins and those of their ancestors (Neh 1:5; 9:2; Dan 9:4–6, 16), because God commanded them to do so (Lev 26:40).

Examples in scripture and modern life where people are influenced by the sins of their families or environments, and they need to repent of it, with that understanding (Jer 16:10–13; Rom 12:2).

Examples of how one generation inherits the obligation to repair the damage their forefathers and foremothers did (Lev 26:40–44), which continue in Jesus's teaching where there is no blood relation, or even causal relation to the suffering (Lk 10:25–37; 16:19–35).

30. For a fuller treatment of the reliance of Christian atonement theology on Jewish debt laws and the Jubilee debt repayment practices, see Mako Nagasawa, "Athanasius as Evangelist, Part 6: Jesus Paid the Debt to God, and Helps You Pay the Debt You Still Owe to God, Too," *The Anástasis Center Blog*, December 21, 2017, accessed May 18, 2023, https://www.anastasiscenterblog.org/athanasius-trinity-nicene-creed/post-6-jesus-helps-you-pay-your-debt-to-god.

31. Ezekiel 18 only had direct relevance to the Israelites under the Sinai covenant, where God's punishment on the Israelites took a specific form: exile. In the Sinai covenant, if the Israelites worshiped other gods or abased themselves before other kings, then God would give them what they wanted. God's consequences on Israel were therefore revelatory, not strictly retributive. God revealed externally what Israel was choosing internally. "Exile" was the umbrella term for that. In exile, Israel's vulnerability to the wild world of the Gentiles mirrored Adam and Eve's vulnerability to the wild creation. And that exile could last for "three to four generations" (Ex 20:5). In that sense, the second, third, and fourth generations from the initial rebellious parental generation would suffer an exile which they technically did not deserve. God's consequences were also restorative, not retributive, because God's goal was that the parents who had harmed their children's faith would participate in the undoing of that damage, a pattern that began in the book of Numbers when the first generation of Israelites failed to have faith, thus damaged the faith of the second generation, and had to help undo that damage. Ezekiel had the insight into, and hope for, the new covenant, which meant this dynamic would no longer be relevant. In the new covenant, each

person would be responsible for receiving the "new heart and new spirit" (Ezk 11:18; 36:26–36) that God provides.

32. See Thayer's Greek Lexicon, s.v. "ἄφεσις." The KJV, for instance, translates "aphesis" as "remission" or "at liberty" or "deliverance" in Matthew 26:28; Mark 1:4; Luke 1:77; 3:3; 4:18; 24:47; Acts 2:38; 10:43; Hebrews 9:22; 10:18.

33. I am aware that there is debate among biblical scholars as to whether the Paul who wrote Romans, Galatians, and 1 Corinthians also wrote Colossians. Still, the question is not crucial for my argument, and so I will for the sake of convenience refer throughout to the author of Colossians as Paul.

34. For recent discussion about the subjective and objective genitive possibilities involved in translating the phrase *pistis Christou*, see Michael F. Bird and Preston M. Sprinkle, eds., *The Faith of Jesus Christ: Exegetical, Biblical, and Theological Studies* (Colorado Springs, CO: Paternoster, 2009).

35. For more on this early Christian understanding, see the resources on this page: www.anastasiscenter.org/gods-goodness-fire.

36. Irenaeus of Lyons, *Against Heresies* 5.17.3. Irenaeus even joined the quote about the handwriting with the language about us owing God a debt. Irenaeus means that since the fall, each human being owes God the debt of our human nature, as God calls us to return our human nature to in a purified and perfected state—something which we can only do with Jesus, by his Spirit.

37. Anabaptist authors who advocate for restorative justice policies and a non-penal atonement include Christopher D. Marshall, *Beyond Retribution: A New Testament Vision for Justice, Crime and Punishment* (Grand Rapids, MI: Eerdmans, 2001); Darrin W. Snyder-Belousek, *Atonement, Justice, and Peace: The Message of the Cross and the Mission of the Church* (Grand Rapids, MI: Eerdmans, 2011); Ted Grimsrud, "Healing Justice," *Peace Theology*, June 28, 2015, accessed May 18, 2023, https://peacetheology.net/2016/12/20/healing-justice-2/.

38. Stephen Pope identifies various Catholics, who generally support Thomas Aquinas's penitential model of atonement, who support restorative justice efforts:

Many dioceses and archdioceses, Catholic Charities, Catholic Relief Services, Caritas Internationalis, the Community of Sant'Egidio, and the Society of Jesus, both the Jesuit Refugee Services and particular provinces throughout the world. Academic research on restorative justice has been sponsored by the University of Notre Dame's Kroc Institute for International Peace Studies and Boston College's Center for Human Rights and International Justice. In November of 2000, the US Catholic Bishops issued a strong endorsement of the restorative justice movement in a statement entitled, "Responsibility, Rehabilitation, and Restoration: A Catholic Perspective on Crime and Criminal Justice." This document addressed urgent pastoral needs, advanced a broad religious vision, invoked practical moral standards, and advocated substantial reform of the criminal justice system by drawing on recent Catholic social teaching regarding the interdependence of peace, justice, and reconciliation. (Stephen Pope, "Restorative Justice as a Prophetic Path to Peace," *CTSA Proceedings* 65 [2010]: 20).

39. https://twitter.com/mako_nagasawa/status/1496242226430726159. The longer blog post is found at Mako Nagasawa, "Atonement Theories & Guilt, Part 2: 'Don't

Make Me Feel Guilty': How Penal Substitution Interferes With Reparations and Reconciliation," *The Anástasis Center Blog*, February 21, 2022, accessed May 18, 2023, https://www.anastasiscenterblog.org/atonement-emotional-development/atonement-theories-and-guilt-part-2.

BIBLIOGRAPHY

Alexander, Michelle. *The New Jim Crow: Mass Incarceration in the Age of Color-Blindness*. New York, NY: The New Press, 2012.

Anyabwile, Thabite. "We Await Repentance for Assassinating Dr. King." *The Gospel Coalition*. April 4, 2018. Accessed on May 18, 2023. https://www.thegospelcoalition.org/blogs/thabiti-anyabwile/await-repentance-assassinating-dr-king/.

Bird, Michael F. and Preston M. Sprinkle, editors, *The Faith of Jesus Christ: Exegetical, Biblical, and Theological Studies*. Colorado Springs, CO: Paternoster, 2009.

Black, Earle and Merle Black. *The Rise of Southern Republicans*. Cambridge, MA: Harvard University Press, September 2003.

Chang, Ha-Joon. *Bad Samaritans: The Myth of Free Trade and the Secret History of Capitalism*. New York, NY: Bloomsbury Publishing, December 2008.

Chapman, Elizabeth N. et al. "Physicians and Implicit Bias: How Doctors May Unwittingly Perpetuate Health Care Disparities." *Journal of General Internal Medicine*. November 2013. Accessed May 18, 2023. https://www.ncbi.nlm.nih.gov/pmc/articles/PMC3797360/.

Christopher, Tommy. "RNC Chair Michael Steele Confesses to Race-Based Southern Strategy." *Mediaite*. April 23, 2010. Accessed May 18, 2023. https://www.mediaite.com/tv/rnc-chair-michael-steele-confesses-to-race-based-southern-strategy/.

The Economist. "Place-Based Economic Policies as a Response to Populism." *The Economist*. December 15, 2016. Accessed May 18, 2023. http://www.economist.com/news/finance-and-economics/21711882-orthodox-economics-distressingly-unhelpful-solving-problem-regional.

Daly, Michael. "Ferguson Feeds Off the Poor: Three Warrants a Year Per Household." *Daily Beast*. August 22, 2014. Accessed May 18, 2023. https://www.thedailybeast.com/ferguson-feeds-off-the-poor-three-warrants-a-year-per-household.

Dingess, Ed. *Reformed Reasons*. https://reformedreasons.com/. Accessed February 21, 2022.

———. "Thabiti Anyabwile, The Heretic." *Reformation Charlotte*. March 24, 2019. Accessed May 18, 2023. https://reformationcharlotte.org/2019/03/24/thabiti-anyabwile-heretic/.

The Editorial Board. "America's Federally Financed Ghettos." *New York Times*. April 7, 2018. Accessed May 18, 2023. https://www.nytimes.com/2018/04/07/opinion/sunday/americas-federally-financed-ghettos.html.

Emerson, Michael O. and Christian Smith, *Divided by Faith: Evangelical Religion and the Problem of Race in America*. Oxford: Oxford University Press, 2001.

Freedman, Lawrence. "Reagan's Southern Strategy Gave Rise to the Tea Party." *Slate*. October 27, 2013. Accessed May 18, 2023. http://www.salon.com/2013/10/27/reagans_southern_strategy_gave_rise_to_the_tea_party/.

Fuchs, Hailey. "Trump Moves to Roll Back Obama Program Addressing Housing Discrimination." *New York Times*. July 23, 2020. Accessed May 18, 2023. https://www.nytimes.com/2020/07/23/us/politics/trump-housing-discrimination-suburbs.html.

The Gospel Coalition Council. "Confessional Statement." *The Gospel Coalition*. Last accessed February 21, 2022. Accessed May 18, 2023. https://www.thegospelcoalition.org/about/foundation-documents/#confessional-statement.

———. "Preamble." *The Gospel Coalition*. Accessed February 21, 2022. https://www.thegospelcoalition.org/about/foundation-documents/#preamble.

Gravlee, Clarence C. "How Race Becomes Biology: Embodiment of Social Inequality." *American Journal of Anthropology*, February 18, 2009.

Gregorian, Dareh. "Trump Digs In On Central Park 5: 'They Admitted Their Guilt.'" *NBC News*. June 18, 2019. Accessed May 18, 2023. https://www.nbcnews.com/politics/donald-trump/trump-digs-central-park-5-they-admitted-their-guilt-n1019156.

Grimsrud, Ted. "Healing Justice." *Peace Theology*. June 28, 2015. Accessed February 21, 2022. https://peacetheology.net/2016/12/20/healing-justice-2/.

Irenaeus of Lyons, *Against Heresies*.

Johnson, Philip R. "Against Mission Drift." *Pyromaniacs: Setting the World on Fire*. February 11, 2016. Accessed May 18, 2023. http://teampyro.blogspot.com/2016/02/against-mission-drift.html.

———. "In Which I Make Some Concessions to Thabiti Anyabwile." *Romans45.org*. Accessed May 18, 2023. http://www.romans45.org/misc/Thabiti.pdf.

———. *Twitter*. April 5, 2018. Accessed May 19, 2023. https://twitter.com/Phil_Johnson_/status/981955880185880576.

Kespert, Debbie Lynn. "Are White Evangelicals Guilty of Assassinating Martin Luther King, Jr?" *The Outspoken TULIP: Discipling Women for Discernment Through Doctrine*. April 13, 2018. Accessed May 18, 2023. https://headstickdeb.com/2018/04/13/are-white-evangelicals-guilty-of-assassinating-martin-luther-king-jr/.

Kristian, Bonnie. "Seven Reasons Police Brutality Is Systemic, Not Anecdotal." *The American Conservative*. July 2, 2014. Accessed May 18, 2023. https://www.theamericanconservative.com/seven-reasons-police-brutality-is-systematic-not-anecdotal/.

Mahler, Jonathan and Steve Eder. "'No Vacancies' for Blacks: How Donald Trump Got His Start, and Was First Accused of Bias." *New York Times*. August 28, 2016. Accessed May 18, 2023. https://www.nytimes.com/2016/08/28/us/politics/donald-trump-housing-race.html.

Marshall, Christopher D. *Beyond Retribution: A New Testament Vision for Justice, Crime and Punishment*. Grand Rapids, MI: Eerdmans, 2001.

Massey, Douglas and Nancy Denton. *American Apartheid: Segregation and the Making of the Underclass*. Cambridge, MA: Harvard University Press, 1993.

McKay, Tom. "One Troubling Statistic Shows Just How Racist America's Police Brutality Problem Is." *Mic*. August 18, 2014. Accessed May 18, 2023. http://mic.com/articles/96452/one-troubling-statistic-shows-just-how-racist-america-s-police-brutality-problem-is.

Moraff, Christopher. "Will Private Money Take the Sting Out of Obama's Police Demilitarization?" *Next City*. May 26, 2015. Accessed May 18, 2023. https://nextcity.org/daily/entry/private-money-police-foundations-obama-police-demilitarization.

Nagasawa, Mako. "Athanasius as Evangelist, Part 6: Jesus Paid the Debt to God, and Helps You Pay the Debt You Still Owe to God, Too." *The Anástasis Center Blog*. December 21, 2017. Accessed May 18, 2023. https://www.anastasiscenterblog.org/athanasius-trinity-nicene-creed/post-6-jesus-helps-you-pay-your-debt-to-god.

———. "Atonement Theories & Guilt, Part 2: 'Don't Make Me Feel Guilty': How Penal Substitution Interferes With Reparations and Reconciliation." *The Anástasis Center Blog*, February 21, 2022. Accessed May 18, 2023. https://www.anastasiscenterblog.org/atonement-emotional-development/atonement-theories-and-guilt-part-2.

News Division. "Thabiti Anyabwile Says All Whites Are Complicit in Murdering Martin Luther King, Jr." *Pulpit and Pen*. April 5, 2018. Accessed May 18, 2023. https://pulpitandpen.org/2018/04/05/thabiti-anyabwile-says-whites-complicit-murdering-martin-luther-king-jr/.

Orfield, Gary. "St Louis, School Desegregation and Housing Policy." *HTH Video*, June 11, 2009. Accessed May 18, 2023. https://www.youtube.com/watch?v=33AgYGJvY8c.

Pope, Stephen. "Restorative Justice as a Prophetic Path to Peace." *CTSA Proceedings* 65 (2010): 20.

Rhodes, Michael. "Should We Repent of Our Grandparents' Racism? Scripture on Intergenerational Sin." *The Biblical Mind*. June 19, 2020. Accessed May 18, 2023. https://hebraicthought.org/repenting-intergenerational-racist-ideology-scripture-intergenerational-sin/.

Rothstein, Richard. *The Color of Law: A Forgotten History of How Our Government Segregated America*. New York, NY: Liveright, May 2, 2017.

———. "The Racial Achievement Gap, Segregated Schools, and Segregated Neighborhoods—A Constitutional Insult." *Economic Policy Institute*. November 12, 2014. Accessed May 18, 2023. https://www.epi.org/publication/the-racial-achievement-gap-segregated-schools-and-segregated-neighborhoods-a-constitutional-insult/.

Rutenberg, Jim. "A Dream Undone: Inside the 50 Year Campaign to Roll Back the Voting Rights Act." *New York Times*. July 29, 2015. Accessed May 18, 2023. http://www.nytimes.com/2015/07/29/magazine/voting-rights-act-dream-undone.html.

Slater, Gene. *Freedom to Discriminate: How Realtors Conspired to Segregate Housing and Divide America*. Berkeley, CA: Heydey, 2021.

Snyder-Belousek, Darrin W. *Atonement, Justice, and Peace: The Message of the Cross and the Mission of the Church*. Grand Rapids, MI: Eerdmans, 2011.

Swann, Ben. "The Root of Police Militarization." *Truth in Media*. December 10, 2014. Accessed on May 19, 2023, https://www.sott.net/article/290512-Truth-in-Media-The-Root-of-Police-Militarization.

Thayer, Joseph H. *The New Thayer's Greek-English Lexicon of the New Testament*. Peabody, MA: Hendrickson, 1981.

Thrush, Glenn. "Under Ben Carson, HUD Scales Back Fair Housing Enforcement." *New York Times*. March 28, 2018. https://www.nytimes.com/2018/03/28/us/ben-carson-hud-fair-housing-discrimination.html.

Totenberg, Nina. "Who Is Judge Gonzalo Curiel, The Man Trump Attacked For His Mexican Ancestry?" *NPR*. June 7, 2016. https://www.npr.org/2016/06/07/481140881/who-is-judge-gonzalo-curiel-the-man-trump-attacked-for-his-mexican-ancestry.

Zengerle, Jason. "The New Racism: This is How the Civil Rights Movement Ends." *New Republic*. August 10, 2014. http://www.newrepublic.com/article/119019/civil-rights-movement-going-reverse-alabama.

Chapter Twelve

Witness: Reparations or Atonement

Searching for an Appropriate Vessel

Rodney S. Sadler Jr.

When any of you sin and commit a trespass against the LORD by deceiving a neighbor in a matter of a deposit or a pledge, or by robbery, or if you have defrauded a neighbor, or have found something lost and lied about it—if you swear falsely regarding any of the various things that one may do and sin thereby—when you have sinned and realize your guilt, and would restore what you took by robbery or by fraud or the deposit that was committed to you, or the lost thing that you found, or anything else about which you have sworn falsely, you shall repay the principal amount and shall add one-fifth to it. You shall pay it to its owner when you realize your guilt (Lev 6:2–5; NRSV).

It was a late spring night in 2020. We had just survived the first few months of COVID-19 and were learning what it was like to live in isolation. It was in the midst of this first crisis that a second began. One evening, the news broke about a recent, brutal killing in Minneapolis. This was an unsanctioned state execution done at the hands—or perhaps I should say knee—of Minneapolis's finest. George Floyd was murdered by one officer who was, in turn, abetted by several others. They kept a growing crowd at bay while those who witnessed the excruciatingly slow-motion execution begged the officers just to let Mr. Floyd breathe.

Black men (and women) die far too frequently at the hands or knees—or tips of tasers, or points of guns—of those who wear blue. A study by the *Washington Post* revealed that though accounting for only 13 percent of the population in the United States, African Americans accounted for 27 percent of those fatally shot by police officers in 2021—more than twice their representation in the general population. The study found that "Black Americans are shot at a disproportionately high rate."[1] Because of idiosyncrasies in policing procedures regarding such murders, many such instances go unreported. I'm afraid to think about how many times such extrajudicial executions have happened in the past. The truth is that we will never know how often it happens; in far too many instances, such acts are not recorded. If they do happen to be recorded, the video evidence is gathered from state-owned dash or body cameras, devices controlled by governmental agencies with significant discretion about what they choose to release to the public.

Were it not for the personal cell phone recording taken by Darnella Frazier, we might never have known that George Floyd was murdered—let alone that as he was being executed, he begged for mercy, for breath, for his mother. But Frazier did record it, and then posted the video on Facebook. Her recording offered a more accurate alternative to the official police statement about an "altercation" gone wrong and that he suffered from "a medical incident during police interaction."[2] That video reverberated around the world during the pandemic crisis, which had forced people around the world to isolate in their homes. Millions of viewers saw graphic images on their video screens of a man dying on camera, confirming what the African American community had been saying for years about police violence against souls in black skin. Protests soon ensued. People of all kinds, ages, and incomes began to rally in what soon became the largest movement for racial justice in history. They began to gather and march in the streets of Minneapolis, Cleveland, Philadelphia, and in cities around the world—even in the streets of the city where I live: the Queen City—Charlotte, North Carolina.

THE DANCE

Then, one evening near the end of May of 2020, I saw a message on social media that there was going to be a local gathering, a march in protest of police violence near the Beatties Ford Police Department. I was initially concerned because I did not recognize the organizers of the march. They were not the familiar names of friends who typically organized such marches in Charlotte.

When I arrived that night on Beatties Ford Road—a main artery in the heart of Charlotte's largely impoverished African American community—many of the people I expected to see were absent. I had marched with the Black Lives Matter protesters and hosts of local activists in Charlotte many times over the years. Those marches were usually well organized, and their leaders kept a tight rein on the protesters, encouraging a certain code of conduct, a moral decorum, and a positive attitude among the marchers. But something was markedly different this evening.

As I walked around the Beatties Ford Corridor, I ran into a friend and colleague, Jennifer Roberts, the former mayor of Charlotte. I had seen Roberts marching in the streets several times before. She had even joined us in Raleigh, North Carolina, when I was working with the Moral Monday Movement before assuming that position. Now out of office, she was again able to stand in the crowd as an advocate for justice.

During the most recent marches in Charlotte, as the crowd came out to protest the Charlotte Mecklenburg Police Department following the killing of Keith Lamont Scott, Roberts had still been the mayor. Two weeks of protests had immediately followed that tragedy, and in the aftermath Roberts had realized that the system was fundamentally flawed and that there was no adequate way for the police, the county, or the city to respond that would really make a difference. Indeed, she saw no clear way to protect the lives of black and brown people from police aggression, misconduct, and harassment.

As we began to march with the crowds that night, Roberts and I began to talk about something we called "the dance." The dance is an elaborately choreographed routine in which leaders from the city and the police department engage disgruntled local grassroots leaders. The first movement of the dance takes place when diverse crowds of people assemble in the streets in massive numbers to protest. The second movement of the dance occurs when the mayor and city council offer a few token concessions concerning city policies and procedures in order to quell the protests. The third movement of the dance is similar to the second: the police chief and his staff offer to make certain policy changes and concessions related to their use of force. The fourth movement is a symbolic gesture in which a commission or committee is empaneled—or "experts" are brought in from national policing organizations—to offer an "assessment" or "report" of some kind. This movement might include an offer to provide better access to state-owned camera footage; changes in the rules concerning state-sanctioned use of violence; modifications regarding the weapons the state uses against protesting citizens; access to safe, affordable housing for impoverished people with extremely limited social mobility; or other incremental steps perhaps representing a modicum of change in a wholly broken system. In the fifth movement, the media announces with great fanfare that certain changes are coming that will dramatically improve the lives of darker-hued Charlotteans.

Once the dance is over, however, nothing in the system really changes. Any promises made are promises soon broken and sooner forgotten. The protests die down, and those organizing them are distracted by other issues. In the final step in the dance, another instance of unnecessary police violence against a black or brown body takes places several months later—in Charlotte or somewhere else in the nation—and the customary, choreographed steps begin again.

This dance, while unsatisfactory, is the norm, and it is altogether familiar. This time, however, the dance did not proceed as expected.

THE DIFFERENCE

As we walked that night, things were extraordinarily different. The unknown leaders of this protest hid their faces behind masks. We were in a pandemic, to be sure; but these people were not just protecting themselves from potential contact with the virus; they were provocateurs hiding their identities. Several civilians in the crowd carried automatic rifles. Others had semi-automatic handguns strapped to their sides. The chants from the crowd against the police were not the normal chants (e.g., "No justice, no peace! No racist police!"; "The people united will never be defeated!") but were much more intentionally provocative, seeking an aggressive response. Police officers were attacked, at times even beaten by the protestors. I used my body, adorned with a clerical collar, to intervene and rescue a few overzealous officers who waded into the incited crowd. I even encouraged another officer to allow a member of the crowd to steal his official, police-issued bicycle—lest he be crushed trying to hold on to it. Things were very different that night.

My time on the street that night ended when bottles of urine were hurled at the police department building and a cadre of armored riot police officers lined up behind shields outside to defend that space. Having lost contact with the former mayor, a ministerial colleague and I decided to call the current mayor in order to ask her to have the police officers stand down. The thought was that if we could get the police to go back into the building, we could perhaps encourage the crowd to disperse and keep anyone else from being injured or killed that night. The loss of George Floyd in Minneapolis was already one loss too many.

That night ended much more violently than we had hoped. Instead of backing down, the police sent out more officers who were better armed. Several people were arrested, including Braxton Winston, a young veteran of the Black Lives Matter movement made famous during the Keith Lamont Scott uprisings. Winston had since become a Charlotte City Council member and, while simply trying to prevent the police from engaging with the crowd, was arrested by the very officers whom, ironically, he employed.

Things were different now. The moment was fraught. We were one lit match away from an explosion that could further devastate race relations in the city—or even ignite a national civil war. In this different world, we needed a different response than the familiar dance, one that would actually address the problems of racism and racial disparity.

In the aftermath of that night, the former mayor, several of our ministerial and civic leaders, and I came together to form an organization that promised to foster true change. Again, the normal dance had proven to be completely inadequate. It was painfully clear to us that the tensions in the city were more than just a policing problem, more than just a school problem, more than just a housing, criminal justice, or access-to-political-power-at-the-polls problem. This was a larger problem than even the well-documented reality that Charlotte ranked 50th out of 50 of America's largest cities in terms of upward social mobility.[3] This was a systemic problem premised on racial identity and we had to do something different to address it this time around.

THE REIMAGINING AMERICA PROJECT

In response, our group of grassroots local leaders formed a beloved community, co-founding something we called the Reimagining America Project: The Truth, Reconciliation and Atonement Commission of Charlotte (RAP). We began to hold weekly meetings, during which we determined that we needed to interrogate every social system in Charlotte in order to determine the manifold ways that race had negatively impacted the lives of black and brown people. It became clear that the problems we were seeing along racial lines were truly systemic concerns that needed systemic solutions.

The goal of RAP is to put every system in the city (and then eventually the nation) on trial to determine what it has done historically to cause racial disparity and what it continues to do to foster imbalanced outcomes that negatively impact African American people. When fully activated, we envision that RAP will be a collaborative effort of activists, governmental groups, foundations, and other organizations working together to foster true systemic change. The founding members—the commissioners—anticipate that this work will take at least a decade to complete, and we have committed ourselves to the long term-goal of fostering a better, more equitable, more just Charlotte—as we develop a model that can prove useful for transforming America.

We began our work in partnership with Rabbi Dr. Mark Gopin of George Mason University in Washington, DC. He directs the Center for World Religions, Diplomacy, and Conflict Resolution, and focuses on resolving matters of international conflict. His work seeks to understand the dynamics of historical conflicts like those in Nazi Germany, while aiming to resolve contemporary discord in places like Israel/Palestine and Syria. As we began our work on race in Charlotte, Rabbi Gopin noted that the divisions we faced here were as dire and contentious as those he had seen in war-torn countries. During the first few weeks of our conversations, we began to consider what

RAP was ultimately seeking to achieve. Very early on, we agreed that we were not an organization attempting to foster "white guilt," noting that all contemporary Americans are recipients of a system that we did not create. We are not "guilty of" fostering our system, but we assert that we are all "responsible to" do something to rectify it. We also noted that because of the way that our system has been intentionally crafted, injustice offers advantage to some by heaping disadvantage on others. We came to see that there is no privilege without attendant under-privilege. Every advantage comes from somewhere; it costs someone something; it is not attained without being extracted from someone. This extraction has resulted in an imbalance of wealth, power, and privilege—with historic roots that continue to feed a supremacist tree today. We recognized our need to do something to address this imbalance. It was then that the concept of reparations first surfaced.

REPARATIONS

As we began to ponder the issue of reparations, we noted that there were numerous people working on the topic. I first became aware of this concept when I worked for the Congress of National Black Churches in the early 1990s and we partnered with Randall Robinson of TransAfrica in work to address the underdevelopment of African peoples in America and on the African continent. He eventually wrote a book called *The Debt*, describing the significant, largely financial obligation owed by the United States to African Americans for centuries of unpaid labor and systemic abuse.[4]

Over the years, I learned of other attempts to seek reparations. For example, US House Resolution 40 (HR 40) has been a decades-long organizing effort initiated by former Detroit Congressman John Conyers. Unfortunately, his resolution never gained the necessary support it needed to be passed on the floor of the House. Since Rep. Conyers's death, however, the resolution has been championed in the House by Barbara Lee and in the Senate by Cory Booker. Still, it seems that the concept of reparations is a hard concept for the American people to rally behind, as many deny the full extent of the harm done to African American citizens as a consequence of this country's racial practices and policies.

In part, reparations are a financial issue. One of the most obvious impacts of our nation's racialized history has been the financial underdevelopment of the African American community. Black people in this country started out at a considerable deficit, having worked for little or no compensation for their first 246 years on these shores—and for but marginally more compensation since "emancipation" was finally granted. So, there are historic reasons for the fact that, on average, African Americans have approximately 1/6th of the wealth of their Caucasian counterparts in 2019 (with Caucasian Americans having approximately $338,093 wealth per capita to African Americans' $60,126).[5] This gross imbalance is not the product of poor financial planning or based on the "laziness" of African Americans. It is instead the result of systemic practices like redlining; denying blacks mortgages for housing in "good" neighborhoods; giving black families mortgages at higher interests rates; enacting restrictive covenants in housing developments that have prevented blacks from owning homes that would appreciate in value; denying black veterans access to the GI Bill; and limiting educational and employment options and opportunities. These are just a few of the policies and practices evident in the United States have that produced such vast economic disparities.

As RAP began to discuss how best to frame what it would seek, however, it became clear that the notion of financial reparations—at a level that would approximate the financial devastation that African Americans have endured—would be difficult to sell to the American public. More importantly, even if we were to attain adequate financial remuneration, the ultimate concern of the African American community would still not have been addressed.

A FULL VESSEL

We do not only seek economic parity, but also full equality and the recognition of our humanity and dignity. This is our ultimate concern. These matters cannot be resolved with the writing of a check, no matter how large that check might be. The term "reparations" has been used in public discourse for the financial remuneration given to the Japanese placed in internment camps by the United States during the Second World War and the compensation given by the Germans to the Jewish people in aftermath of the Holocaust. Many scholars have argued that African Americans deserve financial reparations as a means of redress for the suffering that they have historically experienced in this nation. Consider the following statements from recent analyses:

> Given the lingering legacy of slavery on the racial wealth gap, the monetary value we know that was placed on enslaved Blacks, the fact that other groups have received reparations, and the fact that Blacks were originally awarded reparations only to have them rescinded provide overwhelming evidence that it is time to pay reparations to the descendants of enslaved Blacks.[6]

> The fact that full amends cannot be made for a grievous injustice does not mean significant recompense should not be made. Although the long-overdue bill will not match the price paid by the victims, the bill must be paid.[7]

Though the authors of both of these studies would certainly assert that reparations are more than simply financial remuneration, the concept of reparations today is largely conceived to be a financial entitlement that takes money from an offending group and offers it to a group offended.

I firmly believe that black people deserve reparations, that our society would benefit from providing reparations, and that in instances of intergroup abuse reparations are theologically mandated. But I would argue that such a vision of reparations alone is not enough! The blighted and beset black community needs far more than a mere financial infusion to make it whole. Beyond the fact that I believe reparations are inadequate, there are other issues with the idea of reparations. This concept is laden in our society. Consider the following concerns that RAP has identified:

1. The notion of reparations has been so co-opted in the public square that it has become almost a non-starter as we work for justice. It is a word that evokes powerful negative emotions, and thus it may hamper a larger conversation about RAP's goals for establishing a more just and equitable society.
2. The concept of reparations in the public square is typically associated with notions of financial remuneration. People hear the word *reparations* and assume that the black community is asking for a check that will compensate us for 404 years of oppression. But this too is problematic because:

    a. There is likely not enough wealth in decades worth of the GDP of the United States of America, the richest nation in the history of the world, to compensate black people adequately for what has been taken from us.
    b. Even if there were enough money, financial support alone would not compensate black people for all the harm that they have experienced and to continue to suffer. I often say that even if we gave every American enough money to be a Kardashian, doing so would not keep the next young African American male driving around the city in a new G-Wagon or BMW (purchased with said check) from getting stopped by the police—and then being profiled, harassed, and murdered—all because of the perception that blackness equals danger and criminality.
    c. Also, if financial reparations alone were distributed, I worry that the American people would think that racial disparities had been resolved would require no further consideration—that because the check had been written, members of the traumatized African American community should ask for no more.

d. Thus, although we need to compensate African Americans economically, we have to change more than just our financial bottom line in order to achieve the society that we would like to see. There is ideological and systemic work that needs to be done in order to transform this supremacist society. I firmly assert that, at root, race is an economic idea; nevertheless, its impact on black people extends far beyond economic matters. The full historical and contemporary impact of racial ideas on our nation needs to be addressed and redressed for justice to be possible.

For all of these reasons, RAP decided to adjust our trajectory so as to consider alternatives to the concept of reparations. During one of our earliest meetings, Rabbi Gopin suggested that we make our goal the biblical/theological concept of "atonement."

AN EMPTY VESSEL

Rabbi Gopin described "atonement" as a biblical concept of complete repair. It suggests that the need to repair the breach created by ruptured human relations—a breach perpetuated by graft, fraud, abuse, enslavement, and evinced by sin—is spiritual in character. Gopin's invocation of atonement was an attempt to suggest that in addition to the addressing the financial suffering caused by the race problem in America, we must also attend to the deep spiritual and moral problems caused by the American supremacist system.

In the Hebrew Bible, atonement connotes a range of things. One passage that has proven useful to illustrate this is Leviticus 6:4–5 (NRSV):

> . . . when you have sinned and *realize your guilt*, and would *restore what you took* by robbery or by fraud or the deposit that was committed to you, or the lost thing that you found, or anything else about which you have sworn falsely, *you shall repay* the principal amount and shall add one-fifth to it. *You shall pay it to its owner when you realize your guilt*.

Here we see several concepts employed that address requisite notions of atonement:

- *Shuv*—returning what has been taken (e.g., Lev 6:4)
- *Shalem*—providing restitution for the wrong that was done, and fixing what was broken (Lev 6:5)
- *Capher*—covering over sin and wrongdoing (Lev 6:6)

These and a number of other Hebrew concepts undergird this broad theological notion that relates to the restoration of people who have been abused or defrauded to a place of wholeness (see also Ex 12:35–36, where enslaved Hebrews "plunder" [*natsal*] their Egyptian oppressors as they escape). In fact, the notion of atonement itself is a synthetic, composite term in English created to encompass the semantic range of a Hebrew concept for which there was no English equivalent. "At-one-ment" is the act of making something that has been broken, ruptured, destroyed, and decimated whole. More than anything else, after centuries of systematic dehumanization, devaluation, and denigration, the African American community needs to be made whole.

The tendency in the United States is to evaluate trauma through an economic lens and calculate loss in monetary terms. But as RAP considered the holistic concept of atonement, we realized that such a concept requires far more than a financial response. We imagined that atonement would begin with the elimination of the concept race itself and its constituent hierarchies that control access to wealth, power, and privilege in our contexts. Only then could we imagine a system of equals and identify where systemic choices fostered the intentional imbalances in wealth, power, and privilege evident today.

Thus, atonement would mean the elimination of the view of race as a legitimate means of hierarchically dividing human beings along a color spectrum. It would also require that we examine the systems in which race has operated in order to (1) illustrate the harm that this idea has caused in that system; (2) reimagine what that system would look like if it were just, fair, and equitable; and (3) work to make that just society a reality. This became the way that we envisioned atonement as our appropriate end.

I suppose that I cannot simply say that we need to "eliminate the concept of race" without giving some context to that seemingly nonsensical statement. This is a difficult notion to grasp in a society that has suggested that race is axiomatic, given by God, part of our accepted order. But the concept of race is actually a relatively recent idea born in the time of colonization to provide scientific, moral, and theological cover for those taking people from land and land from people. It is an idea establishing a hierarchy of humanity and a view of the supremacy of those of lighter hue. It is an idea that establishes a social order. It itself fosters inequality.

Thus, the seemingly untenable idea of fighting a concept became an imperative for RAP. As anthropologists, biologists, geneticists, and theological scholars have noted, the concept of race has no ontological, biological, genetic, or theological validity. It exists as a social construct only to delimit access to wealth, power, and privilege along a chromatic spectrum. It divides us into a ladder of human worth that has proven consequential for our very lives. We in RAP determined the need to overcome race as we realized that this concept is the chief factor undermining the potential for equality in our society. Though we have yet to determine what, if anything, should replace that concept as it relates to distinct aspects of people's heritage and culture, we have come to realize that the notion of race with its intended social caste dimensions is irredeemable and inherently problematic, undermining any potential for equality and justice in our nation.

As a note of clarification, the goal of this effort is not to foster a "color blind" society. We are not trying to pretend that we don't see color or foster a fictive notion of equality that ignores our historical and cultural differences a people. Such differences are what make us beautiful as human beings; such differences enrich our common society; such differences should be celebrated. What we are opposed to, however, is that innocuous differences in appearance should lead to differences in human valuation and differences in access to wealth, power, and privilege. These hierarchical dimensions superimposed on human differences are the essence of racialist thought that need to be eliminated from the American psyche. It is for this understanding of race that we need to atone.

The concept of atonement is an empty vessel in our public square. It is not fully formed, and thus not a commonplace term laden with contested meaning, immediately inciting ire when mentioned. Atonement, though an important concept in biblical/theological contexts, retains a plasticity in the contemporary public mind, enabling it to be shaped as necessary to be of best use to us as we think about what it would take to make African American people, our nation, and all of its systems whole.

Thus, RAP seeks atonement by exploring how the very concept of race and its intended notions of hierarchical inequality undermine the possibility of wholeness in any of our systems. Instead of simply seeking compensation, we want to strive for comprehensive justice in every system: education, employment, politics, policing, criminal justice, housing, healthcare, environmental/climate justice—every system in our society. We acknowledge that focusing on only one or two of these systems will never be enough, for they are interrelated. Each impinges on all the others. An underperforming educational system impacts a person's future economic viability, influencing that person's housing options; limiting access to housing causes internal trauma that imperils health; and on and on it goes. In order to make America whole, we need "fusion justice," a comprehensive way of atoning for more than four hundred years of intended imbalance—a reimagining of America. By fusion justice in this instance, I mean a view of justice that de-silos systems and recognizes their interrelatedness. In this regard, fusion justice would suggest that we need to address not just education, but healthcare, wealth inequality, housing, policing, criminal justice, political power, and a host of other interrelated systems—together. In order to achieve that greater synthesis, fusion justice would also anticipate the cooperation of people from different identities coming together at a common table, working to foster Beloved Community—together. Thus, fusion justice is evident when a diverse cadre of peoples come together to address the historic injustice of interrelated social systems.

The concept of atonement holds the key that can open the door to what is really needed to address racism and the host of disparities it fosters.

CONCLUSION?

So, allow me to conclude by saying that we have found *reparations* to be a fraught term coopted in the public square and vilified in typical conversations about healing the racial divide. Viewed as a financial transaction, it does not fully address the plethora of concerns produced by being subjected to a "racial" identity. Eliminating the social construct of race and producing a world that is void of its attendant disparities is necessary if we ever hope to have our nation live into its vaunted ideals. Only in a world where race has been deconstructed and the systems produced by racialized thinking have been purposely dismantled, reimagined, and restored will the American credo ever be more than empty words. Only in such a world freed from the delimitation of racialist thought will we ever be able to honestly say, "We hold these truths to be self-evident, that ALL human beings are created equal." Yes, America and its vision of equality are only possible when we have eliminated the racial hierarchy and atoned for the harm that it has and continues to cause to those in browner skin.

Back in Charlotte, a city still wrestling with its history of racial disparity and lack of opportunity, RAP continues its work. The bond forged on the street between Jennifer Roberts and I that first night; the Beloved Community that grew from our collective work with a group of grassroots activists; the challenge that together we offer to this city and all of its systems—these continue to grow. Nearly three years into its work, the dedicated members of RAP remain convinced that the problems that we see with a color-based caste system will persist until the cancerous concept of race is excised from our collective psyche and our system is reimagined and then renewed. We are neither foolish or deluded: we understand that seeking to reimagine a world without a racial hierarchy is a grand, ambitious goal. But having said that, we realize that unless we dream big, unless we address the impact of this myth on all of our systems, unless we develop a comprehensive, system-by-system strategy to address inequality and injustice premised on racial identity, nothing will change—the dance will continue as it is wont to do.

We have grown weary of doing that old familiar dance and are ready to try something new—ready to seek atonement by reimagining the kind of America that we all want and working to make that vision real. In this regard, traditional visions of reparations are not enough. It is time that America atoned for her sins against her African American citizens. This is a view eloquently expressed by Ta-Nehisi Coates in a recent article:

> An America that asks what it owes its most vulnerable citizens is improved and humane. An America that looks away is ignoring not just the sins of the past but the sins of the present and the certain sins of the future. More important than any single check cut to any African American, the payment of reparations would represent America's maturation out of the childhood myth of its innocence into a wisdom worthy of its founders.[8]

RAP suggests that it is in the process of atonement that "America's maturation" might actually be seen, as she thereby works to achieve the aspirational goals of its Declaration of Independence. It is this broader notion of recompense as atonement that America needs now, both for the sake of African Americans and for the sake of her own soul.

NOTES

1. Curtis Bunn, "Report: Black people are still killed by police at a higher rate than other groups," NBC News, March 3, 2022, Accessed May 15, 2023, https://www.nbcnews.com/news/nbcblk/report-black-people-are-still-killed-police-higher-rate-groups-rcna17169.

2. David Mack, "What Minneapolis Police First Said About George Floyd Vs. What The Jury Found Derek Chauvin Did," BuzzFeed News, April 20, 2021, accessed May 15, 2023, https://www.buzzfeed.com/davidmack/police-statement-george-floyd-chauvin-murder-verdict.

3. Emmanuel Saez, Nathan Hendren, Patrick Kline, and Raj Chetty, "Where is the land of opportunity? Intergenerational mobility in the US," *VoxEU*, February 4, 2014, accessed May 15, 2023, https://cepr.org/voxeu/columns/where-land-opportunity-intergenerational-mobility-us.

4. Randall Robinson, *The Debt: What America Owes to Blacks* (New York: Plume, 2001).

5. Lisa McKay, "How the Racial Wealth Gap Has Evolved—And Why It Persists," Federal Reserve Bank of Minneapolis, October 3, 2022, accessed May 15, 2023, https://www.minneapolisfed.org/article/2022/how-the-racial-wealth-gap-has-evolved-and-why-it-persists.

6. Rashawn Ray and Andre M. Perry, "Why We Need Reparations for Black Americans," *Policy 2020*, Brookings Institution, accessed May 15, 2023, https://www.brookings.edu/policy2020/bigideas/why-we-need-reparations-for-black-americans/.

7. William A. Darity Jr., and A. Kirsten Mullen, *From Here to Equality: Reparations for Black Americans in the Twenty-First Century* (Chapel Hill: The University of North Carolina Press, 2020), 255.

8. Ta-Nehesi Coates, "The Case for Reparations," *The Atlantic,* June 16, 2014.

BIBLIOGRAPHY

Bunn, Curtis. "Report: Black People Are Still Killed by Police at a Higher Rate than Other Groups." NBC News. March 3, 2022. Accessed May 15, 2023. https://www.nbcnews.com/news/nbcblk/report-black-people-are-still-killed-police-higher-rate-groups-rcna17169.

Coates, Ta-Nehesi. "The Case for Reparations." *The Atlantic.* June 16, 2014.

Darity, William A., Jr., and A. Kirsten Mullen. *From Here to Equality: Reparations for Black Americans in the Twenty-First Century.* Chapel Hill: The University of North Carolina Press, 2020.

Mack, David. "What Minneapolis Police First Said About George Floyd Vs. What The Jury Found Derek Chauvin Did." *BuzzFeed News,* April 20, 2021. Accessed May 15, 2023. https://www.buzzfeed.com/davidmack/police-statement-george-floyd-chauvin-murder-verdict.

McKay, Lisa. "How the Racial Wealth Gap Has Evolved—And Why It Persists." Federal Reserve Bank of Minneapolis, October 3, 2022. Accessed May 15, 2023. https://www.minneapolisfed.org/article/2022/how-the-racial-wealth-gap-has-evolved-and-why-it-persists.

Ray, Rashawn, and Andre M. Perry. "Why We Need Reparations for Black Americans," *Policy 2020*, Brookings Institution. Accessed May 15, 2023. https://www.brookings.edu/policy2020/bigideas/why-we-need-reparations-for-black-americans/.

Robinson, Randall. *The Debt: What America Owes to Blacks.* New York: Plume, 2001.

Saez, Emmanuel, Nathan Hendren, Patrick Kline, and Raj Chetty. "Where Is the Land of Opportunity? Intergenerational Mobility in the US." *VoxEU.* February 4, 2014. Accessed May 15, 2023. https://cepr.org/voxeu/columns/where-land-opportunity-intergenerational-mobility-us.

Chapter Thirteen

Reparations NOW
For the Glory of God

Ekemini Uwan

To whom do I belong? Who are my people? Where are my people? These questions intrude upon the subconscious of West Africans, their descendants, and distant relatives due to the impact of the transatlantic slave trade. For the record, I believe reparations are due on a global scale to all Africans and African-descended people who have suffered from the consequences of the transatlantic slave trade, chattel slavery, colonialism, imperialism, neo-colonialism, and the myriad atrocities that are by-products of the brutal legacy of slavery that looms over our people globally. For the purpose of this chapter, however, I'm going to narrow the focus to Black people in America who are descendants of formerly enslaved Africans; Black immigrants, including Caribbeans who are also descendants of enslaved Africans; West Africans; and West Central Africans whose ancestors and relatives were stolen and trafficked in the transatlantic slave trade and shipped to the United States of America. From a Reformed theological perspective, I will argue that reparations are central to the Christian gospel.

There is a tendency to talk about enslaved Africans in generic ways that disconnect them from their homeland, which I've often found disconcerting. To an extent, this is understandable, given that about 12.5 million Africans were stolen from West Africa and West Central Africa and brought to the Americas during the transatlantic slave trade.[1] Due to the sheer volume of Africans stolen, people tend to lose sight of the fact that the enslaved were taken from numerous ethnic groups. Africans have never been, nor will we ever be a monolith. According to Ana Lucia Araujo, during the time of the transatlantic slave trade and into the mid-nineteenth century, African people did not have a pan-African identity, nor did they think of themselves as

"African." Instead, they identified themselves with the ethnic group into which they were born. The pan-African identity and African consciousness developed "much later in the Americas, as a result of the tragedy of slavery, and in Africa, as a response to European colonial rule."[2]

Nevertheless, enslaved Africans were not aliens from a foreign planet. They were image-bearers: flesh and blood, embodied souls. They were stolen from their ethnic groups, villages, states, land, family, and more. In turn, their names, cultures, heritages, languages, ways of life, occupations, and traditions were stolen from them. In an effort to help us resist the urge to think of enslaved Africans in abstract ways, I begin this essay by anchoring them to one of many ethnic groups represented in the transatlantic slave trade: the Ibibio people from Southeastern Nigeria—my people.

This fight for reparations is personal. I am a Black woman, an African American woman, an African woman, a Nigerian woman, and an Ibibio woman. Therefore, I don't speak about slavery and reparations as some distant, outside observer. According to Randy J. Sparks, "1.2 million slaves were transported from the Cross and Niger Rivers in the eighteenth century."[3] That's 10 percent of the 12.5 million Africans stolen during the transatlantic slave trade. Some of the people who were stolen were my people, ancestors, and distant relatives whom I will never meet on this side of Glory.

We West Africans, Caribbeans, African Americans, and Black Diasporans enter into the sordid history of slavery at different points. Nevertheless, our diverse entry points do not negate the fact that it is part of *our* history, collectively. It's time for Africans to speak into this history: the shame, the pain, the loss, the resistance, the resilience, the grim legacy, and the cataclysmic impact that continues to haunt the continent and its people to this day. As an African woman who is Ibibio, this is my offering.

WHO ARE THE IBIBIO?

The Ibibio people are considered one of the most ancient ethnic groups in Nigeria. In *Who Are the Ibibio?,* Edet A. Udo suggests that the Ibibio people are Semi-Bantu people who migrated from the central Benue Valley to the coastal southeastern region of what would become Nigeria.[4] They settled in Ibom and occupied mainland Cross River State. In 1987, Akwa Ibom State was established as a separate state from Cross River State. "Akwa Ibom is bounded by Cross River state on the east, by the Bight of Biafra of the Atlantic Ocean on the south, by Rivers state on the west, by Abia state on the west and north, and by Ebonyi state on the north."[5]

Udo notes that the origin of the name Ibibio is unknown. "The word means short, brief, precise. The Ibibio people do things in direct, precise ways; their language is brief . . . Ibibio words are short and precise and are phonetically spelled. The Ibibio think of their name as meaning 'the people who do things in a precise, brief manner.'"[6]

According to Carolyn A. Brown and Paul E. Lovejoy, "Almost everyone who left the Bight of Biafra boarded at one of three ports, Elem Kalabari (New Calabar) and Bonny (Iboni), both in the delta of the Niger River, and Old Calabar on the adjacent Cross River and its tributaries, the Calabar and Creek Rivers."[7] They write:

> the Bight of Biafra was a major source of enslaved Africans in the terrible forced migration to the Americas, probably involving the departure of 1.6 million people from the 1530s to the 1830s . . . If the numbers of people who were enslaved but never left the region are also included, then the total demographic displacement through slavery was considerably more than this figure.[8]

Brown and Lovejoy continue,

> Before 1740, the Bight of Biafra provided a relatively modest 7 percent of the transatlantic slave trade, but by the 1780s, when the trade was at its peak, the area supplied over 20 percent of all enslaved Africans going to the Americas, a remarkable increase from the early eighteenth century. It should also be observed that 65 percent of departures went on British and North American ships, and this accounted for most people who left before 1808.[9]

Concerning the enslaved Africans stolen from the Bight of Biafra and taken to North America, the primary ethnic groups were the Igbo, Ibibio, and Ijaw (Ijo). Seventy-one percent of these enslaved Africans disembarked in the Chesapeake region, while the other 30 percent disembarked in the Carolinas and Georgia.[10]

It is jarring to note that a significant portion of the 1.6 million enslaved Africans taken from the Bight of Biafra were Ibibio. The impact of the transatlantic slave trade on West Africa and West Central Africa was immediate and persistent. It opened a Pandora's box of oppression, ushering in imperialism, colonialism, neo-colonialism, political instability, economic stagnation, the underdevelopment of Africa, the European scramble for Africa, and the missionary scramble for Africa. Additional deleterious realities that are often overlooked historically and presently are continental warfare, enslaved Africans dislocated to other countries within Africa, severe depopulation of villages due to the capture of men, women, and children trafficked from their homeland, stolen cultural artifacts, cultural traditions, and societies destroyed.

In total, 1.6 million of them were taken from the Bight of Biafra, and a significant portion of them were Ibibio men, women, and children hauled off to Old Calabar to board slave ships from Bristol, Liverpool, London, and even the occasional ships from North America. Ships with names such as *Fair American, Calabar Merchant, Delight,* and *Shepherd*[11] headed for American ports in South Carolina, Maryland, Virginia, and elsewhere, full of West Africans from various ethnic groups, one of which was the Ibibio, my people. The names of the enslaved Ibibios are unknown, but allow me to take some liberties here and imagine some of the Ibibio birth names given to the men, women, and children before they were enslaved. I invite you to lay hold of one of the names in your mind for the duration of the essay.

I imagine that the men had names like Bassey, Asuquo, Edet, Edem, and Effiong. The names of enslaved Ibibio women may have been Iquo, Enewan, Nkoyo, Ekaette, and Atim. Imagine all of them, or even just one, as representative of the 1.6 million stolen from the Bight of Biafra—among the 12.5 million Africans enslaved—loaded onto one of many slave ships like *Delight*, headed for the Americas. Many would not survive the Middle Passage. "While the Delight left Calabar with 211 enslaved Africans, many of them Ibibio, the ship arrived with only 160 people. Fifty-one perished during the journey." Imagine Edet and Atim or Iquo and Bassey on *Delight* as they land in Charleston, greeted by the reprehensible and brutal institution that was American chattel slavery.

When Edet, Nkoyo, Atim, and Asuquo arrived on the shores of Charleston, South Carolina, they were inspected like animals, put on the slave auction blocks, and sold to planters, many of whom identified as Christians. It is a lamentable fact that the church—in both Catholic and Protestant forms—was not only complicit with the institution of chattel slavery but also, more often than not, perpetuated it through theological violence. The Christian faith and the Bible were weaponized against the enslaved.

Katharine Gerbner elucidates this phenomenon in her book, *Christian Slavery*. Gerbner highlights two constructs that ensured for Whites that their enslaved coreligionists would remain in bondage. The first she calls "Protestant Supremacy," which "was the predecessor of White Supremacy, an ideology that emerged after the codification of racial slavery."[12] Gerbner says,

> I refer to 'Protestant' Supremacy, rather than 'Anglican' or 'Christian' Supremacy, because this ideology was present throughout the Protestant American colonies, from the Danish West Indies to Virginia and beyond . . . In these colonies, Anglican, Dutch Reformed, and Lutheran slave owners conceived of their Protestant identities as fundamental to their status as masters. They constructed a caste system based on Christian status, in which 'heathenish' slaves were afforded no rights or privileges while Catholics, Jews, and non-conforming Protestants were viewed with suspicion and distrust, but granted more protections.[13]

Regarding the second construct, "Christian Slavery," Gerbner states that enslavers attacked missionaries in various ways for evangelizing enslaved Africans. In response to the barrage of verbal and physical attacks by the enslavers, missionaries began to promote "Christian Slavery" that married Christian conversion with bondage. Moreover, they worked to pass legislation that sanctioned ownership of enslaved Christians, emphasizing race, rather than religion, as the primary feature of bondage.[14] In other words, both enslavers and missionaries knew that Christian conversion and baptism were incompatible with slavery. As a result, enslavers attacked the missionaries for proselytizing enslaved Africans. In turn, the missionaries preached a counterfeit Christianity that emphasized subservience over against liberation of the body and soul. Their devious attempts to exclude the enslaved from the true Christian faith were futile, as conversion is a supernatural work of the Holy Spirit no human being can thwart.

For the enslaved, the road to salvation, as Langston Hughes aptly stated, "ain't been no crystal stair. It's had tacks in it, and splinters, and boards torn up, and places with no carpet on the floor—Bare."[15] Despite the fact that the enslaved were converted to the Christian faith, those who preached the gospel to them maintained that their conversion had no effect on their status as slaves. This heresy of "Christian Slavery" was ubiquitous due to the idols of white supremacy and the love of money, the latter of which is the root of all kinds of evil (1 Tim 6:10)—evil like the prevalence of rape inherent in chattel slavery, which was recounted by an anonymous formerly enslaved woman to Ophelia Settle Egypt, a scholar who conducted interviews with the formerly enslaved during 1929–1930.

> They would buy a fine girl and then a fine man and just put them together like cattle; they would not stop to marry them. If she was a good breeder, they was proud of her. I was stout and they were saving me for a breeding woman but by the time I was big enough I was free. I had an aunt in Mississippi and she had about twenty children by her master. On Sunday they would get us ready to go to church. They would dress us up after we ask them if we could go and they would have me walk off from them and they would look at me, and I'd hear them saying, "She's got a fine shape; she'll make a good breeder," but I didn't know what they were talking about. Then there was old Sam Watkins, – he would ship their husbands (slaves) out of bed and get in with their wives. One man (a slave) said he stood it as long as he could and one morning he just stood outside, and when he (the master) got with his wife (the slave), he just choked him to death. He knew it was death, but it was death anyhow; so he just killed him. They hanged him. There has always been a law in Tennessee that if a Negro kill a white man it means death.[16]

This haunting account of rape amplifies the inherent wickedness of the enslavers and missionaries' use of spiritual manipulation through exegetical malpractice. Enslaved people could not consent to sex due to the power dynamics, bondage, and restricted agency. Rape, which is condemned in the Bible, was used not only as a capitalistic tool within the institution of slavery; it was also a tool of domination. The enslaved were commoditized and reduced to breeders to ensure that more people would be born into enslavement for sale and distribution. The ideology of white supremacy, to which enslavers pledged their allegiance—believing themselves to be superior to the enslaved—kept the wheels of oppression turning over the bodies of enslaved Africans, who were a means to an end to keep the money flowing.

Moreover, the exorbitant wealth of America and Europe was amassed on the scar-ridden backs of enslaved Africans, who were ensnared by the diabolical, race-based institution of chattel slavery in the United States. As the reprehensible institution continued unabated, Matthew Desmond, author of the *New York Times* article, "American Capitalism Is Brutal. You Can Trace That to the Plantation," says that, "Slavery was undeniably a font of phenomenal wealth. By the eve of the Civil War, the Mississippi Valley was home to more millionaires per capita than anywhere else in the United States. Cotton grown and picked by enslaved workers was the nation's most valuable export. The combined value of enslaved people exceeded that of all the railroads and factories in the nation."[17] The enslaved were America's greatest asset. Human beings, reduced to money-making machines, worked tirelessly for what would become the foundation of American capitalism. After slavery ended, its wicked legacy morphed and led to the evils of sharecropping, convict-leasing, Jim Crow, the great migration due to white terrorism, and lynchings. Presently, the wages of slavery continue in the form of mass incarceration, police brutality, the racial wealth gap, and "medical apartheid,"[18] where Black women are three to four times more likely to die during childbirth.

WHAT ARE REPARATIONS?

In her book, *Reparations for Slavery and the Slave Trade: A Transnational and Comparative History,* Araujo provides both a historical definition of reparations and a distinction between two dimensions of reparations. She writes, "Historically, the term reparation has been employed to convey the idea of making amendments for past wrongs."[19] Regarding the two dimensions of reparations, she says: "The first is moral or symbolic, and usually consists of apologies and actions to help those who were victims of wrongdoing. The second one carries a financial and material scope. In other words, the victim of past wrongs also obtains money or other possessions, such as land, as payment for the misconduct inflicted."[20]

It is a little-known fact that some former enslavers received financial compensation after emancipation. Tera W. Hunter explains that "on April 16, 1862, President Abraham Lincoln signed a bill emancipating enslaved people in Washington, the end of a long struggle. But to ease slaveowners' pain, the District of Columbia Emancipation Act paid those loyal to the Union up to $300 for every enslaved person freed."[21]

There are also historical examples of other ethnic groups that rightfully received reparations for the egregious wrongs committed against them. According to Manisha Sinha,

> perhaps the most successful case is West Germany's 1953 agreement to pay some $845 million (in the dollars of the day) to the Conference on Jewish Material Claims Against Germany and the newly founded state of Israel as reparations for the Holocaust... The U.S. government also formally apologized and paid reparations to Japanese American citizens wrongfully interned in camps during World War II—to the tune of $20,000 each—with the passage of the Civil Liberties Act of 1988.[22]

Several institutions in the United States have examined historical connections to slavery. Some have acknowledged their complicity and participation in slavery and have taken further steps beyond symbolic reparations, providing financial reparations to the descendants of the enslaved. Sinha notes that

> though many universities in the Anglo-American world have recently explored their history of ill-gotten wealth from slave trading and slavery, only a handful of predominantly religious institutions have moved toward reparations. The best-known example is Georgetown University, where Jesuits sold 272 slaves in 1838 to save their college. Not only did Georgetown offer a formal apology, it also tracked down the slaves' descendants to offer them admission.[23]

Unlike Georgetown University, in 2018, Southern Baptist Theological Seminary released its "Report on Slavery and Racism in the History of the Southern Baptist Theological Seminary." The report disclosed that all four seminary founders were enslavers, and, in the early twentieth century, the seminary's faculty was comprised of segregationists.[24] Despite a preponderance of evidence in the report and their anemic apology, SBTS declined to pay reparations.[25]

WHAT DO REPARATIONS HAVE TO DO WITH CHRISTIANS?

First and foremost, it is an indictment of the church that the Christian institutions that were historically the architects of the transatlantic slave trade, chattel slavery, and all of the subsequent atrocities that followed have mostly been silent on the subject of reparations or vehemently opposed to it. In light of the imperatives of the gospel, the church should be leading on this, not the government, universities, or insurance companies. Although all of these institutions are complicit and owe reparations, the church does too. Reparations are part of the very fabric of the Christian faith. In fact, it is central to the gospel.

Before I explain how reparations relate to the Christian gospel, I offer my own working definition of reparations as they apply to the injustice perpetuated against Black people. *Reparations are a gracious invitation to confess, repent, and repair egregious sins from the past and present that have had a deleterious impact on the lives of Black people, with a commitment to never commit such heinous acts again.*

The Triune God is a covenantal God who promised, "I will walk among you, and will be your God, and you shall be my people" (Lev 26:12).[26] Therefore, the Christian faith is a covenantal faith. We are not saved unto ourselves. We are saved unto God and into a glorious covenant community. We are bound to each other covenantally, meaning that we belong to one another. As a result, we have covenant obligations to God and to each other. This is why Jesus said, "You shall love the Lord your God with all your heart, and with all your soul, and with all your mind. This is the great and first commandment. And a second is like it, You shall love your neighbor as yourself" (Matt 22:37–40). When we come to faith in Jesus Christ, rugged individualism and the myth of pulling ourselves up by our own bootstraps has no place. The sin of an individual within the community impacts the whole community and even those outside of the community.

The call for reparations serves as a covenant lawsuit. A covenant lawsuit is legal imagery invoked in the Bible, especially, though not exclusively, in the Old Testament. The lawsuit charges God's covenant people with breaking the covenant with God and with one another by violating covenantal laws. Examples of covenant lawsuits are found, for instance, in Deuteronomy 32, Ezekiel 16, Micah 6, and Revelation 1–3. The pattern usually begins with an imperative command to "Listen!" or "Hear!" Following this initial command, witnesses are called forth, God's loving-kindness and acts of faithfulness to his people are recounted, the indictment is articulated, the sentence is given, and, finally, a promise of restoration and mercy for the repentant is proclaimed.

In that vein, I'm going to explicate one of several biblical views of reparations by utilizing the Reformed Tradition's framework of the four stages of redemptive history: creation, fall, redemption, and restoration. You may hear echoes of the covenant lawsuit spring forth.

CREATION

In the beginning, God created the Heavens and the Earth. All things were created by the spoken word of God: light, seas, earth, living creatures, birds, vegetation, and more. Then God said,

> "Let us make man in our image, after our likeness; and let them have dominion over the fish of the sea, and over the birds of the air, and over the cattle, and over all the earth, and over every creeping thing that creeps on the earth. So God created man in his own image, in the image of God he created him; male and female he created them" (Gen 1:26–27).

Then God planted a beautiful and verdant environment called the Garden of Eden for Adam and Eve to dwell (Gen 2).

God observed all creation and "saw" that "it was very good" (Gen 1:31). Everything and everyone, including Black people. In a fundamental and rudimentary sense, the *Imago Dei* is what made slavery and its subsequent evils, such as rape, heinous and unconscionable. The enslavers that upheld the institution of slavery deemed Africans and their descendants to be inhuman brutes that needed to be tamed and civilized. It was a blatant violation of the image of God within Black people and went against the commandments of God, which are the covenant stipulations for God's people.

Slavery involved what God expressly forbids: human-stealing, covetousness, adultery, rape, idolatry, making oneself god over others, controlling the bodies of the enslaved, and so forth. Enslavers and proponents of the system philosophically and practically denied that enslaved Africans were in the image of God. The fight for freedom from the shackles of oppression has always been theological, because the image of God within Black people has not been recognized and is still under assault when we are denied our fundamental God-given human rights. So long as racist hierarchical structures exist and Black people are relegated to the bottom, the *Imago Dei* is assailed.

Ontologically, humans are the image of God. *Imago Dei* is not an addendum, nor is it incidental. According to Herman Bavinck, "the whole being, therefore and not *something in man* [humans] but *man himself* [humans themselves], is the image of God. . . . In our treatment of the doctrine of the image of God, then, we must highlight, in accordance with Scripture . . . the idea that a human being does not *bear* or *have* the image of God but that he or she *is* the image of God."[27] This has significant implications for Black people globally because our dignity, humanity, and physical appearance have sustained a barrage of attacks over the centuries. Indeed, such attacks continue to the present day.

Our entire being is the image of God, which includes the variegation of our skin tones and our multitudinous hair textures. The *Imago Dei* is reflected in our beautifully defined bone structure, the stride in our step, and the tenacious "souls of black folks." Truly, we are "fearfully and wonderfully made" (Psa 139:14; NRSV). The image of God is humanity's identity; it is the locus from which we derive our dignity and significance. The *Imago Dei* is the *sine qua non* for humanity. Without it, we cease to be human.

FALL

From the perspective of the Reformed theological Christian tradition, Genesis 3 narrates how sin, death, and misery entered the world. The text captures the moment that Adam and Eve fell from the state of innocence into a state of total depravity, confirming that humanity would share in the guilt of Adam's original sin. All humans—in their fallen state—have their hearts inclined toward evil apart from the saving work of Christ. Consequently, sin causes us to want to be god and gods over other people, which is why enslavers, colonizers, segregationists, and the like saw no problem with their insatiable desire to conquer African bodies and their lands. They did what was right in their own eyes.

Due to Adam and Eve's sins of idolatry, lust, and pride, they could not see that they were already like God because they were made in God's image and likeness. Sadly, it was not enough for them to be in God's image; they had to be god. Instead of an elevation from the state of innocence (which means that they were able not to sin) to glory, we observe a demotion.

According to Genesis 3:21, "the LORD God made for Adam and for his wife garments of skins, and clothed them." To paraphrase Douglass Green, "The putting on of new attire implies a change in status. Like when a man puts on a cape, we think superhero." Another example is when a woman puts on a bridal gown with all the accouterments, she becomes a bride. Adam and Eve, "the previously glorious humans have had a change in status. They are now more like the animals they are supposed to rule over than they are like God."[28]

In Adam, all die. As Paul puts it, "as sin came into the world through one man and death through sin, . . . so death spread to all men because all sinned"

(Rom 5:12). The impact of Adam's sin was immediate and comprehensive. Now there is a definitive separation between humanity and God. Sin is dehumanizing, but as wicked as sin is, regardless of how it manifests itself, sin does not remove the image of God from human beings. Sin can and does, however, mar the image of God within us.

The quest for reparations is not only a call to repair sinful acts from the past, which will provide some measure of relief for Black people who have been oppressed for centuries. It also represents an invitation for the oppressor to become what they are—by living into the *Imago Dei* within them—and to fulfill the covenant stipulations God has laid out for us all. When reparations are raised as one of the necessary steps to do justice and bring about healing from the devastating legacy of slavery and all that followed it, there are several predictable retorts from white Christians: "Well, I didn't enslave anyone! I can't be held responsible for the sins committed by my ancestors!" These responses reveal a myopic understanding of the gospel of Jesus Christ. Within the Reformed tradition, there is a theological framework known as "federal theology," which holds that because of the sin of one man, the first Adam, we all die and are guilty, but if we trust in the second Adam, Jesus Christ, we receive the free gift of grace and eternal life. As Lisa V. Fields, president of the Jude 3 Project, poignantly puts the matter in her lecture "Change the Story": "we hold humanity responsible for the sin of Adam. . . . We are not divorced from the father of humanity. So we preach a gospel that connects us from the fall of one man, but when it comes to America, we . . . disconnect ourselves from the original sin of America." Moreover, repentance and repair do not have an expiration date. So long as an individual has breath in their body, there is grace for them to repent of their sins and repair any harm that's been done. As my brilliant *Truth's Table* podcast co-host, Christina Edmondson, said in an episode entitled "Grumbling and Restorative Justice," "the fruit of our repentance belongs to God and our neighbor."

REDEMPTION

In the New Testament, Christ's advent brings into view inaugurated eschatology, which is the arrival of the kingdom of God—the new age. The kingdom of God is not only about the future; it is also a present reality (Col 1:13–14), and righteousness in Christ's teachings is always in reference to the kingdom (Rom 14:17).

Inaugurated eschatology, also known as the "already, but not yet," falls within a two-age eschatological framework. The first is the present-evil age, which is marked by sin, death, and misery (Gen 3:14–15; Eph. 5:16; Titus 2:12). The second is the new age, and in contradistinction to the former, it represents the final order marked by righteousness, peace, joy, justice, and eternal life (Rom 14:17).

The gospel of Jesus Christ holds that we were born enemies of God. According to Romans 5:10, due to Adam's sin, we are born guilty. There was a chasm between God and humanity, and the only way for that breach to be closed was through the sacrifice of a person, the Lord Jesus Christ, who is our reparation. He literally repaired the breach between God and humanity by leaving the Father's side, becoming like one of us in every way except for sin (Heb 2:17). According to the Gospel of John, as the Word of God who became flesh and dwelt among us (John 1:14), Jesus lived the sinless life we could not live.

Then, according to 2 Corinthians 5:21, "For our sake he made him to be sin who knew no sin, so that in him we might become the righteousness of God." Jesus did not sin. He is the only one that is blameless and faultless, yet for the sake of love, He died the death we should have died and secured eternal life for all who believe. He conquered death, hell, and the grave so that we would be reconciled to God and co-heirs with Christ. The gospel is an eternal reparation. Jesus is our reparation. How dare fellow covenant believers balk at reparations when they themselves are living on an eternal reparation wrought by Jesus Christ!

RESTORATION

Redemption is glorious, but that's not how the story ends. The restoration of all things is a present and future reality. Presently, God is still saving people by grace through faith in Jesus Christ. The Spirit is at work in believers and sanctifying us by making us more like Jesus, even when it doesn't seem like we are changing. Such sanctification is progressive, not linear. In the future, Christ will return to judge both the living and the dead for sin and evil. Death will be no more, for God will cast death into the depths of hell. Christ's kingdom will have no end, and all things will be restored.

Reparations can never fully repair and restore Africans on the continent and Black people in the Diaspora to wholeness. Reparation is, however, an act of justice that brings temporary relief, starts the healing process, and points forward to the greater eschatological reality of restoration.

To explore restoration further, I submit a concept I call the "eschatological imagination." While we are unsure of what the eschatological restoration will look like, using our *eschatological imagination*, we can envision what it could be. For instance, in my *eschatological imagination*, I envision God restoring back to my African American and Caribbean siblings their ethnic identity, language, and connection to West Africa. Everything stolen will be restored for my Ibibio people and fellow West Africans whose relatives were trafficked in the transatlantic slave trade. I envision us finally reunited with Bassey, Iquo, Asuquo, Enewan, Edet, Nkoyo, Edem, Ekaette, Atim, and Effiong. I imagine meeting distant relatives for the first time in Glory—African Americans to whom we are related but whom we never knew because of the severed connections wrought by the transatlantic slave trade and chattel slavery.

A time is coming when there will be no more police brutality, no more police, no more systemic racism, no more racial wealth gap, no more white supremacy, no more high rates of maternal and infant mortality, no more mass incarceration, and no more sin!

Revelation 21:1–4 paints a beautiful picture of this glorious future that awaits us:

> Then I saw a new heaven and a new earth; for the first heaven and the first earth had passed away, and the sea was no more. And I saw the holy city, new Jerusalem, coming down out of heaven from God, prepared as a bride adorned for her husband; and I heard a loud voice from the throne saying, "Behold, the dwelling of God is with men. He will dwell with them, and they shall be his people, and God himself will be with them; he will wipe away every tear from their eyes, and death shall be no more, neither shall there be mourning nor crying nor pain any more, for the former things have passed away."

In the meantime, the Christian and Catholic church must bear witness to the coming restoration in concrete ways that reflect the nature of God's reign by paying reparations that address the church's complicity with slavery and white supremacy. Reparations NOW: For the Glory of God and the witness of the church!

NOTES

1. Ana Lucia Araujo, *Reparations for Slavery and the Slave Trade: A Transnational and Comparative History,* HPOD (Bloomsbury Academic, 2017), 14.

2. Araujo, *Reparations.*

3. Randy J. Sparks, "Two Princes of Calabar: An Atlantic Odyssey from Slavery to Freedom," *The William and Mary Quarterly* 59, no. 3 (July 2002): 555.

4. Edet A. Udo, *Who Are the Ibibio?* (Africana-FEP Publishers Limited, 1983), 47.

5. The Editors of Encyclopaedia Britannica, "Akwa Ibom | State, Nigeria," Encyclopedia Britannica, July 20, 1998, accessed January 2023, https://www.britannica.com/place/Akwa-Ibom.

6. Udo, *Who Are the Ibibio?*, 3.

7. Carolyn Brown and Paul Lovejoy, *Repercussions of the Atlantic Slave Trade: The Interior of the Bight of Biafra and the African Diaspora,* First edition (Africa World Press, 2010), 6.

8. Brown and Lovejoy, *Repercussions,* 3.

9. Brown and Lovejoy, *Repercussions,* 4.

10. Brown and Lovejoy, *Repercussions,* 11.

11. Slave Voyages, "Trans-Atlantic Slave Trade-Database," accessed January 2023, https://www.slavevoyages.org/voyage/database.

12. Katharine Gerbner, *Christian Slavery: Conversion and Race in the Protestant Atlantic World* (Early American Studies), reprint (Philadelphia, PA: University of Pennsylvania Press, 2019), 2.

13. Gerbner, *Christian Slavery,* 2–3.

14. Gerbner, *Christian Slavery,* 3.

15. Langston Hughes and Lisa Shea, *The Weary Blues - Poems of Langston Hughes from 1926 - Illustrated Version: Edited and Illustrated by Lisa Shea* (Independently published, 2022).

16. L, "Voices of Slavery: 'They Were Saving Me For a Breeding Woman,'" This Cruel War, August 2016, accessed September 7, 2019, https://thiscruelwar.wordpress.com/2016/08/25/voices-of-slavery-they-were-saving-me-for-a-breeding-woman/.

17. Matthew Desmond, "American Capitalism Is Brutal. You Can Trace That to the Plantation," *The New York Times,* August 14, 2019, accessed March 2023, https://www.nytimes.com/interactive/2019/08/14/magazine/slavery-capitalism.html.

18. "Medical Apartheid" was coined by Harriet A. Washington, author of "Medical Apartheid."

19. Araujo, *Reparations,* 2.

20. Araujo, *Reparations,* 2.

21. Tera W. Hunter, "When Slaveowners Got Reparations.," *The New York Times,* April 16, 2019, accessed December 2022, https://www.nytimes.com/2019/04/16/opinion/when-slaveowners-got-reparations.html.

22. Manisha Sinha, "The Long History of American Slavery Reparations.," *The Wall Street Journal,* September 20, 2019, accessed October 2019, https://www.wsj.com/articles/the-long-history-of-american-slavery-reparations-11568991623.

23. Sinha, "Long History."

24. R. Albert Mohler Jr., Curtis Woods, John Wilsey, Kevin Jones, Jarvis Williams, Matthew J. Hall, and Gregory Wills, "Report on Slavery and Racism in the History of the Southern Baptist Theological Seminary," December 2018, accessed June 2019, https://www.sbts.edu/southern-project/.

25. Samuel Smith, "SBTS Refused Request to Pay Black College Over Ties to Slavery," *The Christian Post,* June 6, 2019, accessed June 2019, https://www.christianpost.com/news/sbts-refuses-request-to-pay-reparations-to-black-college-over-ties-to-slavery.html.

26. Unless noted otherwise, all biblical quotations are from the RSV.

27. Herman Bavinck, John Bolt, and John Vriend, *Reformed Dogmatics, Vol. 2: God and Creation* (Baker Academic, 2004), 554.

28. I owe this explanation to a former professor, Douglass Green, whom I have paraphrased here.

BIBLIOGRAPHY

Araujo, Ana Lucia. *Reparations for Slavery and the Slave Trade: A Transnational and Comparative History*. HPOD. Bloomsbury Academic, 2017.

Bavinck, Herman, John Bolt, and John Vriend. *Reformed Dogmatics, Vol. 2: God and Creation*. Grand Rapids, MI: Baker Academic, 2004.

Brown, Paul and Paul Lovejoy. *Repercussions of the Atlantic Slave Trade: The Interior of the Bight of Biafra and the African Diaspora*, First edition. Africa World Press, 2010.

Desmond, Matthew. "American Capitalism Is Brutal. You Can Trace That to the Plantation." *The New York Times*, August 14, 2019. Accessed March 2023. https://www.nytimes.com/interactive/2019/08/14/magazine/slavery-capitalism.html.

The Editors of Encyclopaedia Britannica. "Akwa Ibom State, Nigeria." *Encyclopedia Britannica*. July 20, 1998. Accessed January 2023. https://www.britannica.com/place/Akwa-Ibom.

Gerbner, Katharine. *Christian Slavery: Conversion and Race in the Protestant Atlantic World (Early American Studies)*. Reprint. Philadelphia, PA: University of Pennsylvania Press, 2019.

Hughes, Langston and Lisa Shea. *The Weary Blues—Poems of Langston Hughes from 1926 - Illustrated Version: Edited and Illustrated by Lisa Shea*. Independently published, 2022.

Hunter, Tera W. "When Slaveowners Got Reparations." *The New York Times*, April 16, 2019. Accessed December 2022. https://www.nytimes.com/2019/04/16/opinion/when-slaveowners-got-reparations.html.

L. "Voices of Slavery: 'They Were Saving Me For a Breeding Woman.'" *This Cruel War*, August 2016. Accessed September 7, 2019. https://thiscruelwar.wordpress.com/2016/08/25/voices-of-slavery-they-were-saving-me-for-a-breeding-woman/.

Mohler, R. Albert Jr., Albert, Curtis Woods, John Wilsey, Kevin Jones, Jarvis Williams, Matthew J. Hall, and Gregory Wills. "Report on Slavery and Racism in the History of the Southern Baptist Theological Seminary," December 2018. Accessed June 2019. https://www.sbts.edu/southern-project/.

Sinha, Manisha. "The Long History of American Slavery Reparations." *The Wall Street Journal*, September 20, 2019. Accessed October 2019. https://www.wsj.com/articles/the-long-history-of-american-slavery-reparations-11568991623.

Slave Voyages. "Trans-Atlantic Slave Trade-Database." Accessed January 2023. https://www.slavevoyages.org/voyage/database.

Smith, Samuel. "SBTS Refused Request to Pay Black College Over Ties to Slavery." *The Christian Post*, June 6, 2019. Accessed June 2019. https://www.christianpost.com/news/sbts-refuses-request-to-pay-reparations-to-black-college-over-ties-to-slavery.html.

Sparks, Randy J. "Two Princes of Calabar: An Atlantic Odyssey from Slavery to Freedom." *The William and Mary Quarterly* 59. 3 (July 2002): 555–584.

Udo, Edet A. *Who Are the Ibibio?* Africana-FEP Publishers Limited, 1983.

Chapter Fourteen

Catholic Social Thought and Reparations

Christina McRorie

How does the tradition of Catholic social thought (CST) orient us toward the conversation of this volume on reparations? Is there a Catholic stance on the issue, or should there be? If not, is there a Catholic way to approach reparations—substantively, methodologically, or attitudinally?

We should start by noting that there has not been any magisterial pronouncement (that is, papal encyclical, conciliar document, or American episcopal letter) on the precise question of whether to endorse a federally-sponsored redistributive program in the name of acknowledging and redressing historic injustices inflicted upon African Americans in the United States.[1] And, although a growing number of Catholic voices have called for the Church itself to make reparations, the subject of federal reparations has arguably not yet reached a critical mass within Catholic ethics (with the exception of a few scholars; more on these in what follows).[2] Even so, the Catholic tradition is chock-full of theological commitments, ethical principles, and socio-analytical methods that are obviously relevant to this question, both within and external to its growing conversation on racism and racial justice.

This essay maps some of these resources, beginning with principles relevant to the duty of reparation and the state's redistributive role, and proceeding to the methodological commitments structuring Catholic social analysis and discussions of public policy. In reflecting on these, this essay will not build an argument either for or against any one specific program of reparations. Instead, it will suggest that CST offers significant grounds for supporting the idea of reparations in principle, and a range of attitudinal and prudential considerations that ought to guide our deliberations over concrete proposals.

THE NORMATIVE COMMITMENTS ANIMATING CST

This essay takes it as firmly established that the Catholic tradition opposes racism, and thus construes both America's history of chattel slavery and legal segregation under Jim Crow law and its ongoing individual and systemic racism as a gross injustice.[3] A growing number of voices have compellingly argued that the institutional Church in the United States has not yet reckoned with either its historic participation in these evils or its ongoing complicity in systemic racism.[4] In so doing, they point out that this places the Church's own witness "at odds" with its teachings "on paper"; Bryan Massingale has called this a "scandalous counterwitness."[5] Since examining that counterwitness is beyond the scope of this essay, this essay focuses on the Church's teaching and on the broader field of Catholic social thought, which alongside magisterial documents includes theological scholarship and reflection on the lived experience of those who practice CST.

The Duty to Make Reparation, Restitution, and Satisfaction

In asking how the Catholic tradition orients us toward reparations, John Slattery proposes we start by considering the Catechism's claim that "Every offense committed against justice and truth entails the *duty of reparation*, even if its author has been forgiven . . . This reparation, moral and sometimes material, must be evaluated in terms of the extent of the damage inflicted."[6] Other passages are even more specific regarding the economic implications of this duty:

> In virtue of commutative justice, *reparation for injustice* requires the restitution of stolen goods to their owner: Jesus blesses Zacchaeus for his pledge: "If I have defrauded anyone of anything, I restore it fourfold." Those who, directly or indirectly, have taken possession of the goods of another, are obliged to make restitution of them, or to return the equivalent in kind or in money, if the goods have disappeared, as well as the profit or advantages their owner would have legitimately obtained from them. Likewise, all who in some manner have taken part in a theft or who have knowingly benefited from it—for example, those who ordered it, assisted in it, or received the stolen goods—are obliged to make restitution in proportion to their responsibility and to their share of what was stolen.[7]

Slattery thus suggests that we approach reparations from the traditional understanding that commutative justice requires making restitution of whatever one has wrongfully taken or even passively received.[8]

At the same time, we might also begin by considering the role that restitution has played in the sacrament of reconciliation over the years. In the Catholic view, confession and true contrition are necessarily accompanied by satisfaction, or action that brings forth "fruits that befit repentance," which is integral for restoring the sinner's relationship with God.[9] One illustration of this in practice can be found in Bartolomé de Las Casas's guides for confessors, which directed them to refuse absolution to Spanish colonizers unwilling to make restitution to indigenous persons they had wronged.[10] Las Casas went so far as to urge the Spanish monarchs themselves to pay for their "sins of conquest in the New World" by returning taken lands, upon pain of their perdition.[11] Although the monarchs declined, other Spaniards did pay restitution, and in at least one instance this was done by a conquistador's heir in accordance with his will.[12]

If this case underscores the economic significance of the link between our reconciliations with God and other humans, it also begins to display the limits of this obligation. Traditionally, reflection on the duty to make restitution and repair harms has been framed as a matter of interpersonal ethics and does not address third-party enforcement or issues raised by the passage of time.

That said, a somewhat clearer picture of how this duty applies to nation states can be found in a 2001 statement by the Pontifical Council for Justice and Peace. It declares,

> From the legal point of view, all persons (individual or corporate) have a right to equitable reparation if personally and directly they have suffered injury (material or moral). The duty to make reparation must be fulfilled in an appropriate way. As far as possible, reparation should erase all the consequences of the illicit action and restore things to the way they would most probably be if that action had not occurred. When such a restoration is not possible, reparation should be made through compensation (equivalent reparation). This is the most common form of reparation, but the calculation of the compensation is often difficult. When compensation does not suffice to make reparation for a moral injury, moral reparation can be made, that is satisfaction. An example of this is the offering of an apology or expression of regret to the victim State by the State responsible for the wrong.
>
> The Holy See is aware of the great difficulty that this "need for reparation" can pose when it becomes a demand for compensation. It is not the Church's task to propose a technical solution to so complex a problem (in this context, one could mention [the claim of the] Episcopal Conferences of Africa and Madagascar: "Not only should the rich nations cancel debts, but they should also agree to compensation for both the debt and the wrongs they have done to Africa"). But the Holy See wishes to emphasize that the need for reparation reinforces the obligation of giving substantial help to developing countries, an obligation weighing chiefly on the more developed countries.[13]

Clearly, existing Church teaching endorses the concept of reparations paid between states, and even identifies reparation as a right on the part of victims.

Citing the logic used in this statement, Nicholas Ensley Mitchell builds a Catholic argument for reparations based in the US government's "intentional pauperization" and systematic denial of what the encyclical *Populorum progressio* calls "truly human conditions" to Black communities.[14] Mindful of the emphasis on offending parties that are directly "responsible for the wrong" done to victims who have "personally and directly" suffered, however, Mitchell writes, "I limit the scope of my argument for reparations to the Jim Crow period because the final victims of Jim Crow and their immediate descendants—the context of whose lives were greatly impacted by segregation—are still alive."[15] Focusing solely on this era and on the government's culpability for harms experienced by persons living today, Mitchell develops a compelling—and even devastating—case for US reparations in a Catholic register.

Other calls for reparations are not so limited in scope and envision them as a means of redress for a more diffuse set of crimes perpetrated by a range of institutions and individuals that include but are not restricted to the state. Given that existing Catholic teaching on restitution tends to presume a present-oriented lens drawn from interpersonal ethics, how can its affirmation of a duty to repair harm speak to this broader vision of the role reparations should play? To answer this, we need to back up and consider how the Catholic tradition directs us to consider the rights and responsibilities of states more generally, and their role in promoting the common good.

Principles of CST Especially Relevant to Redistributive Policies

For this we turn to a set of principles at the heart of CST. These articulate in accessible terms values drawn from scripture and the Christian tradition that should shape Christian expectations for public life, and are relevant for both individuals and groups, including states. What follows is not a complete listing, but an introduction to selected principles especially relevant to taxation and redistribution.

Property as a Right and Responsibility, and Its Social Function

Given that any state-sponsored reparation program would involve redistributing revenues collected via taxation, we begin by asking: what does CST have to say about private property? While CST has long affirmed a right to private ownership (including of wealth), it has never held this right to be absolute or unconditional.[16] This is because this right entails the responsibility to use property in a way that is ordered to the common good.

This responsibility stems from the recognition in CST that property has an intrinsically social character and continues to exercise a social function within and influence upon the wider community even when owned privately. This has sometimes been expressed with the memorable phrasing of a "social mortgage" existing on all private property (again, including wealth). This framing refers us to the social networks within which individual ownership is possible, and which should condition our private use of goods.[17]

Universal Destination of Goods

The theological grounds for the norm imposed by property's social function can be found in the claim that the goods of creation share a "universal destination"—namely, human flourishing—because "God intended the earth with everything contained in it for the use of all human beings."[18] In light of this, human property laws and practices of private ownership are legitimate only to the extent that they facilitate creation's original purpose of supporting humanity, and illegitimate where they frustrate and contravene this end. More specifically, CST follows the early parents of the church in proclaiming that withholding excess in the face of urgent human need is effectively to steal, and even to murder—regardless of local property laws. (Or, in Ambrose's memorable words, that "it is the hungry man's bread that you withhold, [and] the naked man's cloak that you store away."[19]) This applies between states and groups as well as between individuals.[20]

Preferential Option for the Poor

Although articulated in these terms within CST only in the twentieth century, the principle of the preferential option for the poor arises from scripture's consistent portrayal of God as having special concern for the well-being of the most vulnerable (and even identifying with them in Matthew 25), and accordingly directing God's people to show them particular care. In light of this, MT Dávila has called the option for the poor an "incarnational principle."[21] On both a personal and social level, it calls Christians to participate in the divine character by lovingly prioritizing the needs of the suffering, marginalized, and oppressed.

Government as One Medium of Collective Action

CST holds that it is "society as a whole, acting through public and private institutions" that has a moral responsibility to put these principles into practice.[22] Although this "does not mean that government has the primary or exclusive role" in addressing social problems, CST does accord it a "positive moral responsibility" to protect human dignity and promote the common good.[23] This includes the duty to adjudicate conflicts between "private gain and basic community needs," to collect revenues and use them to support those needs, and to institute a system of taxation that is fair and that encourages just economic activity.[24] Given this, in CST taxes "are not intrinsically confiscatory," but an important way that communities act together for the common good.[25]

Subsidiarity and Participation

The role envisioned for government within CST becomes even clearer when we consider the principle of subsidiarity, which holds that social power should be exercised at appropriate levels, with larger and "higher association[s]" helping smaller associations (such as businesses, neighborhoods, nonprofit organizations, and families) achieve their proper social ends.[26] In light of this, "government should undertake only those initiatives which exceed the capacity of individuals or private groups acting independently."[27] Although this is sometimes summarized as a "preferential option for the small," it is better understood as encouraging a nuanced vision of society as made up of overlapping and interdependent groups with distinct capacities and limitations, and thus distinct responsibilities to contribute to and protect the common good.[28]

Subsidiarity thus sits closely alongside CST's use of participation as a criterion of social justice. In their 1986 pastoral letter on the economy, the US bishops identify "contributive" justice as an important dimension of the biblical vision of justice and argue that this is as important as commutative and distributive justice. This recognizes that "persons have an obligation to be active and productive participants in the life of society and that society has a duty to enable them to participate in this way."[29]

Summing Up Thus Far

The Normative Goal of Using the State to Address Historical Wrongs with Ongoing Effects

A fuller accounting of the principles of CST relevant to racial reconciliation would include—at the very least—human dignity (which is grounded in the *Imago Dei*), the common good (the idea that the good of the community is more than just the aggregation of individual well-being), and solidarity (the recognition that our interdependence generates a shared moral responsibility for each other and for all).[30] Nonetheless, this is enough of an introduction to now ask: where does this leave us with reparations? Thus far, it seems clear that the normative goal of using the state to redress historical wrongs with ongoing effects is consistent with the principles of CST.

To start with, this is because CST acknowledges a positive role for the state, which includes its responsibility to collect revenue from our shared abundance and use it for public projects that ensure the ability of the least well off to participate in society, and thus the universal destination of goods. One could, therefore, imagine a Catholic case for reparations simply on these terms (and without reference to the further question of culpability and atonement, which we will take up shortly): as a program to support the agency and participation of the marginalized, in this case Black Americans. To be sure, the principle of subsidiarity does issue a standing caution against "big" projects (and any federal reparations program would obviously count as big!). At the same time, subsidiarity also legitimizes large-scale action in cases where no smaller social body is capable of accomplishing an important goal. The question here would thus not be whether the principles of CST support redistributive programs for specific disadvantaged groups (they clearly do), but whether a federal program is truly necessary to accomplish the goal of their empowerment and participation. But this moves the conversation to pragmatics; at the level of theory and principles, it is hard to see commitments within CST that should lead Catholics to oppose reparations *a priori*.

Indeed, if anything, these values would push us to remember that as a response to injustice, policy is useful and often necessary but never itself sufficient, given that the state is not the only agency tasked with promoting the common good, or the only way Christians act together. A fuller conversation must also ask: how can other groups and institutions contribute to the goals of enfranchising Black Americans more fully in our shared life and combatting inequalities rooted in racism, past and present? And in light of subsidiarity, how can we make sure public policies supplement and support, rather than displace, such private efforts?

One prominent example of such a private effort can be found in Georgetown University's response to a 2019 student referendum calling for reparations to the descendants of 272 enslaved persons owned and sold by the Jesuits in 1838. In response, Georgetown has established and promised ongoing contributions to a Reparations Fund for community projects impacting descendants, and now also offers preferred admissions status to descendants of persons once owned by the Georgetown Jesuits.[31] And, not insignificantly, the creation of the Descendants Truth & Reconciliation Foundation that directs the fund has resulted from and further prompted an ongoing truth and reconciliation process within the larger Jesuit Conference of Canada and the United States.[32] Such efforts illustrate the importance of resisting any temptation to effectively "outsource" responsibility for addressing historically rooted inequality to the government; there is much good that can and should be done by parties other than the state.

The Normative Goal of Using the State to Apologize for Historical Wrongs

We have not yet addressed the expressive nature of reparations as a form of public atonement. As Georgetown's case vividly illustrates, reparations are not being sought simply as a means to address a generic inequality, but as a frank admission and apology for the fact that these inequalities reflect specific wrongdoing on the part of specific institutions and parties against a specific group that still needs addressing. How does CST orient us to this aspect of reparations?

This is an especially important question given that this is a major sticking point in the current conversation. Some Americans who support existing federal anti-poverty programs (and who might even support their expansion) object to the idea of reparations precisely on the grounds that they would require many who are "innocent" to apologize and atone—by paying, literally—for crimes they neither committed nor benefit from. In contrast, advocates of reparations argue that "many Americans are simply wrong about the magnitude and causes of racial wealth disparities," and "the case for justice must include identification of not only the perpetrators of racial harm but also those who gained from the harm—whether or not they inflicted it."[33]

At the heart of this debate lies an empirical question: To what extent do the health, education, income, wealth, and other disparities between races in the United States reflect advantages gained by whites and white institutions at the expense of Black Americans—or, as Protestant womanist ethicist Emilie Townes puts it, the "unjust enrichment of Whites that is not only a past event [but] is also a current event"?[34] In the terms of the Catechism, to what extent do whites and other nonblack Americans living today count as "receiving stolen goods"?[35]

This is an urgent line of inquiry, and not only for the process of calculating the size of reparations owed. Even more importantly, publicly reckoning with the answers to such questions will be a vital part of the process of "truth-telling," which Massingale, following magisterial teaching, underscores as an indispensable part of any social reconciliation process.[36] As he points out, the pursuit of racial justice often involves

> a contest or clash between competing and divergent social narratives. Thus the effort of reconciling social divisions entails debunking the "comfortable fictions"—the deliberate distortions, misleading euphemisms, selective recollections, and self-serving presentations—that societies employ to mask the

presence of injustice or make its existence tolerable . . . telling the truth of our situation, acknowledging our responsibility and complicity, and declaring who profited and how from these estrangements are essential to healing the wounds of racism.[37]

This suggests that full racial reconciliation will not be possible without a public accounting—which should be as economic as it is cultural and historical—of who still benefits from the legacy of slavery, and to what extent.[38]

At the same time, the broader principles of CST suggest that Christian support for reparations should not hinge on the answers to these questions, as if reparations would *only* be appropriate in cases where we can prove and quantify how much whites benefit from the oppression and social exclusion of Blacks. This is firstly because the duty to make restitution does not center on the offender's benefit, but on the harm done to the victim. A thief who has squandered his ill-gotten gains still owes reparation to his victims, despite his destitution. In our case, it is not only clear that Black Americans continue to experience economic harms that have their origins in slavery, legal segregation, and ongoing racism, but also now firmly established that the US government itself is directly responsible for many of these.[39] As Mitchell's Catholic case for reparations for Jim Crow illustrates, we have both a guilty "party" and identifiable victims who continue to suffer from that party's crimes; thus, the duty to reparation need not be indexed to a calculation of the positive benefits passively accruing to whites more generally. Indeed, to make support for reparations contingent on such calculations would be to keep the discussion inappropriately centered on whites, and to fail to consider the problem in terms immanent to those most affected—African Americans (more on this theme in Catholic thought shortly).

Moreover, an exclusively legal and defensive mode of accounting focused on white guilt is unnecessary in light of CST's positive understanding of the state as a medium of collective action for the common good. Because it does not assume that our obligations to each other are grounded in guilt, CST does not frame these as something we discharge by determining the minimal amount of sacrifice we "owe." Instead, our public actions should be motivated by solidarity and the recognition that "we are all really responsible for all."[40] Thus, CST does not envision taxes as a corrective measure punishing wealth, but as an important way to enable property to serve its divinely intended purpose (and reach its true "destination").

Here it is useful to consider comments that the US bishops have made in a discussion of affirmative action programs, which identify both the effective and expressive aims of these as a legitimate response to an obligation incumbent upon society overall:

> Where the effects of past discrimination persist, society has the obligation to take positive steps to overcome the legacy of injustice. Judiciously administered affirmative action programs in education and employment can be important expressions of the drive for solidarity and participation that is at the heart of true justice. Social harm calls for social relief.[41]

In this we see at work CST's vision of the state as one venue through which society meets a shared responsibility for our communal life that is greater than the obligations imposed by individual culpability, and which is organized more centrally around threats to the common good. What calls out for social relief here is social harm—not calculated levels of individual guilt.[42]

A similar logic of positive communal responsibility that transcends individual culpability is visible in reflections on how the Church today should approach its own past sins. A statement issued by the International Theological Commission, *Memory and Reconciliation: The Church and the Faults of the Past*, begins by referencing John Paul II's call for a "purification of memory . . . through a renewed historical and theological evaluation of" past injustices. It continues:

> This should lead—if done correctly—to a corresponding recognition of guilt and contribute to the path of reconciliation. Such a process can have a significant effect on the present, precisely because the consequences of past faults still make themselves felt and can persist as tensions in the present. The purification of memory is thus an "act of courage and humility in recognizing the wrongs done by those who have borne or bear the name of Christian." It is based on the conviction that because of "the bond which unites us to one another in the Mystical Body, all of us, though not personally responsible and without encroaching on the judgment of God, who alone knows every heart, bear the burden of the errors and faults of those who have gone before us."[43]

In a manner perhaps suggestive for politics, this statement indicates that membership in the body of Christ entails bearing the burdens of that body's past sins through a form of moral accounting that transcends our usual focus on present and individual culpability.

From multiple angles, then, it appears there is nothing in the substantive and normative content of CST that should lead Catholics to oppose the idea of reparations *ex ante*—and instead, much to suggest they should support it. This is true when considering reparations purely as a generic redistributive program aiming to empower the full social participation of a marginalized group. Reparations also appear consistent with the Catholic affirmation of a duty to make restitution to compensate victims for an offense, which clearly applies to the US government (as Mitchell has pointed out) where ongoing harms experienced by African Americans stem from racist policies, and which arguably applies to wider society to the extent that disparities between races reflect advantages gained by others at the expense of African Americans. Finally, the expressive dimension of reparations as a form of public atonement for prior injustice is consistent with the positive vision of the state as a medium of collective action in CST. Indeed, to the extent that the shared responsibilities engendered by our incorporation into the body of Christ are analogous to those resulting from our incorporation within a body politic, the tradition offers conceptual resources for arguing that such corporate atonement is not merely legitimate, but even necessary.

We should admit, however, that noticing this consistency at the level of values may not settle all questions Christians might have when considering reparations in practice. We might ask, for example, whether direct payments are the most efficient way to redress inequities and sustainably empower the flourishing of Black Americans, or whether some other form of public investment would be more impactful. Or, we might ask how to balance the different principles sketched here, such as private property and the universal destination of goods. Or, we might have concerns about the trade-offs or unintended consequences of such a massive redistributive undertaking. Even though such questions are primarily about the practicality of reparations rather than their normative legitimacy, they remain central to the current debate. Indeed, there are probably more than a few Christians who might support the goal of reparations in theory but object in practice, citing precisely such concerns about feasibility.

With this in mind, we now ask: how does CST tutor us to enter debates over pragmatic questions when it comes to public policy?

THE METHODOLOGICAL COMMITMENTS STRUCTURING CATHOLIC SOCIAL ANALYSIS

Thus far, this essay has effectively asked *whether* Catholics should join others in supporting reparations on grounds immanent to CST. In turning to methodology, it now asks *how* Catholics should enter into these public conversations. This section begins with CST's foundation in natural law, and then introduces the steps of the See, Judge, Act methodology. The argument here will be that together these encourage a mode of reasoning that is epistemically humble, attentive to the experience and insights of those affected by an injustice, and frank about the way that judgments on social questions inevitably rest on human (and thus contingent) interpretations of social reality.

Natural Law

As an approach to ethics, natural law is founded on the claim that a certain amount of moral insight is available to humans through rational reflection on our nature and our life together in society. That is, it assumes that we can use reason to understand the human good and thus discern what ought to be (or "law") by reflecting on what already is (or "nature"). Due to both sin and human finitude, however, Christian approaches to natural law do not assume that this interpretive process is always straightforward, or that the judgments we reach are automatically valid.[44] Instead, Christian natural law holds that we need to interpret and reflect on our experience in light of scripture and tradition, and in communities of faithful practice. Granting such caveats, this tradition generally encourages confidence in human reason—and, as a result, optimism regarding the possibility of moral agreement and collaboration across lines of difference.[45]

In Catholic social teaching prior to the Second Vatican Council, this confidence led to a mode of reasoning that was largely philosophical, legal, and deductive, and which aimed to build up a body of timeless social doctrine by applying static principles to diverse situations.[46] In contrast, since the Council CST has been characterized by a growing historical consciousness, and the recognition that because human reasoning is shaped by our social contexts, natural law theory cannot "claim to have 'a view from nowhere.'"[47] One implication of this is that the task of reading "the signs of the times" and "interpreting them in the light of the Gospel" cannot be exclusively done "from above," as if the Church could use principles and abstract reasoning to reach solutions for every existing social problem; on many questions, the gospel must be applied to concrete circumstances from within particular cultures and communities.[48]

As we do this, the methodology of natural law directs us to keep in mind the extent to which this application relies on our interpretation of the particulars of our experience—that is, on our reading of nature and of what "is." The closer our moral pronouncements are to the first and most abstract precept of natural law, which is to "do good and avoid evil," the more certain we may be about them. As our judgments descend from this level to prescribe concrete courses of action, however, the more they rely on our grasp and interpretation of particulars, and thus are contestable. This necessarily lends our applied judgments a kind of provisionality: at least in theory, we ought to be open to their revision, if a new understanding of our context prompts us to specify our principles in new ways. In this sense, a natural law mode of reasoning encourages us to cultivate what some have called an "epistemic humility"—or even, as Margaret Farley has put it, the "grace of self-doubt"—that is appropriate to both humanity's fallen condition and our creaturely finitude.[49]

See, Judge, Act

Careful attention to our very human interpretation of reality is also woven into what's called the "See, Judge, Act" method.[50] This offers an approach to social description and problem solving that moves from a critical interpretation of reality through a spiritual and moral assessment of that reality, and toward the goal of transformative social action.[51]

The first step—of "seeing"—directs us to become students of the social systems and problems we mean to address. Above all, this requires that Christians begin by listening to the experiences of the poor, the socially marginalized, and those directly and negatively affected by the problem we are considering. This method assumes that this listening is not only ethically owed to these groups as a way to empower their agency, but also critical as a matter of strategy, given that the suffering have a privileged insight into the dynamics of their own oppression.[52] This has been an especial concern of Pope Francis, who regularly characterizes those at the "peripheries" of society as "see[ing] aspects of reality that are invisible to the centers of power where weighty decisions are made."[53] This step also directs us to consult nontheological sources of insight into the root causes and internal dynamics of the problems we study. Among these external sources, the discipline of economics in particular reminds us to consider the trade-offs and unintended consequences of all policy decisions (including decisions *not* to act), and to attend carefully to the incentives each would create.[54]

Whereas "seeing" focuses on understanding and causation, "judging" moves us to attribute moral responsibility. This unabashedly theological step directs us to use the language of sin to describe where both individual action and social institutions are unjust. It also challenges us to identify our own forms of complicity with and malformation by the sinful structures we're engaging and invites us to a process of conversion from these.

Following this, the final step of "action" invites us into a collaborative process of social transformation. While the practical actions we identify in this step may occur at any level (viz., be undertaken by families, groups and associations, businesses, or government), this method holds that these actions must always empower and be done *with*—and not solely to or on behalf of—those that we intend to serve.[55] In no small part this means following the leadership of those affected and closest to the problem. In so doing, we will come to understand the problems we are addressing—and the path forward to social justice—even more clearly; in this sense, this final step refers us again to the first step of seeing. See, Judge, Act is thus understood as an ongoing and iterative process and is sometimes referred to as a "pastoral circle."[56]

Summing Up Thus Far (Again)

With all this in mind, what can we now say about how CST tutors us to engage the practical conversation on reparations—strategically and attitudinally?

Centering the Conversation on Black Voices

The first thing to be said is that Christians should be working to make sure that discussion centers on—and that we attend closely to—the voices of Black communities, their understandings of the ongoing legacy of racism, and their visions of what it will take to empower their flourishing and full participation in American society. This is important both ethically and pragmatically, given that in different ways both natural law and See, Judge, Act emphasize the inadequacy of abstract and top-down forms of moral reasoning conducted by those at society's "center" rather than its peripheries, and the importance for all ethics of seeing reality rightly—or, as liberationists put it, of being "honest with the real."[57] In our context, this requires collectively listening to African American voices, so as to reach a fuller—and ideally, shared—grasp of the problem at hand.

Massingale has argued that the path toward this shared grasp of reality must be affective as well as discursive, given that the divergent social narratives regarding race operative in the United States today are as much "visceral" and "preconscious" as they are rational.[58] With this in mind, Massingale has highlighted the positive power of lament—of both actively lamenting and receptively witnessing it, and for both victims and the privileged alike—to reorient our sensibilities in a way that "transcends the limits of logic and reason."[59] In this sense, CST's invitation to attend to the voices affected by an injustice is arguably as much about opening ourselves up to being formed by different expressions of spirituality, art, and culture as it is about listening charitably to rational arguments, and as much a call to conversion and liberation from the affective and epistemic bondages of privilege as a call to better understand specific social problems.

Prudential Considerations Shaped by Insights from the Social Sciences

The next thing to be said is that CST also directs us not to enter the fray of policy debates without first being guided by the best available insight into our subject from fields outside theology. In addition to scholarship on reparations and redistributive policies, this would also include research on racial reconciliation and community empowerment. Christians should be wary of taking up a topic as complex as reparations at a merely philosophical level, or of "reinventing the wheel" in our contributions to public discourse.

Instead, we must let ourselves be led by existing scholarship on a range of questions—much of which, not coincidentally, comes from Black scholars. We might ask: what has been learned from the results of reparations programs undertaken elsewhere? Mitchell proposes that in addition to individual payments, reparations could take "the form of large-scale government investments in Black communities for infrastructure development, as well as home and property acquisition."[60] What is already known about the advantages and disadvantages of these various forms of reparations? More generally, what have practitioners and researchers found about what makes racial reconciliation efforts successful? What makes federal policy anti-poverty programs successful, and what works to sustainably reduce entrenched wealth inequalities?

Given the economic nature of these questions, it behooves us to attend especially carefully to insights available from the discipline of economics. It may be worthwhile, for example, to consider the emerging consensus within development economics that cash transfers to the poor can "be *more* effective on a dollar-for-dollar basis than 'traditional' development programming" at improving education and health outcomes and sustainably mitigating poverty.[61] Indeed, against the earlier and paternalistic assumption in development planning that the poor would simply waste any funds given to them directly, studies now consistently find that cash transfers are an effective way to combat poverty (and even negatively impact spending on what researchers call "temptation goods").[62]

At the same time, an economic perspective also pushes us to keep in mind the trade-offs inherent in all policy decisions, and to consider their unintended consequences. And so we might also ask, for example, how to balance various policy priorities, and whether reparations can be put into practice without prompting inflationary effects that would end up hurting the poor most. Fortunately, existing literature already takes up these questions and more.[63] While it is beyond the scope of this essay to summarize or evaluate this growing body of work, a genuinely Catholic mode of entering the conversation will require doing so.

Flexible and Pragmatic, Rather Than Dogmatic

Another observation is that the methods of CST encourage Christians to be flexible and pragmatic when making the concrete judgments that public policy requires, and not to be hung up on the quest to find perfect solutions. While the principles of CST do convey the timeless values of the Christian tradition, the tradition assumes that there are many ways to put these into practice. As the Pontifical Council for Peace and Justice declared in the case of reparations, "It is not the Church's task to propose a technical solution to so complex a problem." And, writing on regulation in general, the US bishops have observed, "The precise form of government involvement in this process cannot be determined in the abstract. It will depend on an assessment of specific needs and the most effective ways to address them."[64]

With this in mind, we should feel a certain sense of freedom when discerning how to address social needs, and not be afraid to experiment and take account of feedback as we attempt to pursue justice and gain clearer insight into the problems of our day. To be sure, such a thing is much easier said than done when it comes to federal policy in a nation as large as the United States—but it should nonetheless be a hallmark of Catholic approaches to public life.

Grace as the Final Word

The methodology of CST also suggests that Christians should approach difficult public discussions with the humility, courage, and sense of freedom proper to our status as beings who are called to share in God's own life through grace rather than through our own efforts—and to whom it has been declared that where sin abounds, grace abounds even more.[65]

We should admit that in the conversation on reparations, we (and whites above all) are going to need this grace. The truth-telling to which Massingale, Mitchell, Townes, and a host of others are calling the churches and American society will not be easy. Like the "judge" step in See, Judge, Act, it will require us to engage racism and racial inequality on a personal as well as structural level, and to grapple with the ways that we participate in, benefit from, and remain indifferent to racial injustice.

For Christians, it is only our wider context of grace that makes such judgment possible to bear. The fact of God's grace reassures us that, although our personal and collective entanglement in and malformation by sin and is not something we can undo alone, help is still available. As Massingale writes, the certain knowledge that "human wrongdoing is not God's final act in the drama of personal and social salvation" is what enables true lament and contrition. Indeed, he adds, "This hope permits truthful and direct acknowledgment of social estrangements and one's participation in them."[66]

Christian hope inspired by grace is precisely what American public conversations on race often lack—at least as conducted within white spaces. Robin DiAngelo has popularized the term "white fragility" to describe the discomfort, defensiveness, insecurity, and even anger whites often feel when discussing racial injustice, and which can include the fear of being wrong or saying the wrong thing.[67] Theologically speaking, it is almost as if American (white) public discourse were subconsciously Pelagian, and thus afraid that there will be no road back from such a devastating reckoning with our complicity with structural sin. As Massingale reminds us, however, in God's story human wrongdoing never has the last word—grace does. Recalling this provides a firm foundation from which to enter public deliberations about race nondefensively, with an eye less toward proving our moral purity and more toward collaborating with others on how to pursue justice.

CONCLUSION: A TRADITION ON THE MOVE

This essay has surveyed conceptual and methodological resources within CST relevant to the subject of reparations and argued that there is much within the tradition to support their use. In so doing, it has drawn primarily upon current magisterial teaching, and used this to extend existing reflection on the duty to repair harms. In a sense, it has focused on CST as it is and has been.

But what about the field as it will be? CST is also a living tradition that grows over time as Catholics worldwide reflect on the praxis of their faith—and in the American context, much of this development is now arising precisely from within reflection on experiences of systemic racial injustice. For example, while the reception of *Open Wide Our Hearts* (the 2018 US bishop's pastoral letter on racism) has been generally positive, many voices have argued that it does not go far enough in identifying and condemning racism as an ongoing structural reality, or in addressing the problems of white privilege and supremacy.[68]

At stake here is not just whether church leaders are taking seriously the experience of Black Catholics, but also whether the current concepts and categories of CST are themselves fully adequate to interpret the "signs of the times." Dávila has argued, for example, that CST tends to emphasize individual conversion at the expense of structural transformation, and should take cues from liberation theology by acknowledging the necessity of conflict for social change in light of structural sin.[69] From a different angle, Massingale has critiqued the focus in official Catholic teaching on our "deliberate, intentional, and conscious" actions as unable to diagnose or combat the way a culture of racism distorts our consciences.[70] Katie Grimes proposes that what is needed is a more "corporate" theory of virtue and vice that can move Catholic ethics past narrowly focused accounts of complicity that are neither descriptively nor rhetorically adequate to the embodied nature of social sins such as racism.[71]

Such scholarship is drawing on and further advancing two ongoing developments within CST, both of which are particularly visible in the writing of Pope Francis. The first of these is a deepening emphasis on the interior, affective, and even visceral dimension of CST's invitation to justice; as Bernard Brady argues, the tradition now is as much "Catholic social living" as it is "Catholic social teaching."[72] The second is a deepening sense of the power of social sin to distort our moral agency, which promises to move Catholic analysis beyond an overemphasis on voluntary actions motivated by a concern not to "diminish[h] personal accountability."[73] These developments are opening up new ways of theorizing about and pastorally reckoning with our shared responsibilities for social and structural evils.

What does this all mean for Catholic approaches to reparations? To start with, it indicates that the map of relevant resources drawn here is necessarily incomplete, given that the terrain itself is continually developing. Moving forward, we might imagine that Catholic reflection on reparations will also examine the issue in light of the connections between social ethics, theology, and spirituality, in addition to drawing upon existing teachings about the duties of states.

As the scholarship just mentioned reminds us, bringing our faith into the public realm is never merely an academic matter of applying moral principles to new social problems, but always also a question of partnering with God's Spirit at work in the world, and of living into our redemption. There are surely many ways to do this with courage and integrity, including and especially when it comes to federal redistributive policies. As we examine the options we have for acting together, however, we should keep in mind our calling to become what we are (as an Augustinian Eucharistic formula has it): the body of Christ. As Shannen Dee Williams writes, in the context of an argument for more truth-telling on race within the Church, "As a leader of anti-racism workshops for Catholic communities, I am often asked what Catholics can do to become a leading force in the fight for racial justice. And my answer is always the same: become truly Catholic."[74]

NOTES

1. E.g., William A. Darity Jr., and A. Kirsten Mullen, *From Here to Equality: Reparations for Black Americans in the Twenty-First Century*, second edition (Chapel Hill, NC: University of North Carolina Press, 2022).

2. These include Nicholas Ensley Mitchell, "A Critical Race Theology Analysis of Catholic Social Teaching as Justification for Reparations to African Americans for Jim Crow," *Journal of Catholic Social Thought* 19.2 (2022): 251–73; John P. Slattery, "A Catholic Case for Reparations," *Daily Theology*, July 21, 2020, accessed May 23, 2023, https://dailytheology.org/2020/07/21/a-catholic-case-for-reparations/; and Katie Grimes, *Christ Divided: Antiblackness as Corporate Vice* (Minneapolis: Fortress Press, 2017), 254 (although the discussion focuses primarily on ecclesial reparations). For other recent arguments for ecclesial reparations, see also Olga Segura, *Birth of a Movement: Black Lives Matter and the Catholic Church* (Maryknoll: Orbis, 2021), especially 75–96; and Shannen Dee Williams, "The Church Must Make Reparations for its Role in Slavery, Segregation," *National Catholic Reporter*, June 15,

2020, accessed May 23, 2023, https://www.ncronline.org/news/opinion/church-must-make-reparation-its-role-slavery-segregation.

3. E.g., see Dawn Nothwehr, *That They May Be One: Catholic Social Teaching on Racism, Tribalism, and Xenophobia* (Maryknoll: Orbis Books, 2008), which offers a collection of official statements on racism from across the globe. See also the "Black Catholic Syllabus" available at U.S. Catholic, a curated reading list "on the history of Black Catholics in the United States and their contributions to Catholic theology, history, and activism," which illustrates the state of current teachings on racism and racial justice—as well as areas for growth in the tradition (more on which subject near the end of this essay) (uscatholic.org).

4. In addition to the above cited sources, see also Bryan Massingale, *Racial Justice and the Catholic Church* (Maryknoll, NY: Orbis Books, 2010); a symposium at *Political Theology Network*, including Shawnee Daniels-Sykes, "Dismantling White Privilege: A Reflection on *Open Wide Our Hearts*," (March 29, 2019); Cary Dabney, "*Open Wide Our Hearts*: The Ups and Downs," (March 29, 2019); MT Dávila, "The Conversion of Hearts and the Sin of Racism," (February 22, 2019); and Ansel Augustine, *Leveling the Praying Field: Can the Church We Love, Love Us Back?* (Maryknoll, NY: Orbis Books, 2022).

5. Mitchell, "Critical Race Theology Analysis," 268, pointing toward *Catechism of the Catholic Church* 1935–38; Massingale, *Racial Justice*, 85, drawing upon John Paul II, *Tertio Millennio Adveniente* (1994), 33.

6. CCC 2487, emphasis in original, cited in Slattery, "Catholic Case for Reparations."

7. CCC 2412, emphasis in original.

8. E.g., Thomas Aquinas, *Summa Theologiae* II-II, 62.

9. CCC 1459.

10. E.g., see Regina Harrison, *Sin and Confession in Colonial Peru: Spanish-Quechua Penitential Texts, 1560–1650* (University of Texas Press, 2014) 23–49.

11. Harrison, *Sin and Confession*, 43.

12. Harrison, *Sin and Confession*, 46.

13. Pontifical Council for Justice and Peace, *Contribution to World Conference Against Racism, Racial Discrimination, Xenophobia and Related Intolerance*, 2001, 12.

14. Mitchell, "Critical Race Theology Analysis," 262.

15. Mitchell, "Critical Race Theology Analysis," 265.

16. E.g., Paul VI, *Populorum progressio* (1967), 23; *Rerum novarum* (1891), 10, 65; and John Paul II, *Centesimus annus* (1991), 6.

17. John Paul II, *Sollicitudo rei socialis* (1987), 42.

18. Second Vatican Council, *Gaudium et spes* (1965), 69.

19. Aquinas, ST II-II 66.7. For other citations to the early church on this theme, see *Gaudium et spes*, 69.

20. E.g., see the claim in *Populorum progressio* that "the superfluous goods of wealthier nations ought to be placed at the disposal of poorer nations. The rule, by

virtue of which in times past those nearest us were to be helped in time of need, applies today to all the needy throughout the world" (49).

21. MT Dávila, "The Role of the Social Sciences in Catholic Social Thought: The Incarnational Nature of the Option for the Poor and Being Able to 'See' in the Rubric "See, Judge, Act," *Journal of Catholic Social Thought* 9.2 (2012): 229–244 (232).

22. USCCB, *Economic Justice for All: Pastoral Letter on Catholic Social Teaching and the US Economy*, 1986, 18.

23. USCCB, *Economic Justice for All*, 18.

24. *Populorum progressio*, 23; for more on taxation, see USCCB, *Economic Justice for All*, 118, 202.

25. Ramón Luzárraga, "Why It Is Still Time for an In-Depth Catholic Treatment of the Question of Taxation," Catholic Theological Ethics in the World Church Forum, February 28, 2023.

26. Pius XI, *Quadragesimo anno* (1931), 79.

27. USCCB, *Economic Justice for All*, 124.

28. I pull this phrasing from David Cloutier, "Getting Subsidiarity Right," unpublished manuscript/forthcoming.

29. USCCB, *Economic Justice for All*, 71.

30. For an accessible introduction to a more comprehensive list of principles guiding CST, see Thomas Massaro, SJ, *Living Justice: Catholic Social Teaching in Action*, third edition (Lanham, MD: Rowman & Littlefield, 2016) 81–121.

31. Rachel Swarns, "Georgetown University Plans Steps to Atone for Slave Past," *The New York Times*, September 1, 2016, accessed May 23, 2023, https://www.nytimes.com/2021/03/15/us/jesuits-georgetown-reparations-slavery.html#:~:text=In%20one%20of%20the%20largest,initiatives%20across%20the%20United%20States..

32. On this, e.g., see Rachel Swarns, "Catholic Order Pledges $100 Million to Atone for Slave Labor and Sales," *The New York Times*, March 15, 2021. See also Georgetown Reflects on Slavery, Memory, and Reconciliation, www.georgetown.edu/slavery.

33. Darity and Mullen, *From Here to Equality*, 4. Important here is the related conversation within economic history on the role slavery played in driving American economic development. Until the mid-twentieth century, the consensus among historians had been that slavery was an unproductive departure from capitalism, which had held back economic progress and did not contribute to American prosperity. Starting in the 1950s, historians challenged this received view by using economic analysis (or "cliometrics") to investigate its importance for the development of the American economy. Although debates about slavery's profitability continue, the emerging consensus seems to be that "capitalism could not have developed as it did without slavery." Stephen Leccese, "Capitalism and Slavery in the United States (Topical Guide)," *H-Slavery*, from *Humanities and Social Sciences Online*, July 8, 2015, accessed February 14, 2023, https://cathstan.org/voices/catholic-news-service/does-the-catholic-church-have-the-strength; see this for a literature introduction to this growing subfield within economic history.

34. Emilie Townes, *Womanist Ethics and the Cultural Production of Evil* (New York, NY: Palgrave Macmillan, 2006), 109.

35. Indeed, insofar as the reparations debate centers on such concerns, it would appear that both sides indirectly acknowledge the validity of the Catechism's assumption that even passively benefitting from a crime entails an obligation to repair it by returning the ill-gotten proceeds.

36. Massingale, *Racial Justice*, 97–100.

37. Massingale, *Racial Justice*, 100. On this theme, Townes argues that the conversation on reparations is stymied by pernicious "legends" about race that are "memories greater than memories" (*Womanist Ethics*, 109, 110).

38. For additional Catholic reflection on the "dangerous memories" hidden behind false racial histories, see M. Shawn Copeland, *Knowing Christ Crucified: The Witness of African American Religious Experience* (Maryknoll, NY: Orbis Books, 2018) and Copeland, *Enfleshing Freedom: Body, Race, and Being* (Minneapolis, MN: Fortress Press, 2009).

39. Ta-Nehisi Coates's influential "The Case for Reparations" especially highlights the ongoing influence of racist housing policies (*The Atlantic*, 2014). Mitchell's account of the "national policy of pauperizing Black people" emphasizes educational policy and the government's failure to prevent or prosecute the vast destruction of wealth in the 1921 Tulsa race riot and in the Red Summer race riots two years prior ("Critical Race Theology Analysis," 259, 262–63).

40. John Paul II, *Sollicitudo rei socialis*, 38.

41. USCCB, *Economic Justice for All*, 73.

42. USCCB, *Economic Justice for All*, 73.

43. International Theological Commission, *Memory and Reconciliation: The Church and the Faults of the Past* (1999) introduction, citing John Paul II, *Incarnationis Mysterium* (1998). Indeed, this statement frequently returns to "The conviction that the Church can make herself responsible for the sin of her children by virtue of the solidarity that exists among them through time and space because of their incorporation into Christ" (3.4).

44. Indeed, the Christian tradition's theological adaptation of natural law arguments for slavery present in Roman law provide one tragic illustration of how this mode of reasoning can go awry. On this history, see John Noonan, *A Church that Can and Cannot Change: The Development of Catholic Moral Teaching* (Notre Dame, IN: University of Notre Dame Press, 2005).

45. Especially when set alongside more distinctively Protestant approaches to ethics that tend to approach human reason with more skepticism and accordingly view reason and revelation as potentially conflicting. For more on these differences, see James Gustafson, *Protestant and Roman Catholic Ethics: Prospects for Rapprochement* (Chicago, IL: University of Chicago Press, 1978).

46. For a fuller accounting of the evolution of the understanding and influence of natural law within CST, see Stephen Pope, "Natural Law in Catholic Social Teachings," in *Modern Catholic Social Teaching: Commentaries and Interpretations*, ed. Kenneth Himes (Washington, DC: Georgetown University Press, 2005), 41–71.

47. Pope, "Natural Law," 62.

48. Second Vatican Council, *Gaudium et spes*, 4. See also Pope, "Natural Law," 57.

49. Margaret Farley, "Ethics, Ecclesiology, and the Grace of Self-Doubt," 55–77, in *A Call to Fidelity*, ed. James Walter et al., (Washington, DC: Georgetown University Press, 2002). See also David Hollenbach, SJ, "Virtues and Vices in Social Inquiry," 39–53, in *The Global Face of Public Faith: Politics, Human Rights, and Christian Ethics* (Washington, DC: Georgetown University Press, 2003).

50. Originally articulated by the Belgian Cardinal Joseph Cardijn in the early twentieth century, See, Judge, Act was most prominently developed within liberation theology, and has now been adopted and almost entirely metabolized within the broader field of Catholic social thought (and is the organizing principle of some of Pope Francis's encyclicals, for example).

51. For a concise introduction to this methodology, see Erin Brigham, *See, Judge, Act: Catholic Social Teaching and Service Learning* (Anselm Academic, 2013), 21–31.

52. E.g., see Francisco Moreno Rejón, "Fundamental Moral Theory in the Theology of Liberation," in *Mysterium Liberationis: Fundamental Concepts of Liberation Theology*, edited by Ignacio Ellacuría and Jon Sobrino (Maryknoll, NY: Orbis Books, 1993), 210–221.

53. Francis, *Fratelli tutti*, 215; see also Francis, *Evangelii gaudium* 198–99, and Clemens Sedmak, *A Church of the Poor: Pope Francis and the Transformation of Orthodoxy* (Maryknoll, NY: Orbis, 2016).

54. For an accessible introduction to what an economic perspective can contribute to Christian social inquiry, see Andrew Yuengert, "What Can Economists Contribute to the Common Good Tradition?" 36–63, in *Empirical Foundations of the Common Good: What Theology Can Learn from Social Science*, Daniel Finn ed., (New York, NY: Oxford University Press, 2017).

55. For more on this as a theme of Francis' papacy, see Darren Dias, "Paulo Freire and Pope Francis on Dialogue: An Anticolonial Interpretation," *Espacio, Tiempo y Educación* 9.1 (2022) 83–98 at 91.

56. E.g., see Joe Holland and Peter Henriot, SJ, *Social Analysis: Linking Faith and Justice* (Maryknoll, NY: Orbis Books, 1983).

57. Jon Sobrino, "Spirituality and the Following of Jesus," in *Mysterium Liberationis*, 677–701, at 681.

58. Massingale, *Racial Justice and the Catholic Church*, 104.

59. Massingale, *Racial Justice and the Catholic Church*, 105.

60. Mitchell, "Critical Race Theology Analysis," 265.

61. Sarah Rose, "The Case for Cash—Beyond COVID—Gains Strength: New Data on Comparative Cost-Effectiveness," Center for Global Development, September 15, 2020, emphasis in original, accessed May 23, 2023, https://www.cgdev.org/blog/case-cash-beyond-covid-gains-strength-new-data-comparative-cost-effectiveness. The nonprofit GiveDirectly compiles and provides access to a database of research involving cash transfers, which currently includes over three hundred studies, peer-reviewed papers, working papers, and program reports, in their "Cash Evidence Explorer." (givedirectly.org/cash-evidence-explorer/)

62. E.g., David Evans and Anna Popova, "Cash Transfers and Temptation Goods," *Economic Development and Cultural Change* 65.2 (2017): 189–221, which provides a

systematic review of forty-two studies. For more on the current move in development economics to attend more closely to the experiences, insights, and preferences—or, in more theological parlance, to respect the dignity and empower the moral agency—of the poor, see Abhijit Banerjee and Esther Duflo, *Poor Economics: A Radical Rethinking of the Way to Fight Global Poverty* (New York, NY: PublicAffairs, 2012).

63. Darity and Mullen in particular take up the concern about inflation, for example (see Darity and Mullen, *From Here to Equality*, chapters 12 and 13).

64. USCCB, *Economic Justice for All*, 124.

65. Romans 5.20.

66. Massingale, *Racial Justice*, 113.

67. Robin DiAngelo, *White Fragility: Why It's So Hard for White People to Talk about Racism* (Boston, MA: Beacon Press, 2018).

68. In addition to above mentioned resources, e.g., see also Andrew Lyke, "Dear White Catholics: It's Time to be Anti-racist and Leave White Fragility Behind," *America Magazine*, November 30, 2020; and Mary Yelenick, "An Anti-Racism Perspective on Open Wide Our Hearts, the November Bishops' Pastoral Letter on Racism," Pax Christi USA, October 31, 2019. (https://paxchristiusa.org/2019/10/31/an-anti-racism-perspective-on-open-wide-our-hearts-the-november-2018-bishops-pastoral-letter-on-racism/, accessed February 14, 2023).

69. E.g., Dávila, "The Conversion of Hearts and the Sin of Racism."

70. Bryan Massingale, "Has the Silence Been Broken? Catholic Theological Ethics and Racial Justice," *Theological Studies* 75 (2014): 133–55 at 141. See also Massingale, "Conscience Formation and the Challenge of Unconscious Racial Bias," in *Conscience and Catholicism: Rights, Responsibilities, and Institutional Responses*, ed. David DeCosse and Kristin Heyer (Maryknoll, NY: Orbis, 2015), 53–68.

71. Grimes, *Christ Divided*.

72. Bernard Brady, "From Catholic Social Thought to Catholic Social Living: A Narrative of the Tradition," *Journal of Catholic Social Thought* 15.2 (2018): 317–52.

73. Kristin Heyer, "Walls in the Heart: Social Sin in *Fratelli tutti*," *Journal of Catholic Social Thought* 19.1 (2022): 25–40, at 30. On the development of the concepts of social and structural sin in contemporary Catholic ethics, see also Daniel K. Finn, "What Is a Sinful Social Structure?" *Theological Studies* 77.1 (2016): 136–64, and Conor Kelly, "The Nature and Operation of Structural Sin: Insights from Theology and Moral Psychology," *Theological Studies* 80.2 (2019): 293–327.

74. Shannen Dee Williams, "Does the Catholic Church have the Strength?" *Catholic Standard/Catholic News Service*, January 2, 2020, accessed May 23, 2023, https://cathstan.org/voices/catholic-news-service/does-the-catholic-church-have-the-strength.

BIBLIOGRAPHY

Aquinas, Thomas. *Summa Theologiae*. Translated by Fathers of the English Dominican Province. Westminster, MD: Christian Classics, 1981.

Augustine, Ansel. *Leveling the Praying Field: Can the Church We Love, Love Us Back?* Maryknoll, NY: Orbis Books, 2022.

Banerjee, Abhijit and Esther Duflo. *Poor Economics: A Radical Rethinking of the Way to Fight Global Poverty.* New York, NY: PublicAffairs, 2012.

Brady, Bernard. "From Catholic Social Thought to Catholic Social Living: A Narrative of the Tradition." *Journal of Catholic Social Thought* 15.2 (2018): 317–52.

Brigham, Erin. *See, Judge, Act: Catholic Social Teaching and Service Learning.* Anselm Academic, 2013.

Catechism of the Catholic Church, second edition. Washington, DC: United States Catholic Conference, 2000.

Cloutier, David. "Getting Subsidiarity Right." Unpublished manuscript/forthcoming.

Coates, Ta-Nehisi. "The Case for Reparations." *The Atlantic*, June 15, 2014. Accessed May 23, 2023. https://www.theatlantic.com/magazine/archive/2014/06/the-case-for-reparations/361631/.

Copeland, M. Shawn. *Knowing Christ Crucified: The Witness of African American Religious Experience.* Maryknoll, NY: Orbis Books, 2018.

Copeland, M. Shawn. *Enfleshing Freedom: Body, Race, and Being.* Minneapolis, MN: Fortress Press, 2009.

Dabney, Cary. "Open Wide Our Hearts: The Ups and Downs." Political Theology Network symposium, March 29, 2019.

Daniels-Sykes, Shawnee. "Dismantling White Privilege: A Reflection on Open Wide Our Hearts." Political Theology Network symposium, March 29, 2019.

Darity, William A., Jr., and A. Kirsten Mullen. *From Here to Equality: Reparations for Black Americans in the Twenty-First Century*, second edition. Chapel Hill, NC: University of North Carolina Press, 2022.

Dávila, MT. "The Conversion of Hearts and the Sin of Racism." Political Theology Network symposium, February 22, 2019.

———. "The Role of the Social Sciences in Catholic Social Thought: The Incarnational Nature of the Option for the Poor and Being Able to 'See' in the Rubric 'See, Judge, Act.'" *Journal of Catholic Social Thought* 9.2 (2012): 229–244.

DiAngelo, Robin. *White Fragility: Why It's So Hard for White People to Talk about Racism.* Boston, MA: Beacon Press, 2018.

Dias, Darren. "Paulo Freire and Pope Francis on Dialogue: An Anticolonial Interpretation." *Espacio, Tiempo y Educación* 9.1 (2022) 83–98.

Evans, David and Anna Popova. "Cash Transfers and Temptation Goods." *Economic Development and Cultural Change* 65.2 (2017): 189–221.

Farley, Margaret. "Ethics, Ecclesiology, and the Grace of Self-Doubt." In *A Call to Fidelity*, edited by James Walter et al., 55–77. Washington, DC: Georgetown University Press, 2002.

Finn, Daniel. "What Is a Sinful Social Structure?" *Theological Studies* 77.1 (2016): 136–64

Francis. Apostolic Exhortation on the Joy of the Gospel *Evangelii gaudium*, November 24, 2013.

———. Encyclical on Fraternity and Social Friendship *Fratelli tutti*, October 3, 2020.

Gustafson, James. *Protestant and Roman Catholic Ethics: Prospects for Rapprochement* Chicago, IL: University of Chicago Press, 1978.

Harrison, Regina. *Sin and Confession in Colonial Peru: Spanish-Quechua Penitential Texts, 1560–1650*. Austin, TX: University of Texas Press, 2014.

Holland, Joe and Peter Henriot. *Social Analysis: Linking Faith and Justice*. Maryknoll, NY: Orbis Books, 1983.

International Theological Commission, Memory and Reconciliation: The Church and the Faults of the Past. December 1999.

Grimes, Katie. *Christ Divided: Antiblackness as Corporate Vice*. Minneapolis, MN: Fortress Press, 2017.

Heyer, Kristin. "Walls in the Heart: Social Sin in Fratelli Tutti." *Journal of Catholic Social Thought* 19.1 (2022): 25–40.

Hollenbach, David. *The Global Face of Public Faith: Politics, Human Rights, and Christian Ethics*. Washington, DC: Georgetown University Press, 2003.

John Paul II. Apostolic Letter for the Jubilee of the Year 2000 *Tertio millennio adveniente*, November 10, 1994.

———. Encyclical on the Hundredth Anniversary of *Rerum Novarum Centesimus annus*, May 1, 1991.

———. Encyclical on Social Concerns *Sollicitudo rei socialis*, December 30, 1987.

Kelly, Conor. "The Nature and Operation of Structural Sin: Insights from Theology and Moral Psychology." *Theological Studies* 80.2 (2019): 293–327.

Leccese, Stephen. "Capitalism and Slavery in the United States (Topical Guide)." H-Slavery, from Humanities and Social Sciences Online (networks.h-net.org), July 8, 2015. Accessed May 23, 2023. https://cathstan.org/voices/catholic-news-service/does-the-catholic-church-have-the-strength.

Leo XIII. Encyclical on Capital and Labor, *Rerum novarum* May 15, 1891.

Luzárraga, Ramón. "Why It Is Still Time for an In-Depth Catholic Treatment of the Question of Taxation." Catholic Theological Ethics in the World Church Forum, February 28, 2023.

Lyke, Andrew. "Dear White Catholics: It's Time to be Anti-Racist and Leave White Fragility Behind." *America Magazine*, November 30, 2020. Accessed February 14, 2023. https://paxchristiusa.org/2019/10/31/an-anti-racism-perspective-on-open-wide-our-hearts-the-november-2018-bishops-pastoral-letter-on-racism/.

Massaro, Thomas. *Living Justice: Catholic Social Teaching in Action*, third edition. Lanham, MD: Rowman & Littlefield, 2016.

Massingale, Bryan. "Conscience Formation and the Challenge of Unconscious Racial Bias." In *Conscience and Catholicism: Rights, Responsibilities, and Institutional Responses*, edited by David DeCosse and Kristin Heyer, 53–68. Maryknoll, NY: Orbis, 2015.

———. "Has the Silence Been Broken? Catholic Theological Ethics and Racial Justice." *Theological Studies* 75 (2014): 133–55.

———. *Racial Justice and the Catholic Church*. Maryknoll, NY: Orbis Books, 2010.

Mitchell, Nicholas Ensley. "A Critical Race Theology Analysis of Catholic Social Teaching as Justification for Reparations to African Americans for Jim Crow." *Journal of Catholic Social Thought* 19.2 (2022): 251–73.

Noonan, John. *A Church that Can and Cannot Change: The Development of Catholic Moral Teaching.* Notre Dame, IN: University of Notre Dame Press, 2005.

Nothwehr, Dawn. *That They May Be One: Catholic Social Teaching on Racism, Tribalism, and Xenophobia.* Maryknoll, NY: Orbis Books, 2008.

Paul VI. Encyclical on the Development of Peoples *Populorum progression,* March 26, 1967.

Pius XI. Encyclical on Reconstructing the Social Order *Quadragesimo anno,* May 15, 1931.

Pontifical Council for Justice and Peace. "Contribution to World Conference Against Racism, Racial Discrimination, Xenophobia and Related Intolerance," 2001.

Pope, Stephen. "Natural Law in Catholic Social Teachings." In *Modern Catholic Social Teaching: Commentaries and Interpretations,* edited by Kenneth Himes, 41–71. Washington, DC: Georgetown University Press, 2005.

Rejón, Francisco Moreno. "Fundamental Moral Theory in the Theology of Liberation." In *Mysterium Liberationis: Fundamental Concepts of Liberation Theology,* edited by Ignacio Ellacuría and Jon Sobrino, 210–221. Maryknoll, NY: Orbis Books, 1993.

Rose, Sarah. "The Case for Cash—Beyond COVID—Gains Strength: New Data on Comparative Cost-Effectiveness." Center for Global Development, September 15, 2020. Accessed May 23, 2023. https://www.cgdev.org/blog/case-cash-beyond-covid-gains-strength-new-data-comparative-cost-effectiveness.

Sedmak, Clemens. *A Church of the Poor: Pope Francis and the Transformation of Orthodoxy.* Maryknoll, NY: Orbis, 2016.

Segura, Olga. *Birth of a Movement: Black Lives Matter and the Catholic Church.* Maryknoll: Orbis, 2021.

Slattery, John P. "A Catholic Case for Reparations." *Daily Theology,* July 21, 2020. Accessed May 23, 2023. https://dailytheology.org/2020/07/21/a-catholic-case-for-reparations/.

Sobrino, Jon. "Spirituality and the Following of Jesus." In *Mysterium Liberationis: Fundamental Concepts of Liberation Theology,* edited by Ignacio Ellacuría and Jon Sobrino, 677–701. Maryknoll, NY: Orbis Books, 1993.

Swarns, Rachel. "Catholic Order Pledges $100 Million to Atone for Slave Labor and Sales." *New York Times,* March 15, 2021.

———. "Georgetown University Plans Steps to Atone for Slave Past." *New York Times,* September 1, 2016. Accessed May 23, 2023. https://www.nytimes.com/2021/03/15/us/jesuits-georgetown-reparations-slavery.html#:~:text=In%20one%20of%20the%20largest,initiatives%20across%20the%20United%20States.

Townes, Emilie. *Womanist Ethics and the Cultural Production of Evil.* New York, NY: Palgrave Macmillan, 2006.

United States Conference of Catholic Bishops. *Economic Justice for All: Pastoral Letter on Catholic Social Teaching and the US Economy.* Washington, DC: United States Conference of Catholic Bishops, 1986.

Vatican Council II. Pastoral Constitution on The Church in The Modern World *Gaudium et spes,* December 7, 1965.

Williams, Shannen Dee. "Does the Catholic Church have the Strength?" *Catholic Standard/Catholic News Service*, January 2, 2020. Accessed May 23, 2023. https://cathstan.org/voices/catholic-news-service/does-the-catholic-church-have-the-strength.

———. "The Church Must Make Reparations for its Role in Slavery, Segregation." *National Catholic Reporter*, June 15, 2020. Accessed May 23, 2023. https://www.ncronline.org/news/opinion/church-must-make-reparation-its-role-slavery-segregation.

Yelenick, Mary. "An Anti-Racism Perspective on Open Wide Our Hearts, the November Bishops' Pastoral Letter on Racism." Pax Christi USA, October 31, 2019.

Yuengert, Andrew. "What Can Economists Contribute to the Common Good Tradition?" In E*mpirical Foundations of the Common Good: What Theology Can Learn from Social Science,* edited by Daniel Finn, 36–63. New York: Oxford University Press, 2017.

PART THREE

Reparations in History and Contemporary Praxis

Chapter Fifteen

The DC Compensated Emancipation Act as Precedent for Reparations

Renee K. Harrison

Reparations are not a new phenomenon in the United States of America. In fact, the US government has a long history of compensating white people, dating as far back as the 1860s.

In December 1861, Ohio lawyer and politician Thomas Marshall Key, with the aid and sponsorship of Massachusetts senator Henry Wilson, drafted a bill entitled "An Act for the Release of Certain Persons Held to Service or Labor Within the District of Columbia." The bill passed the Senate on April 3, 1862, and the House of Representatives on April 12, 1862. On April 16, 1862, President Abraham Lincoln signed the Act into law, releasing all Black women, men, and children forced into labor in the nation's capital. In some sense, the law served as a symbol of freedom for all enslaved persons throughout the divided nation. Though the Compromise of 1850 made slave trading illegal in the nation's capital, the owning and selling of Black people continued in the city until the Act's passage.

The Act physically freed Black people from slavery in the nation's capital. Black people, however, continued to experience violence and hardships while living in the district. The law made no provisions for Black people's safety, well-being, or livelihood, but rather provided economic and social shelter for whites by compensating white enslavers and allocating $1,000,000 to those faced with loss of human property and laborers—and who pledged their loyalty to the Union. Enslavers who filed petitions were eligible for up to $300 per enslaved person working within DC and the surrounding area.

President Lincoln appointed with Senate confirmation a three-member commission—Daniel R. Goodloe, an abolitionist and journalist from North Carolina; Samuel Finley Vinton, Ohio US Representative; and James G. Berret, a Maryland legislator and former DC mayor, to review each petition. Berret declined, so Lincoln appointed Horatio King, former US Postmaster General. Upon Vinton's death less than a month later, the president appointed John M. Brodhead, a DC physician and New Hampshire native. The Emancipation Commission met Monday through Friday in DC's Old City Hall from April to June 1862 to receive and review reparation petitions. The commissioners also hired Bernard Moore Campbell, a slave dealer known for trading Black people between Baltimore and the Deep South, to appraise each enslaved person. Congress also appointed a messenger to publish public notices in Washington area newspapers announcing the commission's work and information on submitting and reviewing petitions.

Within nine months of the Act's passage, nearly 1,000 white people had filed claims, which included the names and characteristics of each enslaved person, their estimated value and skills, proof of ownership (e.g., wills, bills of sale, rental for hire documents, and deeds of trust), and a statement from the owners pledging their loyalty to the Union.

Clearly, the US government understood both the gravity of economic harm and the level of disrespect felt by the owners. The Commissioners approved 909 reparation petitions, which included 2,989 enslaved persons. They rejected 111 petitions because the enslaved were "too young, too aged, or too infirm to merit compensation."[1] According to Kenneth Winkle, Sorensen Professor of American History at the University of Nebraska-Lincoln, "a relative handful of petitions were declined because the ownership of the slaves was questionable, the slaveowners were considered disloyal, or the slaves had run away more than two years earlier."[2] The commission compiled a list of enslavers who filed claims and the names of their laborers and published them in Washington area newspapers. The reparations to owners became known as the District of Columbia Compensated Emancipation Act.

SLAVE OWNER CLARK MILLS APPLIES FOR REPARATIONS

Clark Mills (1815–1883) was among those enslavers who filed for government assistance. Mills, a slaveholder and self-taught sculptor, became noted for developing an advanced method for making life masks—plaster casts of people's faces. Before this innovation, Mills, an orphan at five, lived most of his early life in debt, working as a common laborer, taking handy jobs in cabinetmaking, millwrighting, and house plastering. In the summer of

1837, Mills, age 21, married Eliza Ballentine in Charleston, South Carolina. Subsequently, he purchased a young slave boy named Philip Reid (Reed) and opened a foundry made possible through his wife's $700 dowry given by her father at the time of their marriage.[3] Eliza's father, Alexander Ballentine, was a prominent Charlestown slave owner and harness maker who lived in the Northern Neck of the city.

In 1848, Mills relocated his business, the Mills Studio and Foundry, to present-day northeast Washington on Bladensburg Road. His pioneering ideas resulted in several commissions for sculptures, among them three equestrian statues of two prominent people. In 1848, he designed a sculpture of President Andrew Jackson cast in bronze. It was unveiled outside the White House in President's Park (Lafayette Square) on January 8, 1853. According to the Charleston Renaissance Gallery, the monies Mills "received from Congress amounted to $12,000.00." Because Mills incurred "$7,000.00 for out-of-pocket expenses, Congress awarded him an additional $20,000.00" (a total of $32,000.00 from Congress, approximately $1.235 million in 2023).[4]

New Orleans officials and citizens solicited Mills to replicate the sculpture in New Orleans in honor of Jackson's defeat in the British attempt to overtake the city. The memorial was unveiled in Place d' Armes (renamed Jackson Square) in February 1856.[5] Mills received $35,000 for his work (approximately $1.225 million in 2023).

Four years later, the US government asked Mills to create an equestrian statue of President George Washington, honoring Washington's leadership as Commander of the Continental Army during the American Revolution. The dedication occurred in Washington Circle on the perimeter of George Washington University on February 22, 1860. Congress appropriated $60,000 (roughly $2.145 million in 2023) for the erection of Mills's Washington statue.

In total, between 1848 and 1860, federal and state officials paid Clark Mills approximately $127,000 (about $4.540 million in 2023) for the three sculptures, with minimal labor overhead due to his use of enslaved Black people. But after capitalizing on this free labor, he also successfully petitioned the government for reparations in anticipation of a loss of revenue following the passage of the DC Compensated Emancipation Act (petition number 741; see image below). On June 20, 1862, Mills's petition listed his eleven enslaved laborers—six males and five females. Their names are Lettie (Letty) Howard and her six children Tilly, Tow (or Tom), Ellick, Jackson, George, and Emily; Levi Thomas and his wife Rachel Thomas; Ann Ross; and Philip Reid.[6] Mills had brought all his enslaved laborers from South Carolina except five of Lettie's children, who were born in DC. There is no mention of the father of Lettie's children. In preparation for appraisal, Mills listed each Black person's value as:

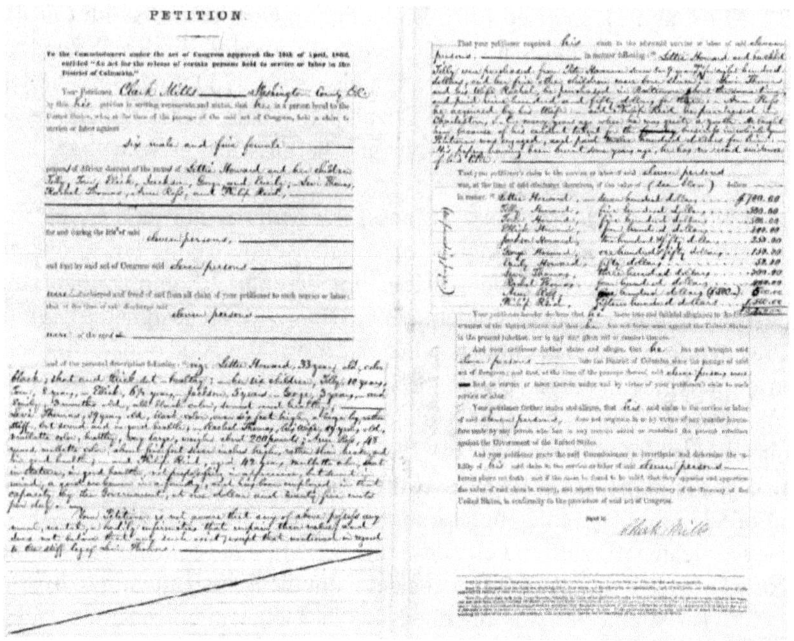

Figure 15.1. Petition by Clark Mills. Source: Records of the Department of Treasury, National Archives and Records Administration.

Lettie Howard, age 33, $700
Tilly Howard, age 10, $500
Tow (or Tom) Howard, age 8, $500
Ellick Howard, age 6 ½, $400
Jackson Howard, age 5, $250
George Howard, age 3, $150
Emily Howard, age 3-months, $50
Levi Thomas, age 59, $300
Rachel Thomas, age 49, $400
Ann Rose, age 48, $500
Philip Reid, age 42, $1,500

Philip Reid (c. 1820–1892), whom Mills purchased at a young age, was valued the highest. In his petition, Mills described Reid, age 42, as "mullatto color, short in stature, in good health, not prepossessing in appearance, but smart in mind, a good workman in a foundry." Reid's potential skills as a master caster who displayed craftsmanship and talent for the foundry business were the primary reasons Mills purchased Reid at a young age. Reid was born into slavery in South Carolina and learned how to work with clay and wood from an unnamed enslaved elder. South Carolina had the highest enslaved and free Black craftsmen population, and many were descendants of craftsmen from West and West Central Africa. Early on, Reid was instrumental in bringing Mills's statues to fruition and went on to play a significant role in casting the sculpture that now sits atop the US Capitol.

PHILIP REID AND THE STATUE OF FREEDOM

In 1855, the federal government commissioned Thomas Gibson Crawford to design a statue for the Capitol dome. Shortly after, Crawford submitted two models, entitled *Freedom Triumphant—in Peace and War* and *Armed Liberty*. Jefferson Davis, a prominent enslaver, and the US secretary of war in charge of the Capitol's construction between 1853 and 1857, rejected Crawford's submissions. Davis was offended by the symbolism of freed enslaved laborers. He did not want any representation of American slavery enshrined at the Capitol.[7] To meet Jefferson's expectations, Crawford, in 1856, submitted his third design for a statue, this one a figure symbolizing American patriotism and conquest atop a globe encircled with the words "E Pluribus Unum" (out of many, one). Davis approved this model, entitled Triumphant in War and Peace, later renamed the *Statue of Freedom*. Crawford died after finishing the full-size plaster model, which arrived from Europe in the United States in six crates and was reassembled in the Capitol in 1859.

The US government appointed Mills to cast Crawford's *Statue of Freedom*, offering him $400 a month to use his foundry and to pay for materials. The statue remained in the Capitol for days because Mills and his workers struggled to disassemble Crawford's 19.5-foot plaster model and transport it from the Capitol to Mills's foundry. Reid "skillfully devised a method of separating and casting the individual sections."[8] He found that using a pully and tackle to pull up on the lifting ring at the top of the model could expose the connections between the sections, thereby allowing separation of the statue at the joints. As a result, the statue was successfully dismantled into five parts to facilitate transportation to Mills's Foundry. The *Statue of Freedom* was closer to resting at its permanent home on top of the Capitol.

At Mills's foundry, under hazardous, humid, and dirty working conditions, Reid helped cast the bronze *Freedom*. Mills did not file his petition to release Reid from bondage until the casting was near completion. Without question, Mills owed a part of the sculpture's successful completion to the craftsmanship of an enslaved Black man. By the time of the passage of the DC Compensated Emancipation Act in April 1862 and the filing of Mills's petition in June 1862, the statue was complete and ready for installation. Reid continued working, now as a free man, helping to install the statue.

On December 2, 1863, while Civil War raged, workers secured the *Statue of Freedom* on the new Capitol dome.

In contrast to Mills, Reid received no pay from the government for working six days per week. His owner, Clark Mills received his pay. Reid did receive $1.25 (between $42 and $44 in 2023) from the government for working a full day on Sundays, the one day most enslaved people were not required to work. Reid received a paltry total of $41.25 (roughly between $1,300 and $1,475 in 2023) for laboring thirty-three Sundays between July 1, 1860, and May 16, 1861. In short, Reid received meager pay for his work on the capital, while his owner, Clark Mills was compensated by the federal government.

Reid Did Not Stand Alone: Enslaved Black Peoples' Contributions to America

In addition to Reid, enslaved Black people contributed to building the US Capitol—which many politicians refer to as the "Temple of Liberty"—and played a role in the capitol's expansion project from 1850 until the enforcement of the DC Compensated Emancipation Act in 1862. Between 1790 and 1863, enslaved laborers comprised more than 50 percent of the Capitol construction workforce. The federal government used enslaved laborers as soon as construction began, renting them from nearby enslavers like Mills. Between 1790 and 1826, an estimated eight hundred or more enslaved Black people were involved in the construction of the Capitol.

Before 1797, the US government paid white slave owners up to $60 per year for each laborer they hired out. In 1797, the amount rose to $70 a year. On average, the owners received $5 per month for their laborers who worked twelve-hour days, six days a week. On occasion, owners paid their enslaved laborers a small portion for their work. Like Reid, enslaved women, men, and children who worked on Sundays received minimal pay for working on the Sabbath. Also, some enslaved laborers were allowed to live apart from their owners and hire out their services. Even then, in some cases, the owner received a portion of their meager earnings.

Enslaved Black people worked as axmen, blacksmiths, brick makers, bricklayers, carpenters, carters, craftspeople, casters, diggers, glazers, haulers, land clearers, masons, miners, rafters, painters, plasters, quarrymen and women, roofers, sawyers, stonecutters, and other positions. They also painted, glazed, and roofed the Capitol building. Many carved and polished the three-story-high marble columns in the Capitol building's Statuary Hall, a large two-story semicircular room devoted to sculptures of well-known Americans. Enslaved Black people performed various known and unknown tasks in the heat of the day and brutal winter without modern-day equipment.

Indeed, the US Capitol was only one of the federal buildings enslaved Black people helped construct. They were instrumental in constructing the

White House, Treasury Building, the Smithsonian, Georgetown University, and other federal and non-federal buildings, businesses, and residences in DC. They were also later made to work as servants inside federal buildings, politicians' homes, and other residences, businesses, and locations throughout the city and nation. Their contributions extended beyond the nation's capital to towns, cities, and states throughout the North American mainland.

From the earliest arrivals to the present-day, Black people have not been "the special object of consideration" of Europeans, early American colonists, and the nation's Founding Fathers. Slavery was the economic engine that ushered in the young nation. At its peak, "slavery was a $3 billion-plus industry and a major engine of the US economy" and a significant contributor to European countries' growth.[9] The early founders and their descendants did not readily turn their backs on the institution of slavery because "slavery's profitability far outweighed the moral outrage it engendered."[10]

William Lloyd Garrison, Frederick Douglass, and others described American slavery as a peculiar institution. An intentional system of abusive labor practices that afforded European immigrants economic, political, and social advantages that would not have occurred without Black people's subjugation and the violent take-over of Indigenous peoples' homelands. The forced transplantation of women, men, and children out of Africa to toil in the American colonies was crucial to America's greatness. The young nation depended on the commodification of Black bodies and the commodities they produced: tobacco, rice, cotton, sugar, indigo, wheat, rum, rubber, whale oil, fish, horses, lumber, wood, silks, furs, and even humans for labor.

As illustrated by the US Capitol building project, enslaved Black people's contributions went beyond agriculture. In addition to what has been mentioned already, enslaved women, men, and children worked in the DC area as domestics, maids, cooks, seamstresses, midwives and nannies, launderers, carriage drivers, butlers, bakers, tailors, stable boys, and waiters. Some were quilters, basket weavers, stonemasons, millers, fishermen, and so forth, working in rural and urban areas and on small farms and lavish plantations—all for Europeans and white American immigrants and their descendants' consumption and advancement. Black people and the commodities produced by their hands, coupled with the indigenous minerals taken from their African homelands, bolstered the economies of the mainland North American colonies, South America, the West Indies, and Europe.

As historian Edward E. Baptist declares: the "commodification, suffering, and forced labor of African Americans is what made the United States powerful and rich."[11] Without a doubt, Americans pocketed "millions of dollars year-after-year from the trading of human beings," and "in several states, money from this industry was the 'chief source of wealth.'"[12] Slave labor provided the capital that financed the Industrial Revolution in England.[13]

Cotton and sugar production alone served as the base of American capitalism and European economic growth.[14] The "American Dream" did not begin with white colonists' quest for independence from Britain. It started when skilled and unskilled Black-bodied people—who brought their crafts with them—were forced onto slave ships, and made to labor on stolen lands in the New World. These laborers and their descendants helped bring into existence regions that now make up the tapestry of the United States and other parts of the world.

The chart below provides a mere snapshot of present-day American companies and universities whose origins or parent companies are rooted in the selling and trading of human beings and their commodities.[15] Many of these entities came into existence directly from the institution of slavery and the slave trade.

Often, Americans speak of slavery and the institutionalized racism and capitalism that have afforded white people economic, judicial, criminal-justice, educational, and socio-political advantages in the United States as something of the past. But today the reality of these systemic and traumatic imbalances continues to plague Black people who are experiencing some of the same barriers and disparities that existed during and post-American slavery. Barriers and disparities do not occur in a vacuum but have been real and potent since slavery.

Table 15.1. **A snapshot of companies/institutions that benefited from American slavery and enslaved labor.** Created and compiled by Renee K. Harrison.

Name	Type of Company/ Institution	Purpose
US government	Government	Used enslaved laborers to build and renovate the White House, the US Capitol, and other federal and nonfederal buildings, roads, canals, and fortifications
Aetna	Insurance	Insured the lives of enslaved Black people
Alex Brown & Sons (acquired by Deutsche Bank in 1999)	Merchant and investment banking	Bought and sold cotton and tobacco from plantations with enslaved labor
American International Group (AIG)	Insurance	Insured the lives of enslaved Black people
The Appeal (newspaper of Memphis; became the *Commercial Appeal*, part of the USA Today Network)	Newspaper	Sold ads advertising sale of enslaved laborers

Name	Type of Company/Institution	Purpose
Baltimore & Ohio Railroad (became a part of CSX)	Railway	Started with money from George Brown's family business that bought/sold products from slave plantations
Bank of America (originally Boatman Saving Institution & Southern Bank of St. Louis)	Banking	Accepted enslaved Black people as collateral
Bank of Charleston (became part of Wells Fargo Bank)	Banking/finance	Accepted enslaved Black people as collateral
Bank of Metropolis (connections with Bank of America)	Banking/finance	Accepted enslaved Black people as collateral
Black Heath Company	Coal mining	Enslaved laborers—miners/blacksmiths
Brooks Brothers	Apparel	Sold clothes to slave owners for enslaved laborers
Brown Brothers Harriman	Banking/finance	Wall Street bank—owned hundreds of enslaved laborers and lent millions to Southern planters, merchants, and cotton traders
Brown Shipley and Company	Investment/banking	Started with money from the Brown family and hid money for plantation owners
Brown University	University	Made use of enslaved laborers
Central of Georgia	Railways	Rented enslaved laborers to work on railroads
The Charleston Courier (became the *Post and Courier*, owned by Evening Post Industries)	Newspaper	Sold ads advertising sale of enslaved laborers
Charter Oak Life Insurance Company	Insurance	Insured the lives of enslaved Black people
Chesterfield Coal and Iron Mining Company	Coal mining	Enslaved laborers—miners/blacksmiths
Christian Index	Newspaper	Sold ads advertising sale of enslaved Black people
The Citadel	Military academy	Made use of enslaved laborers
Citizens Bank & Canal Bank in Louisiana (became part of JP Morgan Chase)	Banking/finance	Accepted 13,000 enslaved people as collateral and took 1,250 from owners who defaulted on their loans
Clemson University	University	Made use of enslaved laborers and convicts
College of Charleston	University	Made use of enslaved laborers

(continued)

Name	Type of Company/Institution	Purpose
Columbia University	University	Made use of enslaved laborers / slave traders
The Connecticut Courant (became the Hartford Courant)	Newspaper	Sold ads about enslaved laborers and products made from enslaved labor
CSX Corporation	Railway	Rented enslaved laborers to build rail lines
Dartmouth College	University	Made use of enslaved laborers
Emory University	University	Made use of enslaved laborers / slave owners
Freshfields Bruckhaus Deringer	Law firm	Clients were slave owners; lawyers acted as trustees of owners' estates
George Mason University	University	Strong ties to slavery; namesake prominent slaver
Georgia Railroad & Banking Company	Banking/finance	Accepted enslaved Black people as collateral
Georgetown University	University	Funded by sale and labor of enslaved Black people
Harvard University	University	Slave owners provided funding
Jack Daniels	Whiskey production	Learned distilling from enslaved man, Nathan Nearest Green
Jean Étienne de Boré (first mayor of New Orleans—willed to Charity Hospital of New Orleans, later owned by Louisiana State University System; closed after Hurricane Katrina in 2005)	Sugar plantation	Enslaved laborers
The Jesuits	Religious institution	Owned and sold enslaved Black people
Knight Ridder	Newspaper	Benefited and profited from slave labor
Lehman Brothers Holdings Inc.	Banking/finance (prior to 2008, fourth largest investment bank in US)	Cotton traders; helped finance Alabama's reconstruction after Civil War and helped found the New York Cotton Exchange
Midlothian Mining Company	Coal mining	Enslaved laborers—miners/blacksmiths
The Mobile Register (became the Mobile's Press-Register and owned by the Alabama Media Group)	Newspaper	Sold ads advertising sale of enslaved Black people

Name	Type of Company/Institution	Purpose
Mount Gay Distillery (Barbados)	Sugar plantation and rum producer	Enslaved laborers
Mount St. Mary's University (Maryland)	University	Made use of enslaved laborers
New York Life	Insurance	Of its first 1,000 insurance policies, 339 were policies on enslaved laborers
N M Rothschild & Sons Bank in London	Investment bank/insurance	Accepted enslaved laborers as collateral on mortgaged property or loans
Norfolk Southern Railroad	Railways	Rented enslaved laborers to work on railroad
Pepperell Manufacturing	Cotton textiles	Bought cotton from the South produced by enslaved laborers and made enslaved laborers' clothing
The Picayune (became the *Times-Picayune*, owned by NOLA Media Group—part of Advance Publications with Condé Nast and American City Business Journals)	Newspaper	Sold ads advertising the sale of enslaved laborers
Presbyterian Church	Religious institution	Owned and sold enslaved laborers
Princeton University	University	Made use of enslaved laborers / slave owners
Providence Bank (Fleet Boston)	Banking/finance	Owned ships used in the slave trade
Rutgers University	University	Made use of enslaved laborers
South Carolina College (became the University of South Carolina)	University	Leased enslaved laborers to cook, clean, and make repairs
Tennessee Coal, Iron, and Railroad System	Coal mining	Enslaved laborers—miners/blacksmiths
Tiffany & Co	Jewelers	Originally financed with profits from cotton mills picked by enslaved laborers
Tribune	Newspaper	Benefited and profited from enslaved labor
Union Pacific	Railways	Bought and used enslaved laborers
University of Alabama	University	Made use of enslaved laborers
University of Buffalo (New York)	University	Made use of enslaved laborers
University of Delaware	University	Made use of enslaved laborers
University of Georgia	University	Made use of enslaved laborers

(*continued*)

Name	Type of Company/Institution	Purpose
University of Maryland	University	Made use of enslaved laborers
University of Mississippi	University	Made use of enslaved laborers
University of North Carolina (Chapel Hill)	University	Made use of enslaved laborers
University of Pennsylvania	University	Made use of enslaved laborers
University of Richmond	University	Built over the site of a plantation and slave cemetery
University of Virginia	University	Made use of enslaved laborers
USA Today (parent company is Gannett)	Newspaper	Links to slavery
US Life Insurance Company (owned by American General Financial and presently known as AIG)	Insurance	Insured the lives of enslaved Black people
Virginia Commonwealth University	University	Enslaved bodies illegally exhumed, used for medical experiments, and then discarded
Virginia Theological Seminary	Seminary	Made use of enslaved laborers
W. & F. C. Havemeyer Company (American Sugar Refining Inc., became part of Domino Sugar)	Sugar production	Processed sugar produced by enslaved laborers
Wachovia	Banking	Accepted enslaved Black people as collateral
William and Mary	College	Made use of enslaved laborers / slave owners
Yale University	University	Made use of enslaved laborers

THE IRONY OF IT ALL

Clark Mills, a highly regarded American enslaver, received $23,796.82 for casting the *Statue of Freedom* from the US government. Philip Reid, an ingenious Black man who lived in slavery for forty-two years, was paid $41.25 for working nearly three years at the Capitol without recognition. A reporter from the *New York Tribune* best describes the irony of this imbalance and disparity, chronicling the day the *Statue of Freedom* was raised above the Capitol and affixed to the cast-iron dome on December 2, 1863, at noon. He recalled the moment, writing,

The Black master-builder [referring to Reid] lifted the ponderous uncouth masses, and bolted them together, joint by joint, piece by piece, till they blended into the majestic 'Freedom' who today lifts her head in the blue clouds above Washington, invoking a benediction upon the imperiled Republic! Was there a prophecy in that moment? The slave became the artist and, with rare poetic justice, reconstructed the beautiful symbol of freedom for America.[16]

A thirty-five-gun salute followed the installation as the Civil War raged in the background. The firing of thirty-five guns represented the thirty-five states, including Confederate states. Service members fired cannons from the twelve surrounding military forts in response to the salute. After that, Capitol personnel raised the nation's flag above the center of the dome, indicating a successful installation. As the symbol of freedom stood defiantly above the US Capitol dome, weary, enslaved Black bodies throughout the nation were still living and toiling under the threat of domestic terrorism.

Eventually, Reid changed his last name to Reed, signifying his freedom from Mills and the institution of slavery in the United States. Reed remained in Washington with his wife and son and worked as a self-employed plasterer. On February 6, 1892, the master craftsman Philip Reed died, nearly thirty years after gaining his freedom. He was born enslaved and died a free man in the city that exploited his ingenuity and labor. One must wonder what Reed contemplated as he passed the statue atop the Capitol on his way to plastering jobs throughout the city—what he felt watching onlookers admire the work of his hands without knowledge or recognition that he, a formerly enslaved Black man, played a role in its magnificent creation.

On April 16, 1862, the US government enacted a law to free Black people working in the district. By the year's end, 3,185 enslaved Black people, which included those named in owners' petitions, were free persons. The date became an official city holiday in Washington, DC, in 2005. But beneath the pomp and circumstance of each year's celebration is the handout the US government provided former white enslavers—and the meager provisions that same government provided generations of Black people who helped build the new republic and its permanent seat of government. The Compensated Emancipation Act physically freed Black people but did not compensate or acknowledge their contribution to the city and the nation. The act also made no allowances for their basic human needs—food, clothing, and shelter.[17] The enslaved who gave years of service to the nation received no compensation from the American government. Moreover, as activists who compiled the "Reparations Now Toolkit" pointedly note, "forms of structural discrimination and exclusion, and racialized criminalization," that persists to this day "have impacted all Black people in the United States, not just those who can prove that their ancestors were slaves."[18]

Though the *Statue of Freedom* now stands at the apex of the Capitol, its symbolism does not represent those involuntarily laboring or hired out by their owners to help build this nation, fiscally and physically. Where are the reparations for these disenfranchised builders and subsequent generations of Black people?

WHY REPARATIONS ARE IMPORTANT

Historically, we know that reparations are important because, in a skewed sense, the US government offered them to white people during American slavery. They gave reparations to white enslavers who treated and saw Black people as property. White enslavers felt entitled and owed for the loss of their enslaved labor force, and the government corrected course, providing them monetary restitution to free their slaves. Through this Act, the US government turned an immoral situation (compensating *enslavers*) into a moral obligation—they acknowledged the loss and set up a process to address and resolve it.

An American story absent of reparations for enslaved Black people and their descendants is a story that seeks to portray American exceptionalism and freedom absent of American hypocrisy and exploitation. The United States of America held Black people in bondage as part of a more extensive European network to cement its presence and advancement in the world. From its inception, the young nation was and continues to be intentionally cruel to Black and Native American peoples.

Systemic injustices, intentional exploitation, and the disenfranchisement of Black people in the United States limit equal economic and socio-political access and infringe on Black people's God-given rights. Because of this, Black activists through the centuries have argued that reparations could provide the United States a pathway to corrective justice. Reparations would allow the United States to correct course. In this sense,

> Reparations require a systematic accounting, acknowledgment, and repair of past and ongoing harms, monetary compensation to individuals and institutions led by and accountable to Black communities, and an end to present-day policies and practices that perpetuate harms rooted in a history of anti-Black racism, along with a guarantee that they will not be repeated. Reparations must take as many forms as necessary to equitably address the many forms of injury caused by chattel slavery and its continuing vestiges.[19]

Since its founding, America prides itself for claiming to be a Christian nation. At the heart of Christian thought is redemption. But how is redemption possible without the acknowledgment of sin and harm? One of America's greatest sins is enslaving Black people, treating them as commodities without their permission, and forcing them into servitude. Proslavery advocates, their descendants, and those who benefited from slavery used the Black population for their national self-interests. It was only toward the close of these individuals' lives, when death seemed imminent and they believed that their souls would be in the hands of a merciful God, that some turned their gaze toward the evils of slavery.

John Washington, George Washington's great-grandfather, for example, in his final days crafted his last will and testament in hopes of being absolved of any wrongdoing in the New World. He writes,

> Being hartily sorry from the bottome of my hart for my sins past, [and] most humbly desireing forgiueness of the same from the Almighty god (my sauiour) & redeimer, in whome & by the meritts of Jesus Christ, I trust & beliene assuredly to be saued, .S: to haue full remission & forgiueness of all my sins. . . . My body at the generall dav of ressurrection shall arise againe [with] joy: through the merrits of Christ death & passion posses & inherit the Kingdom of heauen, prepared for his ellect & Chossen & my body to be buried in ye plantation wheire I now liue.[20]

John went on to say, "It has pleased God to give me far above my deserts," and then proceeded to divide his land estates, human chattel, livestock, and other commodities among family in the American colonies and Europe. Yet John chose not to free any of his enslaved laborers upon his death. Instead, he willed them to his wife and children, and granted his eldest son, Lawrence Washington, George Washington's father, Little Hunting Creek (Epsewasson), which later became known as Mount Vernon. John also gave the rector of his church four thousand pounds of tobacco with orders that a tablet akin to that of the Ten Commandments be his memorial stone.

George Washington continued in his forebear's legacy by not freeing his enslaved laborers upon his death. Though history records Washington as a noble man who made provisions in his will to free his enslaved laborers, it is important to note that Washington made sure such freedom would only come after he and Martha died—when they both had no more use for Black bodies. Most of the Washington's enslaved laborers, like others whose owners died, were separated from their family members, and were willed by Martha, upon her death, to her surviving relatives.

The Washingtons' and other Americans' innumerable sins and harms committed against Black people were not foremost on their minds while profiting from the institution of slavery. It took a DC reparations bill, a Civil War, and constitutional amendments to force enslavers and pro-slavery advocates to rid this nation of human bondage and release Black people from centuries of involuntary labor. But the ethos and remnants of American slavery continued to live on even after the signing of the DC Compensated Emancipation Act, a brutal Civil War, and the passage of the 13th Amendment. Slavery's stronghold remained evident when Texas did not ratify the 13th Amendment until 1870, Delaware in 1901, and Kentucky in 1976. Mississippi finally voted to approve on March 16, 1995, but did not make it official until a mere ten years ago, on February 7, 2013. Further evidence of slavery's stronghold—post-emancipation to present-day—is found in the enactment of Jim Crow laws; racialized domestic terrorism, criminalization, and lynching; mass incarceration; healthcare; medical malpractice on Black bodies; housing discrimination; voting disenfranchisement; educational inequities; food insecurities; economic inequality and racialized capitalism; environmental injustice and harm; and unaddressed intergenerational trauma from slavery.

Though a small percentage of Black people have attained some economic and socio-political success in the United States, these individual achievements pale in comparison to the systemic economic, political, and social barriers that continue to cripple or disadvantage a vast majority of Black people. Since emancipation, Black people have never really had a chance in an American system that has intentionally and disproportionately impeded their presence and quality of life. No doubt, there have been some pivotal moments since slavery in which Black people's wage-earning power increased. Such wage-earning power has yet to translate into the US's collective and sustained economic bargaining, however. When white people arrived in the New World, most had access to—or opportunities to acquire—land, housing, loans, and other assets, which many passed down to their children. The same cannot be said about generations of Black people who were separated from their families after arriving on American soil and lived laboring against their will, without—or with minimal—pay.

The fact that America was built on the backs of Black and Brown people who were never intended to reap the full benefits the New World economy and social systems afforded is an atrocity, and this is a reckoning the United States must face. Another reckoning the United States must face is how American institutions, including the Church, benefited from slavery. Clergymen and members of Congress and the Supreme Court were slave owners and represented states in which slavery was the backbone of the economy.

We must revisit the history of the enslavement of Black people in the United States to see America and its cherished myth of whiteness in their fullest light. Reparation is a gesture of acknowledgment and accountability, and an opportunity to examine the roots of systemic racism and the roots of white America's burden—namely, greed and power weaponized at the expense of those Americans have long devalued and othered. America's ownership of slavery is our freedom. And the elevation, respect, and commemoration of Black people forced to work against their will in the United States is our redemption. Clark Mills and Philip Reed's stories are not aberrations, and their stories are the American story. Facing the truth of our past head-on, making amends for our sins by addressing what is owed—and in what form— is our passageway to something more life-giving and meaningful. We must do the work honestly and with integrity to create a more perfect Nation.

NOTES

1. Kenneth J. Winkle, "Emancipation Petitions: Historical Contexts," Civil War Washington, eds., Susan C. Lawrence, Elizabeth Lorang, Kenneth M. Price, and Kenneth J. Winkle, Center for Digital Research in the Humanities, University of Nebraska-Lincoln, accessed January 19, 2023, https://civilwardc.org/texts/petitions/about.

2. Winkle, "Emancipation Petitions."

3. John Philip Colletta, "Clark Mills and His Enslaved Assistant, Philip Reed: The Collaboration that Culminated in Freedom," The Capital United States Capitol Historical Society, Volume 57, Spring Summer 2020, accessed January 19, 2023, https://capitolhistory.org/wp-content/uploads/2021/09/2020-Dome-1_46_Online.pdf.

4. The Charleston Renaissance Gallery, accessed January 19, 2023, https://fineartsouth.com/pages/about-us/default.aspx. See also (New Orleans) Daily Picayune, June 13, 1880 (Courtesy The Historic New Orleans Collection).

5. The Charleston Renaissance Gallery.

6. A microfilm reproduction of the original document held at the National Archives and Records Administration, Microcopy 520, Reel 5. The original document is held in the Records of the Accounting Officers of the Department of the Treasury, 1775–1978, National Archives and Records Administration, Record Group 217.6.5. Within the National Archives' Archival Description Catalog, see ARC Identifier 4644616 / MLR Number A1 347, accessed January 19, 2023, https://www.visitthecapitol.gov/artifact/petition-clark-mills-petition-number-741.

7. Vivien Green Fryd, "Lifting the Veil of Race at the U.S. Capitol: Thomas Crawford's Statue of Freedom," *Common-Place: The Interactive Journal of Early American Life*, Issue 10, No. 4 (July 2010), accessed January 20, 2023, http://commonplace.online/article/lifting-veil-race-u-s-capitol/.

8. "Philip Reid and the Statue of Freedom," United States Senate, accessed January 20, 2023, https://www.senate.gov/artandhistory/history/common/generic/Civil_War_ReidPhilip_StatueofFreedom.htm.

9. "The Mere Distinction of Colour," James Madison's Montpelier, accessed January 20, 2023, https://www.montpelier.org/learn/6-ways-that-understanding-slavery-will-change-how-you-understand-american-freedom.

10. "Mere Distinction."

11. Edward E. Baptist, *The Half Has Never Been Told: Slavery and the Making of American Capitalism* (New York: Basic Books, 2014), xxiii.

12. John W. Blassingame, ed., *The Frederick Douglass Papers: Correspondences of Frederick Douglass*, vol. 1, 1842–1852 (New Haven, CT: Yale University Press, 2009), 372.

13. Eric Williams, *Capitalism and Slavery* (Chapel Hill: University of North Carolina Press, 1944), Preface.

14. For further insight on the role cotton and sugar played in buttressing the American economy, see R. W. Fogel and S. L. Engerman, *Time on the Cross: The Economics of American Negro Slavery* (New York: W. W. Norton, 1974). See also Baptist, *Half*.

15. This chart is taken from Renee K. Harrison, *Black Hands, White House: Slave Labor and The Making of America*, (Minneapolis, MN: Fortress Press, 2021), 42–47. For a more expansive discussion see Chapter One.

16. "The Civil War: The Senate's Story: Philip Reid and the Statue of Freedom," United States Senate, accessed January 20, 2023, https://www.senate.gov/artandhistory/history/common/generic/Civil_War_ReidPhilip_StatueofFreedom.htm.

17. Important to note, the law did allocate $100,000 toward payment for those willing to leave the US and turn their backs on the country they built and the loved ones they knew. Those choosing to immigrate received $100 from the US government plus transportation across the waters to Haiti and Liberia.

18. Andrea Ritchie and Marbre Stahly-Butts, eds., "Movement for Black Lives Reparations Now Toolkit," (M4BL, 2019), 17, accessed May 18, 2023, https://m4bl.org/wp-content/uploads/2020/05/Reparations-Now-Toolkit-FINAL.pdf.

19. Ritchie and Stahly-Butts, "Movement for Black Lives," 18.

20. Worthington Chauncey Ford, ed., *Wills of George Washington, and His Immediate Ancestors* (Brooklyn, NY: Historical Printing Club, 1891). See also Historical Genealogical Society, The New England Historical and Genealogical Register, vol. 44 (Boston: New England Historic Genealogical Society, 1890), 79.

BIBLIOGRAPHY

Baptist, Edward E. *The Half Has Never Been Told: Slavery and the Making of American Capitalism.* New York, NY: Basic Books, 2014.

Blassingame, John W., ed. *The Frederick Douglass Papers: Correspondences of Frederick Douglass*, vol. 1, 1842–1852. New Haven, CT: Yale University Press, 2009.

The Charleston Renaissance Gallery. Accessed January 19, 2023. https://fineartsouth.com/pages/about-us/default.aspx.

Colletta, John Philip. "Clark Mills and His Enslaved Assistant, Philip Reed: The Collaboration that Culminated in Freedom." The Capital United States Capitol Historical Society, Volume 57, Spring Summer 2020. Accessed January 19, 2023. https://capitolhistory.org/wp-content/uploads/2021/09/2020-Dome-1_46_Online.pdf.

Fogel, R. W. and S. L. Engerman. *Time on the Cross: The Economics of American Negro Slavery*. New York, NY: W. W. Norton, 1974.

Ford, Worthington Chauncey, ed. *Wills of George Washington, and His Immediate Ancestors*. Brooklyn, NY: Historical Printing Club, 1891.

Fryd, Vivien Green. "Lifting the Veil of Race at the U.S. Capitol: Thomas Crawford's Statue of Freedom." *Common-Place: The Interactive Journal of Early American Life*, Issue 10, No. 4, July 2010. Accessed January 20, 2023. http://commonplace.online/article/lifting-veil-race-u-s-capitol/.

Harrison, Renee K. *Black Hands, White House: Slave Labor and The Making of America*. Minneapolis, MN: Fortress Press, 2021.

James Madison's Montpelier. "The Mere Distinction of Colour." Accessed January 20, 2023, https://www.montpelier.org/learn/6-ways-that-understanding-slavery-will-change-how-you-understand-american-freedom.

National Archives and Records Administration, Microcopy 520, Reel 5. The original document is held in the Records of the Accounting Officers of the Department of the Treasury, 1775–1978, National Archives and Records Administration, Record Group 217.6.5. Within the National Archives' Archival Description Catalog, see ARC Identifier 4644616 / MLR Number A1 347. Accessed January 19, 2023. https://www.visitthecapitol.gov/artifact/petition-clark-mills-petition-number-741.

"Philip Reid and the Statue of Freedom," United States Senate. Accessed January 20, 2023. https://www.senate.gov/artandhistory/history/common/generic/Civil_War_ReidPhilip_StatueofFreedom.htm.

Ritchie, Andrea, and Marbre Stahly-Butts, eds. "Movement for Black Lives Reparations Now Toolkit." M4BL, 2019. Accessed May 18, 2023. https://m4bl.org/wp-content/uploads/2020/05/Reparations-Now-Toolkit-FINAL.pdf.

United States Senate. "The Civil War: The Senate's Story: Philip Reid and the Statue of Freedom." Accessed January 20, 2023. https://www.senate.gov/artandhistory/history/common/generic/Civil_War_ReidPhilip_StatueofFreedom.htm.

Williams, Eric. *Capitalism and Slavery*. Chapel Hill, NC: University of North Carolina Press, 1944.

Winkle, Kenneth J. "Emancipation Petitions: Historical Contexts." Civil War Washington, edited by Susan C. Lawrence, Elizabeth Lorang, Kenneth M. Price, and Kenneth J. Winkle. Center for Digital Research in the Humanities, University of Nebraska-Lincoln. Accessed January 19, 2023. https://civilwardc.org/texts/petitions/about.

Chapter Sixteen

Reparation as Reckoning

Malcolm Foley

While I am a historian, the treatment of reparations requires more than a dispassionate historical account of harm caused and payment due. What is required, especially for the Christian, is the connection between that account of harm and what that means for love of neighbor. To me, history, particularly the history of racial violence, is not to be known merely to swell one's mind, but in order to more robustly love our neighbors, especially as we come to terms with the debts that we owe one another. Because the debt incurred is so high, as we consider centuries of exploitation, domination, brutality, and racialization, it is very easy to see the horizon as unapproachable and thus not worthy of effort. Yet that is precisely the ethical option that is not allowed for the Christian. The fact that perfection will not be achieved in this life does not dilute Christ's words in the Gospel of Matthew: "Be perfect, therefore, as your heavenly Father is perfect" (Matt 5:48; NRSV). The only way that we can justly move forward is to view our past and present with moral clarity. Such moral clarity requires us to stare into the seemingly inescapable abyss of the history of racial violence in America.

TWO VIGNETTES

On May 16, 1918, Hampton Smith, a white farmer, was killed in Brooks County, Georgia. The suspected shooter was one of his workers, a Black man named Sidney Johnson. Smith was infamous among his workers as an abusive boss, who took advantage of the debt peonage system of his day, a system we also know by the name of convict leasing. Smith was known to bail Black people out of jail and require them to work for him in order to repay the debt. In so doing, he mercilessly exploited a system that attempted to maintain the second-class citizenry of Black men and women. After so-called Emancipation, newly freed Black people were released into a nation and an economy that had been built upon their exploitation. That exploitation did not stop; rather, in some senses, it accelerated. Before Emancipation, Black men and women were, in the eyes of the economy, both labor and capital, making it largely inefficient, inconvenient and "wasteful" for enslavers to kill them. When racialized chattel slavery perpetuated by individual slaveowners was deemed unconstitutional through the Thirteenth Amendment, corporations and the government took up the mantle, having the recently enslaved arrested for minor crimes and then sold back to plantation owners or growing corporations. Within this milieu of exploitation, violence was a regular risk.

Following Smith's murder, a mob of white people gathered to avenge his death and embarked on what would become known as the "Lynching Rampage of 1918." Over the course of the next week, that mob killed at least seven Black people, one of whom was a man named Hayes Turner. His wife, Mary, grieved her husband's death. But she grieved too loudly.

Local newspapers reported that she intended to seek legal action against the members of the mob. Upon hearing this, the fury of the mob became trained on her. Walter White, then assistant secretary of the NAACP, investigated and explained what happened next: "Her ankles were tied together and she was hung to the tree, head downward. Gasoline and oil from the automobiles were thrown on her clothing and while she writhed in agony and the mob howled in glee, a match was applied and her clothes burned from her person." This brutality was not enough to satisfy the mob, however. Eight months pregnant, Smith was then reportedly cut open with a knife. When the baby fell out of her, a member of the mob crushed its head with his foot. Then the mob riddled her body with bullets.[1]

Forty-six years later, a prominent civil rights leader—and the man after whom I was named—was asked by a reporter whether this country was making progress, presumably with regard to racial justice. Malcolm cut him off, retorting,

> I will never say that progress is being made. If you stick a knife in my back nine inches and pull it out six inches, there's no progress. You pull it all the way out, that's not progress. The progress is healing the wound that the blow made. And they haven't even begun to pull the knife out, much less try to heal the wound. They won't even admit the knife is there.[2]

Malcolm X smirked wryly as he uttered this line, perhaps considering the ignorance behind the question. Progress was indeed elusive. He knew, as did many of the leaders of the civil rights movement, including Martin Luther King, A. Philip Randolph, and Bayard Rustin, that the problem was not merely a problem of laws—or, even beyond that, a problem of hate. Race and racism ultimately come down to a problem of resources. It is no coincidence that when he was asked about the political and economic system he preferred—after a speech to the Militant Labor Forum of New York—he did not choose capitalism or socialism. But he did utter a damning indictment, saying, "You can't have capitalism without racism."[3] Here, Malcolm made the connection that we must all make: that racism is a matter of political economy.

Mary Turner was one of more than three thousand Black women and men killed by lynch mobs from 1883 to 1941.[4] Her story is one of the most brutal stories, but there were many others: accounts of how Sam Hose, Jesse Washington, Luther Holbert, and others were treated will sicken all those who hear of them. Jesse Washington's 1916 lynching in Waco jumpstarted the NAACP's anti-lynching campaigns, as stories of the teenager being castrated, mutilated, and burned alive circulated across the nation.[5] Hearing that the fingers and toes of the lynched Sam Hose were displayed in a meat market in 1899 inspired W. E. B. Du Bois to become an activist as well as a scholar.[6] In 1904, Luther Holbert and an unidentified woman were killed by a mob in Doddsville, Mississippi, but only after their fingers and ears were chopped off and they had been tortured with corkscrews.

In the American imagination and memory, the history of lynching and racial violence is something that we would rather not engage with. A failure to do so, however, restricts our ability to love our neighbors robustly because it is a refusal to reckon with something fundamental to the way that we conceive of white supremacy and the violence that always attends it. That fundamental element is this: white supremacist violence is not rooted in frenzy, emotionalism, ignorance, or hate. It is rooted ultimately in exploitation, greed, and the maintenance of social power. We must remember that Mary's Turner's lynching (and the lynchings of many others) was precipitated by a wage dispute. Nor was the institution that initially created the conditions that Black Americans would suffer under, namely racialized chattel slavery, primarily an institution of hate; fundamentally, it involved the exploitation of labor. Oliver Cox contextualized racial prejudice well after explaining that the slave trade's purpose was to recruit labor to mine American natural resources:

> This then is the beginning of modern race relations. It was not an abstract, natural, immemorial feeling of mutual antipathy between groups, but rather a practical exploitative relationship with its socio-attitudinal facilitation—at that time [in the 1490s] only nascent race prejudice.[7]

This is, in fact, the origin of race and racism—and the origin of the accrual of the debt that requires repayment. While cash payments would likely be an important part of any plan for reparations, what is especially necessary is a different system, a different political economy, and a different way of interacting with our neighbors, our brothers and sisters. The question is whether our consciences have been adequately sensitized to that need.

WHITE SUPREMACY AS THEFT

In their excellent book on reparations, Duke Kwon and Gregory Thompson make a powerful and incisive argument that white supremacy is theft. In their words, "American White supremacy originated in the theft of Black bodies, sustained itself through the theft of Black wealth, and justifies itself through the theft, the erasure, of truths that expose its lies."[8] This insight should not be underestimated, especially insofar as it reorients those who wish to speak of racial justice. We are not speaking abstractly about harm done nor are we speaking of race and racism as though the real problem is merely ignorance and hate, which can be dealt with through education and relationships—often pet projects of evangelical communities. As Malcolm X said, we are speaking of wounds. Yet it remains for us to name the knife so that we can remove it. Only after removing the knife can we heal the wound. Reparations, rightly considered, must address both of those actions.

To that end, the knife must be named: it is racialized capitalism.[9] Obviously, there is scholarly debate over whether or not capitalism is essentially racist. That is not the relevant concern in this particular conversation. One can disagree with Malcolm X's claim that capitalism cannot exist without racism, but it is difficult to argue that racism has not been overwhelmingly characteristic of the capitalism that we have known. The wealth of the United States, insofar as it depended on cotton, depended on the exploitation of Black labor.[10] That association is fundamental rather than incidental; in many ways, the nation's wealth amounts to blood money. In order to build that wealth, it was necessary to transform human beings into exploitable commodities. This was not—and can never be—a nonviolent process. Even if we focus only on slavery, we are considering a fundamentally violent and extremely brutal institution. That brutality was not incidental to the exploitation that it enforced; it was fundamental and instrumental to it.

As Jonathan Tran has recently argued, racial capitalism can be understood as a feedback loop of use, identity, and justification: "how I use a thing tells me what kind of thing it is and the kind of thing it is justifies my use of it."[11] This applies especially to our treatment of our neighbors: if I treat my neighbor, brother or sister, fundamentally as labor, that is how I will see them. If they are meant to be labor, the most important thing to me will be that they are the best labor that they can be. I will seek to maximize their efficiency.

If they will work harder without the familial distractions, I will remove them from their families. If someone protests the morality of my actions, I can fall back on the putative purpose of my neighbor: I am merely treating them in a way that is appropriate to their purpose as labor or, in the case of racialized chattel slavery, labor *and* capital. Here, Tran's description of the system that Cedric Robinson called "racial capitalism" is instructive:

> Racial capitalism's processes are all those technological advances that build out and link into a global political economic complex geared toward extracting consumable and tradable value—critically, in order to serve the ends of profit—in excess to the processes themselves.[12]

This process of extraction is fundamentally and necessarily violent, primarily because people have no desire to be unrelenting victims of extraction. In order to continue the extraction, they must be kept in that position. Thus, Sven Beckert and Seth Rockman argue that in racialized chattel slavery, "no technology was more important than the whip."[13] To use one's fellow human being (exploitation), it is necessary to enforce their use and commodification (domination). This exploitation and domination does not take place without rationalization. From that historical impulse, racialization arose as a justification for a fundamentally exploitative political economy.

We may now extend Kwon and Thompson's argument. White supremacy breaks the eighth commandment because it breaks the tenth commandment. That is, the theft is a result of covetousness and greed. The desire to accumulate precedes the desire to exploit—or, as the brother of Jesus concisely stated, "You desire but do not have, so you kill" (Jas 4:2; NIV). For Kwon and Thompson, framing racism in terms of theft makes reparation the natural and moral response. But we must go deeper than that. Such an evil demands more than just discrete reparations. It demands self-giving generosity as a just response. The debt is actually much deeper than we can imagine.

BLOOD THAT CRIES OUT: THE DEBT OF RACIAL VIOLENCE

While it is easy to point to slavery and see the clear relationship between white supremacy and theft, it is not the only example. Instead, we must look a few years after Emancipation. One of the lessons of the Civil War and its aftermath was that it would take far more than a war to defeat the beast of white supremacy. Although the period of Reconstruction yielded the most continuous progress toward a multiracial democracy seen in American history until that point—and perhaps since—it was also a time of deep, building, and violent resentment from those used to being in the dominant position of exploiter. In fact, in some very important ways, the exploitation continued through debt peonage and sharecropping. Douglas Blackmon, in his excellent book, *Slavery by Another Name,* alternates between calling such systems "quasi-slavery" and "neoslavery," but insofar as they were fundamentally maintained by the exploitation of Black labor, they were effectively a continuation of slavery. As Blackmon notes, the punishments were the same, the people doing the exploiting were the same, and the practices of leasing, bartering, wholesaling, and retailing human beings were the same.[14] In other words, the political economy remained, in some disturbing ways, the same after the Civil War. In fact, the brutality arguably increased with the advent of racialized terror lynching.

Lynching, as a form of extralegal punishment for those accused of crimes, existed before the late 1880s. From 1882–1889, however, the practice became almost exclusively racialized: the proportion of Black people suffering this extralegal and extralethal violence rose significantly while the proportion of white victims plummeted.[15] Such violence required explanation and it became common to describe the Black man, specifically, as a criminal more than as a beast of burden, although the latter description still served to justify the ongoing practice of convict leasing.

Yet Black activists refused to rely on the testimonies of Southern lynchers to their local newspapers, choosing to dig deeper and ask more significant questions. Ida B. Wells was the most significant of these figures, as she methodically dismantled narratives of Black inferiority as well as the narrative that lynching only happened as a response to rape. By investigating and enumerating lynchings as well as the reasons for them, she came to the conclusion, which she repeated in her lectures and editorials around the world, that "the Afro-American race is more sinned against than sinning."[16] Much to the chagrin of white Southern readers, Wells outlined the consensual sexual relationships that were glossed as rape to foment mob violence as well as the fact that there were many situations where sex had nothing to do with the lynching: it was a smokescreen to justify white supremacist violence. Indeed, she found "that colored men and women are lynched for almost any offense, from murder to misdemeanor" and that all that was required was an accusation. The injustice of this drove Wells and others to publicize these facts and to hope that those who heard the truth would act accordingly.

The practice of racialized lynching in the late nineteenth and early twentieth century is often remembered as a time of emotional frenzy. Walter White, who lived during the height of lynching, argued as much when he blamed Christians for its presence. He wrote:

> It is exceedingly doubtful if lynching could possibly exist under any other religion than Christianity. Not only through tacit approval and acquiescence has the Christian Church indirectly given its approval to lynch-law and other forms of race prejudice, but the evangelical Christian denominations have done much towards the creation of the particular fanaticism which finds an outlet in lynching.[17]

For White, the emotionalism of lynching was one of its most disturbing elements, and it could only be described in terms of frenzy and fanaticism. Other contemporary critics, however, saw even deeper reasons for the violence. In the 1940s, sociologist Oliver Cromwell Cox saw a different foundation, arguing that lynching's purpose was not merely to bear explosive witness to the violence of white supremacy but fundamentally to discipline Black labor.[18] Naomi Murakawa, in her treatment of Ida B. Wells, argues that Wells's activism arose from a foundational understanding of the "political economy of racial worth," as she understood the impetus for lynching to lay ultimately in economic struggle. Wells's advocacy for economic resistance resulted from this understanding.[19] She began a chapter on self-help in one of her editorials with an affirmation of the centrality of Black labor in the Southern economy and the suggestion that the best way to stop lynching was by this kind of bloodless revolution. After all, she would say, "the white man's dollar is his god."[20]

When we think back to the case of Mary Turner, we see a mob that appears out of control. I do not wish to speak of intentions beyond what is actually available to us. But it is often the case that "frenzy" is an easy way to ignore the political and social function of the brutal violence of lynching. We also see that the precipitating event was one that could have been avoided, if not for the greed of Hampton Smith and the system that he took advantage of. We see that the mob was protecting a particular status quo: subjection to one's employer is sacrosanct and if it is broken, that is punishable by death. Considering the collective weight of the almost 4,500 lives taken by lynchers, one is faced with blood which, like Abel's, cries out (see Gen 4:10).[21] Although lynching would understandably seem to be driven by hate, hate is not the primary evil in the phenomenon of lynching. From the initial conception of race, greed has been at its center. If, therefore, race is to be evacuated of its oppressive power, it must be evacuated of its economic effect, not only in the past but in our present. For example, we will find, if we investigate the history of incarceration and policing, that moneyed interests often drive policy change rather than actual crime statistics. This then, will demand the attention of all those who benefited—and continue to benefit—from that exploitation. We all have a part to play.

CONCLUSION: WHO IS RESPONSIBLE?

There are, at minimum, three significant institutions from which reparations can be demanded. The first is the government, a case which William Darity and Kirsten Mullen forcefully make.[22] As the institution with the most resources and the one with the most legal responsibility for creating a nation and atmosphere conducive to the exploitation of Black people, the government makes sense as a focus. Kwon and Thompson focus particularly on the second institution, the church, based on their understanding of the Christian's particular moral responsibility to heal wounds, to repair, and to attempt to reverse the death-dealing effects of white supremacy. The third institution consists of a range of business interests. Douglas Blackmon argues that "it was business that policed adherence to America's racial customs more than any other actor in U.S. society," alluding to the history of discriminatory lending practices that continued until the 1960s and were propped up by Wall Street throughout that time.[23] Keeanga-Yamahtta Taylor extends that blame even further, outlining the exploitative nature of the public-private partnerships in the housing market after the explicitly discriminatory policies of Jim Crow.[24] Even after the 1960s, businesses engaged in practices and benefited from policies of predatory inclusion rather than explicitly racist exclusion, with the same effects: Black people were often exploited and white pockets were often fattened. The complicity of essentially every major American institution in the exploitation of Black Americans leads to the conclusion that reparations will require more than we are comfortable admitting: it will require at least as much energy and creativity to remedy as were needed to inflict the wound. We must remember that slavery was not merely a Southern institution; it was a national one. The wealth of Wall Street did not begin with financialized capitalism; it was fed by the slave market that was housed on that street from 1711–1762. The United States' wealth as a nation is traceable in large part to cotton, a good only produced through brutal exploitation. The country's systems of credit were built on the backs of enslaved peoples, viewing them as both labor and capital and in many cases mortgaging them as one would mortgage land.[25] If the major institutions of the nation colluded and commiserated to transform people into profit, repurposing those greedy impulses to human flourishing is going to require widespread systemic change.

Ultimately, reparations—rightly and justly administered—will require a system that does not currently exist. The moral imperative seems to be that we must begin the process of reparations now in the process of bearing witness to a different way of living—as a manifestation of what theologian Antonio González speaks of as systemic change *from below*.[26] Insofar as the gospel of Jesus Christ is a message of reckoning with sin, turning from it and toward the Lord, and being cosmically reconciled with one's neighbor and creation, part of our ethical commitment is to resist domination and exploitation in all of their forms. In order both to recognize the wound and heal it, an unquenchable thirst for profit, otherwise known as greed and also often narrated as a necessity for our current economy, will have to be forsaken, since it is precisely the historical and moral evil that precipitates racialization and the violence and exploitation that plague our history and present. We currently find ourselves in a financialized political economy that obscures these dynamics, yet they still remain. In the light of such national dynamics, the current clarion call is for creativity: the debt is clear and the blood continues to run. We can either stanch the flow, stitch the wound, and form more redemptive and supportive national habits, or we can allow greed and death to continue to wreak the havoc that they have wreaked for centuries.

NOTES

1. Walter White, "The Work of A Mob," *The Crisis* 16, no. 5 (1918): 221–223

2. Malcolm X - *If You Stick A Knife In My Back*, 1964, accessed May 19, 2023, https://www.youtube.com/watch?v=XiSiHRNQlQo.

3. Malcolm X, "The Harlem 'Hate-Gang' Scare," in *Malcolm X Speaks: Selected Speeches and Statements* (New York, NY: Grove Press, 1990), 69.

4. Charles Seguin and David Rigby, "National Crimes: A New National Data Set of Lynchings in the United States, 1883 to 1941," *Socius*, January 2019, accessed May 19, 2023, https://doi.org/10.1177/2378023119841780.

5. Patricia Bernstein, *The First Waco Horror: The Lynching of Jesse Washington and the Rise of the NAACP* (College Station: Texas A&M University Press, 2005).

6. W. E. B. Du Bois, *W.E.B. Du Bois: A Recorded Autobiography, Interview with Moses Asch* (Smithsonian Folkways Recordings, 1961), accessed May 19, 2023, https://www.loc.gov/exhibits/civil-rights-act/multimedia/w-e-b-du-bois.html.

7. Oliver Cromwell Cox, *Caste, Class, & Race: A Study in Social Dynamics* (New York: Monthly Review Press, 1959), 332.

8. Duke L. Kwon and Gregory Thompson, *Reparations: A Christian Call for Repentance and Repair* (Grand Rapids, MI: Brazos Press, 2021), 20.

9. Here, I refer to Cedric Robinson's use of the term, "racial capitalism," but with a bit of a clarification. I am not here making the argument that capitalism is necessarily racial, though it very well may be. In affirming that the only capitalism we know is racial and that such racialization was not accidental but intentional, I use the term "racialized" to affirm the evil and exploitative agency of those who construct and maintain this political economy. See Cedric J. Robinson, *Black Marxism: The Making of the Black Radical Tradition* (Chapel Hill and London: University of North Carolina Press, 2000).

10. For an excellent account of this particular history see Sven Beckert, *Empire of Cotton: A Global History* (New York: Vintage Books, 2014).

11. Jonathan Tran, *Asian Americans and the Spirit of Racial Capitalism*, Reflection and Theory in the Study of Religion (New York, NY: Oxford University Press, 2022), 74.

12. Tran, *Asian Americans and the Spirit of Racial Capitalism*, 76.

13. Sven Beckert and Seth Rockman, *Slavery's Capitalism: A New History of American Economic Development* (Philadelphia: University of Pennsylvania Press, 2016), 15.

14. Douglas A. Blackmon, *Slavery by Another Name: The Re-Enslavement of Black Americans from the Civil War to World War II* (New York: Doubleday, 2008), 8.

15. For more on this process, see this excellent short book: Karlos K. Hill, *Beyond the Rope: The Impact of Lynching on Black Culture and Memory* (New York: Cambridge University Press, 2016).

16. Ida B. Wells, "Southern Horrors: Lynch Law in All Its Phases" (The New York Age Print, 1892).

17. Walter White, *Rope and Faggot: A Biography of Judge Lynch* (New York & London: Alfred A. Knopf, Inc., 1929), 40.

18. Cox, *Caste, Class, & Race: A Study in Social Dynamics*, 548–64.

19. For more, see Naomi Murakawa's chapter in Melvin L. Rogers and Jack Turner, eds., *African American Political Thought: A Collected History* (Chicago: University of Chicago Press, 2021).

20. Wells, "Southern Horrors."

21. For these particular numbers, see Seguin and Rigby, "National Crimes: A New National Data Set of Lynchings in the United States, 1883 to 1941." The 4500 includes Chinese (10 people), Japanese (1), Mexican (71), American Indian (38) and white victims (1082 people), many of whom faced violence both because of their ethnic heritage and because of their economic vulnerability.

22. William A. Darity Jr., and A. Kirsten Mullen, *From Here to Equality: Reparations for Black Americans in the Twenty-First Century*, Second Edition (Chapel Hill: University of North Carolina Press, 2022).

23. Blackmon, *Slavery by Another Name*, 390.

24. Keeanga-Yamahtta Taylor, *Race for Profit: How Banks and the Real Estate Industry Undermined Black Homeownership* (Chapel Hill: University of North Carolina Press, 2019).

25. Bonnie Martin, "Neighbor-to-Neighbor Capitalism: Local Credit Networks and the Mortgaging of Slaves," in *Slavery's Capitalism: A New History of American Economic Development*, ed. Sven Beckert and Seth Rockman, Early American Studies (University of Pennsylvania Press, 2016), 107–21.

26. Antonio González, *God's Reign & the End of Empires* (Miami, FL: Convivium Press, 2012).

BIBLIOGRAPHY

Beckert, Sven. *Empire of Cotton: A Global History*. New York: Vintage Books, 2014.
Beckert, Sven, and Seth Rockman. *Slavery's Capitalism: A New History of American Economic Development*. Philadelphia: University of Pennsylvania Press, 2016.
Bernstein, Patricia. *The First Waco Horror: The Lynching of Jesse Washington and the Rise of the NAACP*. College Station: Texas A&M University Press, 2005.
Blackmon, Douglas A. *Slavery by Another Name: The Re-Enslavement of Black Americans from the Civil War to World War II*. New York: Doubleday, 2008.
Cox, Oliver Cromwell. *Caste, Class, & Race: A Study in Social Dynamics*. New York: Monthly Review Press, 1959.
Darity, William A., Jr., and A. Kirsten Mullen. *From Here to Equality: Reparations for Black Americans in the Twenty-First Century*. Second Edition. Chapel Hill: University of North Carolina Press, 2022.
Du Bois, W. E. B. *W.E.B. Du Bois: A Recorded Autobiography, Interview with Moses Asch*. Smithsonian Folkways Recordings, 1961. Accessed May 19, 2023. https://www.loc.gov/exhibits/civil-rights-act/multimedia/w-e-b-du-bois.html.
González, Antonio. *God's Reign & the End of Empires*. Miami, FL: Convivium Press, 2012.
Hill, Karlos K. *Beyond the Rope: The Impact of Lynching on Black Culture and Memory*. New York: Cambridge University Press, 2016.
Kwon, Duke L., and Gregory Thompson. *Reparations: A Christian Call for Repentance and Repair*. Grand Rapids, MI: Brazos Press, 2021.
Robinson, Cedric J. *Black Marxism: The Making of the Black Radical Tradition*. Chapel Hill and London: University of North Carolina Press, 2000.
Rogers, Melvin L., and Jack Turner, eds. *African American Political Thought: A Collected History*. Chicago: University of Chicago Press, 2021.
Seguin, Charles, and David Rigby. "National Crimes: A New National Data Set of Lynchings in the United States, 1883 to 1941." *Socius*, January 2019. Accessed May 19, 2023. https://doi.org/10.1177/2378023119841780.
Taylor, Keeanga-Yamahtta. *Race for Profit: How Banks and the Real Estate Industry Undermined Black Homeownership*. Chapel Hill: University of North Carolina Press, 2019.
Tran, Jonathan. *Asian Americans and the Spirit of Racial Capitalism*. Reflection and Theory in the Study of Religion. New York, NY: Oxford University Press, 2022.
Wells, Ida B. "Southern Horrors: Lynch Law in All Its Phases." The New York Age Print, 1892.
White, Walter. *Rope and Faggot: A Biography of Judge Lynch*. New York & London: Alfred A. Knopf, Inc., 1929.
X, Malcolm. *Malcolm X - If You Stick A Knife In My Back*, 1964. Accessed May 19, 2023. https://www.youtube.com/watch?v=XiSiHRNQlQo.
_____. "The Harlem 'Hate-Gang' Scare." In *Malcolm X Speaks: Selected Speeches and Statements*, 64–72. New York, NY: Grove Press, 1990.

Chapter Seventeen

Witness: The Call for Truth and Reparations in Minnesota

Jim Bear Jacobs, Pamela R. Ngunjiri, and Curtiss Paul DeYoung

The stealing of land from the Indigenous population, combined with the enslavement of Africans as uncompensated labor, made clear that racism and white supremacy were core to the way of life in what would become the United States of America. The complicity of Christian faith communities further stamped on the nation the imprint of a sinful dehumanization. The State of Minnesota was born out of this blueprint, and the May 2020 killing of George Perry Floyd by law enforcement in Minneapolis became a catalyst for weeks and months of protests and unrest throughout Minnesota, the United States, and around the globe. With Minnesota at the epicenter of a movement for change, the Minnesota Council of Churches (MCC) Board of Directors launched a ten-year racial justice initiative with a three-point platform of truth telling, education, and reparations.

The MCC began as a white ecumenical organization. Today, the Council is a 75-year-old denominational membership organization with twenty-seven member communions from Historic Black, Mainline Protestant, Pentecostal, Greek Orthodox, and Peace Churches in Minnesota. MCC also has strong interfaith relationships, especially with Muslim and Jewish communities. In recent years, four historically Black denominations, one Dakota Native American communion, and one Black-led multiracial communion have joined. The Board of Directors has centered the leadership of historically Black denominations since 2018 by electing as president and vice president the leaders of Black denominations. In 2020, the Board approved a bylaws change to ensure that a majority of its members are Black, Indigenous, Asian, and Latine.

The pursuit of greater racial equity in the State of Minnesota requires a process of truth telling about racism, investment in repairing the damage done by racism, and the transformation of the systems that have caused Minnesota to be ranked with some of the highest racial disparities in the nation in healthcare, wealth, education, public safety, incarceration, employment, home ownership, and the like. Dr. Samuel Myers Jr., at the University of Minnesota has done important research on racial disparities in Minnesota. His research shows that Minnesota is the best state in the United States for whites to live in and the worst for Blacks. He has called this reality "The Minnesota Paradox."[1]

The Council's active truth telling and call for reparations seek to address the historic harm and current disparities experienced by African American and Native American communities in Minnesota. As immigrants and refugees arrive from Latin American, African, Asian, Arab, and other countries, they also feel the impact of pre-existing structures that create inequity. To focus on structures that harm Indigenous and Black communities benefits others thus affected, even economically marginalized whites. The goal of MCC's racial justice initiative is to transform systems that have created such extreme racial disparities in Minnesota.

The MCC's three-point action platform for racial justice is envisioned to operate as follows:

1. *Truth Telling:* MCC offers a strong moral voice that calls for truth telling, welcomes lament, advocates for reparations, and holds systems accountable for change. Faith communities provide a redemptive space for acknowledging past egregious, intentional oppression, and redressing past injustices and present inequities through specific acts of penance and contrition. Truth telling also includes naming complicity by faith communities in racial injustice.
2. *Education:* MCC creates anti-racism and cultural competency training to complement what is already occurring in denominations and congregations.
3. *Reparations in Indigenous and Black Communities:* MCC pursues the goal to repair the harm done by racism in partnership with faith communities and other engaged actors (government, business, academic, etc.). A process for reparations and equity will be developed by MCC throughout the State of Minnesota. The reparations process is coordinated with truth telling.

Each of the three platform propositions presupposes that an organization with a membership of twenty-seven denominational communions (representing one million constituents) and strong interfaith partners is well situated to serve as a catalyst for the envisioned process of racial justice. Much of the work is on a larger scale beyond what an individual denomination could address on their own.

In 2021, co-directors for racial justice were hired to oversee the initiative—Rev. Jim Bear Jacobs (enrolled citizen of Stockbridge-Munsee Band of Mohicans) and African Methodist Episcopal Church pastor, Rev. Pamela Ngunjiri. That same year, truth telling work was formally launched. Acclaimed Black studies historian Dr. Yohuru Williams from the University of St. Thomas (MN) and activist Christine McCleave (enrolled citizen Turtle Mountain Ojibwe Nation), then CEO of the National Native America Boarding School Healing Coalition, were engaged to help shape the public truth telling.

The remainder of this chapter will describe how truth telling and reparations are understood, communicated, and operationalized by the MCC. The faith community brings a unique perspective as a moral voice calling for reparations in society, while at the same time acknowledging and addressing the need to repair the history and present inequity that exist within the church itself.[2]

TRUTH TELLING

> "As we enter into this space, let us remember that we have come to hear, to listen, and to learn. As we encounter someone's story, let us remember that all stories come to us as gifts, and should be received with gratitude. In story we make human connection, and in that connection we are transformed. And so we enter committing to listen deeply and receive gratefully."[3]

The MCC's three-point action platform for racial justice begins with truth telling. Telling the truth is important for shared understanding in any society. Truth is an underlying principle of civil existence that assumes what one is being told is trustworthy. The act of truth telling takes on even greater significance for people of the Christian faith. When Jesus described himself, one of the words he used was *truth:* "I am the way, and the truth, and the life" (John 14:6). This truth does not merely involve a passive understanding of the societal conventions that should govern an ideal society. There is liberative action in truth: "You will know the truth, and the truth will make you free" (John 8:32).

When historically silenced voices from American Indian and African American communities are given platforms to tell their truth, the marginalized speaker can take some initial steps toward healing. The power of this healing is bi-directional. For the recipient of these hard truths, voices from the margins can be a strong medicine, bitter at first, but they are ultimately healing. Indeed, the truth will set us free.

It is imperative that any racial justice work within Christian faith communities leading to reparations begin with truth telling. When we call Christian churches to repentance and reparations, we must be clear about what we are repairing, and what we are repenting from. Truth telling is an act by which communities ensure that they are on the same page when speaking of historical racialized disparities. George Erasmus from the Dene Nation, and co-chair of the Royal Commission on Aboriginal Peoples (Canada) has said, "Where Common memory is lacking, where people do not share in the same past, there can be no real community. Where community is to be formed, common memory must be created."[4] Truth telling is one way of establishing common memory—in the hope that doing so will lead to unified community.

In September 2021, in Minneapolis, the public face of the MCC's focus on truth telling began in earnest with the launch of the first of the truth telling events. Entitled "Minnesota's Racial Legacy: Finally Telling The Truth," this event brought together speakers from our focus communities—Minnesota's American Indian and African American peoples—to share both the history of the impact of white supremacy on their community and the transgenerational and personal impact of that legacy. Due to the still lingering restrictions of Covid-19, the event was held in a hybrid format, with both a live, in-person audience and a larger virtual one. In total, there were over three hundred in attendance for the day-and-a-half event.

The conversation began with a keynote address by Christine Diindiisi McCleave, the chief executive officer of the National Native American Boarding School Healing Coalition. Her presentation focused on the history of the residential boarding school system, with a particular focus on the role of Christian denominations in the establishment and administration of these institutions. While this information may not have been totally new for the audience, the wide scope of its reach was shocking to many.[5] McCleave revealed that in Minnesota there had been at least sixteen residential boarding schools. Given that the number of unmarked graves of Indigenous children in the Canadian boarding school system rose exponentially over time, it is likely that when the United States begins their own investigation, the number of graves on US soil will be alarmingly high. The largely Christian audience began to realize the tremendous scope of necessary repair needed in Minnesota.

The next speaker was Dr. Yohuru Williams, the distinguished university chair and professor of history at the University of St. Thomas. Williams's presentation painted a history of the racial injustice faced by Black and Indigenous Minnesotans. He paid particular attention to the year 1975, when incidents of horrible police brutality against Black and Indigenous people were particularly egregious in Minneapolis. With the eyes of the world still on Minneapolis following the murder of George Floyd, Williams demonstrated how white supremacy continues to show itself in public safety and policing.

Following the keynote addresses, a panel of three community members shared how white supremacy hindered their work toward racial justice. Ebony Adedayo, Anthony Galloway, and Nevada Littlewolf all come from either the American Indian or African American community. These respected activists shared from their own experiences how the institutionalizing of whiteness creates barriers to racial equity. Their personal sharing served to bring issues of racial injustice out of the academic headspace and into the personal heart space.

This type of work can be very traumatizing. The majority of our audience was white, and hearing these stories can trigger trauma responses for BIPOC people. Aware that whitespace is a very uncomfortable place for BIPOC people to process trauma, specialists in trauma from the Native community and the Black community were onsite. A separate space was provided for BIPOC audience members to process away from the white gaze. Also, white people hearing historically ignored truths may experience trauma responses that resemble guilt and shame. White guilt and shame often manifest themselves in ways that create more emotional labor for BIPOC people. So, a trauma-informed specialist from the white community was also onsite.

The audience was divided for a final activity as the program concluded. The white participants were guided into a space where they were led by a trusted white colleague to give voice to their individual and collective practical commitments to carry forward the work of racial justice. The BIPOC members of the audience were guided into a separate space where they were led in a ritual to close their time together with a feeling of solidarity and healing. Several of the BIPOC participants noted that although the event's participants were mostly white, the careful and intentional concern to create space exclusively for BIPOC folks was greatly appreciated.

Since that initial event in 2021, MCC has continued to carry forward the work of truth telling by adapting and creating new formats. We have created some events for smaller audiences that are both shorter and more accessible, and more intimate and conversational. Multiple events have occurred in the Twin Cities and will continue across the decade. Also, MCC has partnered with organizations from around the state to carry this work to the small cities and towns in Greater Minnesota. In the fall of 2022, a truth telling event took place in Duluth, MN. Others are being scheduled in various locations.

EDUCATION

An outcome of truth telling is the education of participants on history and current realities of racial harm. MCC is also focused on creating opportunities for more in-depth racial justice education. Many congregants are not equipped in the language and concepts of cultural competency, anti-racism, and other forms of diversity, equity, and inclusion education. The Council supports the racial justice training efforts of the member denominations. Some have staff designated for this purpose or committees that implement such training. MCC is focused on discovering the gaps in the training or resourcing smaller denominational members. The journey ahead will require unique offerings for rural congregations.

As MCC continues this work for ten years and beyond, truth telling and education will always be essential. We will continue to center stories from Minnesota's Black and Indigenous communities. Stories take this work out of the realm of the abstract and theoretical, center the human experience of marginalized communities, and remind us that we are fighting not for faceless possibilities. Instead, we are fighting for our neighbors, we are fighting for our relatives, we are fighting for real people.

REPARATIONS

"You do not think yourself into a new way of living; you live yourself into a new way of thinking."[6]

William Darity Jr., and A. Kirsten Mullen note that the action of reparation is an "acknowledgment, redress, and closure for a grievous injustice."[7] The goal of reparations is to repair harm done by racism. Truth telling identifies the harm that has occurred. What has become clear in our research and conversations with others in this work is that reparations should be defined as both economic and spiritual repair. Economically, reparations are what should have been granted after slavery ended and honored in treaties that the US government made with Native American tribes. Reparations include money, land, education, and the like. Lack of repair contributes to the ongoing racial disparities in Minnesota, which are among the highest in the United States.

Reparations as spiritual healing is akin to soul repair, which entails repairing the harm done to the soul of those oppressed by racism. Also, the soul of the oppressor needs healing. While whites would not be recipients of reparations, there is certainly a need for healing. What is often missed is how oppressors dehumanize themselves through racist acts and the creation of racist structures. Their repair comes through the dismantling of the myths, lies, and misinformation, which allows for subsequent racist acts and atrocities to be visited upon BIPOC because they are not seen as fully human and, therefore, the harm is not viewed in terms of atrocities against humans, but against "others" or those considered less than human. This dismantling helps restore the biblical notion of the full humanity of oppressed people by inviting oppressors to repair the hole in their soul that hinders their ability to see God in the faces of oppressed people. The work we do in truth telling events moves us toward spiritual repair and ending the perpetuation of white supremacy and its tools of myths, lies, and misinformation.

As a Christian organization, the Minnesota Council of Churches is guided by biblical texts that provide a foundation for racial justice work and offer a biblical precedent for confession (truth telling) and reparations. Two examples are:

- "The LORD spoke to Moses, saying: Speak to the Israelites: When a man or a woman wrongs another, breaking faith with the LORD, that person incurs guilt and shall confess the sin that has been committed. The person shall make full restitution for the wrong, adding one fifth to it, and giving it to the one who was wronged" (Num 5:5–7; NRSV).
- "Zacchaeus stood there and said to the Lord, 'Look, half of my possessions, Lord, I will give to the poor; and if I have defrauded anyone of anything, I will pay back four times as much'" (Luke 19:8; NRSV).

The Council is collaborating with community leaders, activists, and theologians to brainstorm what biblically inspired reparations should look like for Minnesota and its faith communities. Reparations must be defined and determined by the affected communities. The MCC racial justice co-directors have recruited and convened a group of six Native persons and six Black persons for a reparations workgroup / think tank to develop a charge to be given to our member constituents as they begin working on reparations initiatives for their denominations and local congregations. This group of academics, theologians, and community leaders bring a wealth of information and experience to the table. They are connected to persons in all sectors within Black and Native communities.

Our work with denominations and congregations consists of assisting them as they examine their own history—to determine what racial harms their denomination or congregation has participated in and may continue to perpetuate. Many of Minnesota's historic churches were present and complicit as racist systems were built in the State of Minnesota. The intersection of church membership with citizenship formed a backdrop to the harm. For example, we discovered that Brown Chapel AME Church in the city of Hastings, MN, was burned down by arsonists.[8] There was no official investigation. Oral tradition suggests that the local Ku Klux Klan was involved, however. The KKK chaplain at the time was the pastor of the Methodist Church—where the Brown Chapel AME members worshipped before founding their own congregation. This church burning is believed to have contributed to the subsequent exit, over time, of the entire Black community living in Hastings. Reports also say that the church was not adequately compensated for their property loss, and it is unknown whether the families were adequately compensated for their need to relocate. MCC has connected with a local group of primarily white, current Hastings residents who are concerned about what happened and who want to expose this history in order to determine next steps toward repair. MCC is also working with ancestors of the members of Brown Chapel AME Church.

There are Minnesota denominations and congregations that are interested in the work of repair and have taken action to begin a process of acknowledging past and stopping current harms. There are various notions of what reparations means and how faith organizations fit into the work. We engage folks where they are. We begin by helping church leaders to understand that reparations are not charity.

Beyond the faith community, MCC has engaged with the reparations initiatives of local government entities. The St. Paul City Council has established the Saint Paul Recovery Act Community Reparations Commission.[9] The Minneapolis City Council approved a resolution for a truth and reconciliation process that has reparations imbedded in it.[10] MCC has advised and participated in both efforts.

CONCLUSION

The MCC has committed to a process of at least a decade of truth telling, education, and reparations. We intentionally chose a dual narrative approach for truth telling about the historic and current reality of racial harm in Indigenous and Black communities in Minnesota. This will lead to recommendations for reparations uniquely suited for each community. We also envision Black and Indigenous local faith congregations as important vehicles for the delivery of reparations.

This initiative is expanding beyond the constituency of MCC to a broader ecumenical and interfaith effort through the establishment of key partnerships and relationships with Roman Catholics, and with Muslim and Jewish leaders. We believe that a broader faith coalition will increase the possibility of success in this work. In Minnesota, we envision a vibrant interfaith coalition serving as a moral voice to advocate for reparations legislation at the state and local levels.

We have learned lessons in the first two years of our truth and reparations initiative that inform the implementation of our efforts moving forward. We have learned not to underestimate the power of the normative nature of whiteness. While truth telling focuses on the harm of racism in Black and Indigenous communities, we still have to focus intentionally on decentering whiteness. At the same time, in rural communities we are learning that even the notion of whiteness as normative may not be widely held. So we are partnering with local clergy and community leaders who have been working for racial justice awareness in those communities to find a language for discussing truth telling and reparations.

We are hopeful that our decade-long effort will greatly increase the understanding of what is required to repair the harmful results of a long history of racism and begin to position faith communities as important partners in the long process of implementing reparatory justice in Minnesota. The success of reparations for Native Americans and African Americans will ultimately be measured by the achievement of a significant decrease of racial inequities in society, a steady improvement in the daily lives of individuals and families, and the flourishment of community institutions (including congregations).

NOTES

1. Samuel L Myers Jr., "The Minnesota Paradox," University of Minnesota Hubert H. Humphrey School of Public Policy, accessed May 19, 2023, https://www.hhh.umn.edu/research-centers/roy-wilkins-center-human-relations-and-social-justice/minnesota-paradox.

2. For a perspective on the apostle Paul's reparative actions in the first-century church, see the chapter "The Economics of Racial Equity" in Curtiss Paul DeYoung, *The Risk of Being Woke: Sermonic Reflections for Activists* (Valley Forge: Judson Press, 2023), 34–43.

3. Statement of Commitment that greeted participants at the entrance of MCC's Minnesota's Racial Legacy: Finally Telling the Truth event.

4. George Erasmus made this statement in a press release: "From Truth to Reconciliation: Transforming the Legacy of Residential Boarding Schools," *Aboriginal Healing Foundation Press*, 2008. He is quoting theologian H. Richard Niebuhr, *The Meaning of Revelation* (New York: The Macmillan Company, 1941), 11.

5. Minnesota has a large population of Native Americans, with the Twin Cities of Minneapolis and St. Paul holding one of largest urban Native populations in the country.

6. Center for Action and Contemplation, "A New Way of Thinking," October 3, 2019, accessed May 19, 2023, https://cac.org/daily-meditations/a-new-way-of-thinking-2019-10-03/

7. William A. Darity Jr., and A. Kirsten Mullen, *From Here to Equality: Reparations for Black Americans in the Twenty First Century* (Chapel Hill: The University of North Carolina Press, 2020), 2.

8. James Curry, "Hastings, 1907: The Burning of Brown Chapel AME," *MinnPost*, April 19, 2021, accessed May 19, 2023, https://www.minnpost.com/mnopedia/2021/04/hastings-1907-the-burning-of-browns-chapel-ame/

9. Resolution 21–7, City Council, St. Paul, Minnesota, accessed May 19, 2023, https://www.stpaul.gov/department/city-council/reparations-legislative-advisory-committee/resolutions

10. Truth and Reconciliation, Minneapolis, Minnesota, accessed May 19, 2023, https://www2.minneapolismn.gov/government/departments/racial-equity/what-we-do/ongoing-work/truth-reconciliation/

BIBLIOGRAPHY

Center for Action and Contemplation. "A New Way of Thinking." October 3, 2019. Accessed May 19, 2023. https://cac.org/daily-meditations/a-new-way-of-thinking-2019-10-03/.

Curry, James. "Hastings, 1907: The Burning of Brown Chapel AME." *MinnPost*. April 19, 2021. Accessed May 19, 2023. https://www.minnpost.com/mnopedia/2021/04/hastings-1907-the-burning-of-browns-chapel-ame/.

Darity, William A., Jr., and A. Kirsten Mullen. *From Here to Equality: Reparations for Black Americans in the Twenty First Century*. Chapel Hill: The University of North Carolina Press, 2020.

DeYoung, Curtiss Paul. *The Risk of Being Woke: Sermonic Reflections for Activists.* Valley Forge: Judson Press, 2023.

Erasmus, George. "From Truth to Reconciliation: Transforming the Legacy of Residential Boarding Schools." Aboriginal Healing Foundation Press, 2008. Quoting H. Richard Niebuhr. *The Meaning of Revelation*. New York: The Macmillan Company, 1941.

Myers, Samuel L., Jr. "The Minnesota Paradox." University of Minnesota Hubert H. Humphrey School of Public Policy. Accessed May 19, 2023. https://www.hhh.umn.edu/research-centers/roy-wilkins-center-human-relations-and-social-justice/minnesota-paradox.

Resolution 21–7. City Council, St. Paul, Minnesota. Accessed May 19, 2023. https://www.stpaul.gov/department/city-council/city-council-reparations-efforts/city-council-reparations-legislative-0

Truth and Reconciliation. Minneapolis, Minnesota. Accessed May 19, 2023. https://www2.minneapolismn.gov/government/departments/racial-equity/what-we-do/ongoing-work/truth-reconciliation/.

Chapter Eighteen

"Bear Fruits Worthy of Repentance"

A Black Administrator's Perspective on the Challenge and Promise of the Virginia Theological Seminary Reparations Program

Joseph Downing Thompson Jr.

What I bring to the present volume is my experience as the primary architect of one of the first reparations programs for African Americans by a private institution in the United States of America: Virginia Theological Seminary (VTS), a seminary of the Episcopal Church located in Alexandria, Virginia. You might want me to start telling the story by explaining how this came to be. In the weeks and months after we first announced the program in the fall of 2019, I was often asked by proponents of reparations at other organizations, "How did you get them to do it?!?" I found this amusing because I can claim no such credit. The fact of the matter is that the leadership of the seminary—responding to generations of Black seminarians, faculty, alumni, trustees, and their allies who had raised awareness about the realities of slavery and anti-Black racism in the past and present of VTS and the Episcopal Church—was eager to take a substantive step toward making amends for the harm that was done and is still being done through the perpetuation of white supremacy.[1]

Additionally, there was a feeling that the VTS bicentennial, approaching in 2023, would be a particularly appropriate moment for the seminary to tell the most comprehensive truth possible about its history. The bicentennial provided an opportunity to paint a picture of the past, acknowledging the vast debt owed both to the enslaved and to Black persons employed during the exploitative era of racial segregation, those whose labor helped to build and maintain the seminary. The VTS reparations program attempts to center their stories and to build relationships with their descendants. These are the surnames of the descendant families that have been identified up to this point in the research: Casey, Henry, Johnson, Lewis, McKnight, Middleton, Peters, Roy, Simms, Strange, Terrell, Thomas, and Wanzer. First and foremost, this program aims to make amends to the descendants and honor them as the living legacies of individuals who persevered despite facing entrenched oppression. You can learn more about the history that has been documented by visiting the VTS website (www.vts.edu), as we gradually make more of the research available online.

This essay is not intended to share that research, as central as it is. Rather, the focus here is mainly on both the institutional perspective of VTS and my own, in the hope that these reflections will be useful to other institutions that have embarked upon discovering their histories of slavery and racism. As cities, institutions, and families across this nation—and, ideally, the federal government itself—gradually tackle the project of reparations, I seek to share something of my journey participating in the VTS effort and to convey the spiritual underpinnings that have guided the work that I have been privileged to do with this program. My goal is to provide a sense of the reasoning behind the general approach that our institution has taken, rather than to describe the process that went into making every decision—or even every major decision—about the VTS program.

BACKGROUND: PLANTING A SEED THAT CAN GROW

In 2019, in my capacity at that time as the Director of Multicultural Ministries, I was meeting with our dean and president, the Very Rev. Ian S. Markham, about routine matters, when he told me that he had identified a fund of $1.7 million that could potentially be used for reparations. He wanted to know if I thought that the relatively small amount would be insulting, given the enormity of the injustice. Virtually without missing a beat, I told him that as long as this figure was considered a seed that should grow, I would personally support the idea. As an African American who knows about the sordid history of anti-Black racism in the USA from both experience and study, I was certainly not going to discourage the leader of my institution from bringing attention to reparations at our seminary and investing financial resources in the project, even though the amount was admittedly small. Obviously, a strong commitment from those at the highest levels is an invaluable asset for any program, especially a controversial one. For institutional leaders reading this essay, the VTS story illustrates the impact that your power, combined with a sense of initiative, can have on an important social justice issue and the human lives that intersect with it.

After a period of consultation, during which Dean Markham explored the possibility of reparations at VTS with other administrators, faculty, board members, and advisors—particularly the Black members of those constituencies—the program was officially initiated and announced to the public in September 2019.[2] Although the specifics of the program had not been fully determined at that time, I will "fast forward" in the story in order to describe the parameters that were eventually developed. The initiative now consists of several components. The largest of these, by far—and the one upon which this essay focuses—is the effort to identify the names of those who were enslaved at VTS, as well as the names of Black people who were employed by the seminary during the era of enforced segregation; to memorialize them on campus; to connect with their descendants in order to build ongoing relationships (inasmuch as they are willing); and to offer direct financial disbursements from the reparations endowment fund.[3] Another major component of the program is the attempt to provide reparations to the two historically Black congregations in Alexandria that have deep historical ties to the seminary: Meade Memorial Episcopal Church and Oakland Baptist Church. Lastly, there are several small grant opportunities associated with the initiative, including grants for Black VTS alums working in historically Black contexts and for racial justice projects.[4]

Early on, the administration determined that the Office of Multicultural Ministries, which I lead as an associate dean and member of the faculty, would be the best organizational locus for the program. Thus, working closely with our school's leadership, I came to take on primary responsibility for designing and implementing the VTS Reparations Program. While the Office of Multicultural Ministries has taken the lead in shaping and coordinating the project, a number of individuals at the seminary and in the Alexandria historical and genealogical community have had a significant hand in the initiative, offering crucial perspectives on its nature and scope and helping to advance the work necessary in such a complex undertaking. In what follows, I identify these individuals, along with a description of their connection to the program, both to express sincere gratitude and to demonstrate the amount and types of effort that this endeavor has required.

I would like to begin with several of the descendants in the program who were among the first to be contacted and who were exceedingly helpful in connecting us with other members of the descendant community: Toniette Duncan, the granddaughter of Wilmer and Willie Mae Henry, both of whom worked in service positions at VTS from the 1920s until their retirement;

Frances Terrell and Carol Daniels, who are descendants of Daniel G. Simms, a waiter at VTS in 1910; Alfonzo Terrell and Angela Terrell Shivers, descendants of Burney McKnight, who was a domestic worker at VTS in 1870, and of Jacob Terrell who worked at VTS in 1917; and Steve Simms, a descendant of Daniel G. Simms and of John Samuel Thomas Jr., who was a farm laborer and eventually head janitor in the 1920s and 30s.

Among VTS personnel, Ebonee Davis first provided assistance in preserving the program's historical and genealogical research in the VTS Archives. She then went on to become Associate for Programming and Historical Research for Reparations, a position that entails coordinating the team of researchers, with primary responsibility for the day-to-day operations of the program. Ebonee often serves as the initial point of contact for the descendants, bringing her own thoughtful and sensitive vision to the ongoing development of the initiative. She has been a model of skill and grace in all of her work; Christopher Pote, formerly the Seminary Archivist, was crucial in navigating the historical record of VTS, the city of Alexandria, and the Diocese of Virginia from the founding of the seminary to the middle of the twentieth century, and he helped to identify and onboard the historical and genealogical researchers who later became essential to the program.

Char McCargo Bah, an expert on the history of Black Alexandria and genealogist extraordinaire, graciously agreed to conduct research on those who worked at VTS after the Civil War, and she used her many connections in the Alexandria community to help the seminary build trust with their descendants in the earliest days of the program—which would have been a much more difficult prospect without her committed involvement; Elizabeth Drembus, also an expert genealogical researcher, began by offering crucial assistance in finding biographical details about those who were enslaved at VTS. She went on to serve as the main fact checker for the researchers, using her eye for detail to ensure that historical and genealogical claims are well documented; Maddy McCoy, the founder and principal of the Slavery Inventory Database, has been indispensable as the lead investigator on the antebellum research, utilizing her extensive knowledge of the historical record, combined with her determination and dedication, to uncover names and details about more enslaved persons than we ever thought we could identify; the ever-curious and committed Christopher Milko, also with the Slavery Inventory Database, has made lasting contributions to the antebellum research; Curtis Prather, formerly VTS Director of Communications, and Elizabeth Panox-Leach, formerly a member of the Communications team, were at the forefront of managing the significant media interest in the program when it was first announced and, later, when the first disbursements of funds were made to descendants.

Paralleling the research and communications teams was the Reparations Subcommittee of the Dean's Task Force on Diversity, Inclusion, and Equity, the group that functioned as the advisory board for establishing and reviewing the program's policies. As chair of the subcommittee, I came up with the basic framework for the program, which was then vetted and modified by the group as needed. Two people who have already been mentioned, Ebonee Davis and Christopher Pote, were also members of the subcommittee. The other three members of the subcommittee offered invaluable perspectives and guidance: Bishop Phoebe Roaf, a VTS alum and former trustee; Jacqui Ballou, VTS Vice President for Finance and Operations; and VTS alum Riley Temple. Every person I have named—from researchers to descendants—has shown extraordinary dedication to, and passion for, this initiative. It would not have been possible to get the program up and running without significant investments of their time and energy.

VALUES: CULTIVATING THE SOIL FOR GOOD GROWTH

In my own professional visioning over the years, I never imagined that I would find myself at the helm of a reparations initiative. Nevertheless, even though I certainly harbored fears and doubts when my institution requested my service in this regard, I did not hesitate to accept. My willingness came not from a naively romanticized idea of what such a program could accomplish nor from any real confidence that VTS truly understood what would be required of it in the undertaking. Instead, I thought of my people. I thought of my father and grandmothers—all long deceased. I thought of my mother and sisters. I thought of my large extended family. I thought of the pride that all of us have in our heritage as Black people, a people who have somehow managed to survive and even thrive, despite the ways that anti-Black racism has threatened to deform our lives and destinies again and again. It seemed to me that reparations are both about offering restitution and about paying respect to the Black community. It felt entirely natural, then, to assist my institution in approaching this long overdue act of restitution (such as it is) and respect. I can see now that I experienced the possibility of this work as a calling from God and the ancestors. The work represented some small way in which I could play a part in the ongoing struggle against the intertwined legacies of slavery and white supremacy. It also represented a potential contribution to the Black community's agitation for a society that will finally make a serious attempt to rectify the heinous injustices of the past while promoting the spiritual and material conditions necessary for Black individuals and communities to flourish on equal footing with other racial and ethnic groups. I view this agitation as being in itself an important dimension of the ongoing struggle of Black people to heal from the trauma of racial oppression.

But what exactly is the nature of my part in this program, and does a limited initiative such as that of VTS really combat white supremacy, contribute to Black healing, and foster Black flourishing? My colleague Ebonee Davis, who is also African American, has a saying about her involvement in the program that I have often borrowed: "This is not my wrong to right." I understood this idea intuitively from day one, but it nevertheless took me a while to discern how to navigate the strange dynamic of being a member of the aggrieved community while also serving as a public representative of the institution that perpetrated the injury. Over time, I came to view my work in terms of John the Baptizer's saying to the crowds that were seeking baptism:

> You brood of vipers! Who warned you to flee from the coming wrath? Therefore, bear fruits worthy of repentance, and do not begin to say to yourselves, "We have Abraham as our ancestor," for I tell you, God is able from these stones to raise up children to Abraham. Even now the ax is lying at the root of the trees; therefore every tree that does not bear good fruit will be cut down and thrown into the fire (Luke 3:7b-9 [NRSVue]).

The Common English Bible is even more pointed in its translation of the first sentence of verse 8: "Produce fruit that shows you have changed your hearts and lives" (Luke 3:8a). In terms of the VTS reparations program, these verses emphasized to me that I would need to regard the motivations of my institution with some degree of skepticism, looking for signs that might indicate whether the project was bearing fruits worthy of repentance—or if it was merely indicative of an organization seeking an easy salvation without genuine metanoia. Might VTS be behaving in the manner that John associated with the crowds coming for baptism? That is, John suspected that they were coming to him in a first-century act of spiritual "virtue signaling," if you will, mouthing the right words but not allowing God to change their lives.

I also recognized, however, that the descendants directly involved in the program—those whose families have a historical relationship to the seminary and have borne the brunt of the injustice—should judge whether the program is bearing good fruit. At the same time, it is important to stipulate, with James, that "there is only one lawgiver and judge, and he is able to save and to destroy" (James 4:12; CEB). As always, God is the ultimate judge of whether or not the reparations program is an authentic outgrowth of repentance and amendment of life, as true and ongoing conversion in the Christian faith. When an institutional perpetrator attempts to reshape its role in human relationships that have heretofore been defined by exploitation and alienation, however, only those who have endured the oppression can truly determine whether—and, if so, how—the status of the relationship has changed. Only they can say whether or not VTS has acted in a manner that genuinely tells the truth about, and repairs the consequences of, the sins that were committed against the humanity and dignity of their ancestors. It has been crucial, therefore, to design a program that both acts decisively—so that it does much more than merely pay lip service to the idea of reparations—and is living, dynamic, perseverant, and flexible, so that it can be responsive to the legitimate claim of the descendants to be the arbiters of its efficacy. They are the ones who will examine the fruits—holding them, squeezing them, smelling them, and even tasting them—in order to decide whether they are any good.

With that in mind, I came to see myself as being something of a bridge between VTS and the descendants. My role, and that of other African Americans involved in the creation of the program, was first to help the leaders of the institution seriously consider what it might look like to establish a program showing that in some way the very nature ("hearts and lives") of this institution, with its racist past, was changing. To be clear, I could not consider it my responsibility to create such a program because, again, this history is not my wrong to right. But whether explicitly or implicitly, I could keep a fundamentally critical question constantly before the institution: "What must you do to demonstrate that you are committed to treating this descendant community with respect for their dignity and agency and with attention to addressing the sins of the institution against their ancestors?" Along these same lines, I could also make it clear what the seminary would have to do if it wanted me to continue lending my expertise and presence to the program. In the final analysis, no professional position would ever be worth the willing sacrifice of my good name in the interests of an institution, much less one with the seminary's history. So, for example, I would not have continued with the program if the seminary did not at least leave open the option for descendants to receive some sort of direct cash disbursements independent of a grant program or some form of demonstrated personal need. To the credit of Dean Markham and the VTS leadership, there was minimal resistance to the idea of cash disbursements, even though they may not have initially conceived of the program in that way.

The next, even more important, step was to insist that the VTS team had to do everything within our power to ensure that the descendants got as much out of the program as possible, whatever their priorities might be in that regard—whether proper memorialization of their ancestors, disbursements from the endowment, or educational opportunities. Ebonee Davis and I have observed—and it is unsurprising, given the importance of familial memory in many Black communities—that the highest priority for a lot of descendants is honoring their family members who labored at the seminary.

Lastly, as a longer-term goal in the interest of bearing good fruit, it was crucial to develop a means for descendants to offer direct and ongoing feedback to the leaders of VTS. Sometimes, when I mention this particular dimension of the program in conversation, someone will say, "You're giving voice to the voiceless." This is an expression that I almost never accept, however, because, in my experience, virtually everybody has a voice in one way or another. Certainly, the descendants in this program have their own voices. The responsibility of our team is to help ensure that those voices and perspectives are heard in the larger VTS community and by those with the greatest institutional power. A small example of this principle is that every family being onboarded to the program is offered the chance to meet with Dean Markham in order to share with him whatever thoughts they may have at that early stage in their relationship with the program.

MESSAGES AND EFFECTS: THE POTENTIAL SOCIAL FRUITS OF THE PROGRAM

But what of the grand interlocking set of ideas about the possible effects of reparations that to some degree moved me to answer the call to get involved? That is, I would like to think that this type of program might in some small way help to combat white supremacy, contribute to Black healing, and foster Black flourishing. Ideally, reparations would advance these aims by helping to shape a society in which Black people find themselves on a broadly equal material and spiritual footing with other racial and ethnic groups. This would mean that there is equitable financial investment in Black lives and spaces (the material dimension) and that Black lives are seen by the whole of society through a more humane, truthful, and compassionate lens rather than through a distorted lens of inhumanity, deceit, and cruelty (the spiritual dimension). To be very clear on the latter point, I am not saying that society needs to see Black people more often as human, truthful, and compassionate, though this, too, is surely the case. Rather, I am saying that society needs to arrest the now centuries-old and generations-old traditions of treating Black people inhumanely, deceitfully, and cruelly through custom and law because we are judged to deserve no better. And it should be remembered that we are so judged because many white Americans have, for generation after generation, put a great deal of effort into perpetuating an ideology of our racial inferiority, precisely to justify their own avaricious and self-absorbed desire to dominate the resources of this land. Others have simply, and in some ways understandably, acquiesced to the privileges that this white dominance confers.

Does a limited program such as that at VTS help to make progress on the changes that are necessary to redirect this well-traveled trajectory? William

Darity and Kirsten Mullen, in their magisterial book, *From Here to Equality: Reparations for Black Americans in the Twenty-First Century*, have argued that "it will be far more useful for colleges and universities to become sponsors of a national effort for reparations than for them to individually address reparations claims among their immediate constituents."[5] I certainly concur that the ultimate aim of the reparations movement should be a sweeping program at the federal level. Programs offered by private institutions and state and local governments cannot substitute for that broader national reckoning. Such programs, however, can further the larger aims and should make every effort to do so. It seems to me that the constituencies of educational institutions should demand that their schools both institute reparations in their local contexts and advocate at the national level. In fact, starting with the local might serve as a means by which to raise awareness of, and garner support for, the larger cause.

In any case, calling on institutions to demonstrate their seriousness by operating on local and national levels is not asking too much. One of my hopes for the VTS program is that, over time, we can work more closely with organizations, such as the National Coalition for Black Reparations in America (N'COBRA) and the National African-American Reparations Commission (NAARC), that have been laboring in the reparations vineyard for many years and whose work in part inspired and informed the VTS initiative. NAARC has a Ten-Point Reparations Plan, the principles of which, adapted to a local context, were useful in the formulation of our program. Even though we could not engage with all the points that they articulate during these relatively early stages of our efforts, our experience in implementing one or more of them may at some point provide beneficial data, so to speak, to the wider movement.[6]

I do not suffer from any delusion that our program is (1) uprooting white supremacy, nor (2) that it is healing whatever wounds descendants may have due to racial injustice, nor (3) that it is enabling them to flourish. It will take a much longer and sustained effort to dislodge white dominance in institutions such as VTS and the wider Episcopal Church—and in the broader society. To the extent that VTS can promote the healing of Black trauma, it will first have to bear fruit that is good enough to earn the descendants' trust. That, I suspect, will take a very long time. With regard to flourishing, particularly in the financial realm, I have already acknowledged that the funds being offered by VTS are small and certainly cannot be considered a "game changer" for any of the beneficiaries, at least not at this stage. Nevertheless, I would argue that it is a powerful act for a private, Southern institution with deep roots in slavery, segregation, and racism to name the error of its ways; acknowledge that its very existence is owed to the exploited labor of Black people; attempt to retell its history in a manner recognizing that the seminary therefore belongs to those individuals and their descendants as much as it does to the predominantly white generations of people who have inhabited it; and provide cash disbursements to the descendants with "no strings attached."

These actions are intended to send a serious signal that the seminary is not merely taking a stance of tolerating, accepting, or welcoming Black people—a gesture that would, in any case, be rather presumptuous and hollow because simple respect for children of God, whatever their color, should never have been in question. Instead, VTS is acknowledging that it is indebted to Black people, both in terms of the labor that it stole and exploited and the basic human decency that it refused to extend. It is recognizing that this characterization is not some figment of misguided Black imagination, but rather, it is based in historical realities that demand redress. Furthermore, in providing funds without stipulations, the message is that a party who owes something to another party should not get to have any say in what the other party does with it. It is a particularly insulting feature of anti-Black racial ideology in the USA that leads to the argument that a reparations program should involve some sort of mechanism to ensure that the money is not squandered, as though Black people are collectively so much more infantile, incompetent, and reckless than other groups of humanity that we cannot be trusted with what belongs to us.[7] One of the purposes of reparations is that the offending party must name its own wrongdoing and return control of what was taken to those from whom it was taken. I would argue that what the aggrieved party might or might not do with the resources should be totally irrelevant to the offending party. When supposedly making amends, to focus on what Black people might or might not do with reparatory resources simply exposes the resistance of whiteness (as it manifests in white institutions) to (1) relinquish control of resources (even admittedly ill-gotten ones) and (2) take responsibility for their own actions and histories instead of deflecting attention from their own bad behaviors to the lives and cultures of Black people.

DESCRIPTION OF THE PROGRAM'S KEY FEATURES

Having explored a few key theological and ethical themes in VTS's approach to reparations, I will now discuss some of the program's features and the reasoning behind them, beginning with the choice to center the primary component of the program very specifically on the descendants of those who were enslaved at the seminary or worked there during segregation. We could, of course, have chosen a much more general route, seeking, for example, to invest very broadly in the local Black population or in Black organizations nationally. It was well-known, however, that in the neighborhood near VTS there is a longstanding Black community that had a significant history of employment at the seminary up until the middle of the twentieth century. Char Bah, the historical and genealogical researcher mentioned previously, had in fact already conducted extensive research with many of those families and was aware that a significant number of their ancestors had worked both at VTS and its neighbor, Episcopal High School, an elite boarding school that was part of the seminary until the 1920s.[8]

At the start of the VTS program, it was unclear whether these families had ancestors who had been enslaved on the campus. But given that some of the families were working there in the 1870s or 1880s, the researchers reasoned that there was a decent chance they were there before the Civil War as well. The conspicuous, adjacent presence of a Black community with this depth of segregation-era connections to VTS was a strong warrant for extending the initiative's scope beyond slavery. This warrant only bolstered the argument, asserted by many proponents of reparations, that reparations initiatives should not only take into account the era of slavery but also the many decades of racialized terror and malfeasance afterward. The seminary would have been remiss to create a reparations program aimed at making amends for oppression and exploitation without seeking a relationship with these neighbors, many of whose living memory included ancestors who worked at VTS during Jim Crow. If an organization is taking an action to make amends for an institutional sin, should it not express its contrition in word and deed to the progeny of the very people that it harmed, when the opportunity to do so is so evident and concrete? I hasten to add that acts of penitence toward specific families in no way precludes also offering more general acts of penitence toward Black communities broadly conceived.

At this point, a general description of the VTS program seems in order. It has multiple aims, including building relationships with descendants when they are willing, working with them to honor how they would like to see their ancestors commemorated on campus, and offering access to the reparations funds. Descendants are welcome to take advantage of the campus grounds for recreation, eat lunch for free in the refectory, take a class for free, and check out books from the library. If any descendants are interested in a degree program at VTS, financial support is available. Whenever new people are onboarded to the program, these benefits are explained to them. In one case, during the onboarding process, a descendant shared with Dean Markham that he had a major birthday coming up. Dean Markham threw a birthday party for him and his family so that he could enjoy the campus in a way that his ancestor never would have been able to do. Other descendants have utilized campus space for family and professional events. Many regularly take advantage of lunch in the refectory, which has resulted in some of them gradually becoming acquainted with seminarians, faculty, and staff members—thus expanding the notion of who "belongs" there.

It has now become something of an annual tradition that the seminary hosts a gathering for the descendants on campus. This started because two descendants, Mrs. Frances Terrell and Mr. Robert Strange, told my colleague Ebonee that the families from the seminary neighborhood used to get together regularly for reunions, but they had not done so in a while because they no longer had a good space. Ebonee then had the excellent idea that the seminary grounds would be a great place for such a reunion. So, in July of 2021, we held a luncheon for the descendants. In June 2022, there was a gala dinner, for which the research team posted huge genealogical charts for each of the broad family groupings on the walls. Descendants could write comments, update or correct information, and add new information. After dinner, descendant after descendant came to speak at the open mic in order to pay tribute to the strength and resilience of their ancestors. In April 2023, we held a symposium and a family-style cookout as the annual gathering.

Families and individuals whose ancestors were enslaved at VTS or employed there during segregation usually come to the attention of the program either because the research team has come across them in their historical and genealogical explorations or because the descendant reaches out to us themselves to let us know about their family's association with VTS. In the latter case, the research team takes responsibility for documenting the connection using its own methods and sources, along with whatever information the descendant provides. Eventually, the researchers write a report explaining what they are able to document about the ancestor(s) and their descendants in question. They also determine who in that particular family should be considered what we are currently calling "shareholders." These are the individuals who are eligible to receive a share of the earnings from the reparations endowment fund annually, in perpetuity. Shareholders are the members of the generation of a family that is closest to the enslaved individual or segregation-era employee with at least one living member.

To provide a simple example, if my paternal grandfather, who is deceased, had worked at VTS before the year 1950, then my father's generation (he and his two brothers) would be the shareholders because my two uncles are still living. Therefore, the number three would be added to the total number of persons among whom the endowment earnings would be divided in a given year (that is, the total number of persons in the entire reparations program who are considered shareholders). Because my father is deceased, his share would be divided equally among my two sisters and me. If he had no heirs, the funds would be divided between his brothers.

The shareholder alone—or, if deceased, the person(s) to whom the share passes—gets to determine what happens to the money. They can keep it for themselves, split it among their children or grandchildren, give it to a charity or an educational institution, combine their funds with those of other shareholders in order to make a larger contribution to a cause, or whatever else seems right and good to them. Their wish for their annual share is memorialized in a letter to Dean Markham that he countersigns as the head of VTS authorized to pledge the institution to this long-term commitment. The letter is based upon a template that our team gives to each shareholder, which they revise to fit their particular desires. Once each letter is signed, VTS cannot modify the terms. Every letter, however, includes a provision that the shareholder may contact the seminary at any time to alter the disposition of their annual funds. Each letter also details to whom the share should pass in the event of the original shareholder's death.

By setting up the system in this way, VTS has attempted to create something of a trust fund for descendant families. Although the initial fund of $1.7 million was modest, it has the advantage of being a part of the seminary's overall endowment—so, over the long haul, it should increase considerably based upon market growth alone. Beyond market considerations, VTS can also increase the base amount, which, in fact, it did in 2022, bringing the fund to $2.2 million. Donations are another potential source of growth, and the fund has received some modest donations from alumni. Every year, VTS uses the draw rate for diverting funds from the endowment to the general operating budget (currently 4 percent) to calculate the draw from the reparations endowment, which is the sum of money that is to be divided between all of the shareholders in the program. This does mean that the value of a share each year will fluctuate based upon the performance of the market and the number of shareholders in the program. Every year, shareholders receive a report detailing the value of the fund, the size of the draw, the current number of shareholders (in fiscal year 2023, there were 137 shareholders), and the resulting share size. The report also includes other information, such as recent highlights from the historical and genealogical research conducted for the program.

While this system sets up a scenario in which share sizes will likely decrease year over year for some time because the number of shareholders is continually expanding due to new research, it is predicated on the assumption that, at some point in the not too distant future (perhaps three to five years or fewer), the research team will exhaust the available documentary evidence, and the number of shareholders will stabilize because the identification of new shareholders will cease or slow to a trickle. The fund, however, is likely to continue having an overall arc of growth with the market, meaning that in general the value of shares should become more significant over years and decades.

Of course, as families grow, the number of ways that shareholders may wish to divide shares, and the number of ways shares may need to be divided because the initial shareholders are deceased, is likely to increase. One possible solution is that shareholders might begin to utilize the funds to benefit their families and communities in ways that keep the shares intact (e.g., creating a fund to support costs for aging family members or joining with other shareholders to create a tuition fund for extended family groups). An even better solution would be for VTS to figure out how to increase the shares. Indeed, these pressure points in the design of the system put pressure on VTS to monitor closely the size of disbursements that are being provided to descendants over time and to seek ways to make them as financially significant as possible going forward. In fact, in the past couple of fiscal years, the seminary administration has modestly supplemented the basic draw from the reparations endowment in order to augment the share size.

CONCLUDING THOUGHTS

As the program progresses, I anticipate, and will do everything in my power to ensure, that descendants will increasingly voice their wishes for its future as a whole. We acted decisively in the beginning in order to indicate that the institution is serious about the project. Demonstrating that seriousness, it seems to me, has been helpful in attracting the involvement of the descendant community. We have reached a chapter, however, in which the will of the descendant community should become dominant in establishing the course of the initiative. In some ways, the shareholder schema was just as much a means of providing a mechanism for collective descendant control of the program as it was a means to disburse funds. The trust fund and shareholder schema also represents a long-term and open-ended commitment to the descendant community that the seminary is bound to honor and regularly reevaluate. In this way, it is a program that cannot be easily forgotten or undone when the leadership of the institution changes.

I have spent a significant amount of time describing the program's financial model. As I have expanded on those and other details, however, I hope that it has also become evident that the program was designed in such a way as to be proactive and to center descendants. VTS does not ask descendants to prove their family history or apply for the program. Our team takes on the responsibility of doing that research. VTS expects nothing in particular from the descendant community because it has no right to do so. Rather, the seminary is attempting to shine a light on its wrongdoing by opening up a flexible and responsive space in the present moment for a long mistreated but resilient community to explore this piece of their family history, memorialize that history, take an honored seat in the contemporary life of the institution if they so choose, determine to what extent they might want to have a voice in its future if at all, and ultimately let the seminary know whether it is bearing fruits worthy of repentance.

NOTES

1. For more on the history of Blacks at VTS, including advocacy efforts, see Constant, *No Turning Back: The Black Presence at Virginia Theological Seminary* (Brainerd, MN: Evergreen, 2009).
2. For examples of press coverage of the announcement, Rachel L. Swarns,"The Seminary Flourished on Slave Labor. Now It's Planning to Pay Reparations," *The New York Times,* September 12, 2019, accessed February 4, 2023, https://www.nytimes.com/2019/09/12/us/virginia-seminary-reparations.html. See also Meagan Flynn, "Slaves Helped Build Virginia Theological Seminary. The School Will Spend $1.7 Million in Reparations," *The Washington Post,* September 10, 2019, accessed February 4, 2023, https://www.washingtonpost.com/nation/2019/09/10/virginia-theological-seminary-reparations-slavery/.
3. It should be noted here that, about a year into the program, the seminary leadership decided that the $1.7 million fund would be used exclusively for making disbursements to descendants. Other sources of funding were subsequently identified for the other financial commitments made by the program. Also, the financial resources needed for administration of the program and payment of the external researchers are funded from the seminary's operating budget.
4. These grants are not the first way that VTS has attempted to make amends to Black Episcopalians. For example, for many years prior to commencing a program to provide tuition to the overwhelming majority of students in the late 2010s, the Bishop Payne Scholarship provided free tuition to any Black Episcopalian in any order of ministry enrolled in any program at the seminary.
5. William A. Darity Jr., and A. Kirsten Mullen, *From Here to Equality: Reparations for Black Americans in the Twenty-First Century* (Chapel Hill: University of North Carolina Press, 2020), 269–70.
6. Some important and helpful works on reparations include Darity and Mullen, *From Here to Equality;* Ta-Nehesi Coates, "The Case for Reparations," *The Atlantic,* June 2014, accessed February 4, 2023, https://www.theatlantic.com/magazine/archive/2014/06/the-case-for-reparations/361631/; Ana Lucia Araujo, *Reparations for Slavery and the Slave Trade* (New York: Bloomsbury Academic, 2017); and Roy L. Brooks, *Atonement and Forgiveness: A New Model for Black Reparations* (Berkeley: University of California Press, 2004).
7. I do not have space for a thorough account of my understanding of race in the United States of America. I should state, however, that my working definition of racial ideology is as follows: the pervasive and destructive system of social discourse that places people and communities in hierarchies according to racial categories that

are supposedly distinct and innate, with innateness typically understood as being biological or genetic. This racial hierarchization—in this case, belief in the alleged inferiority of persons of African descent—developed, and is still used, to justify the enforcement of drastically inequitable and oppressive social, economic, and political systems. A key point of reference for me on the concept of race as ideology is the work of Barbara J. Fields. One can find elements of this school of thought about race in the work of numerous scholars in the twentieth and twenty-first century, so I will not attempt to list them here. Indeed, in the past twenty to thirty years, it has become much more widespread. Some popular examples by Black scholars that seem to proceed from this understanding of race include Coates (*Between the World and Me* [New York: Spiegel & Grau, 2015]) and Ibram X. Kendi (*How to Be and Anti-Racist* [New York: Random House, 2019]). It can be traced further back than many people today might suppose. For example, W. E. B. Du Bois spoke in 1940 of his "realization that the income-bearing value of race prejudice was the cause and not the result of theories of race inferiority; that particularly in the United States the income of the Cotton Kingdom based on black slavery caused the passionate belief in Negro inferiority and the determination to enforce it even by arms" (*Dusk of Dawn: An Essay Toward an Autobiography of a Race Concept* [Originally published 1940. New York: Schocken Books, 1968], 129–30).

8. VTS has taken the position that there will be no difference in eligibility for the program between those who worked at the seminary and those who worked at Episcopal High School *before* the two entities separated, on the grounds that the high school was truly an arm of the seminary up to that point. In any case, because the governance of the two was intertwined, it is not always a simple matter, or even possible, to determine whether an individual was employed at the seminary or at the high school. Many individuals worked at both places at various times.

BIBLIOGRAPHY

Araujo, Ana Lucia. *Reparations for Slavery and the Slave Trade*. New York: Bloomsbury Academic, 2017.

Brooks, Roy L. *Atonement and Forgiveness: A New Model for Black Reparations*. Berkeley: University of California Press, 2004.Coates, Ta-Nehisi. *Between the World and Me*. New York: Spiegel and Grau, 2015.

———. "The Case for Reparations." *The Atlantic*, June 2014. Accessed February 4, 2023. https://www.theatlantic.com/magazine/archive/2014/06/the-case-for-reparations/361631/.

Constant, Joseph. *No Turning Back: The Black Presence at Virginia Theological Seminary*. Brainerd, MN: Evergreen Press, 2009.

Darity, William A., Jr., and Kirsten Mullen. *From Here To Equality: Reparations for Black Americans in the Twenty-First Century*. Chapel Hill: University of North Carolina Press, 2020.

Du Bois, W. E. B. *Dusk of Dawn: An Essay Toward an Autobiography of a Race Concept*. Originally published 1940. New York: Schocken Books, 1968.

Fields, Barbara J. "Slavery, Race, and Ideology in the United States of America." *New Left Review* 1, no. 181 (May-June 1990): 95–118.

Flynn, Meagan. "Slaves Helped Build Virginia Theological Seminary. The School Will Spend $1.7 Million in Reparations." *The Washington Post*, September 10, 2019. Accessed February 4, 2023. https://www.washingtonpost.com/nation/2019/09/10/virginia-theological-seminary-reparations-slavery/.

Kendi, Ibram X. *How To Be an Antiracist*. New York: One World, 2019.

Swarns, Rachel L. "The Seminary Flourished on Slave Labor. Now It's Planning to Pay Reparations." *The New York Times*, September 12, 2019. Accessed February 4, 2023. https://www.nytimes.com/2019/09/12/us/virginia-seminary-reparations.html.

Conclusion

Drew G. I. Hart

My hope for you is that reading this collection of prophetic voices will not be the end of your reparations journey. I hope you move beyond intellectual activity and into faithful praxis informed by the theological disciplines, leading to a process of remembrance, reckoning, and repair.

The wisdom and perspectives gathered in this book press upon us and compel us to respond. In these chapters, we are provided with a powerful toolbox of persuasive and thought-provoking arguments from different corners of the church, calling for reparations and atonement. From the start, our goal as editors was to address and fill the void of silence from the theological disciplines. The absence of moral clarity on reparations from the scholarship of the theological disciplines for all these years is not surprising, considering how often scholars and Christian leaders used their minds to bolster the status quo and justify the oppression and exploitation of Black people. Academics outside of the theological disciplines have been addressing reparations for some time, and other Christian leaders have done important work to contribute to the ethical reasoning of the church. And yet, these other significant contributions do not erase the moral responsibility of those entrusted in the formation of students and leaders. This book is a resource for the work of remembrance, reckoning, and repair—inviting the church and academy to fulfil its vocation in the shadow of slavery, Jim Crow, and ongoing oppression that stifles human thriving for Black Americans.

Practicing remembrance is a courageous act when the default orientation is historical erasure. As we remember the crucified Christ and see Black suffering through that lens, it should cause us to refuse to forget the harms of the past or willfully ignore ongoing inequities. The church lives out of remembrance, allowing us to recall the devasting legacy of slavery, plunder, and systemic oppression, which has defined so many people's experiences on "Turtle Island"[1] for too long. We cannot turn away from the widespread oppression leading to so much human suffering, the wealth pillaged and accumulated from conquest, and the death-dealing religiosity that vandalized the name of Jesus around the world. We cannot look away or forget how European Christians enacted the theft and dehumanization of Black people for centuries, and how it continues to destroy lives to this very day. The exploitation and racialization have fractured our sense of shared humanity and smothered the flourishing of God's children. Practicing remembrance demands that we confront uncomfortable truths, confess our complicity, and reject the deep denial and history-avoidant inclinations of many white American Christians today.

After the practice of remembrance by scholars within the theological disciplines and the broader church, there is a need for a true reckoning with the scale of the harm caused by the complicity of the Church. Western Christianity has often been an accomplice in the harm caused, and very often it has been a primary perpetrator. Undergoing a reckoning calls for deep lament that internalizes what the Church has done and attempts to see things from the lived experience of those most devasted by this death-dealing legacy. It also demands an awareness of the structural dimensions of society. Together, we must reckon with how we continue to organize our geographies and institutions according to the principle of anti-blackness. This reckoning also means that we must interrogate the adaptions, mutations, and accommodations of our theological systems, biblical hermeneutics, and organizational practices that have so easily partnered with the enslavement and subsequent oppression, exploitation, and exclusion of Black people. If a reckoning were a fire, we might wonder what from the theological disciplines needs to burn like straw and what needs to be purified like gold? Are we willing to be introspective and interrogate our own traditions and religious frameworks that have perpetuated so much suffering? I hope so. A true reckoning not only points outward to the failures of society, of which there are plenty, but especially inward to the life of our own faith communities and institutions.

The practice of repair is restorative justice oriented toward healing harm and the ultimate flourishing of humanity in creation. Our moral responsibility goes far deeper than merely engaging in symbolic gestures or empty apologies. Instead, when we are rooted in remembrance and have gone through a reckoning, we will commit to participating in God's activity of setting things right. Repair is the faithful thing to do even when you are not the perpetrator of a particular harm. Jesus's story of the Samaritan who was a neighbor to the man left for dead (Luke 10:25–37) teaches us that. The Church's vocation is always healing and repair. In the case of western European Christian complicity in the enslavement and oppression of their Black siblings, however, it is morally essential to seek to repair the harms caused by the Church. The body of Christ, as a community, must make amends when it sins against its neighbor. Strangely, or maybe not so strangely, those who have been deeply socialized into whiteness in the United States often frame reparations as punishment for themselves, when the actual goal has always been reparative—with the ultimate goal of Black people's thriving. This reparative work is an anti-anti-blackness practice that rejects the logics of racial inferiority. Repair requires a commitment to truthfully understanding our history, coupled with tangible and adaptive redress for harms, healing for wounds, and liberative interventions oriented toward ongoing Black well-being. Repair must touch every area of life, including economics. It requires the redistribution of wealth, creating equitable opportunities and access for Black people, and investment into Black communities and institutions. It is concerned with soul and body care through physical, spiritual, and psychological healing. My hope is that after reading this book, reparations will no longer symbolize punishment for white people. Repairing intergenerational harm is not a punishment or a burden; on the contrary, it is one more step toward cultivating God's dream for all creation.

The time for robust, holistic, reparations is well overdue, especially since the American church has had the scriptural resources and wisdom of the historic and global Church to help discern its responsibility. The United States of America must remember, reckon, and repair the harm done to Black Americans. And the Church must raise its prophetic voice toward that end. It must also hold a mirror to itself, however, and undergo a rebirth leading to its own repentance and reparative work as well.

This book was pulled together because we identified a missing voice in the swelling call for reparations in the past decade. Too often, the theological disciplines have imagined themselves to be at the forefront of ethical reasoning about major contemporary concerns, and yet in one of the most severe and centuries-in-the-making social atrocities our nation has ever perpetuated (the other being Native American conquest, genocide, and theft), there has been mostly professional silence. Now is the time to reject apathy, to refuse to live in denial, and to renounce indifference to the sufferings of Black people. I hope that this ethical exploration of reparations by a diversity of voices coming from a variety of traditions and perspectives will compel our readers to join the long running river of justice that leads to deepened liberation and beloved community. Indeed, I pray that this resource might be *your* catalyst for joining the movement for remembrance, reckoning, and repair. Then we can be known as repairers of the breach, menders of the brokenhearted, and reconcilers of our dividing walls, demonstrating that the lives of Black people matter to the Church.

NOTES

1. A moniker used for centuries by many Indigenous communities to refer to the land we now call the United States of America.

Author/Subject Index

References in *italic* refer to figures and tables. References followed by "n" refer to endnotes.

The 1619 Project (Hannah-Jones), 27, 93, 126

acknowledgment, redress and closure (ARC), 44–46, 48, 119
Adedayo, Ebony, 275
affirmative action, 27–28, 63, 217–18
Allen, Richard, 82
Anderson, Elijah, 104n33
anti-Black racism, 21, 252, 281, 282, 285
Anyabwile, Thabiti, 155–62, 168, 169, 171n21
Aquinas, Thomas, 174n38
Araujo, Ana Lucia, 193, 198–99
ARC. *See* acknowledgment, redress and closure

Bah, Char McCargo, 284, 291
Baldwin, James, 28, 102
Ballentine, Alexander, 241
Ballentine, Eliza, 241
Ballou, Jacqui, 285
Baptist, Edward E., 146, 245
Baradaran, Mehrsa, 137, 147
Bavinck, Herman, 201

Beavis, Mary Ann, 115
Beckert, Sven, 19, 263
BEDC. *See* Black Economic Development Corporation
Berret, James G., 240
Berry, Diana Ramey, 20
Bilder, Mary Sarah, 20
Birney, James, 85
Black Economic Development Corporation (BEDC), 24, 25
Black History Month, 79–80
Black immigrants, 193
Black Lives Matter movement, 38–39, 102, 182
Black Manifesto, 24–26
Blackmon, Douglas, 147, 264, 266
Blair, William, 87
Boda, Mark J., 60n57
Booker, Cory, 184
Brodhead, John M., 240
Brown, Carolyn A., 195
Brown Chapel AME Church, 277–78
Brown University, 101

Callahan, Allen Dwight, 8, 96
Calvin, John, 47, 49

Campbell, Bernard Moore, 240
Cannon, Katie Geneva, 91
capitalism: financialized, 266; racial, 262–63, 267n9
Cardijn, Joseph, 230n50
Catholic reflection on reparations, 226
Catholic social thought (CST), 209; centering conversation on black voices, 222; duty of reparation, 210, 211–12; flexibility and pragmatic of Christians, 223–24; "government as one medium of collective action" principle, 213–14; grace, consideration of, 224–25; intentional pauperization, 212; methodological commitments, 219; natural law methodology, 220; "preferential option for poor" principle, 213; "property as right and responsibility" principle, 212–13; prudential considerations, 222–23; reparation for injustice, 210, 225–26; restitution, 211; satisfaction, 211; "See, Judge, Act" method, 221, 230n50; using state to address historical wrongs, 214–16; using state to apologize for historical wrongs, 216–19; "subsidiarity and participation" principle, 214; "universal destination of goods" principle, 213
Charlottesville, VA March, 160
Christian Slavery (Gerbner), 196
Civil Rights Act (1967), 126
Civil War, 17, 20, 22–24, 44, 93–94, 101, 146, 182–83, 198, 244, 251, 253, 263–64, 284, 291
Coates, Ta-Nehisi, 6, 137, 296n7; about America's maturation, 191; "The Case for Reparations" essay, 26, 63, 147, 229n39; about white supremacy, 81
Coats, George, 4
The Color of Law (Rothstein), 146

The Color of Money (Baradaran), 137–39, 147
The Condemnation of Blackness (Muhammad), 146
Congressional apologies for slavery (2008 and 2009), 27
Conyers, John, 74n8, 184
Copeland, M. Shawn, 141–45
Cox, Oliver Cromwell, 261, 265
Crawford, Thomas Gibson, 243
critical race theory, 27, 145
CST. *See* Catholic social thought
Cullors, Patrise, 94
Curiel, Gonzalo, 171n18

Daniels, Carol, 284
Darity, William A. Jr., 27–28, 43–56, 57n23, 119–20, 147, 228n33, 266, 276, 288–89
Dávila, MT, 213, 225
Davis, Ebonee, 284–87, 293
Davis, Ellen, 50
The Debt (Robinson), 184
Delany, Martin R., 5
Desmond, Matthew, 198
Dingess, Ed, 156, 162, 168
District of Columbia Compensated Emancipation Act, 22, 240–46, **246–50**, 252–55
Doctrine of Discovery, 160
Douglas, Kelly Brown, 143
Douglass, Frederick, 82, 120n1, 245
Dowey, Edward A., 24
Drembus, Elizabeth, 284
Du Bois, W. E. B., 261, 296n7
Duncan, Toniette, 283

Eder, Steve, 170–71n17
Edmondson, Christina, 203
Egypt, Ophelia Settle, 197
Ellison, Ralph, 83
Emancipation Commission, 240
Emancipation Proclamation, 8
Emerson, Michael O., 159
emotional labor for BIPOC people, 275

emotion of guilt, 155; allergic reaction to feeling of guilt, 158–59; PSA advocates' responses to, 156–57; white guilt, 184
Enns, Elain, 149
enslaved Africans, reparations for, 19, 20–27, 193–98, 200–205
Erasmus, George, 274, 279n4
Evangelical Covenant Church of America, 25
Evans, David, 149
Exagoge (Ezekiel the Tragedian), 4
Ezekiel the Tragedian, 4

Fair Housing Act, 26, 160, 170n17
Farley, Margaret, 220
Fields, Barbara J., 296n7
Fields, Lisa V., 203
Floyd, George Perry, 179–80, 271
Foner, Eric, 20, 21
Forman, James, 24
"forty acres and a mule," 22, 29n18, 35–36, 40, 93–94
Foster, Stephen, 85
Fox, George, 6
Frazier, Darnella, 180
Frazier, Garrison, 93
Freedom Triumphant, 243
Fretheim, Terence E., 49
From Here to Equality: Reparations for Black Americans in the Twenty-First Century (and Mullen), 43, 289
Fugitive Slave Act (1850), 96
fusion justice, 189–90

Gaines, A. K., 99–100
Galloway, Anthony, 275
Galpaz-Feller, P., 10n12
Garner, Margaret, 99–100, 102
Garnet, Henry Highland, 82
Garrison, William Lloyd, 245
Garvey, Marcus, 93
Georgetown University, 199, 215, 216

Gerbner, Katharine, 196; description of Christian Slavery, 197; description of Protestant Supremacy, 196
GI Bill, 26, 185; exclusion of Black families from, 45
Goodloe, Daniel R., 240
Gopin, Mark, 183–84, 187
The Gospel Coalition, 157
Green, Douglass, 202, 207n28
Grimes, Katie, 225
Grimké, Angelina, 82
Grimké, Francis, 85
guilt. *See* emotion of guilt

Hackett, Erna Kim, 3
The Half Has Never Been Told (Baptiste), 146
Hamilton, Victor, 5
Hannah-Jones, Nikole, 30n60, 93
Harding, Vincent, 146
Harvey, Jennifer, 25, 26
Healing Haunted Histories, 149
Henry, Willie Mae, 283
Henry, Wilmer, 283
Holbert, Luther, 261
Horowitz, David, 73n5, 73–74n7, 74n14
Hose, Sam, 261
Howard, Ellick, 241, 242
Howard, Emily, 241, 242
Howard, George, 241, 242
Howard, Jackson, 241, 242
Howard, Lettie, 241, 242
Howard, Tilly, 241, 242
Howard, Tow (Tom), 241, 242
HR 40. *See* U.S. House Resolution 40
Hughes, Langston, 197
Hughes, Richard, 140–41
human dignity, 214
Hunter, Tera W., 199

Ibibio people, origin of, 194–98
Imago Dei, 201–2, 203, 214
Indigenous and Black communities, reparations in, 272, 276–78, 279
Internment, Japanese, 185

Irenaeus of Lyons, 158, 167, 170n13, 174n36
Israelite slavery *vs.* American slavery, 7–9
Jackson, Andrew, 241
Jacobs, Jim Bear, 273
Jim Crow laws, 82, 85, 102, 151, 254, 266
Johnson, Andrew, 21, 23, 29n21, 30n58, 93, 156, 159, 168, 170n4
Johnson, Sidney, 259
Jones, Absalom, 7
Jones, Charles Colcock, 120n1
Josephus, Flavius, 9–10n5, 12n26
Joshel, Sandra R., 97, 114
Joüon, Paul, 11n25
Jubilee, the, 50–51, 54–56, 59n46, 75n27, 162; as formation for reparational reasoning, 67–70; formation, 71–72; legislation, 69–70, 72, 75n23; verse 48:18, 4
Juvenal, 97

Kendi, Ibram X., 23–2, 296n7
Kespert, Debbie Lynn, 156, 158, 162, 168
Key, Thomas Marshall, 239
King, Horatio, 240
King, Martin Luther, Jr., 38, 40, 82, 118, 155–56, 260
Kroeze, Jan H., 11n25
Ku Klux Klan (KKK), 36, 278
Kwon, Duke L., 5, 26–27, 53, 262, 263, 266

Landlines, Bloodlines, and Songlines framework (LBS framework), 149
Leccese, Stephen, 228n33
Lee, Barbara, 184
Letter from a Birmingham Jail, 39–40
libertarian moral reasoning, 63, 66–67
Lincoln, Abraham, 93, 199, 239–40
Littlewolf, Nevada, 275
love, 80, 83, 86–87, 158–59; patriarchalism, 95, 103n13; Paul's cruciform objectives, 110–16; Paul's idea of, 92
Lovejoy, Paul E., 195
Lynch, Matthew, 59n46
lynching: emotionalism of, 265; of Mary Turner, 261; racialized, 264
"Lynching Rampage of 1918," 260

Mahler, Jonathan, 170–71nn17–19
Malcolm X, 94, 260, 261, 262
manumission, 110–12, 114–15
Markham, Ian S., 282, 283, 287, 291, 293
Marshall, Thurgood, 40
Massingale, Bryan, 210, 216, 222, 224
MCC. *See* Minnesota Council of Churches
McCleave, Christine Diindiisi, 273, 274
McConnell, Mitch, 53
McCoy, Maddy, 284
McKnight, Burney, 284
McKnight, Scot, 111, 112, 113
Meade Memorial Episcopal Church, 283
medical substitutionary atonement (MSA), 158; atonement, 163–64; dying and rising in union with Christ in, 166; *vs.* penal substitutionary atonement, 157–58
Memory and Reconciliation: The Church and the Faults of the Past, 218
Merritt, Keri Leigh, 22–23
Meyers, Carol, 10n5
Milko, Christopher, 284
Mills, Clark, 240; injustice to Philip Reid, 250–52; petition for reparations, 240–42, *242;* and Reid's *Statue of Freedom*, 243–44
Minnesota Council of Churches (MCC), 271; 3-point action platform for racial justice, 272, 273–79; call for reparations, 272; white ecumenical organization, 271
Mitchell, Nicholas Ensley, 212, 217, 218, 223

MSA. *See* medical substitutionary atonement
Muhammad, Khalil Gibran, 146
Mullen, A. Kirsten, 27–28, 43–56, 57n23, 119–20, 147, 228n33, 266, 276, 289
Murakawa, Naomi, 265
Muraoka, T., 11n25
Myers, Ched, 149
Myers, Samuel, Jr., 272
Myths America Lives By (Hughes), 140–41

National African-American Reparations Commission (NAARC), 289
National Coalition for Black Reparations in America (N'COBRA), 289
National Committee for Black Churchmen, 85
Native American/Indigenous people, 26, 40, 63, 94, 125–27, 132–34, 148, 149, 160, 162, 211, 245, 252, 271–72, 274, 276, 278–79, 300n1, 311
Naudé, Jacobus A., 11n25
new age, 203–4
Ngunjiri, Pamela, 273
Nixon, Richard, 161
Nozick, Robert, 66

Oakland Baptist Church, 283
Ondrey, Hanna, 25
Open Wide our Hearts, 225

Panox-Leach, Elizabeth, 284
Paul II, John, 218, 229n43
penal substitutionary atonement (PSA), 156, 168–69; and circumcision, 164–65; "forgiveness of sins," 162–63; *vs.* medical substitutionary atonement, 157–58; "possession of stolen property" issue, 160–62; responses to Anyabwile's emotion of guilt, 156–57
Peterson, Lauren Hackworth, 97

Pliny, 96
police, 35, 37–38, 94, 102, 155, 161, 171n19, 180–82, 186, 198, 266, 274
Pontifical Council for Peace and Justice, 223
Pope Francis, 221
Pope, Stephen, 174n38
Populorum progressio, 212, 227n20
Pote, Christopher, 284, 285
Prather, Curtis, 284
"preferential option for poor" principle, 213
Priest, Josiah, 19
PSA. *See* penal substitutionary atonement

race/racial/racism in United States, 25, 39, 63, 81–82, 179–80, 225, 271; capitalism, 262–63, 267n9; origin of, 261–62; prejudice, 261; reconciliation, 214, 217
racial ideology, 288, 290, 295–96n7
racial hierarchization, 296n7
racialized chattel slavery in United States, 17, 146, 148, 263
racialized lynching, 261, 264
racial wealth gap of Black Americans, 43; discussions on *The Color of Money*, 137–38; filling in gaps of historical accounts, 146–49
Randolph, A. Philip, 260
RAP. *See* Reimagining America Project
Ray, James Earl, 155
Reconstruction (1863–1877), 17, 20, 21
Reformed theological Christian tradition: stages of redemptive history, 201–5
Reid (Reed), Philip, 241, 242; craftsmen skills, 242–43; facing injustice for *Statue of Freedom* work, 250–52; and *Statue of Freedom*, 243–44
Reimagining America Project (RAP), 183–84, 188–89, 190, 191; atonement concept, 187–90, 191; for reparations issues, 184–87

remembering: anamnesis, 143–44; Christ crucified body, 142, 144–45; practice of remembrance, 297–98
reparational God, 125–35
reparational reasoning, 63, 67–72; libertarian moral reasoning, 63, 66–67; utilitarian moral reasoning, 63, 64–65
reparations, 35–41, 73nn3–4, 80, 84, 125, 210, 211–12, 219, 225–26, 252–55, 266–67, 272, 276–79, 297
Reparations: A Christian Call for Repentance and Repair (Kwon and Thompson), 5
Reparations For Slavery And The Slave Trade: A Transnational and Comparative History (Araujo), 198–99
"Reparations Now Toolkit," 251
repentance, 80, 84, 86, 87
Rhodes, Michael, 161, 173n29
Roaf, Bishop Phoebe, 285
Roberts, Jennifer, 181
Robinson, Cedric, 263, 267n9
Robinson, Randall, 184
Rockman, Seth, 19, 263
Rose, Ann, 241, 242
Rothstein, Richard, 146
Rustin, Bayard, 260
Ryken, Philip, 5

Sandel, Michael J., 74nn8–9
SBTS. *See* Southern Baptist Theological Seminary
Scott, Keith Lamont, 181
Sechrest, Love Lazarus, 118, 122n36
"See, Judge, Act" method, 219, 221, 222, 224, 230n50
Seters, John Van, 18
shalom, 68–69, 187
Shearer, Tobin Miller, 148–49
Sherman, William Tecumseh, 21, 93
Shivers, Angela Terrell, 284
Simms, Daniel G., 284
Simms, Steve, 284

Sinha, Manisha, 199
Slattery, John, 210–11
slavery, 3, 6–8, 17–25, 27, 35, 39, 44, 50, 59n46, 64, 74nn7–8, 74n11, 74n14, 75n23, 82, 91–93, 95, 99–100, 102, 111, 117, 119–20, 126–27, 129, 133–34, 138, 141, 145–8, 151, 193–201, 203, 205, 210, 217, 228n33, 229n44, 239, 242, 245–46, 246–50, 251–54, 260–66, 273, 281–82, 285, 289, 291, 297, 309, 311
Slavery: Its Origin, Nature, and History, Considered in the Light of Bible Teachings, Moral Justice, and Political Wisdom (Stringfellow), 19
Slavery as It Relates to the Negro or African Race (Priest), 19
Slavery by Another Name (Blackmon), 147, 264
Smith, Christian, 159
Smith, Hampton, 259–60, 265
social discourse, and destructive system of, 295–96n7
social location, 65, 92
Social Security Act, 26
soli, 60n57, 214
Southern Baptist Theological Seminary (SBTS), 199
Southern Homestead Act (1866), 21, 23; exclusion of Black families from, 45
Sparks, Randy J., 194
Special Field Order Number (15), 15, 21
Statement of Commitment, 279
Statue of Freedom, Philip Reid and, 243–46, 252
Stewart, Maria, 82
Stoltzfus, Regina Shand, 148
Strange, Robert, 292
Stringfellow, Thornton, 19

Táíwò, Olúfẹ́mi O., 117, 118–19
The Talking Book (Callahan), 8
ta splanchna in Philemon, 92, 96, 98–101, 102
Taylor, Keeanga-Yamahtta, 266

Temple, Riley, 285
Ten Commandments' negative prohibitions, 49
Ten-Point Reparations Plan, 289
Terrell, Alfonzo, 284
Terrell, Frances, 284, 292
Terrell, Jacob, 284
Tertullian, 5
There is a River (Harding), 146
Thirteenth (13th) Amendment of US Constitution, 254, 260
Thomas, John Samuel, Jr., 284
Thomas, Levi, 241, 242
Thomas, Rachel, 241, 242
Thompson, Gregory, 5, 26–27, 53, 262, 263, 266
Timothy, 108, 120n4
Tran, Jonathan, 262
Trouble I've Seen: Changing the Way the Church Views Racism (Hart), 137
Truth, Sojourner, 82
truth telling for racial justice, 272, 273–75
Tulsa Race Massacre, 94, 229n39
Turner, Mary, 261

Udo, Edet A., 194
"universal destination of goods" principle, 213
University of North Carolina, 101
US Capitol building project, 244–46
US Constitution: Thirteenth (13th) Amendment of, 254, 260; Three-Fifths Clause of, 19
U.S. House Resolution 40 (HR 40), 184
utilitarian moral reasoning, 63, 64–65

van der Merwe, Christo H. J., 11n25
Vinton, Samuel Finley, 240
Virginia Theological Seminary reparations program (VTS reparations program), 281–94, 295n4, 296n8
Voting Rights Act (1965), repeal of, 161

Wallace, George, 155
Washington, George, 253
Washington, Jesse, 261
Washington, John, 253
Washington, Lawrence, 253
Wells, Ida B., 264, 265
We Were Eight Years in Power (Coates), 137, 147
white supremacy in US, 81, 86, 198, 271, 279, 299; Anyabwile's concern for, 155–57; myths of, 140–42, 144, 150; as theft, 262–63, 262–63
White, Walter, 264
Who Are the Ibibio? (Udo), 194
Williams, Shannen Dee, 226
Williams, Yohuru, 273, 274–75
Wilmore, Gayraud S., Jr., 24
Wilson, Henry, 239
Winkle, Kenneth, 240
Winston, Braxton, 182
Wisdom of Solomon, 4
womanist, 91–92, 95, 97, 100, 143, 216
Woodson, Carter G., 79–80
Wright, N. T., 110

Young, Stephen, 112

Scripture Index

Note: References followed by "n" refer to endnotes.

Genesis

1	128
1:26	128
1:26–27	201
1:26–2:9	128
1:27–28	49
1:31	201
2	201
2:18–25	128
3	128, 202
3:14–15	203
3:21	128, 202
4–5	128
4:10	83
6–9	128
12	128, 164
12:3	130
12:10–16	164
12:17–20	164
13:5–12	7
15	128
15:1–3	164
15:4–6	164-165
15:6	164
15:14	6
16	18
16:1–17:18	165
17	164, 165
17:19	165
18:13–15	165
19:18–27	19
21	19
26:12–33	7
30	19
31:9	11n25
31:16	11n25
32:3–21	7
33:1–17	7

Exodus

Ex	3, 19, 27, 39, 41
1–14	129
3	128
3:20–22	6-7
3:21	4
3:21–22	12n28

3:22	4, 6, 7, 10n10, 11n25	6:4	83, 187
		6:4–5	187
5:6–19	23	6:4–7	47-48
5:19	46	6:5	83, 188
11:2	10n10	6:6	188
11:2–3	7	19:33	59n46
11:3	4	19:33–34	75n19, 130
12	5, 41	24:22	75n19
12:21–51	129	25	19, 27, 54, 64, 67, 68, 69, 71, 75n23
12:33	6		
12:35	10n10	25:8–55	50
12:36	6, 11n25	25:11	67
12:35–36	3–4, 5, 10n10, 12n28, 129, 188	25:14	54, 161
		25:16	67
15:3	9n5	25:17	54, 161
15:11–12	9n5	25:20–22	129
20:5	173n31	25:23	67, 68, 129
20:15	46, 81	25:24–28	60n59
21–24	129	25:31	67
21:2–11	17, 18	25:38	162
21:6	18	25:19–55	75n23
21:11	18	25:42	50-51, 162
21:16	47	25:44–46	17, 19, 22, 59n46
21:33–22:5	27	25:55	162
22	83	26	54
22:1	5	26:12	200
22:1–14	159	26:40	173n29
22:5–6	47	26:40–42	54
22:13	10n10	26:40–44	173n29
22:21–24	75n19		
23:4–5	48	**Numbers**	
23:9	75n19		
33:6	11n25	Num	9
		5	83
Leviticus		5:5–7	277
		5:5–8	27
Lev	48	5:5–10	159
6	83	5:7	53, 83
6:1–3	47	5:8	53, 84
6:1–7	27, 47, 48, 53, 54	20:14–21	8
6:2–5	179	21–35	8
6:3	47	21:1–3	8

22:1–24:25	8	*1 Kings*	
33:54	50	3:5	10n10
		3:10–11	10n10
Deuteronomy		3:13	10n10
Deut	19, 25, 27	10:13	10n10
1–3	129	*2 Kings*	
5:12–15	129		
6:4–9	167	4:3	10n10
10:16	161, 164, 165, 166	6:5	10n10
10:16–19	75n19		
15:2	116	*2 Chronicles*	
15:3	116	11:23	10n10
15:7	49	20:25	4, 11n25
15:12	116	29:25	11n25
15:12–15	6, 25, 133		
15:12–18	12n28, 12n32, 17, 18, 116	**Nehemiah**	
15:15	162	Neh	56
15:17	18	1:5	173n29
22:3	48-49	1:6	59n51
24:7	47	9:2	173n29
24:14–15	47		
24:19–21	75n19	**Job**	
27:19	75n19	20:10	84
30:6	165, 166	20:19	84
32	200		
Judges		**Psalms**	
5:25	10n10	21:5	10n10
8:24	10n10	51	159
		105:37–38	6
1 Samuel		139:14	202
30:22	11n25	**Proverbs**	
2 Samuel		3:3	167
12:6	159	7:3	167
20:6	11n25	21:14	12n32
		25:21–22	12n32

Isaiah

Is	56
1	130
1:21–23	130-131
3:14	55
5:1–7	132
57:18	159
58	130
58:2	129
58:6–14	129
61:1–2	159

Jeremiah

1	130
4:4	166
6:13–14	69
8:8–10	69
16:10–13	173n29
17:1–10	167
29:7	131
31:31–34	167

Ezekiel

Ezek	56
11:18	173n31
14:14	5–6, 11n25
18	162, 173n31
16	200
36:26–36	173n31
45:8–9	54

Daniel

9:1–20	59n51
9:4–6	173n29
9:16	173n29

Hosea

| 1 | 130 |
| 2:11 | 11n25 |

Amos

| 5:24 | 144 |

Micah

3	130
4	130
6	200

Wisdom of Solomon

| 10:17 | 4 |

Matthew

5:3–12	159
5:4	159
5:16	132
5:43–47	131
5:48	259
7:24–27	135
18:21–35	122n33, 132
19:16–30	72
22:37–40	200
25	213
25:31–46	75n22
26:28	173n32

Mark

1:4	173n32
10:17–31	72
10:19	58n27

Luke

1:77	173n32
3:3	173n32
3:7–9	286
3:8	286
4:16–21	71
4:18–21	71
4:18	71, 173n32
4:19	71
4:21–27	71
4:28–29	71
10:25–37	5, 132, 173n29, 298
10:35	161
16:19–35	173n29
18:20	58n27, 81
18:41	80
18:42	80
18:43	80
18:18–30	71–72, 76n30
19	26, 27, 80
19:1–10	5, 71, 80, 159
19:2	81
19:3	80
19:4	80
19:7	81
19:8	71, 75–76n29, 76n30, 82–83, 277
19:9	76n29, 84
24:47	173n32

John

1:1–18	131
1:14	204
5:13	155–156
5:19	134
8:32	273
14:6	273

Acts

2:23	159
2:36	159
2:38	173n32
10:43	173n32
20:31	170n13

Romans

1–8	127
1:21–32	163
1:16	131
2:4	86
2:28–29	165, 166, 167
5:10	204
5:12	202-3
6:6	165, 168
6:22	121n7
7:5	121n14
7:7	167
7:8–13	167
7:14–25	164, 167
8:3	167
8:3–4	165, 167
8:9	121n14
8:31–39	127
12:2	173n29
12:10	114
12:10–16	113
12:16	114
12:17	118
13:9	58n27
14:17	203-4

1 Corinthians

1	142
1:27–28	142
6:1–8	99
7:22	121n7
9	110

9:12–19	110	1:18–20	163
11:24–26	142	1:20	163
12:25	114	1:21	163
13	159	1:21–23	164
14:30	121n20	1:22	163, 166, 167
		1:22–23	163

2 Corinthians

3:2–3	167
5:21	204
7	159

Galatians

2:11–14	159
3:24	167
3:28	114
4:3	111
4:7	111
5:13	114
6:10	118

Ephesians

Eph	95, 117
4:17–19	163
4:28	58n27
5:16	203
6:6	121n7

Philippians

2:1–4	113
2:6–8	110
2:8	115

Colossians

Col	95, 117
1:13–14	163, 203
1:14	163
1:15–17	163

2	166
2:11	164, 166
2:11–12	167
2:11–13	166
2:11–15	168
2:13–15	162
2:14	166, 167
2:20	166
3:1	166
3:9–10	166
4:1	117

1 Thessalonians

2:5–8	110
5:15	118

1 Timothy

6:10	197

Titus

2:12	203

Philemon

1	108
1–2	108
2	108
5	108
7	98, 108
8	98
8–9	98, 109, 110
8–10	108
9	98, 108

9–10	108	**Hebrews**	
10	98, 108	2:2	132
11	108	2:17	204
11–12	98	5:7–9	168
12	98, 101, 102, 108, 109	8:7–13	167
13	98, 108, 109	9:12	52
13–14	98	9:14	52
13–17	108	9:22	173n32
14	98, 108, 109	10:18	173n32
15	98	12:1–2	168
15–16	96, 111		
16	98, 99, 107, 110, 111, 112, 113	**James**	
17	98, 109, 110, 121n11	4:2	263
		4:12	286
17–19	98		
18	115	**1 John**	
18–19	107, 108, 115	4:19	132
19	97, 98, 101, 108, 115		
19–20	98	**Revelation**	
20	98	1–3	200
20–21	108	21:1–4	205
21	108, 110, 115		
22	108		
23	108		

About the Contributors

Michael Barram, PhD (Union Theological Seminary–PSCE, Richmond, VA) is Professor of Theology & Religious Studies at Saint Mary's College of California. His scholarship explores the missionally located nature of Christian biblical interpretation and emphasizes the formative function of biblical texts for moral and economic reasoning. Barram has chaired the steering committee of the Forum on Missional Hermeneutics since its establishment in 2005. He is the author of *Missional Economics: Biblical Justice and Christian Formation* (Eerdmans, 2018); *Mission and Moral Reflection in Paul* (Lang, 2006); and, with John R. Franke, is completing *Liberating Scripture: An Invitation to Missional Hermeneutics*, which will appear in a new Cascade series—*Studies in Missional Hermeneutics, Theology, and Praxis*—for which Barram and Franke will serve as editors. Barram and his wife Kelli live in Richmond, California, and have two grown daughters, Jordan and Devyn.

Stacy Davis, PhD (University of Notre Dame, 2003) is Professor of Religious Studies and Theology at Saint Mary's College, Notre Dame, IN. She is the author of two books, *This Strange Story: Jewish and Christian Interpretation of the Curse of Canaan from Antiquity to 1865* and *Haggai and Malachi* in the Wisdom Commentary Series—and a contributing co-editor of *The Africana Bible* and the forthcoming Westminster Study Bible. Davis is also an associate editor for the *Journal of Biblical Literature*. When she is not teaching or writing, she is either running, reading, or watching ESPN.

Curtiss Paul DeYoung, EdD (University of St. Thomas [MN]) is a noted racial justice academic, activist, and author. In addition to his doctoral degree, DeYoung earned a Master of Divinity from Howard University School of Theology (Washington, DC). He is the Co-CEO of the Minnesota Council of Churches, having previously served as the Executive Director of Community Renewal Society in Chicago and as Professor of Reconciliation Studies at

Bethel University in St. Paul, MN. The author and editor of thirteen books on racial justice, reconciliation, social justice activism, and cultural competency, DeYoung co-authored *Radical Reconciliation: Beyond Political Pietism and Christian Quietism* (Orbis) with South African anti-apartheid activist Allan Boesak, and was on the editorial team for *The Peoples' Bible* (Fortress). He has been married since 1984 and has three adult children living in New York City, Seattle, and Washington, DC.

Malcolm Foley, PhD, serves as the Special Advisor to the President for Equity and Campus Engagement at Baylor University, as the Director of Black Church Studies at Truett Theological Seminary, and as a pastor at Mosaic Waco. With his co-pastor, Slim, Foley hosts the podcast *Theology in Pieces*. He writes, speaks, and preaches about how communities united to Christ can resist the death-dealing effects of racial capitalism, work that will be summarized in an upcoming book with Brazos Press, entitled *Children of Mammon*. Foley's writings can be found at *Christianity Today* and blogs like *Mere Orthodoxy* and the *Anxious Bench*.

Michael J. Gorman, PhD, holds the Raymond E. Brown Chair in Biblical Studies and Theology at St. Mary's Seminary & University in Baltimore. He has also been a visiting professor at Duke Divinity School; Regent College, Vancouver, British Columbia; and seminaries in both Cameroon and the Democratic Republic of the Congo. He has also lectured for institutions in Great Britain, the Netherlands, Brazil, and New Zealand. Gorman's publications include *Apostle of the Crucified Lord* and *Becoming the Gospel: Paul, Participation, and Mission*. Active in his local Methodist church, he has supported its anti-racist stance. In his free time, Gorman enjoys spending time with his family and traveling.

Renee K. Harrison, PhD, is a tenured Associate Professor of African American and US Religious History at Howard University. Her doctoral degree in Religion is from Emory University, with an interdisciplinary focus on History, Philosophy, African American Studies, and Black Feminist/Womanist Thought. Harrison's research interests include an interdisciplinary and interfaith approach to African American religious history and culture; Black feminist/womanist thought; aesthetic theory and the arts; phenomenology; and rituals of healing and resistance. She is the author of *Black Hands, White House: Slave Labor and the Making of America* (Fortress, 2021); *Enslaved Women and the Art of Resistance in Antebellum American* (Palgrave Macmillan, 2009); and *Engaged Teaching in Theology and Religion* (co-authored with Jennie Knight, Palgrave Macmillan, 2015).

Drew G. I. Hart, PhD, is Associate Professor of Theology at Messiah University and program director of Thriving Together Congregations for Racial Justice. Hart specializes in Black and Anabaptist theologies and is a sought-after speaker, addressing topics such as Christian discipleship, Christendom, white supremacy, and racial/economic justice at colleges, congregations, and conferences nationwide. He co-hosts the Inverse Podcast and is the author of *Trouble I've Seen: Changing the Way the Church Views Racism* and *Who Will Be a Witness?: Igniting Activism for God's Justice, Love, and Deliverance*. Hart's scholarly contributions and his local, faith-based activism have earned him recognition, including bcmPEACE's 2017 Peacemaker Award and the 2019 W. E. B. Du Bois Award in Harrisburg, PA. He and his family reside in Harrisburg, PA.

Jim Bear Jacobs, MA, was born in St. Paul, MN, and is a member of the Stockbridge-Munsee Mohican Nation, an American Indian tribe located in central Wisconsin. He has degrees in Pastoral Studies and Christian Theology and has served various churches as youth minister, adult Christian educator, and director of Men's Ministries. Presently, Jacobs is parish associate at Church of All Nations Presbyterian Church. He is a cultural facilitator in the Twin Cities, working to raise public awareness of American Indian causes and injustices. Jacobs is the Director of Community Engagement and Racial Justice for the Minnesota Council of Churches, and also the creator and director of "Healing Minnesota Stories," a program of the Minnesota Council of Churches dedicated to ensuring that the Native American voice is heard in areas where it has long been ignored.

Gimbiya Kettering, MFA, rooted in the Church of the Brethren, leads workshops about racism in the church and gospel-based social justice. Since earning an MFA, Kettering's creative writing has been supported by the DC Arts and Humanities Commission, Elizabeth George Foundation, Maryland State Arts Council, Sustainable Arts Foundation, James Merrill House, Yaddo, Callaloo, and VONA. In 2023, *Associated Church Press* awarded her the James Solheim Award of Excellence for Editorial Courage. Kettering lives with her family on unceded ancestral land of the Anacostan-Piscataway. She can be reached at www.gimbiyakettering.com.

Duke L. Kwon, MDiv, ThM (Gordon-Conwell Theological Seminary) is co-author of *Reparations: A Christian Call for Repentance and Repair* and lead pastor at Grace Meridian Hill, a neighborhood congregation in the Grace DC network in Washington, DC. Kwon is active in public conversations around race, equity, and racial repair in the American church, and he writes and lectures on these topics around the country. His work has appeared in

The Washington Post, Christianity Today, and The Witness. He lives in the District with his wife and three children.

Mark Labberton, PhD (University of Cambridge) is President Emeritus of Fuller Theological Seminary, having previously served on the faculty at Fuller before becoming the seminary's fifth president. Raised in Washington State, Labberton graduated from Whitman College and later earned an MDiv from Fuller Theological Seminary prior to completing his doctoral studies. His primary call has been to serve as a pastor, the majority of it at the First Presbyterian Church of Berkeley. Labberton's books include *The Dangerous Act of Worship: Living God's Call to Justice; The Dangerous Act of Loving Your Neighbor: Seeing Others Through the Eyes of Jesus; Still Evangelical? Insiders Reconsider Political, Social, and Theological Meaning;* and *Called: The Promise and Crisis of Following Jesus Today.* He and his wife Janet live in the San Francisco Bay Area and have two grown sons.

Christina McRorie, PhD (University of Virginia) is Associate Professor of Moral Theology at Boston College, School of Theology and Ministry. She is an Affiliate Fellow of the Institute for Advanced Studies in Culture, and a member of the Catholic Theological Ethics in the World Church network. McRorie's research uses resources drawn from Christian theology and ethics, political economy, and economics to consider questions about moral agency and obligation in markets.

Mako A. Nagasawa, MTS (Holy Cross Greek Orthodox Seminary) directs The Anástasis Center for Christian Education and Ministry. Nagasawa and his team teach, train, and write about early Christian restorative justice and healing atonement. He authored *Abortion Policy and Christian Social Ethics in the United States* (2021), contributed to *Honor, Shame, and the Gospel: Reframing Our Message and Ministry* (2020), and wrote commentary for Ezekiel in the *NIV God's Justice Study Bible* (2016). Nagasawa is on the Elder Team of Neighborhood Church of Dorchester and lives in intentional Christian community with his family in Dorchester, MA. He loves food, tea, and stories from around the world.

Pamela R. Ngunjiri, MTS, MSW grew up in a military family and is a transplant to Minnesota. She is currently completing her doctoral dissertation at Bethel Seminary, focusing on white supremacy and its entanglement with the Christian Church. Ngunjiri is currently Co-Director of Racial Justice at the Minnesota Council of Churches, having previously worked as a social worker in child protection and in the chemical dependency field, as a family support services manager, and as an Adjunct Associate Professor of Social

Work at Bethel University. Ngunjiri is an ordained Itinerant Elder in the AME Church, likes to garden, and has two children, six grandchildren, and two great-grandchildren.

Angela N. Parker, PhD (Chicago Theological Seminary) is Assistant Professor of New Testament and Greek at Mercer University's McAfee School of Theology. Prior to her doctoral studies, she received a BA from Shaw University and an MTS from Duke Divinity School.

In 2018, Parker's article, "One Womanist's View of Racial Reconciliation in Galatians," earned second place in the *Journal for Feminist Studies in Religion*'s Elizabeth Schüssler Fiorenza New Scholar Award, and in 2023 she published *If God Still Breathes, Why Can't I: Black Lives Matter and Biblical Authority* (Eerdmans). Parker is ordained with the Missionary Baptist Association of North Carolina, and can be found on Twitter at @anp22fab, Facebook, and the Mercer University website.

Michael J. Rhodes, PhD (Trinity College/University of Aberdeen) is lecturer in Old Testament at Carey Baptist College. An ordained pastor in the Evangelical Presbyterian Church, he has spent more than twelve years living and working in economically marginalized communities. Rhodes is the author of *Just Discipleship: Biblical Justice in an Unjust World* (IVP, 2023); *Formative Feasting: Practices and Virtue Ethics in Deuteronomy's Tithe Meal and the Corinthian Lord's Supper* (Peter Lang, 2022); and *Practicing the King's Economy: Honoring Jesus in the Way We Work, Earn, Spend, Save, and Give* (with Brian Fikkert and Robby Holt; Baker, 2018). He lives in South Auckland with his wife Rebecca and their four children, Isaiah, Amos, Nova, and Jubilee.

Rodney S. Sadler Jr., PhD (Duke University) is Associate Professor of Bible and the Director of the Center for Social Justice and Reconciliation at Union Presbyterian Seminary. Prior to his doctoral studies, he earned degrees from Howard University (BS) and Howard University School of Divinity (MDiv). He is the author of *Can a Cushite Change His Skin: An Examination of Race, Ethnicity, and Othering in the Hebrew Bible* (T&T Clark, 2005), the co-author of *The Genesis of Liberation: Biblical Interpretation in the Antebellum Narratives of the Enslaved* (Westminster/John Knox, 2016), and an associate editor of *The Africana Bible: Reading Israel's Scriptures from African and the African Diaspora* (Fortress Press, 2010). A veteran of many social justice movements, Sadler is co-founder and co-chair of the Reimagining America Project in Charlotte, NC.

Matthew Schlimm, PhD (Duke University) is Professor of Old Testament at the University of Dubuque Theological Seminary. His publications include *70 Hebrew Words Every Christian Should Know* (Abingdon, 2018) and *This Strange and Sacred Scripture: Wrestling with the Old Testament and Its Oddities* (Baker Academic, 2015). Schlimm is currently working on a commentary on Genesis.

Joseph Downing Thompson Jr., PhD (Yale University) serves Virginia Theological Seminary as Associate Dean of Multicultural Ministries and as a member of the faculty in the area of Practical Theology. His courses and administrative work help to ensure that seminarians engage with issues of race, justice, and intercultural awareness as part of their theological education. Thompson's teaching and research interests include the theological and spiritual dimensions of racial ideology in the USA, as well as the moral and ethical implications of the reparations movement.

Ekemini Uwan (pronounced Eh-keh-mi-knee Oo-wan) is a public theologian and co-author of the 2023 NAACP Image Award Nominated Book, *Truth's Table: Black Women's Musings on Life, Love, and Liberation.* Uwan is a Charter Member of the International Civil Society Working Group of the Permanent Forum for People of African Descent at the United Nations. She is a fellow at The Aspen Institute, co-founder and co-host of the award-winning podcast, *Truth's Table*, and also *Get in The Word with Truth's Table*. Uwan's writings have been published in *The Atlantic, The Washington Post,* and her insights have been quoted by NPR, CNN, *The New York Times,* and *The New Yorker.* She has appeared on MSNBC, NPR, and The Grio to provide incisive political analysis. In addition to her writings, Uwan's voice has been sampled on Lecrae's album, *All Things Work Together* and Sho Baraka's *The Narrative.*

www.ingramcontent.com/pod-product-compliance
Lightning Source LLC
Chambersburg PA
CBHW070013010526
44117CB00011B/1553